Rethinking British Decline

Also by Richard English

RADICALS AND THE REPUBLIC: SOCIALIST REPUBLICANISM IN THE IRISH FREE STATE, 1925–1937

ERNIE O'MALLEY: IRA INTELLECTUAL

UNIONISM IN MODERN IRELAND: NEW PERSPECTIVES ON POLITICS AND CULTURE (*co-editor*)

THE STATE: HISTORICAL AND POLITICAL DIMENSIONS (*co-editor*)

Also by Michael Kenny

THE FIRST NEW LEFT: INTELLECTUALS AFTER STALIN

WESTERN POLITICAL THOUGHT: AN ANNOTATED BIBLIOGRAPHY OF WRITINGS IN ENGLISH SINCE 1945 (*with Robert Eccleshall*)

PLANNING SUSTAINABILITY (*co-editor*)

Rethinking British Decline

Edited by

Richard English

and

Michael Kenny

First published in Great Britain 2000 by
MACMILLAN PRESS LTD
Houndmills, Basingstoke, Hampshire RG21 6XS and London
Companies and representatives throughout the world

A catalogue record for this book is available from the British Library.

ISBN 0–333–67965–2 hardcover
ISBN 0–333–67966–0 paperback

First published in the United States of America 2000 by
ST. MARTIN'S PRESS, INC.,
Scholarly and Reference Division,
175 Fifth Avenue, New York, N.Y. 10010

ISBN 0–312–22534–2

Library of Congress Cataloging-in-Publication Data
Rethinking British decline / edited by Richard English and Michael
Kenny.
p.   cm.
Includes bibliographical references and index.
ISBN 0–312–22534–2
1. Great Britain—Politics and government—20th century.   2. Great
Britain—Economic conditions—20th century.   3. Great
Britain—Social conditions—20th century.   I. English, Richard,
1963–   II. Kenny, Michael.
DA566.7.R46   1999
941.082—dc21
99–16305
CIP

This book is printed on paper suitable for recycling and made from fully managed and
sustained forest sources.

10   9   8   7   6   5   4   3   2   1
09   08   07   06   05   04   03   02   01   00

Printed in Hong Kong

To the memory of Bertha English (1930–1997) and
Donald English (1930–1998)

Contents

Preface and Acknowledgements

This book explores one of the central themes of modern British[1] politics: the notion of national decline. The debate about decline – its extent and causes, as well as possible remedy – has generated some of the most exciting intellectual argument in modern Britain. This book aims to assess and further stimulate that debate.

Three crucial questions are reflected throughout the volume. To what extent, and in what precise ways, have arguments about decline improved our understanding of Britain's political and economic development since the late nineteenth century? Why have arguments concerning decline been so frequently and influentially expressed? Are decline debates still pertinent as Britain faces the twenty-first century? *Rethinking British Decline* offers a forum for the restatement and possible revision of important arguments propounded by some of the most influential thinkers on the subject. It also provides systematic examination, by leading academics, of key themes relating to British decline: ideology, the state, the European context, globalisation, and the end of Empire.

In order to achieve this dual purpose the editors have adopted a two-part structure for the book. Part I features some of the intellectual figures whose ideas and theories in relation to decline have played a critical role in the development of debates in this field. Their contributions take the form of structured interviews,[2] in which the various interviewees were asked a broadly similar set of questions. All have been encouraged to reflect upon politics and economy during the 1980s and 1990s, and to consider critically their own and other thinkers' positions on decline in the light of recent intellectual developments. The transcriptions have been edited and rendered into continuous prose by the editors who have aimed to preserve their freshness, vigour and contemporaneity while avoiding some of the repetition and lack of focus which sometimes characterise literally reproduced interviews. The colloquial tone of the discussions has, as far as possible, been preserved.

The editors have written an introduction to each interview, as a guide to the importance and nature of each thinker's contribution to decline

debates. These introductions are intended to provide readers with a suc-
cinct and accessible overview of most of the leading positions relating
to decline, as well as considerable insight into the work of the respective commentators. No collection of thinkers in a volume of this kind
could hope to be comprehensive,[3] yet the voices presented in Part I do
constitute a distinctively vibrant and influential group of thinkers, some
working within the academy, others in the world of journalism. Part I
therefore presents readers with a powerful, innovative and up-to-date
account of some of the most important and exciting controversies ani-
mating intellectuals in contemporary Britain.

Part II of the book consists of newly commissioned essays adopting a
more wide-angled perspective on key themes relevant to decline: party
ideology, and the role that decline has played in structuring party political discourse in the postwar period; the state, and the manner in which
institutions are presented in declinist explanations and theories;
European integration, and the European dimension to British politics;
the implications for decline of globalisation; and historiographical disputes about the end of Empire. These pieces, from distinguished academic experts, provide readers with a profound understanding of scholarly arguments associated with decline.

The two main sections of the book thus complement one another,
and together provide a full appreciation of modern perspectives on
decline. They are set in context by an introductory chapter written by
Andrew Gamble, author of one of the best existing books on decline.[4]
This provides an overview and expertly maps out the contours of the
broad debate on British decline, offering an invaluable starting point for
the material which follows in the book. The conclusion to the volume
has been written by the editors, and addresses the central questions of
the value, causes and continuing pertinence of decline debates.

Academic work on decline has been fascinating in part because of its
interdisciplinary quality. Economic, political, social and cultural historians, together with political economists, sociologists and political analysts, have all made important contributions.[5] This collection leans
deliberately towards the political. We have been keen to address arguments about the Thatcher administrations of 1979–90, the subsequent
Major premiership, and the impact of Tony Blair's New Labour government elected in 1997. The book examines the political constructions
and usages of declinist rhetoric, and considers the political impact of
declinist thinking in and about Britain. But its contributors and the
material which they discuss reflect the diverse quality of decline
debates, and the book is aimed not at one particular discipline, but

rather at people from a wide range of intellectual backgrounds. Moreover, it is hoped that *Rethinking British Decline* might work at different levels: as an introduction to the decline debates for those unfamiliar with the area, but also as a book containing pioneering work which might stimulate and influence experts in the field.

The editors are grateful to the Nuffield Foundation for helping to fund the project with money provided through their Social Science Small Grants Scheme; to the University of Sheffield, the College of William and Mary (USA), and Queen's University, Belfast, for financial support during the research and writing of the book; and to Claire Annesley, Greg Pastor, Stephanie Kaye, Steve Ludlam and Will Hausman. Michael Kenny was aided considerably by the award of a Charter Fellowship, 1997–98, by the Fellows of Wolfson College, Oxford. The editors are particularly indebted to Mrs Helen Pollard for her cooperation subsequent to Sidney Pollard's untimely death in 1998. We are also grateful to our publisher Steven Kennedy for his expert guidance and to all the interviewees in Part I of this book for their time, patience and cooperation. Finally, we have greatly appreciated Andrew Gamble's support, advice and encouragement through every stage of this project.

RICHARD ENGLISH
MICHAEL KENNY

Notes

1. The term 'Britain' is less accurate than 'United Kingdom' when discussing the state comprising England, Scotland, Wales and Northern Ireland/Ireland. But the term 'British decline' is so pervasive in the literature that we have judged it more appropriate to remain consistent with this usage.
2. Conducted by the editors, between July 1996 and December 1997.
3. The absence of a particular author is no reflection of their significance in these debates, but either an indication of their reluctance to be interviewed or the product of insurmountable logistical difficulties.
4. A. Gamble, *Britain in Decline: Economic Policy, Political Strategy and the British State* (Basingstoke, 1994; 1st edn, 1981).
5. Amid the rich literature in this field, some of the finest work has come from political economists and economic historians. See, for example, D. Coates, *The Question of UK Decline: The Economy, State and Society* (Hemel Hempstead, 1994); B. Supple, 'Fear of Failing: Economic History and the Decline of Britain', *Economic History Review*, vol. 47, no. 3 (1994); and the celebration of Supple's work in P. Clarke and C. Trebilcock (eds), *Understanding Decline: Perceptions and Realities of British Economic Performance* (Cambridge, 1997).

Notes on the Contributors

Correlli Barnett was, between 1977 and 1995, Keeper of the Churchill Archives Centre at Churchill College, Cambridge, and Fellow of Churchill College. His many books include *The Desert Generals* (1960), *The Swordbearers: Studies in Supreme Command in the First World War* (1963), *Britain and Her Army: A Military, Political and Social Survey* (1970), *The Collapse of British Power* (1972), *The Great War* (1979), *The Audit of War* (1986) and *The Lost Victory* (1995).

Sir Samuel Brittan has been the principal economics commentator on the *Financial Times* since 1966 and was appointed assistant editor in 1978. His books include *Capitalism and the Permissive Society* (1973), *The Economic Consequences of Democracy* (1977) and *Capitalism with a Human Face* (1995).

Jonathan Clark was Fellow of Peterhouse College, Cambridge (from 1977 onwards) and of All Souls College, Oxford (from 1986). He is currently Hall Distinguished Professor of British History, University of Kansas. His many books include *English Society 1688–1832: Ideology, Social Structure and Political Practice During the Ancien Régime* (1985), *Revolution and Rebellion: State and Society in England in the Seventeenth and Eighteenth Centuries* (1986), *The Language of Liberty 1660–1832: Political Discourse and Social Dynamics in the Anglo-American World* (1994) and *Samuel Johnson* (1994).

Robert Eccleshall is Professor of Politics at Queen's University, Belfast. He has written about English and Irish political thought as well as political ideologies. His most recent book is *A Biographical Dictionary of British Prime Ministers* (1998).

Richard English is Reader in Politics at Queen's University, Belfast. He is author of *Radicals and the Republic: Socialist Republicanism in the Irish Free State 1925–1937* (1994) and of *Ernie O'Malley: IRA Intellectual* (1998); and co-editor of *Unionism in Modern Ireland: New Perspectives on Politics and Culture* (1996) and of *The State: Historical and Political Dimensions* (1999).

Marie-Therese Fay is Research Officer with the Cost of the Troubles Study, a project on the effects of violence in Northern Ireland on the general population. She was previously Research Assistant in the Department of Politics at Queen's University, Belfast, and has written on voter apathy, partisan dealignment and Quangos.

Andrew Gamble is Professor of Politics at the University of Sheffield. His books include *Britain in Decline* (1981), *The Free Economy and the Strong State* (1988) and *Hayek: The Iron Cage of Liberty* (1996).

Stuart Hall was Director of the Centre for Contemporary Cultural Studies at Birmingham University from 1968 until 1979, and was appointed Professor of Sociology at the Open University in 1979. Some of his most influential essays are collected in *The Hard Road to Renewal* (1988) and D. Morley and K. Chen (eds), *Stuart Hall: Critical Dialogues in Cultural Studies* (1996).

Will Hutton became editor of the *Observer* in 1996. He previously worked as a stockbroker, a BBC radio producer, and Director and Producer of BBC 2's *Money Programme*; and as economics editor both of the BBC's *Newsnight* (1983–88) and of the *Guardian* (1990–95); he was assistant editor of the *Guardian* (1995–96). His books include *The Revolution That Never Was* (1986), *The State We're In* (1995) and *The State To Come* (1997).

Michael Kenny is Lecturer in Politics at the University of Sheffield. He is author of *The First New Left* (1995), co-author of *Western Political Thought: An Annotated Bibliography of Writings in English since 1945* (1995) and co-editor of *Planning Sustainability?* (1999).

David Marquand was a Labour MP between 1966 and 1976. He left Parliament to become Chief Adviser to the Secretariat-General at the European Commission. From 1978 to 1996 he was Professor of Politics first at Salford and then at Sheffield University, and is currently the Principal of Mansfield College, Oxford. His publications include *Ramsay MacDonald* (1977), *The Unprincipled Society* (1988) and *The New Reckoning* (1997).

Elizabeth Meehan is Professor of Politics and Jean Monnet Professor of European Social Policy at Queen's University, Belfast. Her main publications cover women's rights at work in the USA, UK and EU;

citizenship in the EU and UK; and Northern Ireland and the EU. She is author of *Citizenship and the European Community* (1993). Her forthcoming research is on British–Irish relations in the context of the EU.

Ritchie Ovendale recently retired as Professor of International Politics at the University of Wales, Aberystwyth. His publications include *'Appeasement' and the English Speaking World* (1975), *Anglo-American Relations in the Twentieth Century* (1988) and *The Origins of the Arab–Israeli Wars* (1992).

Henk Overbeek teaches International Relations in the Department of Political Science and Public Administration at the Free University of Amsterdam. His publications include *Global Capitalism and National Decline: The Thatcher Years in Perspective* (1990) and, as editor, *Restructuring Hegemony in the Global Political Economy* (1993).

Sidney Pollard, who died in 1998, became Professor of Economic History at Sheffield University in 1963, and also held a Chair at the University of Bielefield in Germany, 1980–90. His best known publications are *The Wasting of the British Economy* (1982), *Britain's Prime and Britain's Decline* (1989) and *The Development of the British Economy 1870–1914* (1992).

W.D. (Bill) Rubinstein has been Professor of Modern History at the University of Wales since 1995. He was previously Professor of Social and Economic History at Deakin University in Victoria, Australia. His books include *Men of Property* (1981) and *Capitalism, Culture and Decline in Britain 1750–1990* (1993). He has also written widely on modern Jewish history.

Martin J. Smith is Professor of Politics at the University of Sheffield. He is currently working on the reform of the Civil Service in Britain. His recent publications include *The Core Executive in Britain* (1999) and, as co-editor, *Contemporary British Conservatism* (1996).

Martin Wiener has been a Professor at Rice University in Texas since 1967, and is currently the Mary Gibbs Jones Professor of History. He is the author of *English Culture and the Decline of the Industrial Spirit 1850–1980* (1981) and *Between Two Worlds: The Political Thought of Graham Wallas* (1971).

1

Theories and Explanations of British Decline

ANDREW GAMBLE

Decline has no single meaning. It has always been a contested term and is dependent upon seeing the world and Britain's place within it in a particular way. It does not have a fixed or objective character and cannot be directly observed. It depends on a particular historical and political construction of evidence and experience, which is open to quite different interpretations.

Amidst the mass of assertions and counter-assertions, decline often appears to have as many meanings as there are explanations for it. If a term can be as widely defined as this, does it have any objective reality at all? Like many other contested terms in social science, however, the diversity of meaning arises from the origin of the term in political experience and conflict. Contests over its meaning and its implications have been a key part of the discourse of twentieth-century politics. Decline is a concept which many British politicians from Joseph Chamberlain to Margaret Thatcher have used to understand the world around them and urge particular courses of action. Its different meanings are therefore closely tied to the various strategies for halting or managing it which have emerged at different times and in different contexts during the last hundred years.

Decline has become an inextricable part of Britain's political reality in the twentieth century and has engaged the attention of many leading historians, economists and political scientists as well as columnists and leader writers. It is hard to think of a major public intellectual who has not contributed in some form to the decline debate. It has produced a lively academic and journalistic literature on whether there really has been a decline and if so how it is best measured, and whether there are any policies which might reverse it.[1] Many of the disagreements about the meaning of decline are hard to settle although that does not mean that rules of evidence and relevance which narrow the area of controversy cannot be established. But even if future historians were to agree that in some of the senses in which the term has been used Britain's decline was an illusion, it would still be necessary to ask why so many British politicians on both left and right viewed the world through the lens of 'decline' and advocated ambitious programmes to overcome it.

Absolute and Relative Decline

In assessing any particular piece of writing on decline, a good starting point is to establish what it is that is supposed to be in decline. Decline has been applied to morals, to the economy, to military power, to international influence, to culture, to standards of behaviour, and to democracy. Some writers treat British decline as part of the more general phenomenon of the decline of Western culture and civilisation, others are only concerned with a much narrower topic such as the performance of the British economy, or particular economic sectors.

In understanding how decline is used in any particular literature or context, a useful distinction is that between absolute and relative decline. Absolute decline signifies a permanent fall below a level that had previously been attained. Relative decline, by contrast, is derived from comparing the performance of the entity in decline with that of similar entities. Relative decline is therefore quite compatible with overall improvement. The distinction is particularly relevant to the discussion of British decline. Despite the apocalyptic tone of much writing on British economic performance, British living standards and productivity have continued to rise throughout the century. There have been absolute declines in particular sectors and the disappearance of entire industries, but the overall performance of the British economy in the twentieth century certainly does not show any signs of an absolute decline. On the contrary, the wealth it generates will be approximately three and a half times as great in the year 2000 as it was in 1900. If British economic decline exists at all, it is relative and depends on comparing Britain as a national economy with similar economic entities, estimating the extent to which the British economy grew more slowly and performed less well than economies of similar size and development.

In this 'league table' approach, Britain is typically shown to have progressively slipped down the table according to a variety of indicators, particularly in the 1950s and 1960s.[2] The decline is relative in respect of the particular indicators and countries chosen and in relation to the particular countries. Apart from the objections in principle – voiced most recently by Krugman – to the propriety of treating national economies as though they were a single unit,[3] the data is also difficult to interpret because different indicators and comparators give different results. British performance looks very different in the league tables produced, for instance, by the World Economic Forum and the Institute for Management Development.

The key point is that whatever the final judgement on the performance of the British economy, there clearly has not been anything approaching an absolute *economic* decline. Where there has been an absolute decline is in Britain's position as a world power in the twentieth century. This imperial decline might also be considered a relative decline, since Britain's fall is measured against the rise of other states. At a certain point their power eclipsed that of Britain. What makes it an absolute decline is that Britain has demonstrably less power and influence at the end of the twentieth century than at the beginning. This decline has been a long-drawn out process which is still not complete – Britain still retains some of the trappings of great power status, such as its permanent seat on the UN Security Council and the size and range of its military deployment. But there is no doubt, comparing Britain's position in 1900 with its position a century later, that there has been a qualitative and permanent change in Britain's status in the international state system. Compared to 1900, Britain no longer possesses an *Empire* or the world's top currency; after 1945 it became an important but subordinate partner in NATO and dependent on the United States for military technology; and since 1973 it has agreed to pool its sovereignty in more and more areas through participation in the process of European integration.

The two declines are separable analytically but not politically, and in both popular and elite experience they have been joined together. But popular and elite experiences of decline have been different. Popular discourse has focused on the absolute decline of British power. The loss of Britain's colonial Empire is much more readily communicable (the shrinking of the area of the globe coloured red) than the idea that increasing prosperity signifies decline rather than progress. Future historians may find it puzzling that so much of elite discourse was obsessed with the idea of economic decline at a time when the country was more prosperous than it had ever been. Martin Wiener, for instance, has called (economic) decline the most important problem of twentieth-century British history.[4] But if so it is mainly because it has been defined as such by the political class, which developed a discourse in which Britain was portrayed as constantly underperforming and slipping further and further behind its rivals. The majority of the population has enjoyed rising, not falling, living standards. The quality of life for the great majority of British citizens has improved in measurable ways during the twentieth century. But the British political elite has had a different experience. Its members no longer inhabit a state which is either the leading state in the international system of states or the dominant economy in the global economy, yet today's generation of leaders is constantly reminded in innumerable small ways of what has been lost.

To grasp the dynamics of the decline debate and its impact on British politics and popular opinion, this interrelationship between the two declines needs to be understood. The most potent populist characterisations of decline, such as Social Imperialism and Thatcherism, have always linked economic decline with Britain's place in the world and therefore with threats to British and more specifically English identity. In this way the loss of Empire has resonated in popular experience and imagination, and influenced other perceptions. The tabloid newspapers have helped fuel new forms of English nationalism and xenophobia, particularly in relation to the European Union. Any reduction in British sovereignty is interpreted as a threat to national identity. In this way the performance of the British economy in the twentieth century has often been presented as a symptom of national decline because it cannot be associated with an unequivocal assertion of British power and self-sufficiency, and because other nations to which Britain has been accustomed to regarding itself as superior have had economies plainly performing better that Britain's.

More than any other concept, decline – in this double sense of economic and imperial decline – has been used to interpret Britain's political experience this century. It is not a concept which belongs exclusively to either left or right, but has been used and developed by both. The institutions and policies most favoured by one side have frequently been attacked by the other as the main contributory cause of decline. Decline should not be treated as a single continuous process. There have been different debates and different contexts, and although there has been some continuity in themes and concerns, there are also some quite radical discontinuities and breaks. Changes in the economic and political organisation of the world system have been dramatic in the twentieth century, revolutions and wars have made and remade the balance of power between states and the character of economic and political institutions. These seismic events have created the contexts which express the particular relationship between the political and the economic, between the absolute decline in world power and the relative decline in the national economy, within which the discourses on economic decline have emerged.

The debate in each period has always included competing strategic views of Britain's place in the global economy and the international system of states, and therefore how best to define Britain's economic and security interests and the options for safeguarding and advancing them. Moreover, the very notion of a national economy is itself a construction which depends on a particular view of international politics. In much of the secondary literature on economic decline the national economy is often treated in isolation as though it were a simple natural phenomenon which requires no further explanation. Yet since no absolute decline has taken place, this national economy can only be said to be in decline as a result of a comparison with the performance of similar national economies elsewhere. Understanding British decline requires an appreciation of how the world system has evolved – both the global economy and the international state system.

Decline is therefore politically constructed and needs to be understood through the political debates which have taken place on its dimensions, its causes and its remedies. Three debates have been crucial, and each one is linked to a definite historical and political context which imposed particular constraints on external and internal policy, reflecting Britain's place in the global economy and the balance of interests and the climate of ideas within the state and civil society.

The first debate which lasted from the 1880s to the 1920s was centred on the challenge of Germany and the United States to Britain's dominant economic and military position in the international state system. The key issue for the British political elite was how this challenge might be contained and how the basis of British power in the world – the Empire and Britain's commercial and financial supremacy – might be preserved.[5] The key political battle was fought over the merits of free trade and tariff reform. This was much more than just a dispute over the direction of Britain's trading policy. Free trade had become a symbol of Britain's external and internal policy, and its critics argued that it was leaving Britain seriously unprepared for economic and military competition with its new rivals. The attack on free trade became an attack upon the policy stance and liberal ethos of the British state and civil society.[6] The programme of national efficiency, supported by many on both right and left, made collectivism and individualism the key dividing line in internal political debate. At stake was the issue of how Britain might be turned into a modern state, and how preservation of its Empire was compatible with harnessing the forces of democracy and accepting collectivism without embracing socialism at the same time.

The second debate emerged in the aftermath of the First World War and lasted until the 1960s. Its context was set by the big shift in the balance of power between the leading states in the international system which the First World War signalled and the Second World War consolidated. For Britain the most important aspect of this shift was the rise of the United States to a position of undisputed hegemony, and the exposure of the increasing political and military incapacity of Britain to sustain its Empire or the position of sterling as the leading international currency. In this new environment the principal dispute on external policy within Britain was over how to deal with the United States and how to accommodate Britain to the anticipated loss of its power and status,[7] while the key debate on internal policy became how to modernise the British economy by adopting the best practice methods of American business and commerce and by changing the balance between the public and private sectors. The principal dividing line in political debate became the role of the state in the economy, the free market versus planning. This era saw enormous growth in the size and scope of the state, accelerated by the impact of two world wars, the development of collective bargaining and new forms of economic management.

The third debate emerged in the 1960s and early 1970s from widespread disillusion with the programmes of both left and right to modernise the British economy. These programmes appear in retrospect as the last attempt to create a successful British mass production, Fordist economy.[8] Its context was shaped by Britain's involvement in the development of European integration through the European Community and by the increasing tendencies towards a more interdependent global economy in the 1970s and 1980s. The main external policy issue became whether Britain should seek to advance European integration by participating in plans to form a single currency and a European defence and foreign policy or whether it should resist any attempt to make the union more than a free trade area, a loose arrangement between sovereign states. The central internal policy debate focused on social democracy and how far collectivist institutions should be dismantled and the scope and scale of government redefined.[9] The key issue for economic decline was perceived to be national competitiveness, the kind of supply-side measures which government might introduce to boost the performance of particular sectors and equip citizens with the necessary skills and flexibility to compete in an increasingly uncertain global marketplace. The issue was often posed as the conflict between an enterprise state and a developmental state.[10]

These three debates and their different historical contexts have made decline a long-running theme in twentieth-century British politics, and are the basis on which different explanations of decline have been formed. Ever since it became apparent that the dream of Joseph Chamberlain and the Social Imperialists was not going to be realised, absolute imperial decline has been treated as a painful inevitability. The British Empire was not transformed into a bloc in the world economy sufficiently integrated and powerful to compete with the newly-emerging continent-based Empires of Germany, Russia and the United States.

That option lingered on in a truncated form but the political elite gradually became reconciled to the need to manage an orderly decline of British power through the dismantling of the British Empire. Although there were always romantics (from Enoch Powell in 1948 urging Churchill to re-conquer India by force, to the enthusiasts for the Commonwealth who wished to give it priority over the EEC in the 1960s), the realists among the political elite knew that at best the process might be delayed, but not reversed. Late imperial gestures, like the despatch of a task-force to recapture the Falklands in 1982, did not contradict this assessment. The Falklands war itself had been preceded by British government attempts to negotiate a transfer of sovereignty to Argentina via a leaseback, and was followed by acquiescence in the return of Hong Kong to China in 1997 on Chinese terms. The props to British grandeur – the maintenance of a nuclear deterrent and a state-of-the-art military capability, the diplomatic service, the Foreign Office, the UN role, the secret service and special forces – are all still present at the end of the century, but much of the substance of British power has disappeared and the acceptance of Britain's middle-ranking status is all but complete.

This acceptance of the inevitability of Britain's decline as an imperial and a world power has been the essential backdrop against which explanations of the relative economic decline have been advanced. Some have rejected fatalism, arguing that if the weaknesses of the domestic economy had been tackled the decline in world power might have been arrested.[11] Certainly the Social Imperialist or Chamberlainite wing of the Conservative party always believed so, stressing the intimate connection between economic and military power. Britain proved unable to consolidate its Empire, partly because of a conflict in interest between the priority of maintaining a liberal global economic order and building a self-contained economic and military bloc. The latter was difficult to achieve logistically, and most parts of the Empire made it clear that it was not what they wanted. The settler states wished to exercise the autonomy they had been granted by being given dominion status while the rest of the Empire wanted independence from British rule. Britain lacked either the military or political capability to hold its Empire together in the twentieth century, and the realisation of this steadily sapped the political will of the political elite, and established a mood of resignation and fatalism.

Even if the absolute decline could not have been prevented, however, many have questioned whether Britain's relative economic decline was inevitable. Why could Britain not have prospered by shedding the costs and the burdens of being a world power in the way that Japan and Germany, defeated in war and stripped of their military machines and great power pretensions, had done? The focus of the first decline debate was whether Britain should reorganise its economic and political institutions in order to match the emerging power of the continental-based economies of Germany and the United States, and be prepared to abandon the rules of the liberal economic world order which had been the expression of Britain's nineteenth-century hegemony. The political class was not prepared to make that choice before 1914, and remained deeply ambivalent through the 1920s. National protectionism when it came was a defensive reaction to the collapse of the gold standard in 1931 rather than a proactive policy of national renewal.

The starting point of the second decline debate was this breakdown of the liberal economic world order and the rise of national protectionism. It focused on whether and in what ways the British economy could be modernised through increasing the role of the state. The superiority of American industry over British was now plain. Worries about Britain's relative decline at this juncture were largely about the growing gap between Britain and the United States. By 1945 this gap had become a chasm. But the rebuilding of the British economy after 1945 and the devastation of most other industrial economies by the war left Britain still in a relatively strong position. It was the economic decline which took place in the 1950s and 1960s relative to the performance of the reinvigorated economies of Western Europe and Japan which became the new focus of the debate at the end of the 1950s on why

Britain, despite achieving better growth rates than at any time in the last hundred years, was being outperformed by other industrial economies. This prompted a new bout of plans for the modernisation of British institutions mainly through the enlargement of the role and responsibilities of the state.[12]

It is the last phase of the debate around the theme of modernisation, as well as the third decline debate in the 1970s and 1980s around the theme of competitiveness, which have made relative economic decline so important in British politics in the second half of the twentieth century. Some of the decline literature argues that there was no significant economic decline until the 1950s, and that the prime focus of the decline debate should be on explaining British economic performance in the last fifty years, not in the last hundred.[13] This view has some merit, although it downplays the gap which emerged between Britain and the United States which was so much the focus of concern in the earlier part of the century. Competition from other countries, particularly Germany, was seriously affected by the outcome of the two world wars. Only when the absolute decline of Britain as a world power became plain did relative economic decline emerge as the central concern.

There are many analysts of economic decline, however, who, even though they accept that there has not been a continuous economic decline since the 1880s, do not believe that postwar economic decline can be satisfactorily explained without taking into account its historical roots in the peculiarities of British institutions and British development. The most important dividing line is between explanations which accept that the concept of a national economy is a valid one and that the statement that a national economy can be in decline has meaning, and those which believe that talk of national decline, national competitiveness and national economic performance are fictions. The debate on economic decline can be seen in this respect to be the product of the era of national protectionism, when the formulation of the concept of a national economy for purposes of state policy was very important. Such explanations of economic decline either trace it to particular policies or regard it as deriving from the peculiarities of British capitalism. The latter are the more interesting and the more tenacious. Proponents disagree strongly amongst themselves as to which peculiarities are actually the most significant ones, and they have to contend with alternative theories of British economic development which analyse the British economy in the context of the processes and trends of the global economy, and argue that if there is any reality to the phenomenon of British decline it has to be understood within these parameters and not as something which has been generated from within Britain.

Those explanations which seek to uncover the roots of decline in particular British economic and social institutions all accept the idea that there is such a thing as a British national economy, that it could be in decline in relation to other states, and that there might be measures which could reverse it. The main peculiarities which appear in this literature will be summarised here under the headings of culture, finance, Empire, state and industry. Sometimes explanations of decline which fall under these headings are just seeking scapegoats and offer little theoretical or historical depth. Sometimes they concentrate on making a precise but narrow point about some particular institution or policy. The explanations considered here are those which provide more ambitious general accounts. They reconstruct and reinterpret the past in terms of their favoured *explanans* and point to particular remedies. They have always been contested, empirically, theoretically and politically, and many of them have informed current political debates.

National Peculiarities

Culture

This thesis is known by some of its detractors as the declinist thesis[14] and has become one of the best-known of all explanations of decline. It argues that the principal cause of British decline is to be found in the formation and transmission of an anti-industrial and anti-enterprise culture through the schools, universities and professions. Key occupations for a modern industrial economy, particularly engineering and industrial management, lagged in status behind the professions, the public sector and the City of London. For some of its critics, this 'gentlemanly capitalism' which was averse to industry and technology, was further reinforced by the ascendancy of liberal welfarism over the British Establishment and led, especially after 1945, to greater priority being given to policies of fiscal redistribution and the provision of a welfare safety net than to productive efficiency.[15]

The cultural thesis concentrates mostly upon the British upper class, which is implicitly contrasted with supposedly more capitalist and entrepreneurial elites in other countries. The thesis has been extended to explore the deep conservatism of all sections of the British people and their aversion to change, the lack of social mobility and a dynamic

civil society, the transformation of class into status, and its inappropri-
ateness for a modern industrial society. But in its most popular version
it is the attitude of the elite that is seen as the main cause of the problem and also of the transformation of Britain from the dynamic and
thrusting industrial powerhouse of the nineteenth century into the deindustrialising economy of the twentieth century.[16]

The key assumption made by such accounts is that cultural beliefs
and values play the major role in determining economic behaviour.
They also suggest that in Britain the upper class is both very dominant
and highly sealed. The way in which it was formed has had a decisive
effect upon the way in which the whole society has evolved. The implication for policy is either that the elite institutions need radical reform,
or new elite institutions dedicated to instilling a different kind of culture
need to be created. The main difficulty with the thesis is the quality of
the evidence that is adduced in its support. Much of it is impressionistic
and selective and ignores the prevalence of anti-industrial and anti-bour-
geois cultures in countries which are supposed to have been much more
successful at building industrial economies.[17] It also has to ignore or
minimise the obvious fact that the anti-industrial culture did not prevent
the appearance of numerous new entrepreneurs in the twentieth century
and the founding of major new companies. If elite institutions were so
inefficient at producing industrial managers and technologists, why did
other institutions not spring up to supply them, as happened at earlier
times in British history? The aristocratic ethos in Britain was surely
stronger at the beginning of the nineteenth century than at any time
since, yet it does not seem to have been able to prevent the explosive
growth of industrial capital and the rise of a new class of industrialists.

The cultural thesis has been immensely popular because it suggests
that the ultimate cause of decline is deeply embedded in culture rather
than in policy or interests, and that until beliefs and attitudes are transformed, there is unlikely to be any significant change in economic performance. It was taken up by Keith Joseph and other leading
Conservatives in the 1980s. They argued that creating an enterprise culture and changing popular attitudes towards risk-taking and economic
modernisation were the key to economic recovery. Increasing the role
of the state in the economy was thus a dead-end.

Finance

Britain has always been distinctive among other industrial economies
for the size and role of its financial sector, and, in particular, the way in

which the City has been allowed to regulate itself for long periods with minimal government intervention. The enormous success of the City is contrasted with the poor performance of so much of British industry and the argument advanced that the two are strongly linked. As Will Hutton expresses it: 'The story of British capitalism is at heart the peculiar history of the destructive relationship between British finance and industry.'[18] The hegemony of the City over the British state has meant that in comparison with other countries, relationships between finance and industry have been more strongly geared to the exploitation of global rather than domestic investment opportunities. Managers of companies in Britain have accordingly been forced to maximise short-term returns in order to satisfy the financial markets. The financial system has failed to nurture successful long-term relationships to support investment and development and the kind of culture and practices within firms which promote high productivity. The contrast is both with the United States and its strong system of local and regional banks which do provide financial support for local industry, and with Germany and Japan which have much higher levels of concentration in ownership of companies and close bank involvement in ownership and management.

The consequences of the relationship between British finance and industry have become increasingly serious as the economy has become exposed to international competition in the last thirty years. Large sectors of British industry have become uncompetitive because of their failure to invest, and the result has been a collapse of output and investment. This is the deindustrialisation thesis put forward by a number of economists in the 1970s.[19] They argued that the manufacturing sector in Britain had contracted to the point where it could no longer generate enough exports to sustain full employment.

The main assumption of the finance thesis is that a successful modern capitalist economy requires a close relationship between finance and industry, rather than the sharp divide which has been the British practice.[20] One rejoinder is that the most successful capitalist economy of all, the United States, enforces an even more distant relationship between finance and industry through legislation. But this is partly countered by the existence of different practices in the USA at local and regional level. Another critique is that British capitalism is a unique configuration and has always given priority to finance and commerce over industry. On this reading there never was a period when industry was supreme. Finance did not become dominant sometime towards the end of the nineteenth century; it always was dominant. Britain's particular niche in the global division of labour has always been the provision of financial and commercial services to the world economy.[21] Some versions of this view argue that Britain was never really suited to industry, so that deindustrialisation in the 1970s, far from being a disaster, was an adaptation which allowed the economy to reorient towards what it did best.[22] The issue depends not on how much employment the manufacturing sector provides (because this could be as low as the contemporary agricultural sector) but how productive it is, and whether any other sector can replace the manufacturing sector in generating sufficient foreign exchange to pay for basic imports.

Finance has always been a target, particularly for the Social Imperialist tradition (both Joseph Chamberlain and Oswald Mosley attacked the organisation of finance). But except for the period between 1931 and 1951 there has never been the political will or opportunity to subordinate finance to a national policy aimed at giving priority to the needs of industry, and even at that time no long-term restructuring of financial relationships or company legislation was undertaken. Defenders of finance argue that the financial sector was always efficient and competitive and would have provided long-term finance to industry had industry requested it and shown that the investment could pay. The failures of British industry are regarded as lying within industry rather than in the relationship between industry and finance.[23]

Empire

A third peculiarity is the contribution to decline which possession of the world's largest Empire made. This thesis has been developed in terms of the opportunities during the closing decades of the nineteenth century for British industry to turn away from competing in world markets to the safer and protected markets of the Empire. The Empire therefore acted as a cushion which avoided the need for too much innovation and creative development. Britain could afford such a loss of competitiveness because of the enormous accumulated wealth from its investments and because of the size of its imperial markets.[24] This argument has been further developed in the concept of imperial overstretch, the idea that in common with previous Empires Britain reached a stage at which a conflict developed between the demands of military security and high consumption on one side, and productive investment on the other.[25] The relative neglect of the latter in favour of the former was facilitated by the formation of powerful military and bureaucratic elites keen to preserve their share of the budget. Such theories assume a cyclical view of history, a period of rise followed by decline. The conditions which were responsible for the initial success cannot be indefinitely sustained, and rivals arise to challenge the supremacy of the dominant power. The burdens of maintaining the leading position handicap the dominant power in resisting the challenge, and contribute to the onset of decadence. At a certain point this version of the imperial thesis merges with the cultural thesis.

Critics of the imperial thesis argue that British imperialism was closely tied to the interests of British finance and British commerce, rather than to industry, and that it continued to expand successfully through the first half of the twentieth century.[26] On this view the failure of Britain to develop the new technologies of the second industrial revolution at the end of the nineteenth century reflected the fact that industry had never been an important priority for British policy or for the structure of Britain's formal and informal Empire. This did not stop the continued expansion of that Empire (there was no long retreat), although in the long run it was one of the factors that brought its eventual collapse.

Other critics have challenged the whole notion of a split between British finance and industry, arguing that the leading companies in most sectors of British industry took full advantage of the financial and commercial opportunities which the Empire afforded them. There was therefore a close link between financial and industrial interests of a particular kind. Certain sectors lost out, but the support for the open seas and globally oriented financial and commercial policy came from a bloc of interests which spanned crucial sections of both industry and finance.[27] From this perspective the decline of the British national economy was not the same thing as the decline of British capitalism, which continued to flourish even while parts of the domestic economy languished.

State

A fourth peculiarity that has been singled out is the character of Britain's state. The key argument is that Britain has failed to develop the institutions and policy stance appropriate to a developmental state. It has developed a large public sector, and various kinds of interventionist and planning agencies, but not the kind of developmental role characteristic of other economies. The kind of economic success evident in Japan, for instance, is ascribed to the particular role which the state plays in the economy, creating a framework and infrastructure which promote long-term relationships of trust and close partnerships between finance and industry, and employers and employees, so making possible a dynamic private sector. A developmental state makes growth its chief priority rather than redistribution or welfare, but is also concerned to include rather than exclude its citizens, by providing all with the necessary skills and opportunities to participate in the economy. From this standpoint Britain's problem has been its persistent failure to ensure the creation of the institutions necessary to overcome weaknesses on the supply side of the economy, training and skills of the workforce, research and development of new products.

Arguments about the lack of a developmental state in Britain see the problem not in the particular circumstances of the policy failures and fiscal difficulties of the 1970s which gave rise to arguments about government failure such as the overload thesis, but as an endemic feature in the particular form of state which has been established in Britain. The traditions of parliamentary sovereignty and preference for forms of indirect rule and 'club government' have rested uneasily with the development of modern forms of administration.[28]

These concerns are most vigorously expressed in the characterisation of Britain as an *ancien régime*, the last of the *ancien régimes* in Europe, possessed of a pre-modern constitution and form of state, which in important respects has survived intact to the present.[29] The issue is whether the notoriously peculiar features of the British Constitution such as the absence of a single constitutional document, the prerogative powers of the monarchy, the persistence of the hereditary principle in the House of Lords, the degree of centralisation, and the lack of a systematic code of administrative law, are merely outward, dignified forms or whether they do indicate that the British state is in important respects different from other states.

The developmental state thesis cuts across earlier debates about planning by assuming that the role of the state is to assist a free market economy to work better rather than to supplant it with a different system of production and allocation. It is about different models of capitalism rather than replacing capitalism with socialism. It assumes that the state is able to play a variety of roles in making an economy more efficient and dynamic, and it argues that in Britain the possibility of a developmental state requires radical Constitutional reform to remove the obstacles to the state performing the kind of role which it performs in more successful industrial economies in western Europe and Japan, but also at a local level in the United States.

Criticism of this view comes from neo-liberals who argue that the main cause of decline is not that the state has intervened too little or in the wrong way, but that it has consistently intervened too much. The public sector is too large and places significant burdens on the private sector through taxation, controls and interest rates. From this perspective it is the expansion of the state which has stifled enterprise and fostered inefficiency and is the main contributory factor to decline. The public sector is regarded as a parasite and a drain upon the private sector, because of the inefficiency of the nationalised industries and the cost of maintaining public services. The private sector has been forced to struggle under burdens that inevitably depressed enterprise, discouraged risk-taking, and lowered profits. The remedy is to free the private sector from state control, to deregulate, to privatise, to reduce taxation and to limit the state to maintaining sound money and enforcing contracts, including labour contracts. Britain's economic decline is related directly to a set of policies which failed to give priority to the engine of wealth creation – the private sector. The remedy is to transform the state into an enterprise state. The idea of a developmental state is regarded as just another interventionist programme which will lead to the same government failures as before.

Industry

The final peculiarity which features heavily in explanations of decline has been industry. The problems of the British economy are traced to the poor quality of management and/or the poor state of industrial relations. While there are numerous studies berating either unions or management as the chief cause of decline, there is also an important institutionalist literature which argues that a number of institutional relationships have interacted in a particular way to create decline.[30] The patterns most often mentioned are the relationships between industry and finance, the fragmented unions, and the poor quality of training and education. Such theories draw on the idea of path dependency to suggest that societies can be locked into particular paths of development. Once the initial conditions had been established it proved very difficult to break away from them; the particular institutional configuration that was established was self-reinforcing. Studies of different sectors and industries confirm the destructive spiral of decline which became established in each of them.

One of the main criticisms of such institutional theories of decline is that they exaggerate the strength of path-dependency. Harmful and suboptimal patterns can persist for a time but provided a society remains reasonably open and pluralist, older patterns will become outmoded and will eventually be displaced. Societies and industries that fall behind have a strong incentive to catch up, and before long forces enabling them to catch up make themselves felt. This backwardness thesis suggests that all societies are now interdependent, and that backwardness cannot persist indefinitely. Sooner or later the country or industry that is behind will catch up. Decline is therefore only a temporary phenomenon and to be expected in the normal pattern of development, which will always be uneven, but over time will tend to even up advantages.[31]

This thesis was originally part of classical Marxism, and has been much criticised for being too optimistic about the equalising factors which development sets in train. The hierarchy of wealth and power between groups of nations has barely altered in the last hundred years.[32] But it has also been applied to the analysis of the top group of industrial economies in the argument that the changes of relative position that can be observed among them have been caused primarily by particular events like world wars, and that there is no tendency for cumulative decline or advance. The great strides made, for example, by Germany and Japan in the 1950s and 1960s were a natural example of catch-up. Britain is a special case in this regard because it too, on this theory, should have benefited from the incentives for catch-up. Why Britain failed to respond is ascribed to other factors – one explanation is that institutional sclerosis afflicts countries with open democratic polities.[33] Britain avoided the shocks of invasion and revolution and suffered the price of pluralistic stagnation and a weak, overloaded government. But on a longer view it is argued the shock was only postponed. When it finally occurred in the 1980s it produced a sharp increase in British productivity.[34]

My argument in this chapter is that in historical terms the focus of concern in the political debates on decline has shifted. The concern in the first two debates before and after the First World War was about the British Empire and how Britain's power in the world might be best preserved or prolonged. From the late 1950s Britain's relative economic decline in comparison with similar economies in western Europe and Japan became central. The political debates on decline and what could be done to reverse it reached a peak of intensity in the 1970s. Now the ground has shifted again and the continuing relevance of decline is questioned.

There are several reasons for this. The first is whether discrete national economies any longer exist. During the era of national protectionism which lasted roughly from 1916 (the first suspension of the gold standard) to 1971 (the collapse of Bretton Woods), the concept of a national economy and policy instruments for controlling and steering it were well developed. But this has been put in question by the movement towards deeper European integration through the creation of a single market and the plans for a single currency, as well as the increasing importance of international financial markets and transnational companies in shaping government policies. The European Union is a new kind of state with a fragmented, multi-level authority and a common system of regulation. It undermines unitary states and unitary national economies like the British. Meanwhile the enormous growth of transnational exchanges through corporate, commercial and financial networks makes the statistical definition of the boundaries of national economic space and how its performance can be measured increasingly problematic.[35]

A second reason is that there has been a sharp fall in expectations that governments can change policy and deliver the outcomes they seek. During the era of national protectionism there was greater faith and trust in government. Although the size of the state has barely shrunk at all even in those countries like the USA and the UK where the ideological and political attack has been strongest, the ambition of government has been reduced, and all parties now seek to reduce expectations about what government can do, rather than raise them. The confident programmes of the national protectionist era on full employment, welfare, poverty and economic growth have been abandoned. Even if decline is still thought to exist, no-one really thinks that a problem so complex and deep-rooted could be tackled by government.

The third reason is more prosaic. Many observers in Britain think that the decline is over because the economy has been turned around by the policies of the Conservative governments since 1979.[36] The shock that was administered, partly by accident, at the beginning of the 1980s by the slump in output and the surge in unemployment led to conflicts and changes in behaviour which have altered the path of development of the British economy and broken the obstacles to higher productivity and greater enterprise. The acceptance by the Labour Party of the new dispensation means, on this view, that the key peculiarities of British development which were preventing a more successful economic performance have been overcome. Some observers believe that the Thatcher years in Britain signalled the return to the traditional emphasis of British policy – commercial and financial, preserving the openness of the economy to the outside, and flexible institutions, particular-

ly the labour market, within. In this way the particular, unique form of
British capitalism can flourish again.[37]

A new period has certainly opened, and many of the old concerns
and debates are no longer relevant. Some of the claims being made,
however, are much too sweeping. The loss of power by national governments is much exaggerated, and though there has been a loss of confidence in many of the old ways in which governments acted, the size
and importance of government has not diminished and new ways of
exercising government influence and direction are sure to be developed.[38] The Conservative governments were successful in improving
the supply side performance of the economy in some areas but by no
means all. Investment, innovation, education and training all remain
weak. There was an improvement in the 1980s but no miracle. Many
economists still contend that the improvements in the supply side are
not sufficient to ensure that the British economy has a large enough
manufacturing sector to generate full employment or to prevent further
decline in the future.[39]

The new language in which issues of decline are discussed is the language of national competitiveness. Some economists have rubbished
the notion of competitiveness when it is applied to economies, arguing
that at best it can only be applied to single industries or companies.[40]
An emphasis on national competitiveness, they believe, leads to quite
inappropriate policies which are protectionist because they treat international trade as a zero sum game. National governments can make
supply-side improvements which help particular firms improve their
productivity, but it makes no sense to talk of one nation competing
against another. Thinking in such terms leads to policies which are
harmful because they restrict trade and diminish cooperation and trust.

So long as there are national governments, however, the lure of
thinking in terms of national economic spaces, how such territorially
defined populations and economies perform against one another, and
how policy might improve performance is bound to be strong. But on a
longer view the discourse of decline seems likely to fade away. Many
of the narratives underpinning it have collapsed. The era of national
protectionism and developmental states is over, and Britain's Empire is
becoming a distant memory. Within a single market and single-curren-
cy Europe, national economic decline would have no meaning. But
even if Britain were to withdraw from the European Union or the
European Union were to fall apart, decline will not be the dominant
framework of interpretation in the twenty-first century in the way it has
been in the twentieth. The re-emergence of a unified global economy

and the redistribution of state functions between different levels within
the international state system profoundly changes the concerns of
domestic politics and the way in which these are expressed.[41]
Historians in the next century are likely to see decline, in part, as a specific episode in British history determined by the particular circumstances of Britain's loss of hegemony and the slow adjustment of the
British political class to this change, and in part as a set of discourses
which constructed decline as a problem and urged political action to
remedy it.

Notes

1. See, for instance, N. Crafts, *Britain's Relative Economic Decline:
   1870–1995* (London, 1995); D. Coates, *The Question of UK Decline: The
   Economy, State and Society* (Hemel Hempstead, 1994); D. Coates and J.
   Hillard (eds), *The Economic Decline of Modern Britain: The Debate
   between Left and Right* (Brighton, 1986); D. Coates and J. Hillard (eds),
   *The Economic Revival of Modern Britain: The Debate between Left and
   Right* (London, 1987); A. Sked, *Britain's Decline: Problems and
   Perspectives* (Oxford, 1987); and A. Gamble, *Britain in Decline:
   Economic Policy, Political Strategy and the British State* (Basingstoke,
   1994; 1st edn, 1981).
2. N. Crafts, *Britain's Relative Economic Decline*.
3. See P. Krugman, 'Competitiveness: A Dangerous Obsession', *Foreign
   Affairs*, vol. 73, no. 2 (1994), pp. 28–44.
4. M. J. Wiener, *English Culture and the Decline of the Industrial Spirit
   1850–1980* (Harmondsworth, 1992; 1st edn, 1981). See also the interview
   with Wiener, pp. 25–36 of this book.
5. A. Friedberg, *The Weary Titan: Britain and the Experience of Relative
   Decline 1895–1905* (Princeton, 1988).
6. B. Semmel, *Imperialism and Social Reform: English Social-Imperial
   Thought 1895–1914* (London, 1960).
7. D. Watt, *Succeeding John Bull: America in Britain's Place 1900–75*
   (Cambridge, 1984).
8. H. Overbeek, *Global Capitalism and National Decline: The Thatcher
   Decade in Perspective* (London, 1990).
9. P. Jenkins, *Anatomy of Decline: The Political Journalism of Peter Jenkins*
   (London, 1996; 1st edn, 1995).
10. D. Marquand, *The Unprincipled Society* (London, 1988). See also the
    interview with Marquand, pp. 117–36 of this book.
11. C. Barnett, *The Audit of War: The Illusion and Reality of Britain as a
    Great Nation* (London, 1986); and C. Barnett, *The Lost Victory: British
    Dreams, British Realities 1945–1950* (London, 1996; 1st edn, 1995).
12. A. Shonfield, *Modern Capitalism: The Changing Balance of Public and
    Private Power* (Oxford, 1965).
13. S. Pollard, *The Wasting of the British Economy: British Economic Policy
    1945 to the Present* (London, 1982).

14. The cultural thesis is discussed sceptically in D. Edgerton, *England and the Aeroplane: An Essay on a Militant and Technological Nation* (London, 1991); and W.D. Rubinstein, *Capitalism, Culture and Decline in Britain 1750–1990* (London, 1994; 1st edn, 1993).
15. See C. Barnett, *The Lost Victory.*
16. See M.J. Wiener, *English Culture.*
17. W.D. Rubinstein, *Capitalism, Culture and Decline.*
18. W. Hutton, *The State We're In* (London, 1996; 1st edn, 1995), p. 112.
19. F. Blackaby (ed.), *Deindustrialisation* (London, 1979).
20. P. Anderson, 'The Figures of Descent', *New Left Review*, vol. 161 (1987), pp. 20–77.
21. G. Ingham, *Capitalism Divided? The City and Industry in British Social Development* (Basingstoke, 1984).
22. H. McRae, *The World in 2020* (London, 1994).
23. W.D. Rubinstein, *Capitalism, Culture and Decline.*
24. E. Hobsbawm, *Industry and Empire: An Economic History of Britain since 1750* (Harmondsworth, 1968).
25. P. Kennedy, *The Rise and Fall of the Great Powers: Economic Change and Military Conflict from 1500 to 2000* (London, 1989; 1st edn, 1988).
26. P.J. Cain and A.G. Hopkins, *British Imperialism: Volume Two, Crisis and Deconstruction 1914–1990* (London, 1993).
27. M. Barratt Brown, 'Away With All the Great Arches: Anderson's History of British Capitalism', *New Left Review*, vol. 167 (1988), pp. 22–52.
28. On 'overload' see A. King, 'Overload: Problems of Governing in the 1970s', *Political Studies*, vol. 23 (1975), pp. 284–96. And on 'club government' see D. Marquand, *The Unprincipled Society*, pp. 175–208.
29. See T. Nairn, 'The Crisis of the British State', *New Left Review*, vol. 30 (1981), pp. 37–44.
30. B. Elbaum and W. Lazonick (eds), *The Decline of the British Economy* (Oxford, 1986); M. Dintenfass, *The Decline of Industrial Britain 1870–1980* (London, 1992).
31. C. Feinstein, 'The Benefits of Backwardness and the Costs of Continuity', in A. Graham (ed.), *Government and Economies in the Post-War World: Economic Policies and Comparative Performance, 1945–85* (London, 1990).
32. G. Arrighi, *The Long Twentieth Century: Money, Power, and the Origins of Our Times* (London, 1994).
33. M. Olson, *The Rise and Fall of Nations: Economic Growth, Stagflation and Social Rigidities* (New Haven, 1982).
34. G. Maynard, *The Economy Under Mrs Thatcher* (Oxford, 1988).
35. J. Ruggie, 'Territoriality and Beyond: Problematizing Modernity in International Relations', *International Organization,* vol. 47 , no. 1 (1993), pp. 139–174.
36. N. Crafts, *Britain's Relative Economic Decline.*
37. See W.D. Rubinstein, *Capitalism, Culture and Decline in Britain.*
38. P. Hirst and G. Thompson, *Globalisation in Question: The International Economy and the Possibilities of Governance* (Cambridge, 1996).
39. J. Michie (ed.), *The Economic Legacy 1979–1992* (London, 1992).

40. P. Krugman, 'Competitiveness: A Dangerous Obsession', *Foreign Affairs*, vol. 73 (1994), pp. 28–44.
41. A. Gamble and A. Payne (eds), *Regionalism and World Order* (London, 1996).

Part I

Reflections on British Decline

2

Martin Wiener

Introduction

Martin Wiener has been one of the most important and influential contributors to the decline debates considered in this book. Born in 1941, he was an undergraduate at Brandeis University in the United States, and gained his MA and PhD from Harvard. He was first employed at Rice University, Houston, Texas, in 1967, and is currently the Mary Gibbs Jones Professor of History there. He has enjoyed a distinguished career, holding a number of prestigious fellowships, including awards from the National Endowment for the Humanities, the American Council of Learned Societies and the Woodrow Wilson International Center for Scholars. He is also a Fellow of the Royal Historical Society.

His first book was a study of the Fabian thinker, Graham Wallas.[1] Wiener then began work on his best-known text, *English Culture and the Decline of the Industrial Spirit*,[2] published in 1981. This was awarded the prestigious Robert Livingston Schuyler Prize of the American Historical Association and aroused considerable academic interest. In Britain it figured prominently in the political arguments of the day,[3] its central thesis being appropriated by leading figures within the Thatcher cabinet. In some respects it was the first major 'declinist' text to be taken up by both an academic and a wider audience. In it Wiener offered a powerful critique of 'a distinctive complex of social ideas, sentiments and values in the "articulate" classes, embodying an ambiguous attitude toward modern industrial society'.[4] At a time when concern about the British 'disease' dominated public debate, Wiener provided a potent historical explanation of this phenomenon, placing the blame on the emergence of this cultural complex in the mid-late nineteenth century. It had continued to exert a powerful and harmful effect upon public policy into the contemporary period:

In the world's first industrial nation, industrialism did not seem quite at home. In the country that had started mankind on the 'great ascent', economic growth was frequently viewed with suspicion and disdain. Having pioneered urbanisation, the English ignored or disparaged cities. [5]

Whereas most nineteenth-century historiography focused upon Britain's economic power, Wiener argued that a pattern of decay and decline in fact set in whilst it was the leading nation in the world economy. The forces of economic development that were reshaping British society throughout the nineteenth century were surrounded by a 'cultural *cordon sanitaire*' that was opposed to these changes.

Wiener offered a broad and apparently extensive analysis of middle-class culture at the end of the nineteenth and beginning of the twentieth centuries. He pointed to a mutually reinforcing nexus of sentiments and values which were drawn from different sources, but which were predominantly shaped by the entrenched, landed aristocracy and which, accordingly, celebrated an arcadian vision of rustic England. Thus the middle classes, 'through . . . mechanisms of social absorption', failed to generate a self-sustaining culture around their 'zeal for work, inventiveness, material production and money making', opting for a gentrified cultural style.[6] Even the significant emergence towards the end of the century of a number of modern professions – doctors, lawyers, academics – did not disrupt this hegemonic cultural system, as their mental universe was suffused by values and aesthetics far removed from the mind-set of industrial capitalism.

A central and interesting feature of his analysis concerns the 'capture' of some of the most important middle-class institutions by this gentrified arcadianism and its attendant ideals. Education played an important role in his argument, particularly the classics-dominated curricula offered by the public schools. Likewise, universities in this period were gripped by what he terms a 'conservative revolution', whereby the curricula of Oxbridge colleges were reproduced elsewhere. Wiener also dissected the mental universe of a number of Britain's leading intellectuals, pinpointing their enthusiasm for gentry values after the 1860s. In a range of artistic and aesthetic fields, a highly nostalgic picture of England's idyllic past held sway until 1914. The counterpart to these ideals was the presentation of industrialism and industrial life as antithetical to Englishness. Increasingly, the 'alien' cultures of rival states were perceived as excessively materialistic unlike England's native values.

In the book's second half, Wiener sought to connect this value system to the behaviour of Britain's political and economic elites. 'Politics reflected the general ambivalence about industrial society, and helped in practice to dampen rather than stimulate industrial development'.[7] This also occurred in business, where the industrial 'class' was far less self-confident and expansive than elsewhere, torn between two conflicting cultures. At the heart of Wiener's argument lies the belief that British economic development was severely hampered by a debilitating division between financial and industrial interests. Whereas the former were geographically and socially proximate to the power of the landed gentry and could thus be readily assimilated, industrialists (whose heartlands lay in the 'provincial' north) were culturally isolated as the century developed. The cultural and moral standards that the industrialist inherited were drawn from the world of 'upper Englishry' and refused to take the world of production seriously.

This pattern of development carried serious consequences for Britain. The heartland industries of the 'second' industrial revolution – electricity, gas, motor vehicles – received precious little financial support from the City or government. The two prevailing elites of British capitalism were structurally mismatched, with power and prestige tilting towards finance rather than industry. In the postwar period, the manager and the industrialist were 'leper' figures in cultural terms, lampooned and criticised. Industry drew graduates who were not of the highest calibre: these flocked to employment opportunities elsewhere. Within the business world, he cited numerous examples of the pervasiveness of the gentry ideal: self-made millionaires who tend their newly acquired gardens, and play at being 'lord of the manor', rather than aggressively pursuing the market ideal. Within management, a cautious and conservative atmosphere prevailed so that innovation and entrepreneurship were rare, despite the lip-service paid to free enterprise.

Wiener's arguments proved highly stimulating and provocative for scholars working in these fields. Such has been their influence that he has been described as the progenitor of the 'cultural' explanation of British decline. Some economic historians, particularly W.D. Rubinstein, have issued forceful challenges to Wiener's interpretation.[8] They have focused especially on what they perceive to be his mis-characterisation of the finance-industry divide, and the empirical status of many of his claims. And since the book was written, many of the different domains which he analysed – education, intellectual culture, the views of the political elite, and economic performance itself – have been subjected to close scrutiny as these topics have attracted their own complex and rich historiographies.

In the statement which follows he surveys these intellectual fields, noting areas where his thesis has been refined by other scholars. But he reveals his continued belief that 'decline' should remain a central motif in historical work on the late nineteenth century, and that cultural factors are an important part of its explanation. He also offers thoughts upon the declinist literature which has grown far more extensive since *English Culture and the Decline of the Industrial Spirit* was published. His statement offers some fascinating insights into the different factors which motivated his unusual study. An American by birth, he has been a Professor of History at Rice University for over two decades and has approached British history in singular and insightful ways. He also reveals his reaction to the appropriation of the book by the political right in Britain, and offers some telling observations about contemporary political and economic developments in the UK and elsewhere.

Interview[*]

I began writing *English Culture and the Decline of the Industrial Spirit* in the 1970s. And I wrote it from the vantage point of cultural history, which is the discipline in which I feel most comfortable. I was looking especially at the late nineteenth century, at the plethora of expressions of concern with rural England and the nature of Englishness. And I was living in London in 1973–74, while I was doing this research. I increasingly felt a connection between this project and the personal experience of being an American in England at that time. This was my first time in the country for an extended sojourn. And I picked quite a good year, 1973–74, when the miners' strike, the three-day week and other crises were taking place. All of this seemed a kind of demonstration being put on for the benefit of foreigners. Even celebrations of the Dunkirk spirit reappeared!

The Prime Minister at the time, Ted Heath, seemed to epitomise the anti-modernism at the heart of English culture. He was supposedly the 'moderniser' in the political arguments of the day. Yet he was at best a peculiar kind of moderniser. He really did not like industry or commerce himself. I always thought it particularly inappropriate that *Private Eye* would put him down as 'the Grocer'. *Private Eye* was exhibiting exactly the kind of disdain for commerce that I was talking about in my book. And more generally, it seemed to me that although all three parties at this time were arguing fiercely about how Britain should modernise, all wanted to distinguish themselves

* Interviewed by Michael Kenny: Houston, Texas, 7 April 1997

very clearly from anything American. The modernisers were therefore a peculiar kind, from an external perspective. And so I would come home from the archives in the evening, having studied the phenomenon of anti-industrialism, and I would find it still alive every time I turned on the evening news and heard Heath, or the Liberals, or Wilson! All of them seemed to be saying, 'Don't worry. I won't disturb you, I won't upset your life, I won't introduce any kind of excessively rapid change or vulgar materialism.'

The book gained an audience due to the political climate in which it appeared. Through the 1960s and 1970s concern was growing in public life that something had gone wrong, that Britain was somehow off-track. There was an increasingly pervasive sense of failure. So you have this growing, inchoate mood which crystallised in Thatcher's election in 1979. And at that moment, larger issues about the country's economy and the direction in which society was moving were raised during an election campaign. Now this rarely happens. Thatcher's election seemed at least to signal that some new direction would be tried.

I felt very ambivalent when I realised that political figures were citing my book. I was a little horrified, in part, because I was the typical academic who was not thinking in terms of addressing the immediate national political debate. But the public reaction was also pleasing. I began to receive what you could almost call 'fan mail', which again is not the kind of response we academics expect. I had previously published a book which was read by some minute number of people.[9] And here I was actually getting mail from dozens of people. Typically I would receive a letter, say, from an engineer or small businessman, saying, 'Yes, that's right', or 'That's just what I've been feeling. That's the story of my life.' So I had tapped into a fairly strong current of feeling, especially among these people who felt that they had not been given respect, and that they were working in a society that was continually undervaluing them.

In terms of the broad scope of the book, I think that as an American it was easier to take a wide-ranging look at British history. And I had been teaching British history to American students who knew very little about it. So I had already spent years explaining broad features of British life and culture to people. So perhaps I was more comfortable making generalisations of that kind than more specialist historians within Britain.

I had previously written a book on the early Fabian socialists. It was while working on that study that I began to notice all of these 'ruralist' strains and recurrent anxieties about national culture and identity; particularly from the 1880s to 1914. This was the period I was chiefly looking at. And of course this was when people were first beginning to worry about Britain's economic performance in comparison with the Germans and Americans. This kind of anxiety about imperial rivals and other economic powers really focused people's minds on what England was supposed to be. And what interested me was that few people agreed with Joseph Chamberlain's answer to this question – the idea of imperial preference. They preferred the idea that the English were great 'country livers'. And then I was able to trace this sentiment back to the mid-century, to a point where you first see these preoccupations emerge. So I started my analysis at the moment of the construction of the 'Crystal Palace' and the Great Exhibition as a contrast with what was to come. A decade after 1851, a different world had emerged. It became clear that another (aristocratic) culture had enveloped this rising industrial culture in the course of the second half of the nineteenth century.

I would now emphasise the experience of Empire more in my argument. Empire was important precisely in the sense of encouraging the kind of educational changes, for example, that were going to work against economic innovation. Empire made the figure of the imperial administrator increasingly important, and established this as an ideal career. By the early twentieth century, this figure had become a kind of archetypal civil servant at home. And this was a whole career path that had not existed before. The Empire also promoted what I would term a mentality of maintenance, for which the imperial administrator became the role model. This involved being a 'maintainer' of an existing, already highly successful organisation that everybody else in the world admired. The point was not to find new ways of doing things, but simply to continue the successful, accepted ways, and to adapt them to various particular situations, adapting a given model which, on the whole, one tended to learn in public school. And this continued into the twentieth century. I am in fact just this week having my class watch a film called *Sanders of the River*.[10] It was made in the 1930s, and was very popular then. Of course it now seems extremely archaic, and very politically 'incorrect'. The film was based on stories that were very popular for years. And in it here is this 'model' Englishman, performing an ideal kind of role. And what is he doing? He is maintaining order so that civilisation can do its good works. And how is he doing it? He is not unusually intelligent. But he manages through a kind of personal charisma and force of character, establishing a personal ascendancy over these 'semi-savages', and even over other Europeans, like the evil commercial traders who were selling the Africans guns and liquor. This kind of text offers us images of two kinds of Europeans. There are the nasty, commercial types out to make a buck. Then there is the noble Englishman who is totally uninterested in money, or even in getting the Africans to modernise. Rule is just a matter of maintaining law and order, and allowing everybody to live their tranquil lives. In that sense I think the Empire was very important, in that it undergirded an ideal of maintenance that was linked in some ways to the national character.

Critics of my argument have, wrongly, suggested that I was seeking to offer a complete explanation of British decline. At the time that I was writing, there was no cultural dimension to arguments about decline. I was trying to put forward a point of view, an important part of a total picture, that had not been seen previously. My argument got picked up in a way that suggested it was the sole explanation of decline. I had never intended it to be more than an important aspect of this wider phenomenon. A total explanation needs to look at a lot of other factors – the structure of markets, Britain's early start (which itself was going to create economic problems later by entrenching earlier forms of behaviour and labour relations), and other such factors. There was a penalty attached to taking the lead in economic terms.

But, on the other hand, I think some critics, notably W.D. Rubinstein, go too far. He is so committed to knocking down my argument that he makes some peculiar points. On the one hand he insists that decline is not a problem. And of course, in some ways, maybe he is right. We all know that in absolute terms the British economy has grown for centuries. People are continually better off. And one could also reasonably argue that there were bound to be hiccups in the socio-economic development of a country that leapt ahead in the way Britain did. By the early nineteenth century, Britain was a peculiar place, a tiny island off the coast of Europe that was exercising disproportionate influence and had unbelievable wealth. This was not a stable situation. But to assume, as Rubinstein and others do, that there is no problem with the modern British economy is to fall into the same trap as Marxist historians. The latter are always looking at workers who did not revolt as if they should have. Then they use the idea of 'false consciousness' to explain this. And so it is as if all of the people who have talked about decline in twentieth-century Britain are suffering from false consciousness, a kind of mass delusion. As in anything else, one should generally look for a more straightforward explanation.

So Rubinstein, it seems to me, exaggerates greatly. On some points I do agree with him, for instance his emphasis upon non-industrial sources of wealth in Britain, particularly in the late nineteenth century. Part of my argument was to suggest that the industrialists were not as powerful as we had thought. But Rubinstein tends to identify or measure the importance of industry in terms of the number of millionaires. This is very open to debate and economic historians have argued back and forth on this. I do think that industry was more important than he grants.

Also he draws distinctions that are too sharp. In order to stress how important finance was, he considers the whole service sector and commercial activity under that heading. But commerce and industry are not opposites. Production is not just confined to the field of industry. Products are not always manufactured goods. Increasingly, modern products are intangible. The British economy has also revealed weaknesses in the commercial sector, particularly in terms of salesmanship. I remember that when I was trying to figure out a title for the book, I could not decide between the words 'industrial' and 'commercial'. I wanted to refer to more specific factors than British capitalism, to making things as well as to materialism, commerce and money-making. There is no word in English that has that overtone. So I finally settled on the words 'industrial spirit'. But I kept tossing around in my head 'commercial spirit', which did not quite sound right. In other words, I did not want people to think that I was only referring to the industrial sector.

Rubinstein and other critics have focused too on education. And perhaps in my argument I concentrated too much on public schools. What we need to do is look at educational provision throughout society in this period. But at the time that I was writing, this kind of research just had not been done. And these arguments about decline have now led to more analysis of this kind. Some of the work that has been done since I wrote the book shows that, for example, in the state schools and even the minor public schools, people would emulate both the attitudes and curricula of the public schools, revealing how significant the latter were. And, furthermore, I think that work done since then provides a good deal of evidence that lower levels of technical education were poorly developed and supported. This was true in terms of the education of skilled workers, but was also apparent at higher levels: there has been no equivalent of the Massachusetts Institute of Technology, for example. In general, technical education was underdeveloped compared to what was happening in Germany, France and the United States. There are other ways in which the educational system was inhibiting a faster rate of economic development. I did not deal with these in the book though I alluded to them. I find the evidence about the culture and curricula of public schools overwhelming and vivid, though perhaps the story about these schools was more complicated than I suggested. But I do think that the cultural effects of public school education were, by and large, as I described them.

Some critics have argued that I took professions of anti-industrialism by public figures, especially conservative ones, too seriously; that it is actually an English technique, to put it too crudely, to pretend that you do not care at all about making money simply as a smokescreen to enable yourself to do so, and thus evoke less resistance. Of course there may have been an element of that. Yet I was trying to argue that the rationalisations that people develop, even if they contain strategic elements, tend to rebound and affect these people who are making them. Over generations, what people may think of as purely strategic and almost duplicitous justifications come to shape their behaviour. You come to forget that you are being duplicitous and it begins to sound plausible to you as well. So there were strategic and manipulative dimensions to these professions of rural nostalgia that I did not deal with in the book. Baldwin is a good example, seeking to identify the Conservative party with a broader public. But I think that over time this kind of technique affects the people who are propagating it. You cannot live your whole life as a guise without it partly becoming you.

My book helped stimulate research in this area and others, so that we know far more about them now. Another important field affected by these debates concerned the culture of the mid-nineteenth-century middle class. Economic historians, in general – and even economists – are now far more appreciative of the importance of cultural factors in economic development than fifteen to twenty years ago. In the book I had to state that questions of economic decline are too important to leave to the economists. This is now a much more widely accepted view. Culture has become an extremely popular area of study, perhaps even too much so. The pendulum has swung away from old-style economic history, and cultural history seems about to engulf everything else. And in public debate too, there is far more discussion in Britain about the importance of culture in economic performance, as is evident in recent debates about the Asian 'Tigers'.

One big difference between Britain and the USA has been the absence in the latter of an intellectual culture which crystallised around hostility to economic progress. Certainly there have been people who have deliberately marginalised themselves and become 'beats' and so forth. But they have rarely been people of prestige, wealth and position. And there are certainly different forms of political anti-industrialism in France and Germany. Every modern society has various forms of resistance built into it. So I do not think that the British instance is totally unique in having an anti-industrial culture. It is, though, a matter of degree.

In Britain now, it is interesting that New Labour and associated intellectuals like Will Hutton,[11] who are critical of the Thatcherite legacy, are still very interested in development and innovation. The reaction against unfettered free markets, *laissez faire* and wholesale privatisation that they represent is taking the form of a solid commitment to market behaviour in general, and to understanding that economic growth is critical. Personally, I have never been in favour of 'free' markets everywhere; solutions depend upon particular situations and contexts. From my point of view, the positive aspects of Thatcherism stemmed from the recognition and prestige given to business, efforts to develop technical education and the breaking down of a lot of state control of economic life which tended to work against innovation. Now one might argue that this modernisation project could have been taken further, say in terms of the abolition or reform of some of the archaic parts of the state. But a Conservative administration was never going to abolish the House of Lords! Actually, it was a shame that Thatcher accepted a title. It would have been wonderful if she had refused it. It has always seemed to me a little inconsistent that she took a title, given her own rhetoric.

Economic improvement undoubtedly occurred under Thatcher. On the whole the British economy is clearly performing better. The statistics demonstrate that whereas several decades previously, GNP productivity had been declining relative to most other countries, since 1979 on the whole it has improved relative to France and Germany, and even in comparison with the United States. That is pretty striking, because productivity usually changes only gradually. It seems to me that the economy has been freed of a lot of inhibitions, and people who are interested in economic growth have been given greater power. And most of the privatisations have been economically beneficial. Moreover, a fundamental realisation has dawned that you cannot escape from international economic pressures. You must figure out a policy to work within them. That is partly a legacy of Thatcher. She shifted political perspectives. So, to some degree I think she changed the mental set, very broadly speaking, of the middle classes in England.

I recall that when I was in England in the seventies, we were living in a middle-class suburb, Edgware, and I got to know a few of my neighbours. I was struck by the fact that they were natural Conservative voters. Their parents had generally voted Labour and they themselves had grown up in working-class areas, and then succeeded sufficiently to move to Edgware. They had now entered the middle class, were committed to improving themselves, did not want to pay high taxes and saw their own interests bound up with economic growth and development. Yet they were very frustrated because they did not have anyone to vote for enthusiastically in the 1974 election. They were feeling some of the frustration that I felt, since Heath was the candidate whom they would 'naturally' vote for but they did not like him, though they did, for the most part, vote Conservative. He evoked no enthusiasm on their part because he seemed to be upper class. Perhaps he was not in objective terms. But, nonetheless, he had absorbed this whole anti-urban and anti-enterprise culture. These people felt he was not somebody who understood them. It seemed to me then that there was a job vacancy for a Conservative leader who could reach these people, who could speak in their terms and not seem upper class; someone who seemed to care about the issues that they did. Thatcher fitted that job description perfectly.

Looking back, I see my own book as part of a larger reaction against an earlier historiography that I absorbed when I became a British historian, back in the 1960s. This was really a historiography from the 1940s and 1950s. It consisted of a celebratory, 'Whig' consensus about British social development, seeing in Britain the inexorable rise of the world's most civilised society, humane and balanced, successful even in giving up an empire so peacefully (this view was so predominant that historians did not seem to notice that hundreds of thousands of people killed each other in India in 1947!). Of course continental Europe was in ruins at this time, and German history appeared to be a story of total disaster. I was reacting, I think, against that whole framework, which did not square with what I was finding out about the nineteenth century. The first sentence of the book expresses this frustration: 'The leading problem of modern British history is the explanation of economic decline'.[12] So I was rebelling against this historiography and suggesting that important parts of the story of British development had been missed. My position became exaggerated in 'translation' by others.

Actually I had a problem with putting 'decline' in the title as well as the word 'industrial'. My original idea for the book was 'English Culture and the Containment of Industrialism'. I was persuaded, partly by the publisher, to change it because 'decline' grabs readers more and this helped no doubt to get it picked up politically. What I was really trying to argue was not that after the mid-nineteenth century everything deteriorated in English life, but that development did not occur as it might have: an alternative history was possible. And when industrial culture was emerging, it was enveloped and contained by this highly effective aristocratic culture which was already there. So the book was really an effort to explain a change that did not occur, rather than a deleterious change happening to a successful state. I think some of the criticism I received stems from a misunderstanding of this. I always thought of my function as being to raise questions that might subsequently be modified and complexified. And these questions were easier for me to raise because I was outside the culture. I particularly wanted to connect public discourse about the state of the country in the 1970s with the concerns of historians, because these seemed – unfortunately – to be totally separate in Britain.

Notes

1. M. J. Wiener, *Between Two Worlds: The Political Thought of Graham Wallas* (Oxford, 1971).
2. M. J. Wiener, *English Culture and the Decline of the Industrial Spirit 1850–1980* (Harmondsworth, 1992; 1st edn, 1981).
3. References to Wiener's book are legion in political commentary, journalism and the academic literatures on British politics and economic development. For discussion of the reaction to his book, see: K. Robbins, 'British Culture versus British Industry', in B. Collins and K. Robbins (eds), *British Culture and Economic Decline* (London, 1990), pp. 1–21; W.D.

Rubinstein, 'Cultural Explanations for Britain's Economic Decline', *ibid.*, pp. 59–90; and C. Harvie, 'Liturgies of National Decadence – Wiener, Dahrendorf and the British Crisis', *Cencrastus*, vol. 21 (1985), pp. 17–28.
4. M.J. Wiener, *English Society*, p. ix.
5. *Ibid.*
6. *Ibid.* p. 13.
7. *Ibid.* p. 96.
8. W.D. Rubinstein, *Capitalism, Culture and Decline in Britain 1750–1990* (London, 1994; 1st edn, 1993). See also the interview with Rubinstein, pp. 61–75 of this book.
9. M.J. Wiener, *Between Two Worlds. op. cit.*
10. *Sanders of the River* was released in 1935, and directed by Zoltan Korda.
11. See the interview with Hutton, pp. 50–60 of this book.
12. M.J. Wiener, *English Culture*, p. 3.

3

Correlli Barnett

Introduction

Correlli Barnett's work has had a profound influence on the shape of the British decline debate. Born in 1927, he was educated at Trinity School in Croydon and Exeter College, Oxford. His many books include *The Desert Generals* and *Britain and Her Army*;[1] but it is less in his military histories than in three other highly important books[2] that his work relates most closely to the question of British decline. Barnett has argued that the causes of Britain's weakness as an industrial country after the Second World War lie 'not in the events and policies of the post-war era, but in the British record during the war itself'.[3] But this focus on British policies and performance during the Second World War forms part of a wider argument about British experience. Barnett holds that by the mid-1930s Britain was already enfeebled and that, contrary to widespread assumption then and later, the country was in fact already a second-rate power. The demands of the 1939–45 war, he suggests, revealed the nature and extent of longstanding British weaknesses: the poor quality and widespread ineptitude of industrial management; the uncommitted, ill-trained, ill-educated, smugly conservative and obstructive workforce; the narrow base in high technology resources and skills, and the consequent overdependence on imports of foreign technology (a dependence combined during the war with a reliance on massive but temporary American financial support);[4] the weak provision of education and training facilities;[5] the misconception that Empire and Commonwealth were evidence of strength as a first-rank power, rather than a drain on resources which contributed to Britain's second-rate standing; and the fragmented industrial organisation and serious deficiencies in key sectors of the economy (coal, iron and steel, shipbuilding, aircraft).

What is commonly identified as the British disease of the 1960s and 1970s was, therefore, already widely evident in the 1940s; for the cru-

cial period of British commercial defeat was between the 1870s and the
outbreak of the Second World War. Part of the problem lay in the nature
of the governing elite, one which was too preoccupied with romantic
idealism and moral purpose and insufficiently concerned with questions of power and strategy. This attitude had produced the anti-techni-
cal bias which marred so much of British industrial performance. The
Oxbridge and public school culture which produced the Establishment
elite was crucial here, for these institutions saw their duty to lie in an
Arnoldian preference for gentlemanly, Christian leaders rather than in
the provision of technical education for the governing of an efficient
industrial nation.[6] Education was seen by the late-Victorian public
schools not as a preparation for the world, 'but as an inoculation
against it'.[7] Consequently, Barnett argues that the elite which had been
produced by the 1840–1940 period was one which was high-minded
but essentially hopeless: moral fervour, honour, balance, detachment
and nineteenth-century romanticism were no match for the challenges
of the 1939–45 conflict and, in particular, for the planning necessary
for postwar reconstruction. Late nineteenth- and early twentieth-century British public schools were woefully lacking in awareness of the
newest scientific and technological innovations; and British educational
developments were unrelated to one another, this lack of coordination
being typical of a British way which eschewed centrally administered,
coherent organisation.

But in addition to the liberal and romantically idealistic educational
bias there was also the problem of the cult of the 'practical man'.
British industry was typified by people who sneered at technical or scientific preparation and development, and who emphasised their capacity for pragmatically learning on the job. According to Barnett, therefore, the Second World War demonstrated that Britain required a fundamental and long-awaited overhaul of industrial infrastructure.
Investment was needed in rebuilding and re-equipping the obsolete
industrial structure, and a new approach to education was definitely
required. It was 'shortage of resources – economic and financial –
which posed by far the gravest question of all for the British government after the fall of France in 1940'.[8] At the end of the war, Britain
was 'a war-impoverished, obsolescent and second-rank industrial economy'.[9]

The roots of this went deep. The moral, Christian and romantic
strains in nineteenth-century British life elevated emotionalism and
sentiment over hard-headed, rational calculation of interests. And,
interwoven with this, Britain from the 1840s onwards had been failing

to adapt speedily and effectively enough to meet the challenges of technological change. Much of the nineteenth century had seen Britain failing to develop science and technology at rates comparable with her rivals; quality of technology and of management were serious problems in British industry, and government policies during the 1939–45 war worsened this situation. In the coal industry, for example, wartime policy fudged the link between productivity and reward as between different coalfields. Coal productivity actually fell during the 1942–45 period; and the combination of historic weaknesses, wartime performance and government planning during the war meant that the development of a strong postwar coal industry was very difficult.

Crucially, Barnett holds that during the immediate postwar period Britain missed 'a unique and irrecoverable opportunity to remake herself as an industrial country while her rivals were still crippled by defeat and occupation'.[10] But governmental planning for the postwar period was, in fact, unrealistic and inadequate. This point is central to Barnett's overall argument. The wartime and postwar combination of two misconceived and burdensome projects crushed what could have been a resurgent Britain: first, the overambitious attempt to create a New Jerusalem ('a society in which poverty, ill-health, slums and unemployment would all be abolished by beneficent state action');[11] second, a continued belief that Britain's Commonwealth commitments (and the Sterling Area) made her a world power and that these huge commitments were therefore justified. Too much of Marshall Aid was used to prop up the Sterling Area's gold and dollar reserves, and to support current government expenditure at home and abroad; and too little on the root and branch reconstruction of industry and infrastructure. Only superficial changes were wrought, and Britain's shaky Victorian edifice was essentially left in place.

Illusions, dreams and romantic ideals obscured realities and obstructed realistic, practical planning. The elite nurtured on romantic idealism cherished an unrealistic New Jerusalem project which a financially drained and industrially enfeebled country simply could not afford. Just as there had been a contradiction between the unsullied idealism of nineteenth-century elite education and the grubbier industrial world which funded it, so too British wartime planning concentrated more on desirable social change than on economic realities, and more on ethical concerns than on the question of resources. War stimulated impracticable social ambitions and expectations, and there was a stark contrast between, on the one hand, self-congratulatory celebration of achievement and potential and, on the other, a grimmer industrial reality. For example, the plans for post-war reconstruction concentrated on housing, rather than on recreating a strong industrial base which could fund housing that Britain could actually afford. And British wartime forecasts failed dismally to recognise the radical recasting of industry which was to characterise much postwar European development. Britain was left ill-prepared for the challenge posed by her rivals. Whitehall was itself Victorian, and this was reflected in the weaknesses of her wartime policies and planning. Strategy for the postwar era was piecemeal and tentative rather than radical, centrally coordinated and profound.

After the war, only inadequate changes were made. Educational change was based on wartime New Jerusalem convictions about equality rather than on hard-headed recognition of industrial need. Postwar planning during the war had relatively neglected the improvement of technical and higher education, and this was to have damaging consequences after the war. There remained the British educational preference for supposedly high or pure culture rather than for the practical and the industrial.

Barnett's *Collapse of British Power*, *Audit of War* and *Lost Victory* constitute, in effect, a continuous and threefold argument: first, that there existed longstanding problems with Britain as an industrial nation; second, that the Second World War reflected these deficiencies, and that government policies and planning during the war exacerbated them; third, that there was in fact a unique opportunity to reconstruct Britain as a European industrial power in the immediate postwar years but that this was wasted (in substantial part because of British policies and vision during the war itself): 'Britain's post-war decline began in wartime British dreams, illusions and realities'.[12] Correlli Barnett's arguments have had an extremely powerful impact on decline debates. Many scholars have responded to his theses, and a lively exchange has ensued.[13] Politicians, too, have adopted his arguments. Keith Joseph was among those who endorsed Barnett's views, and the latter's suggestion that the British elite had been unhelpfully hostile to science and technology plainly fitted in with aspects of Thatcherite ideology.

Interview[*]

Declinism and anti-declinism are concepts of a kind absolutely beloved of academics. I myself prefer not to talk specifically about decline in any of my

[*] Interviewed by Richard English and Michael Kenny: Cambridge, 16 July 1996.

books. Indeed, I do not really think my books are about decline as much as about more specific issues. These issues include the imperial overstretch (totally out of kilter with the actual military and wealth resources of the country); they include Britain's unquestionable backwardness in education generally (and particularly technical education) and our failure to educate and train the nation as well as our competitors. So I am more interested in competitiveness than in decline. Another aspect is the question whether or not Britain was laggardly in getting into new markets for new products and new technologies. Again that is something which I explore in my work, but whether this amounts to decline I would leave to other people.

People have sometimes linked my work with that of Martin Wiener. Wiener's book[14] appeared roughly a decade after *The Collapse of British Power*. It does have, in some respects, a similar kind of argument about the antipathy of British nineteenth-century elite culture towards industrialisation. But Wiener leaves out some things that I try to tackle, including the question of the 'practical man' in industry who did not particularly value training and education in a very formal way. So Wiener's book is a one-track argument, and I think there is more than one track in this question of how the country, as a whole, approaches industrial competitiveness. But there is a similarity between our arguments in so far as Wiener and I both look at the ways in which the mental climate which prevailed among the governing elite and intelligentsia was hostile to competitive industrialisation.

In relation to authors such as Professor Wiener and myself, some have suggested that, rather than being primarily an industrial nation, Britain was a commercial trading nation. But I would not have thought that this was really possible to assert in view of the amount of British economic and social life locked up in industry. The importance of that great weight of industrial production and export within the overall economy was crucial. So I think it is exaggerated to say that Britain's was essentially a trading rather than an industrial economy.

In my own work I have drawn attention to the importance of the Second World War in relation to British competitiveness. The First World War was hardly less important, both in itself and in its effects. We came out of it relatively lightly. The Germans were not only financially ruined but politically ruined; their entire society was turned upside down, with revolution and civil strife. The French had a savage war fought over their northern departments, and had a great swathe of enormous devastation; they lost twice the numbers of men that we did in proportion to population. We were indebted to the United States, but then so were the French and so were the Germans. Our loss of merchant ships was about the limit of our physical damage. What I do think the Great War did, and I said this in *The Collapse of British Power*, was

to break our nerve – or, at least, break the nerve of our governing classes and intelligentsia.

This question of when problems first emerged in the British industrial economy is important. Just as somebody may be going along, looking terribly robust and hale and hearty, while in fact their cells have already begun to divide in the wrong sort of way, so also with the economy there were problems in Britain – and other nations were beginning to go about things in a different way – as early as the 1830s and 1840s. It seems to me that when you look at this early period, the difference between us and the continental Europeans – say the French or the Germans – is that we had already achieved this absolutely astonishing industrial success and predominance (which I do not suppose is even equalled by modern-day American predominance, in relative terms). Just at this time when we were beginning to congratulate ourselves – 'We have the secret. We are absolutely tremendous' – other nations were thinking hard how to catch us up. Foreigners came to Britain, visited the works, talked to the workmen, talked to the bosses; and these new competitors thought about faults in British performance, and about how they themselves could do better.

One important feature of British experience is that the industrial revolution was something that happened from the grassroots; it was not masterminded in any way by government. So in a certain sense government, the state, was something that went on separately and concerned itself with foreign policy, fighting Napoleon and gradually building an Empire. In contrast, in European countries, the state made conscious decisions: 'We are going to become an industrialised country – how do we set about it?' And therefore there was not in Europe the same split between, say, Westminster and Mayfair on the one hand and central Manchester on the other.

As to the later period, and in particular the 1940s, the importance of the Second World War seems vital to me. Before working on this area I wrote military history in the pure sense, and right from my first book (*The Desert Generals*) it seemed to me important that one questioned any received account, that one asked, 'Can this really be true?' When I came to write *The Audit of War*, I asked the same question about the legend of British technological triumphs in the Second World War, and of how we had all pulled together as a national team in industry. In questioning these legends, I stuck close to what was in the documentary sources, like the civil official histories – in which there is a vast deal of valuable information – and the original Cabinet and Ministry files relating to production, labour and so on. Most of my analysis is warranted by the information *at the time* in the official papers.

In the late 1940s Britain had a unique opportunity because of her position *vis-à-vis* the defeated Europeans. It was a window of opportunity: it was certainly five years before our trade rivals began to come back fairly strongly, and ten years to the end of the postwar decade when they really were running up fast behind us, although I know that they did not formally overtake us until later. Given the deficiencies that have been revealed by the war-time record, and given the sorts of things that were being planned in 1945, even in terms of education and training, then that first postwar decade was an opportunity to put ourselves right while our competitors were still in fact recovering from occupation and defeat: a crucial moment. Also, at that time, world markets would literally take anything we cared to export, largely because people were so starved of goods. We had an easy run. And of course we were given the $3.75 billion loan in 1945, then Marshall Aid, and other help as well. I think it is reckoned that between 1945 and 1950–51 we received handouts or loans of about $8 billion and so here again was an opportunity to use this bunce from a rich uncle, to do something constructive with it. In my view, we were too self-indulgent to seize that moment of opportunity. There was a mental climate favouring idealistic politics.

And there is in Britain a very strong idealistic lobby which reproduces itself down the generations. Their ideals, their hopes and their morals are of course absolutely impeccable. But the question is the practicality and the consequences. Certain aspects of morality may be sound in themselves but hopelessly inappropriate when made the basis for decision-making in international relations. One has to see the world as it really is, to see the realities of power, the realities of leverage and of course the realities of your own interests.

The picture I paint of the 1940s decade is a rather bleak one, and it certainly serves as a corrective to more celebratory approaches to Britain's victory in the war. Militarily, the essential part of winning the war was done by the Red Army on the Eastern Front. That is what really did for the German army, which after all was the great engine of German military power. We certainly helped with bombing to some extent, but in a military sense we rode on the back of the Red Army. The Mediterranean and North African campaigns were simply matters of expediency; but at the end of the day they were not a decisive help in winning the war. So that is the first point, the military point that the Russians – the Red Army – did the lion's share. The other point about our entire war effort – which people continually lose sight of, despite its being widely documented – is that from April 1941 we were absolutely living off American subsidies. And the entire British war effort from then on was made possible by those American subsidies. It would be interesting to ask the question: 'What sort of a war could we have fought from our own resources?' And I should think that would amount to sending somebody out in a rowing boat once a week, and firing a catapult at Calais! Seriously, I do not think one can overestimate the importance of the whole British war effort being understrapped by the Americans. Again, as I point out in *The Audit of War*, in terms of vital pieces of industrial equipment, or actual industrial end-products, we were crucially and repeatedly dependent on America.

So what people sometimes refer to as 'the British disease' – usually locating it in the 1960s and 1970s – is evident much earlier. The problems concerning management and labour are clearly there in the 1940s. Now, politicians have sometimes addressed themselves explicitly to dealing with this British disease, most obviously perhaps the Conservative Party under Margaret Thatcher. It seems clear to me that here in labour relations, as in any kind of conflict, you think of leverage. It seems to me equally clear that under conditions of full employment, however induced, the strength of leverage is shifted from management to the workforce. Other jobs are available, people actually poach labour. If you therefore wish to cure these labour problems you have to change the leverage. I think it was only Thatcher's willingness to deflate the economy, to produce more widespread unemployment, and then to fight battles when it came to painful restructuring (with the miners, for example) – it was only this type of approach that could actually cure our chronic labour problems. Neither Labour nor Conservative governments in the immediate postwar era contemplated such policies.

It seems to me quite clear that whatever one's general economic and social philosophy (and whatever the government or party), the education and training of the nation as a whole must be a state concern and it must be a matter of a state strategy. And when it comes to how you actually achieve the right kind of education and training, you first decide what your objectives ought to be, and you then come to the means. Obviously, with the latter, there is room for discussion: whether you run the thing through local authorities, or directly delegate from a Ministry of Education down to schools, or whatever. The whole belated development of education and training in Britain was reluctant, against the grain of traditional British prejudices. In the mid-Victorian age there was a sense that somehow or other you left it to private charity and the market to deliver. And it did not deliver. Therefore it was the state which gradually filled the vacuum. So I have no doubt about that, that the state must take responsibility for the nation's education and training in a systematic way.

I suppose what surprises me about the postwar Labour government is that it did not fulfil Labour Party rhetoric. Since 1918, or even before then, they had been banging on about the state as the instrument of the collective will and the collective interest, and how the state would plan and enforce industrial reform. And then when it came to the actual event, their industrial policies lacked bite between 1945 and 1950. There was a vast deal – in education as well as elsewhere – of advisory councils, consultative boards and so forth. But where was the actual leverage?

The Attlee Labour government believed in the command economy, but surely the leverage in a command economy must involve the state definitely intervening. According to such a view, the state must surely not just nation-alise old dinosaurs, but actually take a mess like the British motor industry and do what the Germans were planning to do, back in the 1930s, and ratio-nalise it. That would be one route, from the left. And by contrast, of course, if you adopt the Thatcherite answer the leverage is provided by a free market where, if you do not succeed then you go bankrupt and nobody helps you. The crucial test is the effectiveness of the approach rather than its ideologi-cal complexion. The key question is whether something functionally suc-ceeds.

In my work I have concentrated on the idea of a hard-headed calculation of national interest, and in particular the ways in which such calculation was neglected in favour of unrealistic ambitions and ideals. In terms of New Labour today, one gets the impression of great caution, especially over the possibilities of doing things and the cost of doing things; this is very much in contrast to the sort of euphoria of the last two years of the Second World War in terms of the New Jerusalem. So I think that is a tremendous change and I get the broad impression that it will probably be a very pragmatic gov-ernment rather than an ideological one. I must say I am all in favour of that, because I think where I would part company with the Thatcher government, certainly in the latter years, is that having started off by applying some effec-tive solutions to practical problems, they then became sold on their own ide-ology. I think it is always a calamity when a political party actually comes to believe its ideology.

People from various shades of political background have cited my work. I have had favourable responses from Marxist periodicals and also from Fascist ones, so take your pick! Certain Conservative Ministers in the 1980s used some of my arguments. They were then the government in power, and if one's work is having an impact on the government in power then obviously one is pleased. You do not write in a vacuum; you hope what you say will be taken on board and scrutinised, and that it will be taken into the thinking of the people who are actually running the business. So I was pleased.

One key question is to compare different interpretations of British interests and how best they might have been pursued. This is vital when considering the Empire, an Empire which might be seen after the war as a drain on resources, a terrific expense. The notion that the Empire indicated strength was an important part of British mythology, as was the idea that we had all pulled together and performed successfully to win the war almost single-handed. This brings me back again to the point about suspecting the validity of myths. You should always suspect a myth or a legend: the things that people tell each other because it makes them feel good to do so. You really have to look at them and say, 'Yes, but is this really true?' Regarding the Second World War, people have felt very happy to go back in memory to those days when, as legend has it, we all pulled together, we were top dogs, we were winning and we were all absolutely splendid. That must be especially true for the older generation. For anybody who actually fought in the war, that must be a very strong sense.

Another of the great myths which I have challenged concerns elite education: Oxbridge and the public schools. The problems of British education have still not adequately been addressed. When one reads the comparative investigations of the performance of British school children at different ages in maths and so forth, one feels that perhaps we still have not actually caught up with our competitors. We are still not producing a large enough proportion of young people who are educated beyond school leaving age, in part-time education and training. I can remember various reports on our general training record (reports from the early 1990s, for example), which were deeply worrying. I can remember Geoffrey Holland, when he was Chairman of the Manpower Services Commission, saying in about 1990–91 that according to their analysis of training in Europe, Britain was not only not in the same league as the opposition, but was not in the same game. And so I think we have probably still got quite a long way to go. As of the late-1990s, Tony Blair is saying exactly this.

Now my own experience of British educational life has to some degree influenced my views here. I went to a direct grant school in Croydon, and we were fortunate because, unlike many other schools where Humanities and the Classics dominated the agenda, we were able to study Economics and Economic History. So in a certain sense my own interest in these matters dates from this. You were straightaway brought up with the question of the poor performance of British industry during the slump. So that was an advantage. But on the other hand there were a fair number of modern factories around the old Croydon Airport, making things like airscrews and so forth and nothing in our schooling had anything to do with that. This was a separate world altogether; somewhere out there were factories making airscrews, but no connection was made between this and the schooling process.

Going up to Oxford after the war, on what was called a Further Education and Training Scheme, I enjoyed my three years enormously. But when I look back on it I am in a state of complete paradox about it, because here we all were a first generation of semi-detached youngsters going up to Oxford on, naturally enough, fairly small government grants. But there we were in the austerity period of the late 1940s living a kind of sub-Evelyn Waugh life with boat-club dinners. Can you imagine? Here we were on an emergency Further Education and Training Scheme to refill the reservoir of trained talent which had not been produced during the war and you were asked to go up with a kit which included dinner jackets and boiled shirts. I do find that strange. Also, of course, if you are not used to it because no other member of your family has ever been to university, the whole casual way in which the place worked seemed bemusing. Even looking back on it now, I feel that one could have been steered much better; the whole thing could have been organised better. And certainly I think that British education in that period did tend still to be more of an inoculation against the world, rather than a preparation for it. There is no question about it. You spent three years in a place like Oxford, living this sort of sub-Evelyn Waugh life with lots of fun and all the rest of it. And so the idea of going into industry was an absolute joke; and when people who had gone down the year before came back and told us about stacking *Daz* packets in village stores we just fell about screaming with laughter.

At Oxford I read Modern History, and Modern History at Oxford went from AD 410 up to the early twentieth century. But the stuff that was rammed down your throat included boring studies of the medieval administration of the King's household, or studies of the relations between church and state in the twelfth century. I can safely say there were only two books that I read at Oxford which strongly influenced my subsequent approach – one part of the Special Subject, and the other something which a friend recommended to me. The first was Clausewitz's *On War*, which was part of a Special Subject on military history and the theory of war. The other was Lewis Mumford's *Technics and Civilisation* – if I read it again now I do not know what I would think of it, but certainly that was a starting point for my interest in looking at history in technological terms rather than in the constitutional/political terms prevalent at Oxford.

Churchill College in Cambridge, where I have been a Fellow since 1977,[15] is a rather different story in that the College was originally founded because Sir Winston Churchill and his advisers believed that Britain was backward in higher technological education. This, remember, is some 12 years after the Percy Report on Higher Technological Education. It was originally hoped to found a British version of the Massachusetts Institute of Technology, but we finished up as constitutionally a Cambridge College, though with a 70 per cent bias right through the College body for the sciences and technology. That is written into the statutes.

One theme which my work has persistently pointed to is the contrast between Britain's pretensions and desires on the one hand, and its actual wealth and weight on the other. And I think this contrast still persists now. We still cannot make the fundamental adjustments. When right through the 1960s and 1970s we retreated step by step from global commitments – east of Suez, then in the Middle East – it was not because the government said, 'This is absurd', and took a far-sighted decision, but simply because we had run into some stunning balance of payments crisis and some Chancellor would say, 'Look, we simply can't afford these new attack carriers, we can't afford TSR 2, we can't afford to stay east of Suez'. But it was always because we had come up against some sort of crunch. Even in more recent times, the tendency to think in terms of Britain 'punching above her weight' has a rather hollow ring to it.

In my contributions to debates on British history, I have sought to avoid the ivory tower, self-referential approach sometimes favoured by academics. To be perfectly candid, I am not enormously concerned about an academic audience. If I were to ask for whom I am writing then it would be, generally speaking, a reader of a quality Sunday or daily newspaper and also, prefer-ably, people who actually are either in politics or industry and who actually themselves have got clout – people who might think, 'Well these ideas are interesting' and might act upon them. So it is a broad, and hopefully also an influential, readership that I want to reach. I have a fair correspondence with people who have been in British industry, in various aspects, people who have actually read my books and who write to me. Sometimes they say, 'You have got it wrong' and sometimes, 'You are spot on'. But the thing is to have direct contact, not with other academics, but with people in industry or in pol-itics who have practical experience and influence – those are the people with whom I want to interact.

Notes

1. *The Desert Generals* (London, 1960), *Britain and Her Army: A Military, Political and Social Survey* (London, 1970).
2. *The Collapse of British Power* (Stroud, 1984; 1st edn, 1972); *The Audit of War: The Illusion and Reality of Britain as a Great Nation* (London, 1987; 1st edn, 1986); *The Lost Victory: British Dreams, British Realities 1945–1950* (London, 1996; 1st edn, 1995). A fourth volume, provisionally entitled *The Chains of History*, on the period 1950–56, is in preparation.
3. C. Barnett, *Audit of War*, p. vii.
4. '[T]he entire British war economy was sustained, its artificiality made pos-sible, by American aid' (*ibid.*, p. 59).
5. Of the period immediately prior to the Second World War, he comments on 'the crushing inferiority of British output of well-educated and well-trained personnel at every level' (*ibid.*, p. 205).

6. The 'victory of the Victorian lobbyists for a "liberal education" in the public schools and ancient universities must be accounted one of the crucial factors in Britain's loss of technological leadership between the 1860s and the 1940s' (*ibid.*, p. 220).
7. C. Barnett, *Collapse of British Power*, p. 37.
8. *Ibid.*, p. 586.
9. C. Barnett, *Lost Victory*, p. 45.
10. *Ibid.*, p. xii.
11. *Ibid.*, p. 1.
12. C. Barnett, *Audit of War*, p. 8.
13. See, for example, D. Edgerton, 'Liberal Militarism and the British State', *New Left Review*, vol. 185 (1991) and C. Barnett, 'A Reply to David Edgerton', *New Left Review*, vol. 187 (1991); D. Edgerton, 'The Prophet Militant and Industrial: The Peculiarities of Correlli Barnett', *Twentieth Century British History*, vol. 2, no. 3 (1991); J. Tomlinson, 'Correlli Barnett's History: The Case of Marshall Aid', *Twentieth Century British History*, vol. 8, no. 2 (1997); P. Clarke, 'Keynes, New Jerusalem and British Decline' in P. Clarke and C. Trebilcock (eds), *Understanding Decline: Perceptions and Realities of British Economic Performance* (Cambridge, 1997); J. Harris, 'Social Policy, Saving and Sound Money: Budgeting for the New Jerusalem in the Second World War' in *ibid.*; 'Symposium: Britain's Post-war Industrial Decline', *Contemporary Record*, 1, 2 (1987), with Barnett responding in *Contemporary Record*, vol. 1, no. 3 (1987).
14. M.J. Wiener, *English Culture and the Decline of the Industrial Spirit 1850–1980* (Harmondsworth, 1992; 1st edn, 1981). See also the interview with Wiener, pp. 25–36 of this book.
15. Between 1977 and 1995, Barnett was Keeper of the Churchill Archives Centre at Churchill College, Cambridge.

4

Will Hutton

Introduction

Born in 1950, Will Hutton was educated at Bristol University and
worked as a stockbroker, a BBC radio producer, and Director and
Producer of BBC 2's *Money Programme*, before becoming economics
editor both of the BBC's *Newsnight* (1983–88) and of *The Guardian*
(1990–95). He was assistant editor of the *Guardian* (1995–96), and
became editor of the *Observer* in 1996. A respected and influential
commentator with broad-ranging economic and political expertise,
Hutton has diagnosed Britain as being 'a third-class state'.[1] He argues
that the weakness of the British economy, especially regarding the level
and character of investment, originates in its financial system: 'The targets for profit are too high and time horizons are too short'.[2] Financial
institutions' indifference to the long-term is crucially damaging; banks
borrowing large amounts in short-term money markets are unlikely to
be attracted by the prospect of long-term loans to industry at fixed rates
of interest. Reform of the financial culture and system are required if
British decline is to be reversed. But Hutton argues that equally extensive political reform is required: the nature of the British state is also
important in producing British economic and social problems. The situation in Britain is desperate; both economic and political reform are
needed.

Economically, an increase in public and private investment is
required in order to boost the growth potential of the economy. This
can only be done with a recasting of the financial culture and institutions of Britain. The structure of British finance was crucial in ensuring
that Britain was unable to exploit the wave of new inventions in the late
nineteenth century; by the time of the First World War a pattern was
established with a banking system divorced from production, a risk-
averse stockmarket in London focusing on international investment,
and an industrial base losing out relative to foreign competition. The

City, rather than industrialisation, was the central project of the British Empire.

Politically, a modern constitutional settlement is required. The old Labour Party held that economics determined the political culture and that once the former was addressed, the latter would be sorted out. The fact that the nature of the political institutions might itself help determine economic performance was therefore missed.

Many of Britain's problems are identified, in Hutton's analysis, with Conservative Party government from 1979 onwards. Rising inequality under the Conservatives led to economic instability. Both economically and politically Hutton is critical of free market philosophy: in part *The State We're In* and *The State To Come*[3] are attacks on the Thatcherite attempt to reverse decline. The idea that private-sector activity in an unregulated market would improve the economy was misguided: 'the major tenet of free market economics – that unregulated markets will of their own accord find unimprovable results for all participants – is now proved to be nonsense'.[4] The monetarist theory of inflation is misconceived. Once free and flexible labour markets had been constructed, the results were more disappointing than free market theory would have led us to expect. For, in fact, wealth generation is a social act as much as an individual one. Human relations within organisations are more important to productivity than are wage structures. The mixture of rivalry with cooperation is the hallmark of the world's most powerful economies (US, European, East Asian) and it is this pattern which Britain must follow.

Hutton is a neo-Keynesian, representing part of a resurgence of Keynesian ideas. He argues that Keynes' *General Theory* is 'the nearest anybody has ever come' to the holy grail of economics,[5] and that it 'offered the outstanding alternative theory of capitalism'.[6] Keynes opposed the short-termism of the financial markets and, to neo-Keynesians, high investment will produce high savings rather than the other way around. Thus Hutton's ideas are underpinned by a Keynesian foundation.

In order to improve the dire situation Britain faces in the 1990s, social inclusion, a properly functioning democracy, and a business culture characterised by high investment and long-term thinking are all necessary. A new conception of citizenship is also needed, with an emphasis on strong social institutions. It is important to recognise the relation between social cohesion and wealth generation; and social rather than individualistic capitalism has to be the way forward. The marketisation of society has led to anxiety and communal breakdown, and has further entrenched short-termism. Housing, pensions, education, health and transport are all increasingly marketised and this has tended to expand the division between those respectively on upward and downward spirals: 'The introduction of market principles into education, health, criminal justice, housing, television, pensions and social provision is actively eroding social cohesion, and undermining society'.[7] Indeed, Hutton has criticised free market thinking in its wider international context as well, calling for greater global regulation of the financial markets in the face of 'wild swings of confidence and of capital movements'.[8]

In order to harmonise capitalist dynamism and the public good, Britain needs: a written constitution, reformed finance, democratised civil society, regulation of the market economy, and the maintenance of a properly functioning welfare state. Social fragmentation, pervasive marketisation, structural short-termism, political decay: all are so dire that a revolution of sorts is required. Hutton's is 'a demand for a more inclusive, fairer, higher-investing Britain with a well-functioning democracy . . . a vision of a stakeholder economy and society, but constructed by a contemporary state in contemporary conditions'.[9] In the following interview, Will Hutton defends this vision and relates his economic arguments to the politics and society of modern Britain.

Interview*

I have argued that Britain needs profound economic and political reform: that the nation accustomed to success has, by the late twentieth century, experienced profound stagnation and decay. The necessary changes require some political party (or combination of parties) committed to their achievement. So, how are we to assess the attitudes of Tony Blair's Labour Party in relation to this? Tory Central Office talked about a political phenomenon called 'close marking' which developed, with all of their effective ministers close marked by their Labour shadows. Whatever Michael Howard or Gillian Shephard said, you could rely on Jack Straw and David Blunkett to 'close mark' them with comments that were almost exactly the same, or certainly from exactly the same culture. And that was true of everything: Labour 'close marked' the Tories on Euroscepticism, on monetary fiscal policy and so on, and there are really only two areas left where there is clear water between the two parties. The first is the labour market and the second is the Constitution. On the first,

* Interviewed by Richard English: London, 12 February 1997.

Blair assures us that even after the minimum wage, the changes that he proposes would still leave the British labour market the most deregulated in Europe. On the second, the truth is that it is impossible given the past commitments, and given the representation of the Scottish and Welsh in the Parliamentary Labour Party, to drop Scottish and Welsh devolution (although I think that if he could he would, and I think the same is true on the commitment over the referendum on proportional representation). Reform of the House of Lords is long overdue and recognised as such by many Conservative peers. So New Labour have got to a liberal Conservative position as it would have been recognised in the late 1970s. It is broadly the sort of portfolio of views with which Douglas Hurd or Kenneth Clarke joined the Conservative Party to defend England from socialism. It is a sign of how far they have got that they have reached this position. Blair's claim even to sit in the twentieth-century social democratic tradition is really very faint. And he would probably regard himself as an Asquithian Liberal. In the Whig–Tory divide he is a Whig.

However, to be positive, there are two or three things that might follow from a Labour victory and which might tend to be underestimated prior to their election. One of the most amazing developments would be a recapturing of language. 'Independence' has come to mean independence from the state; now even Tony Blair would not use that language in that way. There has been a colonisation of the basic vocabulary of western liberal thought by the right so that 'freedom', 'flexibility' and other terms have come to have set meanings suitable to the right. And this has been fantastically corrosive. Blair's election might lead to an integrity again in the language of political discourse and this would be important. The mere fact of Labour victory might lead to the recapturing from the right of the vocabulary of western liberalism. The second thing is that although the Labour programme is minimalist – Whig rather than social democratic in its ambitions – that does not mean that it will not set in train very important dynamics. Blair's thinking is liberal Conservative, right-centrist, and he is much more comfortable with right-wing intellectuals than with left-wing intellectuals. But he does come from the Whig side of politics. He is a progressive reformist. And I think that there could be a cascade of consequences from some of these small reforms which will lead inexorably in the direction in which I am pointing.

And here there is also something else that is important: the climate of ideas. Tory strategists have talked about 'close marking' and, facing the 1997 general election with the prospect of huge defeat in front of them, they still dominate the political agenda. They set the agenda completely. I think with Labour in power, recolonising the rhetoric and just having different kinds of policy priority (the windfall profits tax, the attempt (however tepid) to make the City more long-termist and corporations more far-sighted, the attempt to narrow inequality through moving people from welfare rolls into employment), there will be powerful generative and reflexive effects on political debate which are very hard to estimate. Once these effects are in train there is a lot of intellectual progress being made by a wide range of thinkers who have been arguing that the job is to remake, to socialise capitalism. I think that these small policy manoeuvres and the regaining of the language will refract into that and we could quite quickly see things moving on from what appears to be a minimalist starting point.

I also think that this is true on the Constitution. Some of these changes have a cascade of consequences which we cannot predict. I think devolution in Scotland and Wales will open up the demand for devolution in the English regions and will help produce more autonomy of action by mayors and towns and cities. I think the delegitimising of the hereditary principle in the House of Lords will ultimately be very dangerous to the monarchy. These are dynamics being set in train. It is fashionable to say that Tony Blair is a liberal Conservative and will make no difference. He *is* a liberal Conservative, he *has* a minimalist programme, the strategy up to the election *is* to 'close mark' Conservative spokesmen who still set the agenda completely; he is extraordinarily uncourageous in advancing arguments which challenge the status quo, and himself professes allegiance to the Whig tradition in British politics. But that is maybe all one can expect. Britain is a very conservative country, it has been governed for 18 years by Tories, the whole climate of opinion is ratcheting to the right in a fantastic way; there are no exemplars of economic and social models which are on the left now, and even the ones on the right which are corporatist and which put an accent on social cohesion are sclerotic and are suffering from high unemployment. These are very right-wing times. The credibility of the Labour Party – which was shattered by four election defeats and the 1974–79 period in government – needs to be regained by having a successful programme in government and maybe the only way to be successful in government is to govern from the right. And there are positive aspects to the dynamics which might be set in motion by Labour victory.

And Constitutional reform relates directly to the redress of Britain's economic problems. I have stressed the connection between profound Constitutional change and economic improvement; and have criticised the old Labour Party view which involved the quasi-Marxist notion that economics would produce politics, whereas in fact the nature of a country's political structures itself affects economics. Economics works at a lot of different levels. There is getting the macro-economic policy right – balancing monetary fiscal policy etc. – and that plainly is hugely important. But I have always regarded that as the necessary but insufficient condition for sustained growth. The sufficient condition involves micro-structures or supply-side structures which produce investment and innovation, and that is a much more subtle process of wealth-creation than metric models or the socialist tradition or indeed the right-wing tradition in Britain think. The right-wing idea that it is all about micro-efficiency, by having less red tape, less labour market regulation and so on, is as pathetic as is the socialist view that you have to maximise investment as a proportion of GDP. Wealth-creation is about recognising that there are macro-efficiencies for the behaviour of the system, and that you have got to get hold of and offset the spillover effects of the system on micro-behaviour. And rising inequality is an economic bad; it makes the economy more unstable. And also it gives people on the bottom rungs no incentives to train or commit to work. And the same is true of investment and the successful firm. A successful enterprise is also a just enterprise in the sense that it treats people properly. There is a kind of moral capital inside the firm. People come into the enterprise from civil society and they bring to it expectations and values from that civil society. And if you take the view, as I do, that those values do not just lie about but that they are generated by the history and culture of institutions and by patterns of institutional behaviour, then the way you organise your political system is fundamental. It is very difficult for the English regions to generate a local business class that is grown up and adult and loyal to that region because political power does not reside there. If you want to make it in Britain you come to London: in journalism, television, politics, finance. The consequence is that the provinces – as they are called by Londoners – have less talent in them and operate in a financial framework which is set by London, either by the public sector as the public expenditure framework or within the private sector by budgets set by London in terms which maximise their share. Middle managers in Manchester, Birmingham, wherever, find themselves downsizing corporations or closing them and there is no countervailing power, no countervailing elite; they themselves are just the instruments of head office. Because everyone knows this, therefore people are stoic and uncommitted. That is an important explanation of why Britain has a 'falling off a back of a lorry' approach to enterprise. Or at least, it is part of the explanation of why we have got to where we are.

In terms of economies which are more successful than Britain's, I have referred to the US and European models as well as to Southeast Asia as places which Britain should emulate. Probably some combination of Australia and Holland might provide the best model for Britain. As to the USA: I think people do not understand America very well in Britain. My argument is that American capitalism should be seen as red in tooth and claw, which it is: it is driven by shareholder value, there is no welfare system to speak of, and the incarceration of so many American blacks is an important way of lowering unemployment totals. So let us be clear-sighted about this. But there are off-setting characteristics too. There is a very deeply embedded democracy at state and city and town level which gives a tradition of citizenship which informs American corporations, particularly medium-sized corporations, in a way that you would not find here. I cite Bill Gates. And I still think it is remarkable. For example, Lord Hanson has made a small fortune here and there is no chance of Lord Hanson giving away a large percentage of his fortune to endow some trust for even educational prospects. Lord Hanson feels that he owes Britain nothing, he feels that he owes his workforce nothing, he feels he must put nothing back in. And this view is widely held in Britain. It involves the idea that owners of firms make as much money as possible for shareholders, employ workers, and that when profits are dipping there is nothing wrong with selling one's shares before others do and saying, when the share prices drop, 'that's your problem'. It is an immoral approach. And there is a kind of morality about American capitalism. It is partly to do with the role of religion in American life still, and it is partly to do with the Tom Paine citizenship tradition. It offsets the harsher aspects of American capitalism. And I think that the managers of American capitalism are more honourable and more anxious to treat people properly than their British counterparts. That does not mean that there is not vicious racial prejudice, and considerable aggressiveness. My point is that once they have made their pile, they are prepared to put something back in. And – apart from the Quakers in Britain like Rowntree, Cadbury – that is a tradition conspicuous by its absence here. People running utilities and investment banks have no conception that they are lucky to have this kind of money, that that kind of money is really only proper if you have taken real risks and put something into the system. They are rentiers scrabbling for their piece of the action in terms of rent.

Decline debates involve the search for alternative ways of approaching the economy. And if we are lookng for alternatives, then I think stakeholding is vital. Some have suggested that the idea of stakeholding is unconvincing because it sounds as though nobody will suffer, as though all stakeholders will benefit and all will be happy; and that this is implausible in terms of the way that society is run. I tend to get angry about this. Tony Blair was looking for a big idea and stakeholding seemed like it and then he discovered that John Monks liked it and Will Hutton liked it, so he ran a mile. It was the politics of funk. As soon as David Willetts or Michael Portillo said, 'Aha, this means you're going to try and change the constitution of the market economy. That's interventionist; we don't want that, do we?' Labour reacted with a staggering lack of self-confidence, produced by the loss of four successive elections. Having lost four elections it became imperative to win the fifth. Not to win would devastate the Labour Party and devastate democracy in Britain. So I quite understand why, when stakeholding had that spin put on it, he reacted in the way he did. As to those who have expressed criticism of stakeholding along the lines I have just mentioned: well, this is where the people who talk about 'declinists' are right; there is a whole bunch of people on the left who are so fundamentally pessimistic and oppositional that they are unable to think positively. They consider stakeholding a right-wing idea and reject it as such. And there is a lot of that about on the left and I do criticise it very aggressively. I think it is second-rate.

I myself was never a socialist, and there is an irony in my being presented as a left guru. I never believed in socialist planning, in the socialisation of private property, powerful trade unions and so on. That is not where I have come from. I am an economist by training who believes in the price mechanism, and that people respond to incentives. So I find myself in this astonishing position where I am painted as a left guru, well to the left of Blair. And it is comic, because what I am trying to say is that market economies have constitutions. Social behaviour has – in the language of Tony Giddens – a reflexive relationship with institutions. And markets will run away with themselves. So you have to put in place reflexive dynamics that run against those trends, otherwise you get booms and bust, monopolies, exploitation. And the notions that the market is self-regulating, or that parties to free market transactions do not have a fundamental asymmetry of power where the worker is helpless and the employer is all-powerful, seem to me to be so self-evidently wrong that I am speechless when I find people who think otherwise. And stakeholding is saying: the job is designing capitalisms where there is a reasonably equitable distribution of risk, where your trade efficiency gains off against equity, where you operate the system for the benefit of the whole – that means an accent on citizenship, on social inclusion, universal welfare. It is about designing micro-structures that actually incorporate that value system, and if you get that right you get nearer to the good economy of a society than you do if you have other kinds of capitalism. A lot of people say, 'I don't understand what Will Hutton means by that' or they say that all this stuff is for the birds. That seems to me to be a kind of hangover of battles fought and lost on both sides. To people who mock stakeholding, I would say: What's your project then? What are you going to do about it? What body of ideas are you going to put together that are going to challenge the way that capitalism operates today? What is your reform programme? Are you going to make common cause with the right? Are you merely going to mock those who come up with alternative projects?

And then there are people on the left who say, 'What about multinationals? What about international financial markets? You can't get this project off the ground, can you?' And I say: What's your alternative then? Give me three coherent sentences which are going to win you a majority in the House of Commons and will command a majority of the British people, that will reform British capitalism, instead of standing there and telling me that multinationals are very powerful and exploit British workers. When I see Tony Blair privately he tells me that stakeholding as I define it is integral to his thinking and to his project. So perhaps I was overly extravagant at the beginning of this interview when I talked about him as a liberal Conservative; mind you, many liberal Conservatives would also buy the stakeholding argument.

The supposed division between right and left – where you are supposedly one or the other – is something which has been challenged. Arguments around decline often involve people crossing those boundaries of left and right in terms of their influences and their thinking. Some of my arguments have been adopted by Labour Party figures; it is also true that some of what I say echoes people who have been adopted by sections of the right. In terms of my attack on short-termism, or my stress on the need for research and development, for example, there are echoes of Correlli Barnett's work. I would have to say that there are also aspects of Barnett's work with which I disagree. The idea that after 1945 governments could not put the welfare of the people high on its agenda is fanciful to the extreme. And also, while it might look now to have been foretold that the Russians were not going to sweep over western Europe after the war, it was not clear in 1945–48. Keeping a lot of men in arms was sensible enough. So I think parts of Barnett's work are uncontextualised.

Keynes has been a profound influence upon my thinking. It has been suggested that the globalisation of capitalism has ruled out the possibility of Keynesianism in the nation-state, in one national economy. Certainly, global financial markets make it very difficult to operate a very discretionary monetary fiscal policy in one country and to capture all the benefits of it in one country. But I have never understood Keynesianism to be simply about running a discretionary fiscal policy. My first book, *The Revolution that Never Was*,[10] set out a view of Keynes saying that what this is about is how the interaction of uncertainty and money destabilises, via the financial markets, the operation of market economies. It is the different speed of adjustment, the different pace of changing expectations in financial markets and goods markets in an economy, which fundamentally destabilise it; and the locus for taking interventionary action is the financial markets. Now I have always taken the view that the best kind of market economy is one that regulates itself, and one that does that better is one whose financial system is less prone to these instabilities than others. And in *The Revolution that Never Was* I set out using Keynes as I read him – his *Treatise on Money* as much as *The General Theory* – with the view that that is what the man was about; and that you are trying to use interest rate structures, you are trying to use intervention in the money markets (and everyone does that now, it's no longer an issue), you are trying to get bond holders and equity holders to be more long-termist and more far-sighted in their view, and that that may require different institutional structures. Almost as a last resort, if you cannot get the market to regulate itself, then the state comes in – as a borrower of last resort, or as a taxer of last resort in a boom – to settle the whole thing down. Now if you look at Keynes through that perspective I do not think globalisation has really affected it that much. But if you look at Keynesianism as an attempt to use discretionary fiscal policy to generate demand permanently above whatever the level of output is in order to persuade entrepreneurs to invest (which is the conventional way of looking at Keynes), then yes.

But the globalisation argument is again complex. We have globalised financial markets. We have globalised communication markets up to a point, particularly Anglo-Saxon products. But in product markets and goods markets there are limits to globalisation. Secretarial functions, financial services, haircuts are unglobalisable. You get to some threshold of import penetration above which you cannot go. I am also impressed by the argument that multinationals are very vulnerable, as much as they are powerful. So the globalisation question has to be looked at quite carefully. It is possible that the globalisers have in fact overstated their case.

As to other intellectual influences, one or two people on the left got rather ratty that I have not acknowledged my debt to Perry Anderson. To tell you the truth, I have never read Perry Anderson, actually. I have met Perry, but I have never read his work. I have read Martin Wiener's *English Culture*[11] which made an impact on me. And I have read Sam Beer.[12] Philosophically, I'm a Rawlsian.[13] Politically, I'm a *Rights of Man* man, Tom Paine: the rights of man being a bourgeois as much as a radical concept. So, my influences would be Paine (politics), Keynes (economics), Rawls (justice), and on decline: Wiener and Beer. Cain and Hopkins[14] in terms of gentlemanly capitalism. Geoffrey Ingham.[15] David Marquand: David and I are the closest intellectual soulmates. I remember reading *The Unprincipled Society*[16] when it was first published and being absolutely thrilled. Marquand was a huge influence on me. He and John Gray and I are very close. John has moved a bit: he is much less of a protectionist than he was, and he has moved to a position quite close to my own and David's. We spend a lot of time together around Oxford: I have a place near there, and John and David are often all around Oxford as well. So there is a cluster of us. And Vernon Bogdanor also pushes quite hard at Constitutional change. So there is a bit of an Oxford-based mafia (which has come together quite recently) and we do talk a lot.

Notes

1. W. Hutton, *The State We're In* (London, 1996; 1st edn, 1995), p. 10.
2. *Ibid.*, p. xxvii.
3. W. Hutton, *The State To Come* (London, 1997).
4. W. Hutton, *The State We're In*, p. 237.
5. W. Hutton, 'Keynes still has the Answers', *Guardian* 1 April 1996.
6. W. Hutton, *The State We're In*, p. 239.
7. *Ibid.*, pp. 283–4.
8. *Marxism Today* November/December 1998, pp. 28–9.
9. W. Hutton, *The State To Come*, p. 64.
10. W. Hutton, *The Revolution That Never Was* (London, 1986).
11. M. J. Wiener, *English Culture and the Decline of the Industrial Spirit 1850–1980* (Harmondsworth, 1992; 1st edn, 1981). See also the interview with Wiener, pp. 25–36 in this book.
12. S.H. Beer, *Modern British Politics: Parties and Pressure Groups in the Collectivist Age* (London, 1982; 1st edn, 1965); *Britain Against Itself: The Political Contradictions of Collectivism* (London, 1982).
13. J. Rawls, *A Theory of Justice* (Oxford, 1973; 1st edn, 1972).
14. P.J. Cain and A.G. Hopkins, *British Imperialism: vol i, Innovation and Expansion 1688-1914; vol ii, Crisis and Deconstruction 1914–1990* (London, 1993).
15. G.K. Ingham, *Capitalism Divided? The City and Industry in British Social Development* (Basingstoke, 1984).
16. D. Marquand, *The Unprincipled Society: New Demands and Old Politics* (London, 1988).

5

W. D. Rubinstein

Introduction

The 'cultural critique' of British decline, most famously associated
with Martin Wiener and Correlli Barnett, has been systematically challenged by Professor W.D. (Bill) Rubinstein. Born in New York in 1946,
Rubinstein was educated at Swarthmore College, Pennsylvania, and
Johns Hopkins University in the United States. While at University he
became immersed in studying British history. At Johns Hopkins, he initially intended to write on the Edwardian Conservative Party but shifted
instead towards the study of British wealth-holders. Information concerning these people was available and clearly significant, yet they had
largely been ignored in systematic scholarly enquiry. It was by this
route that Rubinstein became involved in work crucial to decline
debates. So, while his 1993 book, *Capitalism, Culture and Decline*, is
the volume of his most clearly related to decline debates, it is also
important to note that the implications of his previous work – *Men of
Property* and *Elites and the Wealthy* – are also crucial to this area.[1]

His research led him to a position which differs starkly from that of
authors associated with the 'cultural critique', and which has established him as an iconoclast within the decline literature. He disputes
Wiener's and Barnett's argument that aspects of British culture have
worked against a dynamic and competitive British industrial performance. Indeed, he holds that Britain was never primarily an industri-
al/manufacturing economy – even at its most successful – and that,
therefore, to allege that Britain declined owing to its anti-industrial culture misses the point entirely. Britain was always, according to
Rubinstein, a commercial/financial/service-based economy, even at the
height of the industrial revolution. During 1815–70, and even more so
afterwards, the British economy was primarily financial/commercial,
with bankers, merchants and financiers being more crucial than factory
capitalists. Heavy industry and manufacturing never predominated;

'The British wealth elite during the eighteenth, nineteenth and twentieth centuries has been one where land and commerce predominated, and where industrialism in the strict sense comprised a surprisingly small fraction of the total number of wealth-holders.'[2] 'Despite the Industrial Revolution the most important element in Britain's business wealth structure during the nineteenth century was commerce and finance.'[3]

Britain's relative industrial decline – which Rubinstein also considers to have been exaggerated in some quarters – merely reflected a working out of the process of commercial/financial advantage. If people concentrated on finance/commerce rather than on industry, then this made economic sense and had nothing to do with decline: 'What is so often seen as Britain's industrial decline or collapse can be seen, with greater accuracy, as a transfer of resources and entrepreneurial energies into other forms of business life.'[4] In Wiener's argument, for example, it was industry rather than finance which was hampered by the deleterious effects of culture: financial and professional classes were anti-industrial, while industrialists wanted to become gentlemen. According to Rubinstein's view, if finance and commerce have been the basis of British economic success then the period of psychological and intellectual de-industrialisation described by Wiener would be much less significant, even if true.

But Professor Rubinstein also argues that, far from being anti-capitalist, British culture has if anything been strikingly pro-capitalist: he questions the very notion that British culture was damaging in its impact on British capitalism. In so far as one can relate a national culture to economic performance – and Rubinstein is sceptical – Britain can be seen to have possessed a more capitalist-friendly culture than the 'cultural critique' might suggest. And in so far as one can assess British high culture in relation to the economy, it emerges from Rubinstein's work as being less hostile to entrepreneurial/business life than that of Britain's competitors: less anti-capitalistic, and more sympathetic to business life than the equivalent influences in Germany, France, Italy and America. Critics of capitalism, liberalism and modernity were far less extreme in Britain than elsewhere.

Key to the 'cultural critique' is the role of elite education in cultivating and sustaining an anti-industrial, anti-competitive ethos. Rubinstein rejects such an argument. He argues that public-school influence simply was not wide enough to achieve what is claimed for it by authors associated with the 'cultural critique'. Too few people attended the schools in question, and in particular too few sons of businessmen.

Moreover, he argues that it was not the case that sons of businessmen/industrialists went, via elite education, out of their fathers' economic world. Family background was far more important than public school education in determining choice of career. He also points out that it was more common for those engaged in financial/commercial activities to be educated at public school than for industrialists to attend them: yet it was industry which supposedly declined and finance/commerce which thrived: 'Those who argue that sociological factors were of primary importance in explaining the decline of British entrepreneurship ... must explain why this failed to affect Britain's commercial and financial dynasties'.[5] In Rubinstein's view it is certainly far from clear that the public schools actually engendered an anti-business, anti-entrepreneurial mood through their ethos and education.

He also argues that it is wrong to see Britain's political traditions (of the right or the left) as inherently damaging to economic dynamism. It would be wrong to link Britain's supposedly poor economic performance with an anti-capitalist polity. 'Both British culture and British politics have thus clearly worked to limit and to marginalise the intellectual and ideological extremes which threatened to undermine the cultural foundations of capitalism in other societies.'[6]

In so far as Britain has experienced economic decline, therefore, Rubinstein is sceptical of explanations for this phenomenon which emphasise cultural factors rather than economic or fortuitous ones. Moreover, he holds that Britain's decline has been exaggerated. He argues that between 1870 and 1914, for example, the British economy fared much better than is suggested by its declinist critics. He also disputes the widespread assumption of post-Second World War dramatic decline. Living standards – which he holds to be no less significant than growth rates as a test of economic performance – have risen strikingly in the supposed era of decline and have remained similar to those characterising Britain's rivals. The economy has never, in Rubinstein's opinion, performed more strongly than in the post-1970s era. The City has prospered and continues to do so (being one of the three great financial centres of the world). The immensely important role of London in British economic life, and indeed London's great success, reflect Rubinstein's argument regarding the true basis of British economic strength. London (rather than the manufacturing towns) and commerce/finance (rather than manufacturing/industry), provided the most significant foundations for wealth creation in modern Britain.

Interview*

The 'cultural critique' associated with writers such as Martin Wiener, Correlli Barnett and Anthony Sampson[7] forms part of Britain's post-Suez malaise. One did not find these arguments before that. In the nineteenth century, self-evidently, nobody would have argued that Britain was not a leading industrial power, that the British spirit was not pro-business or that it did not engender business life. It would have seemed a ridiculous argument. Nor did anyone really argue about Britain's decline for the first half of the twentieth century, until the Second World War. It comes about, chiefly in my view, as a result of the post-Suez malaise, which has affected everything about the way Britons view themselves. If you look at manufacturing industry and Britain's role and share in the world output in manufacturing, the evidence is there of course. My argument is that, first of all, there is no evidence to link the usual suspects – that is, the public schools and the universities – with this. There is really remarkably little hard evidence, and what evidence there is suggests the exact opposite. Secondly, you are ignoring the financial and commercial sector, which has not declined. And thirdly, you are ignoring the growth in the standard of living of the average person in Britain, which has increased enormously and relentlessly in this very period.

Wiener raises the interesting question of the part played by culture in determining economic development. The role of intellectuals is key here. But Wiener is selective in his choice of examples. There are vast numbers of intellectuals, of whom only a very small number are remembered. With so diverse a range of figures to draw upon, one can identify almost any intellectual tradition (most of which have been forgotten). It is perfectly true that there is a mainstream of British culture which was pro-rural. But there were also other intellectuals with very divergent views, and Wiener selects figures to suit his argument. The other question is whether such intellectuals had any influence on the economy. Even if they had, it is probable that in other countries, such as Germany or the United States, the anti-capitalism of intellectuals was *more* pronounced than in Britain. If such trends had no retarding effect on those economies, why should they do so here? Britain certainly had fewer ideologues, fewer fascists and communists than other countries.

So why, given all this, has the 'cultural critique' become so popular? It is a kind of self-flagellation, which I think the British indulge in, especially post-Suez. There is an aspect of British culture which is prone to self-flagellation. The British love to hear no good said of themselves. I do think that is quite

---

* Interviewed by Richard English and Michael Kenny: London, 12 December 1997.

true, in a way which is in a sense the opposite of the United States. Given Britain's present performance, which is so good, one does not hear this argument made as often. It is quite paradoxical and impossible to argue that Britain is somehow predisposed to fail in business life when it is running rings around everybody else in the world – or virtually – at the present time.

It is always very confusing to talk about relative versus absolute decline. There are areas of British manufacturing industry which have declined in absolute terms. I imagine that there is less coal produced now than 70 years ago. There are probably also fewer automobiles manufactured here than there were 30 years ago. But if you look at that sort of thing the absolute decline has probably not been as great as people imagine. What has happened is that Britain lags far behind other countries in terms of total output, other countries which have competed in these areas. There is no doubt there has been a relative decline in terms of manufacturing industry in those areas. But the British economy has always rested primarily on finance and commerce rather than on industry. There has, however, remained a fixation with evaluating Britain's economic position in terms of manufacturing industry. This might be because it is more visible. It is much easier to add it to the gross national product, or to find it there. And also there is a greater linkage with jobs, or at least a more subtle linkage with jobs in the cases of finance and commerce. There is a feeling that unless something is produced, in the sense of being manufactured, it is not really there, that there is some kind of sleight of hand involved; and that the people who sit in the City and make millions doing nothing, pushing things around on computer screens, or converting currency on the sly between one and another, are not really doing anything. In contrast, it is supposed that if one manufactures electronic equipment or software then one is doing something, and this is good. Now, my argument is that a pound is a pound. It does not matter what you do: if it turns up in your bank account then it is good (for you). In fact the twenty-first century's information technology and globalisation will heavily favour the type of approach that Britain is good at, in a very striking way.

I became immersed in the decline debate through my study of wealth-holders in the nineteenth century, work based on the probate records. The thing that strikes you from these sources is that finance and commerce and London are much more important than manufacturing industry. This is also backed up by the income tax records and the geographical picture they paint: incomes were higher per capita, and the middle class was situated by and large, in the south east of England. There was a middle class in the main manufacturing cities but it was a smaller and weaker one. This was the case when Britain was indeed an industrial country, and therefore *a fortiori*, it would be true now, I would have thought, when Britain is no more an industrial country. All the evidence suggests that indeed London and the City have not declined as rapidly as other sectors of the economy, if in fact London and the City have declined at all. I published *Capitalism, Culture and Decline* in 1993. I wrote it in 1991–92. One starts with the proposition that all predictions and prophets are wrong. But I am rather proud of what I said in the book. I think I got it right almost consistently, and not only in the British case. With regard to Britain I did not make any predictions; but if you infer from what I said what was likely to happen, Britain has done exactly as well as one would expect it to have done, based on this pursuit of its natural advantages in finance and commerce. It is now reaping the benefits of that approach. Another point I made in that book was that Japan was going to decline. And that was by no means a commonplace view when I said it. So I am rather proud of that: I do not think I got it wrong at all. I read someone like Will Hutton and what is striking about him is that his prophecies bear the same relationship to actual facts as the predictions of Mystic Meg do to the National Lottery numbers! They simply have not come about. Britain has done well by doing exactly the opposite of what Hutton (and those who echo him) say it should have done.

Of the other writers in this area, I admire Martin Wiener – though I disagree with him. He and I use different kinds of evidence. I use evidence which is quite objective, from the probate records; I did not leave anybody out. In contrast, Wiener's use of literary evidence seems to me to be somewhat selective, but it does produce an arresting thesis. Yet Wiener's approach is different from Hutton's in important ways. Wiener says nothing about what Britain ought to do, about how it should pull itself out of its malaise. He does not say it should develop manufacturing industries or anything like that: he is a very clever American, and he knows that such a view would be facile. I think he is talking in purely historical terms. Economic historians have debated the 'cultural critique' now for a generation and the usual view is that it is wrong, that even Britain's manufacturing industry did not underperform. There were reasons why Britain did not move into the so-called second industrial revolution in the way that America or possibly Germany did, but you cannot pin them on the entrepreneurial abilities of British manufacturers who were doing well at that time. This has been debated in the literature now for a generation and the weight of opinion is that this view – that British manufacturing industry failed – is wrong. There are economic historians, such as William Kennedy,[8] who argue that it did fail, that it was not up to scratch. But by and large the weight of opinion among economic historians is that it did not fail.

Why is the 'cultural critique' popular, why did it hit a note? In Wiener's case it appealed to the right and the left in British politics in an odd sort of way at the same time. Curiously it appealed to Thatcherites. Thatcher did not resurrect British industry. In so far as she was successful it was by allowing Britain's natural comparative advantage in finance and commerce to work itself out,[9] which is the opposite of what Wiener is suggesting. Of all the things the Tory governments of 1979–97 did, probably their most important means of getting Britain back on its feet again was cutting direct rates of taxation in 1986 to their present levels. Britain had crippling rates of direct taxation. It is absolutely impossible for individuals to save under such conditions. It was imposible for the average person to save, and there was no investment culture being built up, which has occurred, very largely since 1986. And this is one of the main reasons why Britain is doing so well in precisely those areas. In 1997 the total market value of all UK registered equities – in other words stocks and shares – was £1.1 trillion. In 1987 it had been £374 billion, in other words a third of that. In 1979 when Thatcher came to power it was £67 billion. It has risen by 15 times in 18 years. Unit trusts are worth £163 billion at the present times, investment trusts are £50 billion. Those are two of the main ways that the individual can save and invest. Thatcher in effect created a new investment culture, one which was not there before. As a result there are something like £40 billion of investment in venture capital and small company shares in this country which were not there before. That is all to the good, that people are investing in that sort of thing. I have some investments in venture capital unit trusts/investment trusts, and one of the things that some of the companies say in their prospectuses is that they cannot find new enterprises to invest in, that they have to go to Europe. In other words, there is more money chasing venture capital initiatives than there are venture capitalists, which is a unique turn of events. Now what Thatcher and the Tories did not do as effectively was to build up an investment and savings culture among ordinary people, which takes advantage of this as much as it might have done. In America 40 per cent of all households, and probably 80 per cent of households with middle-class incomes, own mutual funds (which is what Americans term unit trusts/investment trusts); in Britain it is still only 10 per cent (15 per cent to 20 per cent at most), which is far too low. Some of the best-performing unit trusts/investment trusts which specialise in venture capital have microscopic numbers of investors. More people put money in Tessas or ordinary Building Society accounts, which offer a much lower rate of return. So what has not happened is an explosion of investment of the more lucrative kind. Most people in Britain are still extremely conservative in their saving and investment habits. But at least they can save and invest, which was not true before.

The other good thing which has come out of all of this is that people no longer automatically put their money into property. That is one reason why the value of houses has not escalated so dramatically in the last five or ten years. I lived in Australia for 20 years: there, people put money into house property rather than into the stock market because it is house property which will double your money and entitle you to tax advantages. This is not the best way of running an economy. What the Tories did in Britain – too late, in my opinion – was to create an investment culture apart from house properties, which had been one of the banes of British investment and savings before that. In fact, if the Thatcher government had cut taxes to the 1986 level when they first came in, they would probably still be in power. They would have been reaping the benefits by now. They delayed until 1986, then came the stock market crash of 1987 and the exchange rate crisis with Europe in 1992, and it is only now that the benefits are being reaped in a big way. Unfortunately, the Labour government has inherited it. It has inherited the pot of gold which was left there.

Thatcherism has been criticised regarding the geographically uneven effects of its economic policies. That is quite wrong. One of the remarkable features of the 1979–97 period is that the gap between the north and south has declined, almost to vanishing point, in terms of income. Places like south Wales, which was devastated by the closing of coal mines and so on, are actually doing all right. Indeed, the south-east has been more heavily hit by the last recession.

Thatcher was paradoxical in that she made noises about getting back to manufacturing; but, as I say, this is exactly what did not happen. In fact she stopped trying to make water run up hill (in the sense of trying to reinvest in the north, in order to resuscitate manufacturing industries) and she also lowered direct taxes. And those two moves produced highly beneficial results. Her regime was successful in that it allowed the financial and commercial strengths of the British economy to flourish. This did not necessarily reflect any sharp recognition on Mrs Thatcher's part of the kind of argument I have propounded regarding the relative unimportance of industrialisation. The sort of developments which occurred under Thatcher, in terms of finance and commerce increasingly flourishing, might well have happened under other governments; but they happened faster under her because of the way she cut taxes. If *I* were the Chancellor of the Exchequer I would abolish income tax! There is an ongoing and fairly serious campaign in the United States to abolish income tax. I would also abolish death duties and capital gains taxes. Income tax only raises 22 per cent of central government revenues. Nearly 80 per cent of central government revenues are raised by all the other taxes. I would simply put up VAT. You would have to protect the poor. But once you withdraw the argument that income tax was meant to redistribute income, which the Labour government has explicitly said it no longer believes in now, there is no reason to have the thing. People would get exactly what they are paid. They could save more. You would tax foreigners and tourists here. There would probably be less evasion. The other thing I would do, which has also been proposed in the States, concerns old age pensions – with which there are going to be huge problems. I would propose that, when anyone is born in Britain, a deposit of £1000 should be registered in that person's name in the stockmarket. They could not touch this until they were 60 or 65. That £1000, even with a moderate rate of return, would grow to something like half a million pounds in 60 years and I would give them a lump sum at 60 or 65. That would be it. There would be no other state old age pension. That would absolutely cure the taking out of money to pay for old age pensions (of course, in 60 years, not before that). It would solve the problem, which is going to be huge. It is going to be a very big problem in Japan, for example. Those are the two things I would do: abolish income tax, and adopt that scheme to deal with pensions.

Who would have thought the day would come when Britain's unemployment rate was virtually a third of Germany's or France's? Or that the British economy was doing better than Japan's? Given the current success of the British economy, there is some irony in that fact that during the last ten years there has been so much mention made of other models, which Britain should supposedly emulate. Events have caught up with such speculation, with Britain outperforming numerous of the supposedly superior economies. While people such as Will Hutton have presented Britain as being in crisis, reality is far different. It may be that the world is entering a period of worldwide deflation and declining profits. Some economists have argued this, and the news from east Asia would suggest that, in which case there might be higher unemployment and lower returns to the economy here than we are currently experiencing. But that would be an aspect of the world economy, not something rooted in specific British faults. Some economists have suggested that we are entering a period which is very similar to that of the late nineteenth century – the long boom between 1865 and 1914. During that period a worldwide boom was generated by lower prices, in turn generated by more technology, globalisation, the emergence of markets like America, Australia and so on. It was not a boom generated by state government, or by Keynesian mechanisms. One of the features of that period was deflation; the cost of living went down in the late nineteenth century/early twentieth century.

There are aspects of the present situation, and what is likely to occur in the next generation, which are similar to that: the end of the Cold War, the coming of economic stability to places like Latin America (and indeed everywhere: even places like India are starting to climb up the ladder). So you have new areas being brought in which will be centre zones for productivity.

There is a globalisation of the world's economic structure which was not the case even 15 or 20 years ago in quite the same way; the end of the Cold War has been crucial here. And this development will probably lower prices and mean that manufacturing industry here, at the lower end of the scale, will be uncompetitive. It will only be competitive at the luxury end. The schlock stuff will be made in Haiti and so on. The famous ambiguity of British foreign policy since the Second World War (whether it belongs to the North Atlantic Alliance or to Europe or to the Commonwealth) is actually a source of great strength, in many ways, to Britain's financial and commercial lead. The City of London does have certain unique features to it. It does look out to the North Atlantic *and* to the Commonwealth *and* to Europe, which gives it very great advantages over competitors. If you read economic prognostications or economic advice from New York, in American financial magazines, you find that there is a great deal of naivety about them. Those who produce them think in terms of economic man and how this model will be adopted everywhere, whereas the British in many respects are much more realistic about the worldwide differences in culture. This reflects, I think, a greater sophistication in the City of London. There is no reason why the City should not become – if not the world's most important financial centre again, as it was a hundred years ago (it will not overtake New York – there is just too much money in the United States, and *they* are doing the right things) – certainly the second most important. It will overtake Tokyo. There is no reason why Britain is doomed to failure. It was the world's premier power for two hundred years. It made the industrial revolution, the commercial revolution, had an empire, was the first democratic society. Why should the same people, or their descendants, now be doomed to failure? Of course, they have a lot of competition now. But there is no reason why the cleverness which they demonstrated a hundred and fifty years ago should not be replicated in a different situation now. It is not mandated in advance that Britain will fail. In fact, all of the signs today suggest that Britain can, if it plays its cards right, once again get almost on top – not in the sense it was when Britannia ruled the waves, but definitely in a perceptible sense.

As I say, Labour has inherited what the Conservatives created. The New Labour government is not as bad as I had thought they would be. However, I am a dyed-in-the-wool Tory and my view is that the worst Tory government in the world is better than the best Labour government. As Chancellor of the Exchequer, Gordon Brown is marginally worse than his predecessor [Kenneth Clarke]. He has made some mistakes. I do not like giving the Bank of England the power to raise interest rates without the Chancellor doing it. The Bank of England is allergic to prosperity, it is wildly exaggerating the amount of inflation here and it is going to use its new powers like Tarzan to jack up the interest rates when they do not need to be raised. We are not going to have 15 per cent inflation any more. No country has that. The world is less inflationary now. Whether inflation is 2.5 per cent or 3.5 per cent is almost irrelevant. It is of microscopic importance compared to the harm that jacking up interest rates can do to the prosperity in Britain.

What Brown may be doing with savings schemes, abolishing Peps and so on, is a grave mistake. That is one of the major reasons that Britain has done well. And we cannot look forward to further cuts in income tax rates under Labour. So we are stuck with a 40 per cent top rate. This is lower than it is in many other countries but it is not as low as it should be. Under the Tories every year there was a slight cut. Under Labour you will not get that. They still have a working-class clientele. There is still an expectation that left of centre means 'slug the rich' (except when they are in the Labour Party, of course). Also, I do not like its noises on Europe. I am not a gung-ho anti-Europeanist. I think that the EU is okay, if it is simply a tariff barrier. But if it means federalisation then I am against it. It is, however, refreshing to see the more realistic approach which Labour now has, compared with their attitude ten years ago. There has been a definite improvement. They have moved in a conservative direction which reflects British realities more accurately than did their previous radicalism.

One key aspect here concerns the notion that the state should be about public service. This was a very strong element in Fabian socialism, the idea that an elite would govern the nationalised industries, and eventually all industries, in the interests of the whole public, of the country as a whole. Such thinking was behind a good deal of the work of the 1945–51 Labour government: there is a public service which, by acting in the public interest, will benefit everybody. That has gone now from Labour thinking, except in a very limited sense. That is a great change. For it would have been an absolute disaster if Labour had tried to redistribute income or wealth, or to nationalise businesses. I cannot imagine that any but a small minority of the population (except among intellectuals, of course) would have favoured that or seen it as a solution to anything. Privatisation, with an element of competition, is so much more efficient than a nationalised industry.

Another change is that they have lost faith in progress or science. The idea of science and technology as a panacea for the world's ills – you do not hear that any more in European socialism or on the left generally. Indeed, there is a great distrust of science and technology on the left. That is a great difference, and in many respects a regrettable one. The vanishing of that undermined Marxism, especially Soviet communism which was built on a faith in technology being harnessed to the public good.

So, I have argued that Britain's comparative advantages lie in finance and commerce and that by allowing those advantages to work themselves out, Thatcher essentially strengthened the economy. Now some have argued that the post-1979 era witnessed problems with social cohesion, that allowing comparatively free play to market forces hastened social fragmentation. Certainly, the relative unity of British culture which existed, say, in the 1930s or perhaps even until the early 1960s has gone, but it has gone everywhere in the world and for a variety of reasons: multiculturalism, the rise of local nationalisms, generational issues, the decline of symbolism and tradition (which in many respects is regrettable), the decline of religion. Also, in Britain the BBC had a monopoly of radio/television broadcasting until 1958; that has gone. All printed communications in effect came from Fleet Street, Oxbridge and London until the 1960s; that has also gone. In many ways it is regrettable, but on the other hand choice is a good thing. The question is how you live with it without a societal breakdown. If you ask whether 15 per cent unemployment means that you are going to have people who are hostile dropouts and so on then the answer is yes, and the obvious solution is to have lower unemployment.

But the changes which have generated social tensions do not necessarily relate to the strength of finance and commerce. The end of Empire, the loss of symbolism, the loss of Britain's great power status have generated independence or quasi-independence movements in Wales and Scotland which are now very important. The presence here of two million people of non-European origin has generated certain obvious racial tensions. But these have nothing to do with Britain's financial economy. Also, there is probably less social tension in Britain than in many other countries, and perhaps less now than there was ten or fifteen years ago. What objective evidence do we have of social tensions? We do not have riots, the crime rate is the same or lower than it was, more people are at universities, people are not holding massive demonstrations, there are virtually no strikes. None of the negative prognostications has eventuated.

Declinism reflects much about British culture, particularly higher mass culture, the better newspapers and so on. The idea that Britain is pre-ordained to fail appeared around the time of Suez, and had become dominant by the mid-1960s. There was enough evidence to confirm that Britain was no longer a great power, that its manufacturing industries were going down. But this argument is wildly exaggerated, and is certainly not true now. Britain is *not* pre-ordained to fail. Many academics are sceptical about declinism, including most economists. Leftists accept the declinist thesis, because under capitalism a middle-ranking nation like Britain cannot easily compete without basic reforms. A certain type of extreme rightist might also accept it. But the objective facts simply do not bear it out. In my view it is less a case of explaining British decline in some objective sense, than of explaining why declinism has held such an appeal for some people. There is a national spirit of self-flagellation, which may be part of Britain's national character. It may be that there are certain identifiable psychological types, in different countries. One would not want to pursue this too far down the road of racial characteristics. But it may be that one finds a certain kind of authoritarian personality in Germany; while the equivalent in Britain is a schizoid personality. The latter is the eccentric: a person who talks to himself and is a loner, but not in a harmful or anti-social way. Usually that type is pretty harmless and endearing. But there may be something in this personality which cannot understand success and this might relate to declinism: one does not brag, one dampens downs one's good qualities, one assumes inferiority. These are not cast-iron types, of course, but might provide some clues to the declinist mentality.

Some people hold that if the state had been harnessed to economic development in a direct way, then Britain would have been better off. But there are several problems with that. One is that it carries certain totalitarian implications. More importantly this assumes that the state knows what to do, which of course it does not. For example, in the 1945–51 period why should the government have pursued the development of computers (as Correlli Barnett has argued)? Were they supposed to know that computers would some decades later be at the centre of the world's economies? This would assume an ability to predict the future, to sense a teleological development, which is unrealistic. If the state had undertaken to direct what Britain should have produced at that time, the most likely outcome is that the state would have got it wrong. Its guesses would have been mistaken.

One of the great changes which has come over Britain in the last generation is the vast increase in the numbers of university students. The increase has been astronomical. The proportion of the population entering third-level education now is probably fairly similar to that in the United States. This was not the same two generations ago. This does not mean that the students are better than they then were. In fact, they are worse. They cannot write a sentence in English without making five grammatical mistakes. Also, they have absolutely no self-confidence in themselves to say anything original, and simply parrot their readings. That is one of the most striking things you see. They do not challenge received opinion. That is a regrettable feature of the increase in numbers entering university education. I also think that the fact that they cannot write is an indictment of primary and secondary education. Such trends will not serve Britain well in the long term. On the other hand, one should not be too disconsolate. I remember when Sputnik went up in 1957, a panic set in in the United States. One thing I remember in particular is that *Life* magazine – this must have been around 1959 – had a cover story comparing two high-school students, one in Chicago and one in Leningrad. This made an enormous impression on me. The kid in Chicago was a virtual juvenile delinquent. He never read anything weightier than a comic book. The only things he thought about were girls, hot rods and Elvis Presley! The student in Leningrad was carrying a huge pile of thick scientific tomes, already knew five languages and looked like he was in line to win the Nobel Prize before graduating from high school. Now panic set in throughout the West around this period about how the Soviets were going to run rings around the West because of their emphasis on science. And one would have assumed, looking at American popular culture at that time, that this might well happen. Yet here we are 40 years later: the Soviet Union has collapsed and the United States is the world's leading power. So maybe there is some hope for the British riff-raff today!

Indeed, given the optimistic possibilities inherent in contemporary Britain, there is no reason to believe that the country is foredoomed to failure. It might take a long time to persuade people of this. It has become second-nature to British psychology to expect failure. Many people think that the current strength of Britain is a flash in the pan, that something will go wrong and that there is a flaw in it somewhere. Certainly the adjustments of the 1970s and 1980s were not without their painful side. But that seems to be behind us now. Precisely when people will accept that the worst is behind us, it is difficult to say. But it is hard for people to sustain the argument that Britain is lagging behind the world when, by any rational standards of comparison, it plainly is not.

Notes

1. W.D. Rubinstein, *Men of Property: The Very Wealthy in Britain since the Industrial Revolution* (London, 1981); W. D. Rubinstein, *Elites and the Wealthy in Modern British History: Essays in Social and Economic History* (Brighton, 1987); W.D. Rubinstein, *Capitalism, Culture and Decline in Britain 1750–1990* (London, 1993).
2. W.D. Rubinstein, *Men of Property*, p. 247.
3. W.D. Rubinstein, *Elites and the Wealthy*, p. 54.
4. W.D. Rubinstein, *Capitalism, Culture and Decline*, p. 24.
5. W.D. Rubinstein, *Elites and the Wealthy*, p. 63.
6. W.D. Rubinstein, *Capitalism, Culture, and Decline*, p. 87.
7. M.J. Wiener, *English Culture and the Decline of the Industrial Spirit 1850–1980* (Harmondsworth, 1992; 1st edn, 1981); C. Barnett, *The Collapse of British Power* (Stroud, 1984; 1st edn, 1972); C. Barnett, *The Audit of War: The Illusion and Reality of Britain as a Great Nation* (Basingstoke, 1987; 1st edn, 1986); C. Barnett, *The Lost Victory: British Dreams, British Realities 1945–1950* (London, 1996; 1st edn, 1995); A.

Sampson, *The Changing Anatomy of Britain* (London, 1983). See also the interviews with Wiener and Barnett, pp. 25–36 and 37–49 of this book.

8. See, for example, W. P. Kennedy, *Industrial Structure, Capital Markets and the Origins of British Economic Decline* (Cambridge, 1987).

9. Cf. 'Thatcherism at its heart *was* simply the admission, as the centre-piece of governmental policy, that Britain's comparative advantage in the international economic sphere lay in the services, finance and commerce, and that deliberate attempts by the government to focus economic policy on the fostering of a truly revivified manufacturing sector were likely to be quixotic and counter-productive' (Rubinstein, *Capitalism, Culture and Decline*, p. 154).

6

Sidney Pollard

Introduction

Sidney Pollard enjoyed a distinguished career as one of Britain's leading economic historians and a highly respected observer of economic policy. He published widely on different periods in British economic history, as well as on the history of Sheffield and developments in the international economy. Born in 1925, he was educated at the London School of Economics and then became Knoop Fellow at Sheffield University. He held academic posts at Sheffield University since 1952, becoming Professor of Economic History in 1963, and at the University of Bielefeld in Germany, 1980–90, and became a Fellow of the British Academy in 1989. He died in 1998.

Pollard has addressed the question of decline in a number of important texts.[1] These draw upon an intimate knowledge of many of the controversies and arguments which have animated economic historians on questions relating to decline. He has recently focused upon arguments about whether the origins of decline can be detected in the late nineteenth and early twentieth centuries. In *Britain's Prime and Britain's Decline*,[2] he considers in some depth different explanations of Britain's supposed decline in the late nineteenth century. His starting point is the difficulty of pinpointing the precise causes of the recession which appeared to take hold in this period. A particularly popular theory stresses the uniqueness of Britain's early start in terms of industrialisation, so that 'early success in capital goods exports was accompanied by capital exports, which in turn created financial intermediaries geared to channel exports abroad rather than into British industry'.[3] Other commentators stress the alleged decline of entrepreneurship and managerial skills in this period, and for some the weakness in scientific and technological training and research was all important. In terms of theories that stress other variables, he notes the popularity of explanations that highlight the role of Britain's ageing industrial structure. There are different variants of this view, which either assert that economic strength lay in industries developed earlier, or stress the early shift from agriculture, or the cost of replacing much of a complex structure if innovations were to be introduced at any one point, or the reluctance to innovate, characteristic of British workers and industrialists. Other factors that crop up in the historiography of this period include the fatal embrace of the aristocracy by the industrial bourgeoisie, the absence of a mass market, the preference for 'soft' imperial markets in the face of German competition, and the defensive and conservative attitude of workers and trade unions to innovation. The bulk of *Britain's Prime* involves a critical examination of these theories, and a rather sceptical consideration of whether it is appropriate to talk of 'decline' in this period. For a start there is no evidence for the idea of an absolute decline in the rate of growth at this time, though it is true that 'in spite of the variations between the different estimates, it is clear that British growth rates, both in absolute terms and in per capita terms, are falling seriously behind those of the major new economic powers, Germany and the USA, especially after about 1890'.[4]

Pollard's preferred way of measuring decline is to adopt a sectoral approach. In engineering and shipbuilding we can perceive the first signs of foreign superiority emerging, though this conclusion has to be qualified to recognise the 'extremely strong export potential' in these and other industries. His conclusion is that '[t]here seems to be no single characteristic, or no particular feature, within British industry which can be made responsible for such weaknesses as appeared in the period 1870–1914'.[5] Rather than decline being the problem, focus should be on slow growth. His general conclusion is that decline really has to be pinpointed at a later date, well into the twentieth century.

This thesis provides the backdrop to his well known book, *The Wasting of the British Economy*.[6] This begins with a discussion of contemporary national awareness of 'staggering' relative economic decline, an assertion confirmed by GNP figures. From 1950 to 1978, Britain's growth rates were substantially lower than those of her main rivals. Moreover, decline can be detected within particular industries, a more meaningful level for analysing such phenomena. He examines the different causes of decline, focusing especially on the lack of productive and investment capacities within the economy to enable Britain to catch up. The low levels of investment in capital and equipment are a recurrent motif in the book. Pollard explains the low annual rate of investment to income in Britain compared to some of her rivals. He also asks why investment has been so low from 1945 to 1973. Of particular significance in understanding this, Pollard argues, is the pre-dominant cycle, known as 'stop–go', which has characterised British policy in this period. During the 'go' or expansionary phase of this cycle, growth has risen to European levels, but during the 'stop' peri-ods, governments have repeatedly tried to prevent balance of payment deficit and focused on combating inflation. As a result the economy has come to a grinding halt and investment in particular has suffered badly at such points.

An important reason for the failure to maintain investment stems from the 'contempt for production', a characteristic feature of British political culture: 'investment in Britain was low because the whole panoply of government power, as exercised above all by the Treasury, was designed to keep it so'.[7] Governments and the Treasury are then the chief culprits in this story. The Treasury is identified throughout as perhaps the principal locus of damaging macro-economic thinking, and a key part of the institutional matrix that shapes economic policy. Pollard is especially critical of what he perceives as the unwarranted focus upon 'symbolic figures and qualities, like prices, exchange rates and balances of payment to the neglect of real qualities, like goods and services produced and traded'.[8] In the mind-set of the Treasury, issues like the balance of payments or inflation are considered more urgent than 'real productive power and real goods and services available for consumption which were repeatedly sacrificed for the sake of the sym-bols'.[9] The principal results of these preferences are a critical lack of capacity in key industrial sectors and delays in meeting orders in cer-tain industries which have hampered competitiveness.

There are, however, some alternative causes for the lack of invest-ment which merit consideration. He thus focuses upon other possible causal factors, paying particular attention to the failure of the econom-ics profession to provide an alternative framework for understanding economic growth: 'the economics profession has proved incapable of dealing with a problem that can be solved not by devising better theo-ries, in which British economists excel, but by altering the premises and the possible range of variables within which policy can operate'.[10] Also significant was the failure of different political parties when in power to develop viable 'counter-poles' to the Treasury, around which alternative macro-economic priorities could have been maintained and defended. There thus exists in British central government no tradition of planning and social 'steering' which might be compared with those that exist in other industrialised states.

Pollard ends *The Wasting of the British Economy* with an analysis of the Thatcherite attempt to reverse decline. He is scathing about the policies pursued in these years, excoriating the deflationary strategy pursued by the Conservatives. Mass unemployment, in the early years of the 1980s, was the most obvious and painful symptom of such misguided policy. Whilst other commentators stress the discontinuities in British policy after 1979, Pollard in fact sees Thatcherism as representing the intensification of earlier trends, particularly the unhealthy obsession with inflation at the expense of 'investment, innovation and improvement'.[11] In the second edition of *The Development of the British Economy*, he takes this analysis up to the 1990s. The 'experiments' pursued by the Thatcher governments represent an unmitigated failure. By 1990, Britain had a higher rate of inflation than any other advanced economy, as well as higher interest rates and unacceptably high levels of unemployment. He points also to the high number of bankruptcies, falling levels of output and the largest balance of payments deficit in history.

Pollard poses a pertinent question towards the end of *The Wasting of the British Economy*: 'Is decline inevitable?' He answers this by citing a range of institutional and cultural factors which meant that the legacy of the past hung heavily on the British economy in the postwar period. This was a 'formidable, mutually reinforcing historical burden to carry'.[12] Yet he also observes that, in certain respects, Britain enjoyed considerable advantages over competitors, yet contrived to waste these. In conclusion he offers a plea for a macro-economic strategy which might 'divert enough resources from consumption to investment, and likewise to expand the capital goods industries to supply the . . . buildings and machinery on which economic prosperity must be based'.[13] Ultimately the remedy for Britain's problems lies in the attitudes of administrators and policy-makers. In the interview which follows, he expands upon some of these arguments, explaining the biographical and intellectual influences upon his work, and updating his critique to cover government policy in the 1990s.

Interview[*]

I have been interested in economic decline for a long time and I have located it throughout my work in the post-1945 period. The economy was growing quite well then, but compared with how it might have performed, it was a

[*] Interviewed by Michael Kenny: Sheffield, 28 November 1997.

very bad show. So it is a relative decline that we are discussing. That is very important. It is not a total decline; at least not in this period. We should ask why and how the rest of the world, or particularly the rest of Europe, managed to maintain a very fast rate of growth from practically nothing at the end of the war. Clearly one explanation was new investment, which is necessary both to expand the economy and to modernise it. You cannot modernise unless you put in new equipment and have new investment.

Most of the other economies in Europe were run by people who were well aware of that. If you look at the literature and the statements by their central banks and so on, they knew jolly well that the only way to get a faster rate of growth is to have higher investment. Of course not every investment is productive and you can have some bits of growth which do not require much investment. But overall investment was an absolute necessity and the appropriate rate depends on the mix of the particular economy. Some industries need relatively little and others need high investment for a given rate of growth. But since most economies are mixed, the overall rate is important. So that is what you would look for even if you never saw the statistics. If you then look at the statistics it is very obvious that the British rate of investment is much lower than that of the continental countries in the post-war period. And the continental European countries' investment is much lower than in Japan.

My interest in these questions also stems from personal experience. Very soon after I came to Sheffield in the early 1950s there was a great campaign to link the University with local industry. The industrialists came to the University and we were led round the works, and I could see what the steel works looked like. And then sometime later I went round German works and found myself in a different world. And it was obvious that our people could not produce and expand at the rate the Germans could. The principal difference between us and them was that they had had their economy destroyed and had therefore to start from scratch. Our tendency is to patch rather than build anew, and to hang on to traditional methods. There was also a certain amount of trade union power here which would either stop new investment or insist that nobody got the sack even though half the labour force was probably superfluous. I also went around Japanese motor works about thirty-odd years ago. Even then they were in a different class compared with our motor car works.

I remember when I was in the Economics Department here at Sheffield and everyone laughed at me when I talked about this, and they said, 'Well, they're only catching up, you know'. At the time, you have to remember, we were streets ahead. We had won the war. The continentals could not run the factories because they had no coal; they had no coal because the railways were not running; and the railways were not running since they could not be repaired because there were no factories. And the Germans, particularly, used to spend their time in overcrowded trains travelling to the countryside to pick up a sack of potatoes, and anyone who had a sack of potatoes was king for the winter. From this position it is astonishing to me that they caught us up at the rate they did. Whilst we were staggering from one crisis to another, their vision was of constant growth and in their minds if they could not grow it was due to a bottleneck in some particular item which you could pin-point and cure. If on the continent – think of Germany – you hear a sentence beginning with 'In the light of the economic position', you know you are talking about expansion. If in Britain somebody said 'In the light of the economic position', you know that we are going to be talking about cuts. So it is not merely that our rivals grew faster. They had a more dynamic and positive attitude.

The next question is why our investment was very low. There has been a lot of talk about the faults of the British economy, that manufacturers and business men were not enterprising. Well, my experience from contacts I had with the local steel industry is that they were very enterprising. And it did not seem to be plausible that there was a failure of enterprise in forty different industries all at once. If there had been, there would have always been a new generation taking over and pushing the old ones out. So one should look for a more generally applicable factor, in particular economic policy at the centre. So that is what I looked for and it seemed to me that policy was precisely geared to prevent the sort of investment that was necessary. It was partly because government investment itself was always the first thing to be cut in every stop phase in the stop–go cycle, to make it less worthwhile for British manufacturers to invest. As soon as they got going again there would be another stop and the manufacturers who had been rash enough to invest could not get their money back. So it seemed to me then that while there are various other reasons too, the main explanation would have to be government policy which produced the strange stop–go cycle. And then the question is why did we have this kind of government policy? Then you come up against the traditional view of British policies being governed by the interests of the City. The Treasury and the Bank of England misunderstand the priorities that ought to be governing their actions. The central economic policy-making bodies in all other countries known to me – including even Switzerland, which also has a very large financial sector – look to the economy as a whole if they make policy changes. Ours always look to some tiny aspect: *either* interest rates *or* the inflation rates; *or* the rate of the value of the pound; *or* the balance of payments; always some non-concrete factor which interests the City.

The Treasury focus upon one or another of these symbolic entities. Throughout the 1950s, 1960s and 1970s it was mainly the balance of payments that concerned them. And now nobody cares about the balance of payments. Our balance of payment deficit is ten times larger than it was then, which makes me think it was not important then really. Another refrain from that period up to Thatcherism was about the external value of the pound. Terrible. Nowadays, the pound is dropping in value and nobody cares. On the contrary we think the pound is still high. These are symbolic things which are unreal. And today of course it is inflation. Go to an economist and ask: 'What's the main problem now?': 'Inflation' is the answer. So these symbolic goals were not sensibly chosen. There are different reasons for the evolution of what I term the Treasury 'mind-set'. Traditionally, going back to the nineteenth century, the British productive economy was better than anybody else's. You could maintain policies without worrying about the productive economy. Then, until the end of the century – 1900 or so – the American economy was better. Well, it would be. Their resources were infinitely greater. In any case they were led by people of British origin so that they were successful as a son or daughter enterprise. Still policy-makers in Britain felt that they did not have to worry about making the economy more productive.

Moreover, the long tradition of non-interference by the state is very important in the nineteenth century. It is astonishing how little the state and, especially, government did. So economic policy was not really made by the state at all. It was made by the Bank of England. And the Bank of England had its own very curious set of concerns. The main one was to keep its gold reserve intact. The last thing the Bank of England worried about was the state of the economy. It worried about the gold reserve because it had to back its bank notes. Anybody could take bank notes into the bank of England and demand gold. And at any sign of trouble people did and so it had to worry about its gold reserve. The way to protect the gold reserve was through various open market operations, as they called it: selling assets and securities but mainly, of course, raising the interest rate. So the notion developed that the Bank of England's job was to keep the gold reserve going and not to worry about the real economy. And that mind-set has persisted.

Then, during the First World War government was very much troubled by the balance of payments. The British could not pay for their imports so they had a lot of debts in America. By the time of the First World War the productive economy did begin to matter – how many tanks, guns and weapons you could turn out. But as far as the Treasury was concerned, the problem was to balance the books. And then after the war there was the Cunliffe Committee[14] and everyone was obsessed with the idea of returning to the days of the gold standard. In fact even Keynes was not interested in rapid economic growth. His interest was in employment, which may be similar but is not quite the same thing. So again you have the whole balance of government and Treasury thinking concerned with preserving the value of the pound or keeping it up, having raised it to look the dollar in the face. By this period, of course, unemployment became another issue and the Treasury refused to have anything to do with it. So there is a long tradition of this disregard of real goods and services, apart from very special war-time needs, when it was obvious that the productive economy mattered. And this still seems to be the case. One thing always struck me when I was in Germany for ten years: if there was a news item on television to do with the economy, the background picture was of cranes and a ship yard. On the British news, in contrast, if you have an item on the news about the economy, the background is a picture of stockbrokers. That is our notion of what the economy is about.

There is a social dimension to this mind-set in that the top people in the civil service and the City are the same sort of people. Their training is in the Arts and Humanities, and they come from public schools, and they intermarry a lot. Provincial industrialists are not quite in the same circle, they do not belong to the same clubs. There is a sort of social linkage between the top bankers, top officials, top financial civil servants and so on which provincial industry is kept out of. This is hotly debated by historians but I still think it is very important.[15]

There have been attempts by British governments to build 'counter-poles' to the influence of the Treasury. The only one I really know a lot about at government level was George Brown's Department of Economic Affairs in 1964. He simply fell victim to the Treasury. There were other factors as well but I think the politics of vested interests in the civil service power structure and the Treasury simply were not prepared to have a second economic ministry. They thwarted him. The first thing they said was 'Get the balance of payments right'. But nowadays the balance of payments has ten times the negative value of then and nobody bothers. So George Brown, apart from his personal failings, was swimming against the stream and he had the most powerful ministry against him. His little Department of Economic Affairs just could not get off the ground. You simply have to destroy the whole set of priorities which were governing policies up to that point for somone like George Brown to succeed. Instead the belief was that you set the scene by altering the interest rate and everything will take care of itself.

An interesting thing that I found in Germany was that when they talked about expansion or dealing with unemployment, the mental process and in fact even the language they used, were different to ours. They assume that if you want to create employment you have to invest a certain amount of capital. They see employment as – they call it *Arbeitsplatz* – a place where people work. This makes you visualise a machine or a desk or something. They realise that if certain industries employ an extra ten thousand people, that means, say, thirty million pounds. British government never thinks like that. They say, 'If you want employment, lower the interest rate'. And they do not realise – the present government included – that to employ ten thousand people you need to invest so many million pounds. There is no other way. Of course different industries have different capital-worker ratios. But you cannot employ people simply by lowering interest rates. Somebody has to create *Arbeitsplätze*, places where people work. I was very struck by this.

After the Second World War in Britain, people expected the rewards of victory after a lot of hardship. British people expected rising expenditure, rising consumption. So did the Americans. The Germans, Japanese, French and the Belgians knew very well that they could not have rising incomes. So for some years they were quite prepared to accept very low incomes and their economists then fixed upon about 25 per cent of GNP to go on investment. Ours settled for about 14 per cent of GNP. But immediately after the war our economy was on a much more even keel and so the absolute level of production mattered less. Instead, the first task for Attlee's government, at least on that level of policy, was to balance the books externally. And analysts said we needed a 75 per cent increase in exports to meet the loss of foreign earnings by capital going abroad and to get back to the prewar position. So that was the first task: produce for exports and the balance of payments. For a while this was a good policy but soon nothing else mattered but the balance of payments, whereas in Germany and France the priority was to get the basic economy moving. So when Marshall Aid came, we used it to clear the foreign balance of payments and other countries used it to increase investment. That in a sense reflected what were then considered to be our priorities. The British basically thought the economy could take care of itself: 'We have to worry about the balance of payments, prices, inflation and wage explosion'. The continentals had to worry about building steel mills and power stations. The French had several major industries they were going to build up: concrete and cement, power, coal mining and others. We had no real priorities. Our priority was to balance the books. In the long run this made a difference.

I have been increasingly struck by the view that economists, financial journalists and people in the Treasury, people who are all opinion-formers, are like sheep. If somebody says 'inflation', everybody shouts 'inflation'; if somebody says 'balance of payments', everybody shouts 'balance of payments'. It is extraordinary that there are no lateral thinkers. It astonishes me today since they are such clever people, these economists, and yet they take as the framework for their thought the consensus of everybody else even though it is clearly in conflict with reality. It is still the same today. We wait until the Bank of England raises interest rates even though this makes absolutely no difference to inflation but hits a lot of exports. And yet we sit there and nobody says: 'Why the hell do we do this? Why do we have 7 per cent interest rates when everybody else's is 3 per cent? Why do we price ourselves out of the foreign markets?' It is totally unnecessary. It seems to me that there is a consensus of thoughtlessness. I must say that after *The Wasting of the British Economy* appeared, a lot of people wrote to support me – including former Ministers. But what can we do about it? It seems to me that it is not merely a material loss that our national income per head should now be 50 per cent more than it is. It is the atmosphere of defeat, of constant struggle, of finding that if someone says 'Because of the economy' you know jolly well what is going to come is an argument for cutting something. That dispiriting view of the economy is pervasive, but it need not be so.

Matters are different now in that the British position has not improved but everybody else's has deteriorated. So we are now no longer out of line except at an absolute level. We ought to be 40 per cent, or whatever, higher than we are in terms of national income per head. And I think that it is absolutely disgraceful that we have 7 per cent unemployment 'officially', when in reality it is 12 per cent or 15 per cent. And so we keep on saying: 'Look, we are ahead of everybody else, they all envy us, our unemployment rate is so much better'. This sort of dishonesty came in with Thatcherism. Even anti-Thatcherites keep on saying: 'Well at any rate we have such a low rate of unemployment'. But there is a lot of dishonesty about this. At one time you could trust British official figures. You could not necessarily trust other people's but you could trust ours. But you cannot now. They are all tainted.

The first two or three years of the Thatcher administrations set the scene. They destroyed three million jobs and we never got them back although they pretended that we had. Those parts of industry have gone; thirty thousand jobs in Sheffield, gone overnight. Admittedly the productive manufacturing sector had to shrink. Every economy – even the successful ones – finds that this shrinks but it certainly should not have shrunk by three million people overnight. And that was due to the fact that they had, on top of the oil bonanza, a very high interest rate which meant that the pound shot through the roof. Even Milton Friedman, the great monetarist whom they were supposed to follow, threw up his hands in horror. He did not want anything to do with it. He is not as stupid as that. Some work has been created for women in part-time, unskilled jobs but three million full-time skilled jobs went and have never been replaced.

What also distinguished Thatcherism was the enormous redistribution of income which occurred, taking wealth out of the hands of the poor and giving to the rich. I think that is what Thatcherism was essentially about. I am sure that some people really believed that private enterprise is better. But it is such a weird notion that I do not think that many think so. What all this is about is redistribution of income: make sure that people who live on profits do well and people who live on wages do badly. It is ludicrous to make inflation a major target and destroy jobs and exports. The Labour Party has made it even worse by taking the Treasury's hand off the steering wheel, leaving it all to the Bank of England with a number of tame economists to sit around the table and be told what the position is.[16]

Now, it is quite true that certain sectors would have had to shrink anyway; even in Japan they have shrunk. But ours shrank far too much by comparison with other countries. One wonders, for instance, why shipbuilding collapsed. Admittedly, shipbuilding declined everywhere, but ours just collapsed despite its leading position. And why, for example, did motor-cycle production collapse? Why could we not produce motor cars? No one in Britain can produce bicycles. No one in Britain could produce the Sheffield Supertram. It had to be made in Germany. A lot of industries in which you would expect Britain to have expertise have simply been destroyed and I do not think that was necessary. The fact is that we now have hardly any productive sectors. Even the City of London has not been successful. Bill Rubinstein may think that the City of London is great.[17] Yet it has made one calamitous mistake after another. The City has had no end of catastrophes because its leaders are so incompetent. Look at the Baring disaster when this chap Leeson lost them several hundred million pounds and they interviewed him and there were public enquiries about what happened at the head office. And they turned out to have been totally incompetent, totally idle, these chaps in charge. Do you remember about three years ago that the Midland Bank wanted to buy an American bank? Of all the banks they could find in America, they found one that was totally bankrupt. They lost seven hundred million pounds. And these are the top people: Barings, the Midland Bank and the top people in the City – totally incompetent. So even the City is not successful although it is much more so than, say, the motor car industry. Those three million people who lost their jobs, as well as all the industrial exports we lost, and the penetration of foreign exports in Britain, cannot be made up by services. There simply are not enough services and there is not enough productive capacity in the services. And this is apart from the fact that we are not terribly good at services production.

I reviewed Rubinstein's book and I remember saying that it is a very important text. I think he is wrong, not totally wrong, but very much mistaken. The Industrial Revolution was not a commercial, but essentially an industrial, revolution. It started from Britain being very successful up to 1850 industrially, in coal mining and so on. On that basis Britain could balance its books and develop services that other people were not yet ready to develop. So it left us a step ahead in banking, insurance, leisure industries and in all sorts of services; not in every service though, as British education was always lagging a bit. But the notion that you can be a successful country nowadays and keep 55 million people going on services is just wrong. I think the Swiss have a wonderful tertiary sector, well two really. They have a banking sector which is as good as ours and they have tourism. And yet they have some of the biggest chemical firms in the world. Even the Swiss – and there are only six million of them – cannot live on services. It is just absurd. You do not necessarily need 40 per cent employment in industry but you need whatever it takes.

One reason why I did not subscribe to the view that decline set in during the late nineteenth century is that the British Treasury and the Establishment and, later on, Thatcherites, were trying to off-load their failures by saying we could not help it, the rot set in around 1900. But the statistics are against this argument. We were still on top on the world in 1914 except for America. American resources were immense, especially in agriculture and the provision of high-grade iron ore and cheap coal; America was an outgrowth of the British economy with the same sort of people running the same sort of society. We were still leading. The Germans were nowhere compared with our economy in terms of industrial output and industrial exports, and everybody else was a long way behind. The Germans were the only ones really at our heels. Why should we say that we were declining then? It was true that the gap between Germany or the rest of Europe and us was closing but you would expect it to be. If it had not been for the First World War, you could easily say that they would never have overtaken us. All this is very tricky because we do not know what would have happened. Part of *Britain's Prime* is centred around the many signs of the British making good their weaknesses: the founding of this University, Sheffield, as well as others, was an attempt to remedy our weakness in technical education at a higher level. In terms of statistical evidence there is no sign that we were losing out. You can work back and find signs of weakness though. Of course the main one was that we relied far to much on skilled labour and not enough on brain power.

One thing I learned in Germany was that they tend to exaggerate their successes and we tend to exaggerate our failures. At a personal level people will say: 'Well of course twenty years ago we (not 'we' as a country but 'we' as a family) could not afford that but nowadays we have a big car and go on holiday three times a year'. But no British person would ever say that. It is seen as bad form to boast about your wealth, but they do. And the Germans did before 1914. Partly because they were on the up and had an Emperor with a loud mouth. The British were disturbed about no longer being the top dogs. It is similar to when the Americans were so concerned as the Russians sent the Sputnik up. But there was no reason before 1914 to panic really. If you control 60 per cent of the world's productive capacity and then you only control 30 per cent, it may seem terrible. But 30 per cent is perfectly good if you are only a small country. The British were used to being totally dominant in most industries. They were no longer and so they panicked. They should have thought that this is very reasonable; there are 60 million Germans and they have got to make a living. They were an industrial nation by 1900 and had not been in 1850. Why should they not become a major power? In fact the liberal free trade doctrine should have made people quite happy about this. Those thinkers said – quite rightly, I think – that it is always better to have a trading partner who is efficient than one who is backward.

I would rather talk about the wasting of the British economy than about decline. The argument is not about absolute decline, but is about Britain not using all of its historic opportunities. And there are many areas of Britain – Sheffield is one – that are desperately poverty stricken in a way that you do not see in Germany. You may see it in France but not in Holland, or the Scandinavian countries or Austria. There is such a culture shock when you come from Germany or Scandinavia or Holland to a place like Sheffield; we are 50 years behind in terms of dirt, neglect and sordidness. The city has no money and a lot of people are in an 'underclass'. It is true that the economy as a whole has been rising but that is because there is an underlying growth in the world economy largely due to inventions and improvements in Japan and America. We simply get cheaper television sets and cars every year. We did not do anything to bring this about. There is an underlying growth of perhaps 2 or 2.5 per cent. I think there are good reasons for deploring the failure to keep up with Europe in the early 1950s, 1960s and 1970s which now have come home to roost. This poverty, this sordidness and dirtiness; the way that people accept low standards which Germans would not. Here they take it for granted that shop fronts have flaking paint and so on; that nobody clears the streets. You go round Sheffield and all the bushes in the city centre are full of rubbish. No one picks it up. In cultural terms – theatres, cinema and so on – Britain has done 'very well. It has been a glorious country to be in. But in terms of culture defined as self-respect and hope for the future, respect for public figures and so on, we have done very badly by comparison with others. And in terms of the behaviour of people to each other, and so on, we have done very badly. Selfishness is rife despite the long tradition of charitable giving.

I am not terribly impressed by New Labour but they have only had six months in rather curious circumstances. They imposed a straight-jacket on themselves to have Thatcherite economic policies for two years. It was not necessary. If you want to create jobs then you have to put money into industry or agriculture or forestry or whatever. Simply setting the scene by freeing people to enter the labour market is not itself going to create a single job, except for the carers in these kindergartens. To that extent there is nothing in New Labour attitudes that makes me very hopeful.

In terms of Europe, my own view is that it would have been better if they had not started upon integration and monetary union, but since they have, we had better be in it. I felt like this right from the start, with the EEC. It would have been much better if they had left it alone but now we are thinking of a powerful economy run from Frankfurt. It would be fatal really if we kept out of it. The Bundesbank is at least worrying about the real economy whereas our central Bank worries about interest rates. They may not be concerned about Britain as such but they would be much cleverer than our Bank in running the economy. At least they start on the right lines. But I am not an enthusiastic pro-European. I do not think that politically they are a very happy crew. In political terms this country is still very much better organised, as you can see from the issue of restricting refugees from other countries, from the amount of money which goes into maintaining incompetent farmers in Greece and in Spain, and from the corruption evident in some states – the way they falsify their accounts to get EU money, that sort of thing. Other nations – the Scandinavian, Dutch and Germans – have political systems as least as stable as ours, so there is no problem linking up with them.

As a historian I would say the role of the state – the necessary or optimal role of the state – changes very much over time. I am not sure that I would say that the state's role should be larger. On the contrary in some ways it should get out of the way. It should be doing different things but not necessarily nationalising everything. On the contrary I object to the way in which it presently interferes and raises interest rates when nobody wants them raised. It is not the quantity of intervention that is wrong but the quality of what it does. I do not think it should interfere much more in areas like the law or the welfare schemes. And again I do not think, historically speaking, that there is an ideal proportion of state activity which is right. On the contrary it is very much a question of where you are in development terms and where you are in relation to other countries. The lead country, the USA, needs far less state action than a country desperately trying to catch up. Certainly, as far as Britain is concerned, I am not saying the state should do more; in fact in many ways it should get out of the way. It is doing a lot of damage. But it should certainly be better at whatever it is doing. Under Thatcher the pendulum swung too far in favour of the merits of private enterprise. But there are other forms of public intervention than the state itself. There are various other municipal schemes, like housing associations that do not have to be profit-making or state run. There are various forms of enterprise that lie between the public and private spheres. So I do not automatically think that anything that is not profit-making is therefore run badly. The BBC is run extremely well by comparison with commercial operations. Profit-making does not guarantee efficiency. While the state is doing all sorts of things wrong, it does not mean that private industry is doing very much better. The way in which big industries were privatised was an absolute scandal. The notion that private monopolies are better than state enterprises is totally wrong even in terms of the ideas of the Adam Smith Institute. But that does not mean that we should immediately go back to nationalising everything.

In order to get the 'underclass' and the deprived people up to a decent level, everybody else's position has to improve. We have found no way of ending the poverty of the lower third of the population in industrial societies except by raising everybody's living standards. But of course progress does not necessarily just mean higher incomes in material terms. It could mean more leisure, better television sets not more television sets, better books not more books. But I cannot see any way of improving the lot of the worse-off without some redistribution.

Notes

1. Apart from the texts discussed here, see S. Pollard, *The Development of the British Economy 1914–1980* (London, 1991).
2. S. Pollard, *Britain's Prime and Britain's Decline: The British Economy 1870–1914* (London, 1989).
3. *Ibid.*, p. x.
4. *Ibid.*, p. 3.
5. *Ibid.*, p. 55.
6. S. Pollard, *The Wasting of the British Economy: British Economic Policy 1945 to the Present* (London, 1982).
7. *Ibid.*, p. 7.
8. *Ibid.*, p. 72.
9. *Ibid.*, p. 73.
10. *Ibid.*, p. 150.
11. *Ibid.*, p. 184.
12. *Ibid.*, p. 186.
13. *Ibid.*, p. 187.
14. A reference to the Cunliffe Committee on Currency and Foreign

Exchanges which reported in December 1919, recommending the restoration of the gold standard at the earliest possible opportunity.

15. These issues are discussed in the interviews with Martin Wiener and Bill Rubinstein, pp. 25–36 and pp. 61–75 of this book.

16. A reference to the decision of the Labour government, immediately after its victory in the general election of May 1997, to grant substantial autonomy to the Bank of England in determining interest rates.

17. W.D.Rubinstein, *Capitalism, Culture and Decline in Britain 1750–1990* (London, 1994; 1st edn, 1993). See also the interview with Rubinstein, pp. 61–75 of this book.

7

Samuel Brittan

Introduction

Sir Samuel Brittan is one of Britain's best known economic journalists and political commentators. He has been the principal economics commentator on the *Financial Times* since 1966 and was appointed assistant editor in 1978. His ideas span the fields of political philosophy, ethical debate and economic history. Brittan is well known for his critique of Keynesian economics and advocacy of market friendly and politically libertarian ideas. But his thinking cannot be neatly pigeonholed in ideological terms: he remains an iconoclastic libertarian, as concerned with moral and ethical questions as with formal economic arguments.[1]

Brittan attended Kilburn Grammar School and Jesus College, Cambridge University, from which he graduated with first-class honours. Though he was taught by Milton Friedman and Joan Robinson whilst an undergraduate at Cambridge, he did not espouse neo-classical views until some time later. His original political sympathies lay with the left, and he was especially interested in foreign policy questions. After Cambridge he joined the *Financial Times* and published his first book, *The Treasury under the Tories*.[2] In 1965 he left journalism briefly and worked for the newly created Department of Economic Affairs. He was subsequently appointed to the post of economics editor at the *Financial Times*. During this period he propounded his belief that the pound was overvalued. But he became increasingly critical of the underlying assumptions of Keynesian orthodoxies, especially of the idea that the state could orchestrate growth by spending to increase demand. These views were expressed in the final edition of his book, *Steering the Economy*.[3] After 1969 his thinking on inflation was taken up by the Conservative intellectual Keith Joseph, among others, and Brittan became an important sceptical voice within economic policy circles. He began his study of the relationship between a 'free' economy and a 'free' society (a relationship which has become a key theme in his work), published as *Capitalism and the Permissive Society* in 1973.[4]

In certain respects Brittan's heterodox economic ideas overlapped with the free market policies and monetarist ambitions of the Thatcher administration elected in 1979. Yet he has always been critical of aspects of Thatcherite politics, notably over what he perceived to be their 'illiberal' nationalism. During the mid-1980s he became a convert to the idea of the European Exchange Rate Mechanism, though he has indeed expressed regret at the timing of British membership which was delayed until 1990. In 1993, his contribution to political and economic debate in Britain was recognised in the form of a knighthood. Several themes have flowed consistently through his writing. Perhaps most importantly, he remains a skilled economic analyst who is sceptical of many of the assumptions of fellow professional economists. He has always sought to broaden the scope of economic debate, adroitly incorporating traditions of political and ethical theorising in his writing. He has thus been concerned to think through the ethical implications of his liberalism, especially how economic 'freedom' can be connected with socially and politically liberal policies. From the late 1960s, he played a key role in attacking the intellectual foundations of orthodox Keynesian economics: his critique of the 'conventional' belief that there was no long term trade off between unemployment and inflation was a critical component of first New Right and subsequently New Labour thinking. Yet he did not view government policy in the post-war period as simply 'Keynesian' in inspiration. He argued that in this period policy was shaped most of all by the Bretton Woods system which fixed currencies against the dollar (and the latter against gold) and which ensured low inflation while it lasted.

Brittan has made indirect contributions to the decline debates that became prevalent from the late 1960s. In the 1970s he was very critical of corporatist thinking and incomes policy. Yet his work has always undercut some of the central assumptions of 'declinism' too. Critical of those who have fretted about balance of payments deficits, for example, he argued that strong economies can run deficits whilst important features of national economic life are not measured in such a calculation. Even more important is his critique of the notion of national economic competitiveness – which for him, as for many economic theorists, is almost meaningless. He has repeatedly observed that the only level where competitiveness can be measured is that of the economic enterprise. He explains why in the statement which follows: 'I reject the whole notion of competitiveness. We cannot all be more competitive'.

Equally, he dislikes the 'chauvinistic' assumption behind competitiveness talk. Trade, he has repeatedly asserted, should not be conducted as a form of economic war.

Of particular interest now are his views on the Thatcher 'experiment' and what we are to make of this latest attempt to reverse Britain's perceived decline. His response to Thatcherism was ambivalent. Outspoken about some of the societal consequences of policy in the 1980s, he was also sympathetic to central parts of the Thatcherite programme – notably privatisation, the abolition of exchange controls, and trade union legislation. As he demonstrates in the interview below, he shares the Thatcherite hostility to union power and monopoly: 'The unions played an important role in holding back British performance'. Yet social equity and stability, he believes, can only emerge from a much more systematic attack on the fiscal privileges of pension funds, home owners and landowners on the one hand, and more targeted and generous distribution of resources to the less well off, on the other. The gravest error Thatcher and her ministers made, in Brittan's view, was to underestimate the rigidities of the labour market which took longer to 'loosen up' than was realised. In economic terms, the Conservative government's policies brought some, perhaps unexpected, benefits, engendering massive internal reorganisation within the manufacturing sector and increases in productivity during the 1980s and 1990s.

Interview*

I have always thought that individualism represents a vital aspect of the climate of ideas which influence economic performance. If you look at my book, *A Restatement of Economic Liberalism*,[5] there is an essay there, called 'Capitalism and the Permissive Society', where I point to the limits of individualism in the nineteenth century, how it affected only adult heads of families. There were not enough people then in a position to take advantage of individual freedom. But by the late nineteenth century these ideas were being hotly disputed, and Gladstone and Joseph Chamberlain were partly falling out over them. Then along came the New Liberals, like Bosanquet, who somehow found their niche within the Liberal Party. But there was still a streak of tolerant individualism in the pre-1914 Liberal government.

But then the First World War brought back collectivism, militarism and dictatorship. And ever since, the right has succumbed to the great fallacy of try-

* Interviewed by Richard English and Michael Kenny: London, 12 July 1996.

ing to marry economic individualism with nationalism and a very pronounced non-pacifism. In fact, Michael Oakeshott said that the biggest influence in favour of what he disparagingly called the enterprise state, as distinct from a civil association, is war.[6] War always leaves a legacy of more government authority, more rules and regulations, which it takes many decades to get rid of. And war played a major role in moving Britain down a collectivist path. There were other causes too. There was the triple alliance of the unions, the imperial preference movement and monopoly minded businessmen, all of which existed before World War One. But I do think that the war put back for many decades the prospects of a civilised capitalism.

Immediately after World War Two, the public spending proportion, after disarmament was over, was not much more than 30 per cent. Somehow, when nobody was looking, it started creeping upwards, and by the 1970s, governments had to fight very hard to stop it getting above 50 per cent. I am not against the postwar welfare state, but if we were starting again, would we not organise it on a different basis? This is a complex area of debate. But one aspect of collectivism involved the expansion of government services which in some ways went too far. Despite the concern about relative economic decline, by 1960 the UK was a prosperous society even though growth rates were not as high as they could have been. Nevertheless there was a great outcry about relative deprivation. I think we could have tried to consolidate the welfare state as it was about 1960 with some rule that increased expenditure in one direction would involve retraction in another. Equality took over from freedom, and that, I think, was what went wrong with progressive education too.

I have generally been very sparing in talking about the 'British disease' in my work. But the unions played an important role in holding back British performance. They are not terribly significant now, except in odd areas like urban transport. One could not help noticing that the reason why British governments used to say that they had to put on the brake was because of inflation, which was then blamed on the unions. That was the argument used by Labour governments even more than Conservative ones. And though they sometimes blamed the balance of payments, the trade unions came in as a cause of every economic fault. Governments would say: 'We would like to expand the economy faster, but we need pay restraint as a *quid pro quo*'. But it always broke down, one way or another. The unions still seemed to exert an influence even within a more monetarist framework, because, it seemed to me, their habits increased the amount of unemployment involved in getting down the rate of inflation, and increased the amount of unemployment prevailing in a steady state once you had got the rate of inflation down. These are proximate influences on public events. I had always thought that unions are essentially monopolistic organisations. Just like monopolistic employers, they operate by control of entry. Even if they do not control entry themselves, they do not go for a market-clearing payrate: they try to fix it as high as possible. They settle for higher pay per head at the expense of lower employment. Some neo-classical economists, like Patrick Minford,[7] say that this is only possible because of the benefits floor, but even if that is so, you could have the benefits floor doing much less harm to employment if labour markets were much more competitive.

Perhaps I lacked the typical formation of a British economic intellectual who is brought up to denounce monopoly but who regards union monopoly as something different. Unions also always appeared to me in a threatening pose. When I was at university, I used to believe in a 'socialist foreign policy', which really meant a liberal foreign policy. Now the great Praetorian Guard which protected the Labour right against the foreign policy liberals were also the union barons, who ruthlessly used the block vote to try to stop dissent. Later these people relished the thought of bringing London to a halt. There are other lobbies of a similar kind: there is the farming lobby, for example. And I do not see any real distinction between the unions and the lawyers' organisations who stopped Lord MacKay from liberalising the law profession as much as he wanted.[8] That is the nature of trade unionism. In the 1970s, it was impossible to imagine that the National Union of Mineworkers would become a minor organisation and that the Coal Board would be sold off to a small private company. It would have seemed a utopia. What I did not look at sufficiently were what the obstacles to performance would be if the unions were reduced in influence. But I do not want to take back anything I said about the unions. God help us if they return.

The 1972–79 period was one in which interest group coalitions increased in influence. Why were we able to have full employment earlier? One influence at work here was that for a long time in the postwar period there was a surprising amount of 'money illusion'. People thought that a 5 per cent pay increase was a good one, and did not say that they wanted it after inflation and tax. At a certain point that was punctured. Some commentators would say that this was because of a new generation of trade union leaders. More important is the fact that when inflation began to accelerate you had a shattering of 'money illusion', and full employment could not be sustained because of this illusion. The postwar decades were charactersied by mass production (I think the Marxists call it 'Fordism') and for that period there was no great difference between the supply and demand situation for different types of labour, so you could conceive of an incomes policy with an average of 3 per cent or 5 per cent, without asking too many questions about some people needing to have minus 5 per cent and others plus 25 per cent. You could think of realising this through pay policy, as perhaps the Germans and the Scandinavians did for a time. Once we moved away from 'Fordism', from mass production, to secure full employment it was necessary to have the pay of different groups of workers moving in radically different directions. Those on the losing end could not be expected to like that. So we had both more militant trade unionism, and also demands to use the public sector to redistribute income. But it is not possible to redistribute more than there is. Thus we got into problems in the 1970s which helped generate the overextended state.

I have not really changed my values since the age of 16. I did support Keynesian full employment policies when I thought they would work. The difference between myself and some other people was that they thought these policies could be made to work by corporatist institutions. I did not. If an incomes policy simply meant some nice man in the Treasury working out that we all have to get a 3 per cent rise then that might be acceptable. But once it involved Jack Jones telling Denis Healey what he could put into the 1978 budget, it was too much.

Considering the 1970s from the vantage point of the 1990s, a number of developments have occurred which I did not anticipate. There is now an obstacle, not so much to growth and productivity, but to full employment in the preference of 'macho' employers for what they call a small, highly paid labour force, rather than for a larger and less well paid one. They are acting almost as if they are internalising the union role. If you divide the union effect into two – first, the purely monopolistic effect on higher pay and lower employment; and second, the restrictive practices effect – the restrictive practices effect is now very much reduced, but employers themselves are very reluctant to take on a great number of low-paid employees. Clearly, one can see the temptations here. For if they have well-paid but scarce jobs, they can ration entry. And they can therefore discipline the people who are there. The internalising of labour monopoly by companies is perhaps something which I should have foreseen. But the other part which I could not have foreseen (although occasionally I did say it might be possible) was that technical progress would be so unfriendly to the less-skilled or less-lucky workers. I need to put this very carefully, because I do not buy all the propaganda about training and education. But clearly there are widening differentials. I do not mind widening differentials between the medium and the top, but the widening differentials between the medium and the bottom reveal that some workers are not trained, or are unlucky, or are simply not 'street credible'. The spread of market clearing pay has widened. And it has moved very much against the less skilled or unlucky workers. It may also have moved in favour of capital and against labour.

If one thinks about these issues on a comparative basis, it is clear that nobody has solved these problems entirely. The Americans have a more flexible labour market, but they have a greater problem of poverty at work. The Europeans have much less poverty at work, but they have worse unemployment than we have. And they have managed to keep a so-called safety net but at the expense of very low employment rates. They even have more retired workers than we have. And with the tendency for the population to age, they will have a problem of very few productive workers to produce the national income on which all the rest will depend. I would like to see more of the social security budget spent on top-up payments for people in work; and therefore less spent on the dole. But if you ask me whether there is a society which has got there and from which we can learn, there might be a little trick which we can learn from one country and another little trick from another. But there is no obvious role model. In fact, I think that the problems of Britain, France, Germany and, to some extent, the United States are very similar.

I reject the whole notion of competitiveness. We cannot all be more competitive. I remember somebody saying: 'Whom should the whole world be more competitive against?' We can all perform better, we can all be better off. We cannot all be more competitive. 'Competitive' is a comparative notion. If you restrict it to a very boring macro-economic sense, each country needs to have a real exchange rate that is competitive enough not to have a current payments deficit greater than what can be met from long-term foreign capital imports. But the fixation upon competitiveness is not merely a mistake, it is harmful because it makes trade into a form of war. And it suggests that Britain cannot do 'better' without other countries doing 'worse'. Now, I do think that – partly because of Thatcherism – there is less difference between the various European countries. There is talk about Rhenish capitalism being on the wane. Problems now are common ones. The question is no longer why Britain is performing so badly in relation to other countries. Studies are appearing on German economic performance, French development, and even on the Japanese economy, making many similar critical points about each. In a sense, I would have been more prepared to accept the 'What's wrong with Britain?' conversation in the 1960s or the 1970s than I am now. I do not think it is a very helpful approach always to be wearing the dunce's cap and asking why you are the dunce. It is really more sensible to ask why the whole class is not doing better. Today a discussion of the economic and social problems of one country is much like a discussion of those in another. And by asking what is wrong with particular countries you get the wrong emphasis because the argument always then hangs on slight differences. And it always assumes that the country in which one is having the conversation is much worse than all the others, which is untrue. There is a major difference between Europe and North America, with Britain coming somewhere in between. There was supposed to be at one time a distinctive Scandinavian model, but that has gone.

Thinking specifically about the decline debate, it is important that after the Second World War Britain started with a higher standard of living and a higher GDP per head than most other European countries. Now you would have expected some catch-up by these other nations after the war, but the catch-up continued for a suspiciously long time and by about the late 1960s – about fifteen to twenty years after the war, and going by very imperfect statistics – they seemed to catch us up and then carried on overtaking us. So there did seem to be a performance gap.

British institutional peculiarities have also been historically important. I have already discussed the unions. We could also consider the class system. In the 1950s and perhaps early 1960s people did get jobs because they were somebody's nephew or had been to a certain school. Oddly enough Wilson and Thatcher between them symbolised the end of that. A culture dominated by union obstructionism on the one hand and upper-class twits on the other was not a great recipe for success. Britain is now much less 'class-ridden' than it was. I suppose what 'class-ridden' means is that the vicar who comes to sherry regards himself, and is to some extent so regarded, as socially superior to a cockney industrialist who could buy him out a million times over. This has implications, because this cockney industrialist will want his son to go to Oxbridge, and then go into the civil service or go into one of the professions, and will have some sort of bias against business. All that has declined; it still exists, but is much less prevalent than before.

On this question of anti-business bias, I liked Martin Wiener's book.[9] He makes very good observations about how the business classes reached their high point at the time of the Great Exhibition in 1851, and from then on were mainly hoping to join the landed gentry. Now, this book has supposedly been answered by W. D. Rubinstein.[10] I do not think it has been actually. People might expect me to think so, but I do not. Wiener laid himself open to criticism by talking about the industrial classes, and the industrial spirit. If he had said business or commercial spirit, his argument would not seem so out of date. But at the moment if you draw a graph relating GDP per head to the proportion in manufacturing, you will find that it is an inverse graph – the higher the GDP per head the fewer the number of people in manufacturing. Wiener was nevertheless largely right, more so with his literary illustrations perhaps than with his numbers. He has all these wonderful quotations from Baldwin saying the Englishman was a countryman at heart. And Ramsay MacDonald was not much better: he was supposedly a Scottish countryman.

But by then well over 90 per cent of the British population was urban. And to some extent this myth was held by people lower down who as soon as they could afford a car, would take a picnic and sit in it on the fringe of the road thinking they were in the country. What has gone wrong with the Wiener argument is that the word 'industrial' in his title has been taken too literally.[11] I am not sure how far you could apply the Wiener critique today. When he was writing, the typical City company director would, by mid-Friday afternoon, have long been in the country. Today, however, he would be unnecessarily in his office at seven o'clock in the morning to keep in touch with the Japanese market and stay there in case something from the USA comes in later. Now, it is not clear that this makes for any greater efficiency than reading Trollope or hunting, shooting and fishing because it is the sort of thing that you could leave to an assistant. Probably those do best who do not frenetically try to follow every twist of the market which you cannot forecast in any case. Most of it is noise. If you substitute the word 'business' or 'commercial' in place of 'industrial', then I think Wiener's thesis would apply from about 1850 to about twenty years ago, which is quite a good run. Then came 'Thatcherism', though in fact a lot of people, including many in the civil service, will tell you that the real change came in 1976, triggered by the International Monetary Fund. If you look at the Denis Healey period, you might well feel that Thatcherism had come in then, because there were clear commitments to reducing the public spending proportion, and the borrowing requirement. So at the macro-level it started then.

It is obvious that I have never been a Tory. I have never liked the Conservatives very much. So I was not dancing in the street at the prospect of a Thatcher government. There was something paradoxical about using authoritarian means to bring in a liberal order. If you look at her speeches, you will find that she rarely spoke about a liberal order. She always used language which she thought would mean more to people in the street. She left it to Keith Joseph to put it in other ways. She did not talk of a liberal order, but about people's responsibilities, the need to wake them up and to see that the state could not provide them with everything. In her view, of course, decline came to an end in 1979 and started again in 1990!

In economic terms the Thatcherite record looks quite good, better than I was prepared to admit, in fact. Privatisation was more important than I perhaps realised at the time. And so were the union reforms. Now, it would be perverse to say that it was 'fortunate' that there was a recession at this juncture, but sometimes chance lends a hand. The fact that the union reforms came at a time of recession meant that people thought the effects of the laws were greater than they really were. There should be no apologies whatever for taking on the unions. Thatcher made a lasting contribution in challenging the unions. She made enterprise profit respectable. People felt less apologetic about making profits. And she did raise a query about whether more state spending was the answer to every problem. These are much longer cultural changes that you cannot 'graph' in terms of national income figures.

There are less-favourable aspects of her governments' record though, especially concerning some 'technical' issues. They were, for example, looking for a magic monetary solution, but did not discover it, and in fact no one has found it. There was also the fact that under Thatcher herself there were lots of reserved areas in policy terms, such as mortgage interest relief. Thatcher's great advantage was that she could ignore the paradoxes of her position on questions like this. She was in favour of getting the state off the backs of the people, and so encouraged people to buy their own houses, which meant that she did not tax mortgage interest. This is not entirely a minor point. This 'special favours' approach to housing had quite a lot to do with the housing boom of the late 1980s. Now you might say that credit expansion was more important; but when you remove credit controls there is bound to be an outburst of lending and it would have been better if mortgage interest relief had been removed in the early or mid-1980s.

She was utterly confident about the link between economic liberalism and a strong sense of nationalism. So we had the Falklands war, which I was totally against, because I think people lost their lives for insufficient reason. This nationalism became important in economic policy towards the end, with Thatcher's attitude first to the European Exchange Rate Mechanism and then European Monetary Union ('I will not have my monetary policy controlled by Belgians'). She began this chauvinistic response, but it has been exacerbated by other people. This is a definite inhibition on the conduct of British macro-economic policy and on other matters too.

As for the Conservatives in government post-1990, there was much less of a u-turn in policy than a change of tone. For instance, Michael Heseltine would say that manufacturing industry was very important. But he did not have a large enough budget to do much about it. And in some respects, such as in denationalising in areas where Thatcher did not dare to go, there was some progress. What went wrong is something that cannot be shown in the numbers, but is what happens when a conviction politician is replaced by a manager. When Margaret Thatcher was leader of the Conservative Party, she did not have to work over the weekend to think about how to answer Labour. She would tell you for an hour or two, and there was no stopping her! Major's Conservatives tried a different approach. First they said that Labour represented just the old type of socialism. Then they claimed that Blair had stolen their ideas. Subsequently they moved to a third position, that he had got a new set of ideas but they were dangerous. The fact that the Conservatives moved from one argument to another the whole time suggests that they were troubled by the question 'What should we be thinking and saying?' Sometimes people have convictions which prudence prevents them from uttering. But these people seemed to have no convictions, except the desire to retain power.

If you were to look at the numbers in the 1970s, the British growth rate was very low indeed. You could say it was because this was between the oil crisis and the discovery of North Sea oil. After 1979 two major developments occurred. First, the British growth rate reverted back to the trend of the 1950s and 1960s. Second, the European and Japanese growth rates slowed down. So there was no longer a significant growth gap. It is possible that in the 1990s the British expansion will be stronger. So the Conservatives were not just talking nonsense. On the other hand, if you look at some of what James Callaghan was saying from 1976 to 1979, he had the same sort of ideas about shaking up labour in Britain. A similar point could be made about what Peter Jay was then arguing as Britain's Ambassador to the USA. It looked as if such thinkers were inaugurating a new era. The big difference was that Callaghan was politically indebted to the unions and he knew it. He grew up within the labour movement, and if he went against the unions he felt bad about it. So his emphasis was always on aiming to get union leaders to come out with some statement which supported his views.

Economic liberalism and other forms of liberalism should be tied together. You get, on the one hand, so-called liberals, who are mostly interested in equality, and who do not see that the liberty to change your money into a foreign currency, to start a business, to go where you like, even to determine how to spend your income, are important liberties. On the other hand, you get so-called economic liberals, who draw up tables of economic freedom, in which South East Asian dictatorships become tolerable. They are *both* in danger of making themselves absurd; these views are not convincing if held in isolation. I am a little bit out on a limb here, because you will find that most of the economists around the Institute of Economic Affairs either find reasons for supporting the non-economic side of the Conservative project, or they just keep very quiet about it. My view is that it is important to consider the non-economic aspects of liberalism in conjunction with economic liberalism itself.

Notes

1. The breadth of his interests is well exemplified in his recently published collection of essays, *Capitalism with a Human Face* (London, 1995); and *Essays, Moral, Political and Economic* (Edinburgh, 1998).
2. S. Brittan, *The Treasury under the Tories 1951–64* (Harmondsworth, 1971).

3. S. Brittan, *Steering the Economy* (London, 1971).
4. S. Brittan, *Capitalism and the Permissive Society* (London, 1973).
5. S. Brittan, *A Restatement of Economic Liberalism* (London, 1973).
6. M. Oakeshott, *On Human Conduct* (Oxford, 1970).
7. See, for instance, P. Minford, *The Problem of Unemployment*, Selsdon Group pamphlet, Selsdon Group Policy Series, no. 5 (1981).
8. A reference to Lord MacKay of Clashfern, Lord Chancellor from 1987–97.
9. M.J .Wiener, *English Culture and the Decline of the Industrial Spirit 1850–1980* (Harmondsworth, 1992; 1st edn, 1981). See also the interview with Wiener, pp. 25–36 of this book.
10. W.D. Rubinstein, *Capitalism, Culture and Decline in Britain 1750–1990* (London, 1994; 1st edn, 1993). See also see the interview with Rubinstein, pp. 61–75 of this book.
11. This is an a particularly interesting comment when considered in the light of Wiener's observation about the title of his study, in the interview in this book, p. 32.

8

Stuart Hall

Introduction

Born in Jamaica in 1932, Stuart Hall has become one of the most prominent interpreters and critics of cultural and political life in contemporary Britain. He was educated first at Jamaica College, and then in 1951 began a Masters degree at Merton College, Oxford University, as a Rhodes Scholar.[1] After 1956 he was a central figure in the fledgling New Left movement that emerged in towns across England and Scotland, and became the first editor of the celebrated journal *New Left Review*. His early writing reveals his acute sensitivity to the overlap between cultural developments and social life, and the political significance of anxieties about national identity and nationhood in the British context.[2] As the second director of the Centre for Contemporary Cultural Studies at Birmingham University, from 1968 until 1979, he played a major role in developing the discipline of Cultural Studies. Since then, he has become one of Britain's best known intellectuals through his skilful commentary on a range of social and cultural developments. He was appointed Professor of Sociology at the Open University in 1979.

In recent years Hall achieved prominence for his interpretation of the ideological aspirations behind 'Thatcherism' in British politics during the 1980s. He has also helped refine understanding of political discourse and debate more generally, exploring how political 'common sense' and ideological arguments rely upon (often subterranean) invocations of racial and ethnic imagery and identification, which have significant social effects. In the light of Hall's work, generations of scholars are far more sensitive to the ideological and symbolic character of the deployment of terms such as 'nation', 'nationhood' and 'English'. His thinking has never been easy to classify in ideological or intellectual terms. It has been shaped by an extensive engagement with Marxism, yet he has never been a particularly 'orthodox' type of Marxist. He has incorporated the insights of a number of other major social and cultural theorists – Michel Foucault and Antonio Gramsci most significantly – in his work, but has always maintained his own distinctive intellectual voice and style. There are a number of central themes around which his work has been organised, especially the question of how the left should respond to social change and how it might conceive and construct an alternative, counter-hegemonic politics to that offered by the political right. In the course of his writing, he has ranged widely in subject matter, ignoring conventional academic demarcations. Hall has offered some of the most insightful, and at times influential, analysis of contemporary British politics to have emerged from the left of the political spectrum in the last twenty years.

Throughout his work he has considered the notion of 'decline' far more broadly than most other commentators, attending to ideological and cultural dimensions of the phenomenon often ignored by participants in decline debates. With his colleagues at Birmingham University, he began to argue in the mid-1970s that Britain was drifting towards a 'law and order society', as more authoritarian regulatory measures were deployed by the British state in response to relative economic decline and novel forms of social conflict. He was perhaps the first commentator to grasp the significance of the gathering of a new alliance of forces on the right of British politics in the mid-1970s, which drew on a range of intellectual and political sources – from the ideas of 'gurus' such as Milton Friedman to the heterodox policy recommendations of think-tanks such as the Institute for Economic Affairs and the Adam Smith Institute.[3] In his analysis of the 'great moving right show' which characterised British politics at this juncture, he showed how this 'new right' was gaining ideological momentum and legitimacy as the worldwide recession exacerbated the weaknesses of Britain's economic and social life.[4] As the following statement reveals, in Hall's mind declinist arguments are indissolubly connected to struggles over race and nationhood in Britain: 'the notion of decline is caught up with the question of an embattled national identity even though nobody will say that is what they are worried about'. From an early stage he understood Thatcherism as a misguided but ideologically potent attempt to provide a solution to the problems attendant upon relative economic decline and social fragmentation. Hall argued that Conservative discourse on race, national identity and crime was central to its ideological appeal, whilst many other analysts remained reluctant to grasp the significance of these issues in contemporary political debate.

Hall's ideas have proved both politically and intellectually controversial. Many on the left were reluctant to accept his reading of the 'hegemonic' dimensions of Thatcherism, though for many others Hall played a crucial role in defining what a 'New Left' politics might be in the dynamic and threatening conditions of the 1980s. A recurring, though arguably misplaced, criticism is that he overstated the ideological hold of Thatcherite ideas on the British public and the coherence underlying the Thatcherite 'project'.[5] Whatever the merits of these different arguments, there is no doubt that Hall's ideas about the nature of Conservatism in the 1980s occupy a central place in debates about the Thatcher administrations. In the statement that follows, he discusses the crisis facing the British 'psyche' in the post-colonial era as well as the deeply rooted anxieties underlying today's arguments about Britain's role in the European Union. He also reflects more generally on his understanding of 'decline' and questions whether New Labour has the capacity to reverse this phenomenon.

Interview[*]

Debates about British decline have often been formulated in terms of exceptionalism. But I have always regarded my work as emphasising the particularities of British development rather than exceptionalism. I am uncomfortable with the idea that there is a general type of successful state to which Britain does not conform. A lot of accounts of the United States have used an extreme form of exceptionalism, claiming that it is the *only* leading capitalist country that does not have a class system of the old type, and so on. I do not believe that. I just think that each specific national formation is quite dense and concrete, that you can read off only very general features in terms of the mode of production. That Britain is a capitalist formation tells you, of course, a certain amount, but only so much. After that, you have to think about how capitalist relations are embedded, and how they are historically embodied in a specific formation. So I think about this more on the model, as Marx said, of there being language, but all languages having certain features. So what we are interested in is what he called the *differentia specifica*: what is specific and different about each individual language, or, in this case, state.

There *are* certain features which belong to what the nature or the type of society is, which one might begin to try to predict at a general analytical

* Interviewed by Richard English and Michael Kenny: London, 15 July 1996.

level. But what I am calling the more extreme form of exceptionalism thinks that all the others belong really to one broad type, while Britain is somehow evading or escaping this. This is what happened in the great debate that took place between the 1870s and the 1890s about Prussia, a state-driven model of capitalist development. I do not myself think that there is any ideal-type combination of state and market which is the only one under which capitalism prospers. And I do not believe that comparative work is usefully done like that. This is the problem with how the South East Asian model is sometimes discussed. People say: 'They're doing better than us. So they must be doing something that we are not doing and ought to have done.' But I do not trust this kind of thinking when it is put in terms of the one true path, because I think that this relies on a model which suggests that the logic of capital drives everything. And this kind of thinking assumes that there is equally an ideal form of family, politics and sexuality that goes with it. I do not believe that history works like that: it is much more of a grounded and specific combination of forces that unfolds in particular ways.

A related controversy – which is one that interests me, and which I have been thinking about again – is that to which Martin Wiener contributed.[6] But this is also very much a New Left argument – exemplified by the debates between Perry Anderson, Tom Nairn and Edward Thompson.[7] I think an ideal type predominates in Anderson and Nairn's contributions to these arguments. The ideal type is the French Revolution and French development more generally. Their argument was that there must have been a moment, which coincides with industrialisation, at which the bourgeoisie manifestly takes command. And this sets up the appropriate level of polity, which is the republic, and it moves to the highest level of bourgeois conceptualisation in the figure of the citizen. When does this happen in Britain, they asked? It perhaps occurred in the seventeenth century, or maybe in the nineteenth. What happens in the nineteenth? Well, Wiener tells us: no sooner were the middle classes on stage than they were buying themselves into the aristocracy. They never became citizens. I thought Edward Thompson's response to this kind of thinking was absolutely right. It is because Anderson and Nairn have a kind of ideal type of what the bourgeois revolution is that they did not understand the degree to which Britain became a bourgeois society really very early on, in which the market did penetrate very deeply. And this happened in a funny, peculiarly English way. Britain became the leading bourgeois society in the nineteenth century.

Just because modernisation stalled in Britain, it does not mean that elsewhere the ideal model was being followed. Britain *was* exceptionally placed at that stage. It was very early in its industrial revolution, a whole century before everybody else. And Britain made the industrial revolution on the back of the first technological revolution. And then other states came along and made it on the back of the second, which was the chemical and electronic one which we never quite caught up with. So it is not surprising that Germany, the United States and Japan took advantage of their place in that sequence. It is not that Britain was simply exceptional, though there was something specific about the way in which Britain moved through that moment. This explains why, having once led, it no longer did so after 1900. It explains why there is a very profound fault line somewhere around the 1880s and 1890s in British social development.

Now, I argued in a piece I wrote with Bill Schwarz[8] that in a way this moment coincides with the beginning of what we call modernity. It coincides with the beginning of modernism, certainly. This is when the modern forms of labour movement emerge in the whole of Europe. So it is a pretty historic moment to slip from being the nation in the vanguard to being the one that is not making the transition very effectively. And it is also the moment of high imperialism, which, of course, neither Nairn/Anderson nor Thompson wrote about. The other countries enter the imperialist race, but not in that deeply formed way; they have not been 'inside' imperialism for two hundred years in exactly the same way as Britain. And their institutions have not been hauled around as a consequence nor their investment priorities shaped in the way that Britain's were. Therefore, I do think that there is a certain, 'real' way of dealing with and entering modernity, and Britain did not do that. And this has had important consequences. To have the relations between men and women that the British have at the end of the twentieth century, for example, is just not to live in the modern world. British culture is so archaic in some respects. It is caught in a sort of time warp.

I have found myself drawn back to these debates by the emergence of Tony Blair and New Labour and the discussion of other successful 'models' of capitalism, particularly the Southeast Asian 'tigers'. Both left *and* right are riveted now by this other model and so it is playing the kind of role, I suspect, that Prussia played in the 1870s. 'Whatever they're doing, we have to follow'; a kind of model for want of another. As for Blair, I think he has settled for the management of decline. I suppose it is a different version from the Tory one. But his mission is to lower expectations: 'Very little can be done; we are not in charge of our destiny'. And some of that is true. I am not denying that the global conditions have changed, although I think a lot of rubbish is talked about globalisation. But from somewhere Blair has got this notion that part of his task is to lower the expectation that everybody has about what Britain can ever do. People might say: 'Don't you think the poor need support?' He would say: 'Well, yes, but the government can't do it, we cannot deliver at that level any more'. I think the idea of decline is very deeply embedded in British culture and it underwrites the debate with Europe too.

A crucial dimension of these debates concerns the loss of Empire. The conventional teaching of history which separates 'British history' from 'imperial history' and 'Irish history', for example, has disabled us from understanding how profoundly every middle-class person in the mid-nineteenth century knew about Empire, was touched by Empire, or had missionary sons; many were members of churches that were part of the abolitionist movement, and went to those meetings. A great deal of thinking about democracy and the degree to which 'men' could be independent, was infused by models drawn from Australia, New Zealand, India and so on. So I think that the imperial culture runs fantastically deep and then reaches – politically and economically – a really profound climax towards the end of the nineteenth century. The loss of empire is profoundly traumatic. We have to understand that when people say, 'Well what does Britain mean anymore?', a good half of the answer is still about imperial images.

That is why I think the notion of decline is caught up with the question of an embattled national identity even though nobody will say that is what they are worried about. That is what people are concerned about in relation to Europe, and that is why they are worked up now about the Far East. On and on and on, it is the question of what on earth can we be now in the aftermath of this past? So, in that sense I think decline is very tied in with Empire – at the level of a collective psychic understanding of what Englishness means. Englishness is special – Britishness to a certain extent – and the play between those two entities is quite important. It is difficult to explain to anyone why the English, and the British, are so confused about identity. It is a complicated matter. You find yourself frazzled about whether you are talking about the English or the British, whether the words are interchangeable. And that is because of the complicated relation between different parts of the UK.

Decline debates have tended to obscure these questions. But then I am not surprised by that. Look at how many historians write wonderful and well-respected tomes about Empire in which the capital race does not exist. They really do write about India and Africa without the metropolitan race appearing. They talk about power and colonisation and native peoples and so on, but the notion that the definition of Englishness has always carried a racial signature is just never brought to the surface at all. So I am not surprised that it is not reflected on in the decline debates. This is a different question from talking about how the relation between the British and the Afro-Caribbean community is going, which is a specific negotiation. I am talking really about the degree to which Englishness has depended on a particular racial definition of national identity and what travails that notion must be experiencing within an increasingly globalised world in which it is never going to carry that signature ever again. So what on earth can Englishness mean and how do you think about national greatness without thinking about a national/imperial character that is pre-eminent in popular thinking? Unless you grasp this, you cannot understand why the Tory Party could conceivably tear itself apart over Europe. If the question here was straightforwardly an economic one, the Conservatives would not rip themselves apart like that. They would adopt some more rational discussion of how much Britain can get out of Europe. Clearly it is not a discussion about that but about power – who is on the stamp? It is a discussion about symbols, at least a lot of it is, that is generating all this heat. So, as usual, the British talk about what they are really concerned about in some other way – never directly. They find some other coded language and talk about Europe or South East Asia. These are the signifiers, which relate to this other, deeper question.

Though formal decolonisation began after the Second World War, it feels as if Britain is really decolonising now. They took the flag down then. But what decolonisation really means is never going back to an older historical era. So, of course, it seemed to have happened relatively painlessly, partly because the really difficult wars were kept under wraps. You can say to people in Britain, 'What about the colonial wars in Malaysia?' Nobody knows what you are talking about. They really do not know that there were any. But let me use an old phrase: 'lost an empire, never discovered a role'. And it is true; I do not think that the significance of decolonisation has really come home, though it has been slowly beginning to do so for a long time. Direct migration is another issue. I do think it hugely ironic that it is at the moment of decolonisation that the colonies come home! That must have been a cruel dilemma for the British. Because they had just got rid of these people, thinking that they could now cut the umbilical cord, give them independence, and not have to deal with them in Wolverhampton, Bradford and Oxford, and so on.

Mixed up with these issues after the Second World War was the increasingly global role of the United States. The war absolutely confirmed that this was how global wars were fought and Britain could not fight one without the economic power of a much larger market. It signalled the emergence of an American empire. It was a neo-imperial empire, based on war and surveillance, not necessarily an empire of occupation, flags and administration. Not only was a different power the leading imperial nation, but it ushered in a different form of global economy. So I think that the Second World War had a lot to do with dramatising that shift in fortunes for Britain. The war also locked Britain into an Anglo-American relationship in a subordinate position. It became manifest, immediately afterwards, that Fordist forms of production were going to come through much more strongly and energise the American economy, with Britain falling behind. From then on Britain resentfully learned the game from the USA. The position had been exactly the reverse. In the middle of the nineteenth century everybody had been learning the game from Britain. It had been a case of coming to Britain in order to discover how to be up-to-date. Now it was a case of coming to Britain to learn how to be traditional!

At a popular level, decline has been 'managed' in different ways, often through sport, which is one of many barometers signalling long-term secular adjustments and compromises, and also eruptions. Think about the history of the absorption of blacks into the central areas of sport. The sequence has varied. But I think that the process of decline has been reflected by spasms at a popular level. These moments of popular concern have been expressed in relation to defensive targets: race is one, and Europe has become one. These are very difficult developments to read; you have to be very careful to avoid overreading them, making them too clear-cut. What about travel, for example? Unprecedented numbers of young people travelling abroad: has that helped to shift attitudes? Well, it has in one sense and not in others. It certainly has, in that they know more about different food and foreign cultures. But it does not always mean that they are necessarily more sympathetic to a European perspective, or that it has made them feel more like European citizens. We used to read a lot of the signs like that; when the Vespa came, this was Italian modernity at last. Turin was going to take over British popular culture and streamline it. In fact, this culture only got as far as the south coast, and then the young men affected by it beat each other up! Like anything else, these developments are quite hard to read. But I think we have become closer to other cultures. There genuinely was a kind of opening in the 1950s and 1960s, and not only to Europe: there was also Americanisation, which involved a kind of relaxation in mores connected with sexuality and music, most obviously. I do not think that you can say that recently there has been a receptivity to foreign influences – I mean other European and North American influences penetrating British culture. In fact, I can feel our culture clenching again after a moment of openness. Perhaps this is not surprising given the nature of Thatcherism.

In a sense, Thatcherism occurred partly because the left as well as the right thought that Thatcher herself was right! There was a widespread recognition that the 1970s simply could not go on. The question was whether the social democratic 'solution' was any longer affordable – both politically and economically. After 1968 – with the surge of stronger bargaining powers by the left, equal opportunities legislation and so on – we almost got to the point of a kind of stasis, a Gramscian situation, in which one side cannot manage and the other side cannot lead. We almost got to that. And since there was never the political opportunity to go beyond that on the left – I do not think that the land that Tony Benn would have taken us into ever existed – we had to step in the opposite direction. It was almost as if at some moment in the 1970s we got to the point of thinking: 'It doesn't matter. There are no real economic costs. We don't need to ask that question.' And I think, in their heart of hearts, people felt it could not go on like that. Even if you decide not to pay the cost, you must work out what it is, you *must* know what it is. You cannot avoid asking this. So I think there was, even among the left, a kind of awareness that we had gotten ourselves into a sort of 'cuckooland'. So, the question is whether that was itself just a perception or whether there was some truth to it; whether by then the fiscal crisis of the state was of such a degree that actually we were not producing enough to go on extending the welfare state in the form in which we had it. I do not know the answer to that. But I think we are obliged to ask that question. Because we all felt that Thatcherism indicated some limits or parameters. We thought it had, partly because, for whatever reason, Britain was no longer at the top of the tree. So there was just an air of unreality as to whether the country could go on in the same way. Did it really not matter that British industry had no investment and was technologically backward and could not run a sweetstall? Did it not matter that the managerial class could not put two words together? Did none of these things matter? British capitalism ran on the basis of a shrinking economy, a declining social formation, was less confident than it had ever been before, had less of a world role, and was more dependent on the United States. I think there was a bubble about to burst before Thatcher applied the pinprick.

I tend to think now that the problems she was pointing to were 'real' but it is hard to separate that from her particular way of talking about them, which led to particular solutions. The latter – her remedies for these problems – were not inevitable. But there were some external parameters that nobody could have evaded. Thatcher let people into the conversation about these realities in ways that nobody on the left was prepared to do in the 1980s. For the left it was considered treason even to talk about such things. And this, of course, is exactly some people's quarrel with Blair. He has acknowledged that some of the parameters are real, but he has not been able to think of any other way of addressing the problem, except in thinly remodelled Thatcherite terms.

If I am resentful about the intellectual debates surrounding Thatcherism, it is towards those people who quoted British social attitudes at me: 'Yes, but the British electorate says that collectivism is okay, and that they're perfectly willing to pay a lot for that'. This was nonsense. It did not recognise the degree to which ideology had hit home. This whole area got away from us and has made the argument about inequality, the division of the spoils, and indirect redistribution through the taxation system and the welfare state, impossible to acknowledge. So we have been driven back to the position of either scrapping the welfare state or defending it. Neither of these is a tenable position. We are talking now about two alternatives: either, having every individual dealing with his or her own insurance and so on; or having a welfare state and not touching it. And yet we have known for twenty years that these are not the only alternatives. We knew that many of the forms of welfare delivery were bureaucratic, top-down, undemocratic and unresponsive. But we have never found out how to give form to these elements of our critique of the welfare state. Because it seemed that in doing so you were giving assent to the assault on the welfare state.

On the left in the 1980s there ought to have been debate about the changing economic constraints in the context of an increasingly global and competitive market system, when one of the traditional alternatives – large-scale economic planning – was now no longer viable. This would have been a difficult conversation for the left to have. But we should have wanted to know 'what are the parameters?' We should have wanted to know how to strike a balance between being relatively well-off in global terms, but certainly not at the top of the tree in terms of Western standards of living. So a certain lowering of expectation was inevitable. We see that in a much wider context now: a lowering of expectations is coming to everybody, throughout Europe and North America. I am very persuaded by the argument that if you look at the number of workers who are involved in enterprises which are producing goods and services for global markets, and think of those who will enter the market by the end of this millennium, no matter how rapidly the global economy grows, the share-out cannot leave the same proportion for Western Europe and for North America. The shares in the Third World are going to be much more unequally distributed too. And it is also important to reconsider the kind of internal share-out which we will have in Britain. This involves thinking about the welfare state because it concerns the social wage and forms of distribution – whether this will be via the market or taxation. But I think the debate about the internal share-out has been lost for the time being; and I do not think it will return whilst we are trying to figure out the effects of globalisation. I have defended stakeholding as potentially a notion which could be disarticulated and rearticulated in different ways, and still think that is probably true. Behind it is a notion of a more responsible corporate sector tied to social goals that are larger than itself, which is important.

If you are going to have capitalism in some form, the question is, can you set the agenda by arguing for certain ways of behaving, and regulate capitalism according to that agenda? There are a lot of fantasies on either side of that, but that seems to be where the real argument is. And if Blair had really wanted to have that debate he should have done something extremely bold, which was to launch this agenda three years before the election. He would have endured a terrible six months, in which his opinion polls would have sunk through the floor, and then gradually began to inch their way back up. And he would have had to be very clever about it. He should have picked for redistribution only those areas where he knew there was some broader class consensus. He could have touched on the ones that the famous south-east, one-nation Tories wanted to see dealt with. The one-nation Tories are convinced that Thatcherism was not very good for the social fabric and think that though one does not want a swingeing level of taxation, one does want something done about the roads, schools, education and the health service. So I think he could have staged a debate around some of those issues. But I am not suggesting it would have been easy. There are about four or five targets and I would have gone for those, held the debate around them. That is where the climate has altered. People are shifting away from the Thatcherite consensus, though not very far. So Blair is right in the sense that launching the red flag would be the way to oblivion. The question is whether there is any virtue in not staking out some difference in these political debates. And if you decide to do that, you would have to weather some storms. He could have faced up to it in a very limited number of cases, saying: 'We can't take back everything, but rail privatisation is the stopping point. It's going to cost money, but I do believe that you will choke to death on the roads in Surrey as well as anywhere else, unless we can have all the elements of transport policy in our hands. So, we can't get everything, but we're going to do something about the railways.' Then there would have been no question about the difference between the two parties.

I do not think that New Labour has a strategy to reverse decline, but I think they may make it more tolerable. They talk about the adverse effects of risk and anxiety, but I think they accept the persistence of social anxiety. Their position appears to be that the state cannot protect people from anxiety. Their new 'concordat' between the individual and the state, with the state helping the individual to make do for him/herself, means that the state can never now guarantee long-term employment and so on. It just is not possible. So, we think of that as the experience of decline – long-term unemployment, middle-class unemployment, people in their fifties being made redundant, unable to get another job. There is nothing in Labour's programme that will touch these issues. You could believe there might be if they were going to expand the welfare state in a more selective way. And Blair's recipe for managing the economy is not going to turn the rate of growth around. Nor are they going to make major institutional shifts. So I think that this strategy amounts to the more gentle management of decline.

The centrepiece of British decline is economic performance, in particular the rate of growth, the rate of investment and the history of manufacturing industry. But we should also consider some other aspects of economic performance. We have a horrendously philistine managerial class: unbelievably stupid, one-dimensional and uncultivated. That is a major problem. Another is the unthinking way in which the language of the new managerialism has spread from top to bottom. I think that the new managerialism was the missing piece of my analysis of Thatcherism. In assessing how 'ideology' was to be put in place, in transforming institutions, it is now clear that it was through the medium of the language of the new managerialism: empowering, scaling down bureaucracies, delayering and all of that stuff which has been taken up. The public sector has been transformed by it more than the private sector. This is how the market has been imported. And this has transformed the public sector from top to bottom. Bringing management consultants in, drawing up mission statements, delayering and so on. It is heady stuff, and it is exactly because of its technical neutrality that the left uses it as much as the right. Think of those who are just about to make the transition from heads of department to line managers in universities, for example; they have never been endowed with such goodies as this rich language. This is very important. In Thatcherite terms, how do you make this country – which used to know how to make a buck and go out and sell goods to the natives out there – regain its entrepreneurial past? Thatcher said to the British people: 'We are the last political chance you'll ever have. If you miss this one, social democracy will kill you. You'll just endlessly decline.'

The other important dimension of decline concerns the Constitution, citizenship, the monarchy, and all of that. Why do my spirits not surge at all of this? I think these are important areas but they can be exaggerated. It is true that Britain's retention of its archaic institutional structures is important. I suppose I cannot get excited about reforms here because I think that in the last ten years these institutions have been a slight buffer between the social fabric and market forces driving through with unyielding force. I prefer old Toryism to new Toryism. But of course it is bizarre that we should still be without a written Constitution, and without a Bill of Rights. I think that the conception of citizenship is important.

The final dimension of decline that I would emphasise has to do with the question of risk. It seems that there was a point in the sixties and early seventies when people recognised what greater exposure to market competitiveness meant, and acknowledged the need for compassion, care and support. And the left missed out on that moment. It has gone completely. Now

116   *Interview*

there is much more of an abrasive ethic abroad: 'Nobody can protect you but yourself. If you don't want to see your house disappear when you're sixty then take out a pension or private insurance.' And this ethic is underpinned by a 'market-man' model which is deeply archaic. It so manifestly does not deliver the unadulterated positives that are tagged for it. It takes inspiration from Adam Smith. But the notion that this is the only viable model of the social individual does seem bizarre at the end of the twentieth century. It is as if we have learned nothing from psychology, psychiatry, the unconscious, the complexity of life, the idea of people playing multiple roles and so on. It is as if all that we have discovered about the complex ways in which we manage ourselves and our lives in modernity counts for nothing.

Notes

1. For a thoughtful autobiographical discussion of his early years, see D. Morley and K. Chen (eds), *Stuart Hall: Critical Dialogues in Cultural Studies* (London, 1996), pp. 484–503.
2. See M. Kenny, *The First New Left: British Intellectuals after Stalin* (London, 1995), pp. 54–68, for a consideration of the impact of some of his ideas on the early New Left.
3. S. Hall, *The Hard Road to Renewal: Thatcherism and the Crisis of the Left* (London, 1988).
4. See S. Hall *et al.*, *Policing the Crisis: Mugging, the State and Law and Order* (Basingstoke, 1978).
5. See, for instance, B. Jessop, K. Bonnett, S. Bramley and T. Ling, 'Authoritarian populism, two nations and Thatcherism', *New Left Review*, vol. 147 (1986), pp. 32–60.
6. M.J.Wiener, *English Decline and the Industrial Spirit 1850–1980* (Harmondsworth, 1992; 1st edn. 1981). See also the interview with Wiener, pp. 25–36 of this book.
7. See especially P. Anderson, 'Origins of the Present Crisis', *New Left Review*, vol. 23 (1963), pp. 26–53; T. Nairn, 'The English Working Class', *New Left Review*, vol. 24 (1964), pp. 43–57; T. Nairn, 'The British Political Elite', *New Left Review*, vol. 23 (1963), pp. 19–25; and E.P. Thompson, 'The Peculiarities of the English' in *The Poverty of Theory and Other Essays* (London, 1978), pp. 35–91.
8. S. Hall and B. Schwarz, 'State and society, 1880–1930', in M. Langdon and B. Schwarz (eds), *Crises in the British State 1880-1930* (London, 1985), pp. 7–32.

9

David Marquand

Introduction

Throughout his career David Marquand has crossed the divide which separates the political and intellectual worlds in Britain. He has done so with greater agility than most other figures of his generation, establishing himself as a well-known and highly regarded political observer. He has written on a range of subjects, many of great relevance to the question of decline.[1] In addition to his many essays and articles, three of his books stand out as especially influential: his vivid reinterpretation of the 'progressive' tradition in British political life since the nineteenth century;[2] his well-received biography of the Labour leader and Prime Minister Ramsay MacDonald;[3] and his sharp and influential exploration, in *The Unprincipled Society*, of the interconnections between Britain's ailing economy and the governing philosophies of its ruling class.[4]

Born in 1934, he was educated first at Emanuel School, then at Magdalen and St Antony's Colleges at Oxford University. He graduated with first-class honours in Modern History in 1957, and soon found himself a leader writer for the *Guardian*, a post he held from 1959 to 1962. In 1966 he stood for Parliament for the second time, winning the seat of Ashfield for the Labour Party. He was one of the most promising young MPs of his generation. 'Despite being singularly ill-suited to the feverish inconsequence of Parliamentary life', he sat in the House of Commons for 11 years, 'the first four of them fulfilling enough; the remaining ones increasingly, and in the end mind-numbingly frustrating'.[5] He served as a PPS during 1967–69[6] and was a member of the opposition's Frontbench team during 1971–72.[7] Within the Parliamentary Labour Party, Marquand was associated with a group of so-called 'revisionist' MPs who looked to Tony Crosland for intellectual guidance and to the political leadership of the Home Secretary (until 1970), Roy Jenkins.

As he has recently recalled, Marquand experienced a growing sense of unease about some aspects of Croslandite thinking during the 1970s, though he was even more convinced of the inadequacies of the rival orthodoxies of the day – neo-liberal political economy and the neo-socialism of a reviving Labour left. The themes of 'decline and modernisation – or, as I later came to see it, of change, adaptation and failure to adapt – had a special resonance for revisionists',[8] but increasingly he had 'a nagging sense that Britain had failed where others had succeeded'.[9] The revisionist case, he came to believe, had to be reconceptualised in the wake of the rising tides of economic and social instability affecting the British state. He moved gradually towards an enthusiastic pro-European position in debates over British membership of the Common Market. Following Wilson's retirement in 1976 and Roy Jenkins' failed bid for the leadership, Marquand accompanied Jenkins to Brussels, becoming Chief Adviser to the Secretariat-General at the European Commission.

Shortly afterwards, he changed tack in professional, if not intellectual terms. Between 1978 and 1996 he held professorial posts in the Departments of Politics at the Universities of Salford and Sheffield. In 1996 he was appointed Principal of Mansfield College, Oxford University. But he has continued to figure in national political developments. In the early 1980s he was one of the high-profile recruits to the newly founded Social Democratic Party, serving on its National Steering Committee until 1988. He subsequently joined the party which emerged from the SDP's merger with the Liberal Democrats – the Social and Liberal Democrats. He has latterly found himself attuned to the reforming Labour leadership of Tony Blair, and, in a welter of articles and essays, dissected the slow disintegration of the Conservatives' stranglehold on British politics. In the interview which follows, he builds upon these insights, raising some important and critical questions about the directions taken by New Labour in office.

Marquand's contribution to academic and political debates about decline has been considerable, particularly through *The Unprincipled Society*. Here he recalls the different influences upon this study, and offers some slight amendments to the arguments contained in it. Yet he holds to the central tenets of its innovative and striking analysis. He has recently described the book as containing three principal elements:

> a critique of neo-liberalism and the historiography of the New Right . . . an alternative account of the rise and fall of the post-war social democratic consensus and of the secular relative decline of the British economy . . . [and] the tentative outlines of an alternative, communitarian public philosophy,

centred on what I now realise was a civic republican notion of 'politics as mutual education'.[10]

The argument was set against the background of the increasingly fraught international economic context in which Britain was operating in the 1970s and 1980s and the efforts of the Thatcher governments to restructure the British economy. But he considered the 1980s from a much longer historical and intellectual perspective than most other commentators. Relatively poor performance dated back to the end of the nineteenth century:

> Though the curve of relative decline since then has been jagged and irregular, the forces behind it have been in operation throughout. Britain has had to face the world-wide upheavals of the last fifteen years from the position of a chronic invalid exposed to a snowstorm. [11]

The historical dimensions of decline were thus inescapable. In certain respects, 'twentieth-century Britain has been the prisoner of her nineteenth-century past':

> [B]ecause she was the pathfinder – because she made the passage to industrialism early, at a time when the technology was still primitive, when the skills it required were still the small-scale, fragmented structures of liberal capitalism – the experience taught the wrong lessons.[12]

The focus throughout *The Unprincipled Society* was on the governing philosophies that had prevailed amongst Britain's political elites, and which 'lie behind the economic record'.[13] The book's distinctiveness stems from this concern to pinpoint the values and assumptions of the ruling elite, which have framed and constrained the policies pursued in economic matters. Early industrialism was enabled by the doctrine of individualism, but a political culture organised around this was damaging by the time of the next major phase of industrial development – the so-called second industrial revolution of the late nineteenth century in which scientific-based industries, such as chemicals, were to the fore. 'In the age of the industrial laboratory, the chemical plant, and later of the computer, [Britain] stuck to the mental furniture of the age of steam'.[14] He combined this analysis with discussion of a range of social, institutional and economic factors which also militated against economic success from the late nineteenth century.

Comparing Britain unfavourably with her rivals, he employed a term which has become central to recent debates in comparative political economy – the notion of a 'developmental state'. In the interview which follows, Marquand describes the different intellectual influences which shaped his adoption of this concept. It was used to describe those states which relied upon the forging of an institutionalised partnership between different economic groups and interests and the more sophisticated deployment by the directive intelligence of the state of a wider set of policy instruments. Developmental states, he argued, were characterised by state-led and negotiated forms of adjustment. This pattern was thus powerfully contrasted with the apparent inflexibility and rigidity of the response that competition and recession elicited from Britain's managerial class in the 1970s. 'Britain's inability to adjust to the economic upheavals of the 1970s and 1980s lies in her failure to become a developmental state'.[15]

In the postwar period he highlighted the failure of Keynesian social democracy – defined very broadly as the governing philosophy of the 1940s to 1970s – to cope with the crises of the 1970s. This body of doctrines was crippled by the absence within it of a strong normative sense of the public realm or public good. Yet the political-intellectual alternatives of the day – neo-liberalism and neo-socialism – were equally flawed in their comprehension of political economy and the remedies for problems that they proposed.

The Unprincipled Society ends with a lament for the social and cultural consequences of decline, and a call for a reorientation of political culture along communitarian ethical lines: the idea of politics as 'mutual education' has to supplant 'politics as . . . command and exchange'.[16] This tantalising suggestion was developed more fully in Marquand's subsequent writing on constitutional reform and citizenship. It also found expression in the political arguments he outlined in his next book, *The Progressive Dilemma*. Here he 'called for a new bottom-up "progressive coalition" based on a marriage between communitarian, decentralist, participatory radicalism to which the Liberal Democrats are heirs and the communitarian, decentralist participatory strands in the socialist inheritance'.[17]

Interview*

Looking back, I think that the argument I put forward in *The Unprincipled Society* was, in some respects, too simplistic. This is partly because a lot of economic history has been published since. Or maybe some of it had

* Interviewed by Michael Kenny: Sheffield, 17 July 1996.

already been published, but I did not know about it. Some of these findings have now drifted to a broader community, and I have become aware of them. I think that the writing of Cain and Hopkins on the relationship between British imperialism and capitalism, and also the arguments that W.D. Rubinstein has developed, have produced a much more nuanced picture.[18] What emerges from their work is a model of British development which says that the real strength of the economy always lay in the financial services sector concentrated in the south east. That was always where Britain's comparative advantage was, even at the time of the Industrial Revolution. This is a bit reminiscent, oddly and interestingly I think, of some of the views that figures like Perry Anderson offered in the 1960s.[19] You have to see Britain as a kind of city-state, almost like Holland, with this extraordinarily dominant and powerful financial metropolis which, almost by accident in the periphery, developed industrial capitalism.

But industrial capitalism was always in fact secondary within the economy. What we then see in the nineteenth century is – partly because of the extraordinary gains that were made by being a pioneer in the Industrial Revolution, but also because of the success of the financial services sector – that Britain was able to win the battle for empire with France in the eighteenth and early nineteenth centuries, and became the first global power in the world; the first truly global power which then created the first truly global market.

The British state, then, is locked into this pattern of development almost inextricably. If you look at it this way, such an argument does not invalidate some of the theses in *The Unprincipled Society,* but I do think it makes the whole argument that I would now offer more complicated. In particular, it renders my notion of the failure of Britain to develop a developmental state not exactly wrong, but over-simplified. I would still claim, on the basis of this literature, that Britain did not have a developmental state. It certainly had a state which believed it had a very important role, to maintain and protect the economic strength of Britain. But the state was geared towards the financial sector, because that was, in fact, the strongest part of the economy. It did not try to turn itself into a sort of modern industrial capitalist state like that in Wilhelmine Germany. But then, in a way, it would not have made great sense to do that, given the inheritance from the past. So whilst the behaviour of the British state might have been damaging to the industrial sector, it was not really damaging to financial interests. State policy always privileged the financial sector because that was the pivot on which the whole imperial complex turned.

Something like this represents my current understanding of British development and I do not think that it involves the total revision of the argument in

The Unprincipled Society. My original position was that the British model fitted the sort of primitive industrialism of the early nineteenth century quite
well, but did not suit the more sophisticated science-based industry which
started to develop in Germany and America at the end of the nineteenth century. There would have had to be a quite drastic reorganisation of the state
and a reconceptualisation of the role of the state for that to have happened.
But now I think that the refusal to change was not just the product of a pig-
headed, irrational attachment to the past. It was in a sense a perfectly rational decision, even if not always taken specifically in this way: 'Look, we are
the financial capital of the world, this is what the British Empire means, this
is what the British state is all about and we want to carry on being like that'.

In terms of the cultural argument about decline, I do find the Rubinstein
critique of Martin Wiener totally convincing.[20] I think Wiener's book is rather
unimpressive, to be honest. I happen to have some personal knowledge of
this in that he quotes me in one passage, but in fact what he has done is lift
a quotation from my biography of MacDonald completely out of context! I do
think that the cultural argument is potentially extremely promising as culture
is a critical part of the story of Britain's development. But you cannot infer
what the culture actually was from a promiscuous reading of bits and pieces
of literature and polemic, particularly if you take out all the bits that confirm
your thesis and ignore all those that do not fit. So Ramsay MacDonald, for
instance, was a much more complex figure than Wiener suggests. This particular quotation expressed the part of MacDonald which was a sort of premature environmentalist, ideas that can be found in early socialism, in the
Independent Labour Party, and particularly the ethical socialism of William
Morris. In the biography I argued that this was one of the sources of his
appeal to the Labour movement. But there is also a completely different
strand in MacDonald's writings, which was also quite common in the socialism of that time: this was a national efficiency argument. In other words, he
was not purely and simply a romantic believer in the virtues of the countryside who rejected economic change. Maybe this is a small point. Why should
one invalidate the whole book on the basis of this? Yet this is exactly what I
think Wiener does in his analysis of most other figures too.

I have actually been more influenced recently by Jonathan Clark's work.[21]
I think he is very convincing in terms of his basic thesis about the eighteenth
century, when Britain was still an *ancien régime,* and in characterising the
values of the elite as essentially aristocratic, not bourgeois. And he suggests
that Lockean individualism was a minor current in the debates of the time; it
was not central at all. People were very much more concerned with theology
than they were with politics. That was what the elite argued about most pas-
sionately. I found this a very convincing argument. And I do not think that it

invalidates my basic position but can be deployed to render it more subtle and complicated.

Elsewhere, in a much shorter essay, Clark says that the English political tradition can be regarded as that of authoritarian individualism.[22] I think that this can be used to qualify the argument I offered in *The Unprincipled Society* very fruitfully. *The Unprincipled Society* was in many ways a preliminary exploration of a number of these themes. I genuinely did not know how it was going to end up when I started it. I was at first influenced by a number of debates about comparative advantage, especially as defined by the New Right. They argued, particularly in terms of international trade, that if your comparative advantage is in producing cheap cotton staples, then you should be producing cheap cotton staples. You should not try to produce something else because somebody else is doing that. It is irrational to do anything else. This is linked to the debates which have gripped economic historians working on the 1870–1914 period. Some are now saying that the entrepreneurs of that day were not mistaken in their investment priorities; they were 'rational actors' making the most of their comparative advantages. It would not have been rational for them to invest in more expensive machinery because someone else was doing it.

Then, as I was thinking about competitive advantage, I came across an article by Colin Leys in *New Left Review*.[23] In it there is a point where he says that comparative advantage can be made, and that struck me as true. It is not the case that comparative advantage is always a question of natural endowment. It is in earlier periods, but it is not now, nor even at the end of the nineteenth century. I also came across a piece by Ronald Dore, a sociologist, which affected my thinking.[24] He talks about the developmental state being one that sees the world not as a sort of self-regulating market, guided by Adam Smith's 'invisible hand',[25] but a cut-throat jungle where you have to fight for national competitive advantage, and where countries often construct their comparative advantage. Dore's argument was very much drawn from Japan. Armed with that notion, you can see so many parallels between the Japanese state and, say, Germany, in the latter part of the nineteenth century, and France, for instance. So I stitched these different ideas together in the book.

I still think that Britain has to be considered as in some respects an exceptional state. Britain and Russia were the two countries that defeated Napoleon. They were *not* conquered by revolutionary France and did not have revolutions in 1848. The trajectory of British history compared to the history of the rest of Europe has been exceptional. Only one European country became the centre of a worldwide empire, and that was Britain.

Since *The Unprincipled Society* appeared, I have been greatly influenced by Cain and Hopkins.[26] They suggest that Britain's victories in the struggle for Empire in the eighteenth century were *not* contingent. All wars are contingent in a way; the outcome of battles can always go the other way. But by having this very close relationship between the state and the financial sector, Britain was able to mobilise credit on an unparalleled scale. And that is why Britain won, despite being, for instance, a smaller country than France. That is something that needs to be explained. Britain was on the periphery of Europe with a population of five million while the French had 30 million. If you thought in terms of the indicators of military strength in the seventeenth century, it is very odd that Britain should have beaten France. What gave the British the edge was that they were able to mobilise credit on a scale that the French state simply could not. And they could do this because people thought they were creditworthy and were willing to lend, and Britain paid its debts. I think that Cain and Hopkins have quite a powerful argument. They talk about the military fiscal state in the eighteenth century, a highly efficient machine for mobilising resources for war.

One of the central questions now facing us is how we understand the role of Empire in British development. Of course arguments about decline and Empire go back a long way, particularly to debates about what our role should be 'East of Suez' in the 1960s, and before that to the 1950s when Andrew Shonfield was a major figure in an emerging declinist literature which linked decline to Empire and the role of sterling, and to the cost of maintaining a world role.[27] I was elected to Parliament in 1966, a young man, and very quickly became a part of a sort of right-wing element in the Labour Party which was critical of the 'East of Suez' role. Actually this is a period which I do not think has been adequately described by historians yet. There was a very important division within the Labour right between what I would term the Denis Healey right, who were believers in a world role for Britain and were Atlanticists (wishing to remain closely linked to the United States and being prepared to pay quite heavy costs to do that) and another section of the right in which Roy Jenkins, I suppose, ultimately emerged as the key figure. The latter were pro-European rather than Atlanticists. They saw the 'East of Suez' role as an appalling drain on Britain's actual resources, and, more important still, a terrible sort of psychological weight, because it locked Britain into a view of itself and its position in the world which was completely out of date.

The latter was the position that I held in my early thirties, back in that pre-devaluation period from 1966–67. When I was writing *The Unprincipled Society* this was still an important part of the way that I looked at the world. In my youth it seemed to me that a lot of the old brigade could not see that the world had changed from 1950, and I thought that they were unable to adjust because they were too old and did not understand that the world had moved on. By the time I came to write *The Unprincipled Society* I was becoming a bit more sophisticated in my thinking. I was beginning to feel that the structures and operational codes of the British state were permeated with the assumptions of Empire, and it was very difficult for the establishment to reject these.

Having read Cain and Hopkins, and Rubinstein, I now see this as a conflict between competing 'rationalities' facing the British state. There were, in fact, very important short-term gains to be made by remaining part of the sterling area and in a sense there was a perfectly 'rational' case for the Empire. Thus a writer like Correlli Barnett, in his book *The Audit of War*, is still stuck in that old way of thinking.[28] He is not willing to say that in 1945 it was not necessarily irrational to believe that it was important to preserve the sterling area. I think Barnett is hopelessly muddled between two different lines of criticism which he wants to make at the same time. They are logically entirely distinct. It does not mean to say that they cannot both be true. But at least he should acknowledge that they are not the same. One line of criticism, in terms of economic factors, is that Britain was very negligent in terms of industrial production in the 1940s. Then there is another argument which says that the British state is not an interventionist, Germanic type of state. To me, one of the strange features of the reception of Barnett was that he should become a kind of guru of the Thatcherite right when this second line of argument is completely un-Thatcherite. What he supports, in the end, is a Prussian or Japanese developmental state. A lot of the argument is, for example, like a modern version of the thinking of the Milner Circle and the Webbs and the national efficiency people before the First World War. This strange tension in Barnett's writing comes out repeatedly. But what is more important in the middle of a war – making cheap planes or ones that shoot down the others? Maybe our planes were rather expensive. But they do seem to have been good though! I think what emerges after the war is more an extremely painful dilemma than an obviously clear-cut choice in which all the sensible people are on one side and all those on the other side are idiots. It is not that simple.

But in thinking about popular, as well as elite, concerns about decline, the loss of Empire is tremendously important. I really do stick to an exceptionalist view of Britain here. You only have to walk around the streets of London to see this: every square is full of monuments to obscure Afghan wars and generals that nobody has ever heard of, who went off to India or elsewhere. Our culture is absolutely saturated with this. It still retained its hold on the people of Britain, as well as the elites, well into the postwar period. And the Commonwealth seemed a sort of surrogate for Empire for a long time. The left's view was, 'Look, we are not any longer going around oppressing all these people in the far corners of the earth. Instead we are being very nice to them. Our role and unique vocation in the world should be as a marvellous multi-racial commonwealth which has absorbed British values. We may not be the workshop of the world, but we are the great exporter of constitutions to the rest of the world.' My father was a typical example of this kind of thinking. He was a Minister in the postwar administration, very much involved with India.[29] This was a pretty universal view on the left and right. It had enormous resonance among the population at large. It provided a self-image for the British people. But it became impossible to believe in it eventually.

This change occurred in the postwar period when popular attitudes to British development began to shift. The general view in the immediate postwar years and up into the 1950s is that we were simply the best. We won the war. British institutions were vindicated. And the economic forecast looked very good. By the 1950s some people were starting to say that the German and French rates of growth are much faster than ours, but on the whole the predominant view is, 'So what? You would expect them to be. They were smashed to pieces in the war. It is catch-up, and once the initial catch-up is finished it will taper off and they will start to come down to much the same level.' In the 1950s on the left the most powerful argument about this – and it was my 'bible' – was Tony Crosland's *The Future of Socialism*.[30] Yet it was an extremely complacent book in a way, certainly about this kind of question. He argued that the mixed economy was delivering the goods. There was no need to change the mix. We knew how to achieve full employment, and how to get growth, and we would go on achieving both and redistributing the fruits. And that would produce a better, more comfortable society.

It is really in the early 1960s that you start to get an important change of climate because of the difficulties of redistributing the fiscal dividend. Now people said, 'We are in decline and what are we going to do about it?' The 1964 election was entirely fought about decline. You could argue that every general election since has, in a sense, been fought about decline. Then, in the 1970s both parties are discussing decline a lot. They offer different versions of how to deal with it. In the 1980s the Conservatives were saying that we had been declining, but that they had now stopped the rot.

Linked with this change of mood is the question of entry into Europe and of course the great tragedy for somebody like me, who is a pro-European, is that this was presented as a response to decline and failure: 'We were once a world power. We are not anymore. And what we have to do now is rather strange, but Europe is the only place left to go.' It was not a very thrilling rallying cry on the whole. There were some people for whom that was not the rallying cry, some European idealists. But broadly speaking that was the argument that prevailed. Thus there is a sort of down-beat element to British entry into the European Community which is absent from the other European countries. It is almost a kind of response to defeat and a sense of national failure: all the rhetoric which was quite strong in the 1960s, the 'cold bath' stuff, and 'Europe is going to sort us out; we are going to have to compete with all these people and be forced to be efficient by going into Europe'. It is a horrible argument if you think about it, really quite nasty.

Added to this, I think that there is a very serious problem about identity in terms of the British state. The Scots and the Welsh – particularly the Scots – are able to produce a kind of myth of nationhood. I think all nationhood is mythical to a considerable extent; not myth in the sense of being utterly false, but the sort of myth with a capital 'M'- a myth of their own nationhood which says, in the case of the Scots, 'We are an ancient European country with a proud European history, a European identity. Edinburgh is a great European capital, we had the old alliance with France in the middle ages, and we had the Scottish Enlightenment.' The Welsh can produce a slightly different version of the same thing – as a mystical, Celtic, poetic people who are also part of mainstream European culture. They can construct a national identity for themselves which is both European and national. But no one has managed to do this for the English. That is the problem. Perhaps because in fact England is not European. Maybe we could be if we tried very hard, but I am not sure if anyone would believe it.

John Mackintosh [31] once said to me that if you want to understand what is happening in Scotland you have to realise that the British Empire was a Scottish empire, too; in fact, arguably more so per head of population, so to speak. The Scots got more out of Empire than anybody. Clever Scottish lads went off to India, got into the Indian Civil Service and came out with lots of money. And they were happy to be British when Britain was a pretty important concern. But now we have become a shoddy little power sinking into the North Sea off the coast of Europe. Why should they be British? They could go back to being Scottish. It is much better, and small countries do very well in Europe.

Now the question is whether decline has been reversed in the 1980s. I think it is a bit too soon to tell because it is still so recent. A lot of the indicators are still obscure and point in different directions. I think people have got to take on board the argument that the global economy has changed the contexts in which we operate. The Germanic model has not provided the solution. The very features of this model, which were the sources of this extraordinary strength in the post-war period, are now sources of weakness, though I think that British shouts of joy at German failure are a bit premature.

After all, Germany has only recently been unified, and East Germany is a massive burden in the short term. There is a huge transfer of resources going on here. It is only when you go to East Germany that you realise how large this is.

In fact, if you look at different national economies and how they fared in this period, you could say that the British have done better than Germany, but not much better than Singapore, for instance. So it is not easy to give cast-iron answers about relative decline in the 1980s. In coming to terms with Thatcherism, we must – strange to say – accept that it actually happened and a lot of restructuring took place. It is not possible to reinstate what existed before it. For better or worse, we cannot turn the clock back to 1979 and say we wish we had taken a different path, now we are going to do so. The other point that strikes me about Thatcherism, in relation to decline, is that I am much less sure that as a project it was 'market-led'. Another book which appeared after *The Unprincipled Society*, and which I have been greatly influenced by, is Harold Perkin's *The Rise of Professional Society*.[32] I find this extremely interesting and rich on these issues. His argument, in a nutshell, is that Thatcherism provided camouflage for a battle between the private and public sectors. He suggests that the professional class ran away with the spoils of the struggle between the entrepreneurial class and the aristocracy in the last century, and the hallmark of the twentieth century has been the development of the professional society. However, professionals are divided between the public and private sectors. Initially these two sectors were not in conflict with each other. The postwar settlement represented a sort of symbiosis between the professionals in each sector. The attitudes, ethos and behaviour of the private sector professionals were extraordinarily like those of the public sector. They had a public service ethos in a way. The people who ran ICI and Unilever were not too different in their attitudes, outlook and behaviour from the people who ran the National Coal Board or staffed the Treasury.

However, Perkin demonstrates that there is a contradiction built into this symbiosis. The public-sector professionals are located within various professions, and each one has a strong vested interest in boosting its own claim to resources by saying that the services it provides are actually essential to society. This part of the argument resembles the public choice theory of the Virginia school.[33] There is a built-in pressure within the public sector to expand itself, and to take a greater share of the social product than it had before. Problems emerged in the 1970s when there was not enough money to go around. The private-sector professionals started to see the public sector as a rival, instead of being an ally. Thatcherism, on this reading, is about the revolt of the private-sector professionals against the public sector. New

Right ideology is a camouflage for the vested interest of the private-sector professionals. Thatcherites said that they were trying to recreate the entrepreneurial ideal and society of the early nineteenth century. Of course they were not doing anything of the sort. This is completely impossible anyway, because we are not living in the early nineteenth century. The large modern firm is not remotely like the atomistic, owner-manager, capitalist industrialist of revolutionary Lancashire. It is absolutely light years away. Yet Thatcherite ideology justifies and enables the claims of these professional groups against the public sector. I do not think that we should take this line of argument too far. But it is an interesting way of looking at the 1980s. The business classes are not believers in the free market. They never have been. Adam Smith was actually right about that. The business class want some 'freedom', and want to deregulate the labour market, for example. They want to have a lean, mean welfare state because they would not have to pay taxes to finance a big and generous one. But the idea that they want free competition is really complete nonsense. J.K. Galbraith has also influenced me on this point.[34]

I think you can maybe understand Thatcherism in this way, therefore. And in different policy areas we should possibly interpret Thatcherism as the use of the power of the state to create large powerful firms which can be competitive in world markets. That is the logic of privatisation. British Telecom is the supreme example of this, British Airways another. The argument was that as long as you are tied to the apron strings of the Treasury, you will never be able to be a really competitive player in world markets. The two great success stories of privatisation are these two companies. They are both now giant firms, highly competitive in world markets. They do not have any competition at home to speak of.

Now if you start to think of Thatcherism in that way, it is not really about market-led adjustment, is it? That seems rather simplistic. If it was market-led adjustment, it is the global market that matters. Thatcherism was about using the power of the state enormously to weaken organised labour; there is no question about that. And of course the Conservatives were using the power of the state to strengthen the financial services sector as well. The deregulation of the City of London was very much a part of that story.

We can return to our earlier theme of comparative advantage here. The Tories came to power in 1979. Here is this clapped-out economy, as all the debates on decline have shown. And they asked, 'Where does our comparative advantage really lie?' In considering this, they threw sentimentality out of the window. What they found was a rather peculiar mixture of activities. A highly competitive financial sector was one. Potentially powerful players in the global economy existed here and there, if they could be liberated from social responsibilities, from the terms imposed by organised labour, and from the strings of the Treasury which always stop firms from behaving efficiently. The economy also excelled at producing poor, bad, shoddy goods based on low wages and unskilled labour. Plus if you could crush the labour movement enough, it might be possible to turn Britain into a site for Japanese inward investment. And that is what they have done. So Thatcherism was not really a way of going back to a nineteenth-century market because they could not have done that even if they had wanted to. It was actually the use of the power of the state in a very active way. This is also perhaps the reason why the paradox that Andrew Gamble has identified, of the free economy and strong state, really is a paradox.[35] It is not a free economy in the classic sense.

If you follow Perkin's argument through, the suggestion is that the private-sector professionals were bound to go for Thatcherism. That was the obvious creed for them to follow. Here I am not sure that he is correct. Why was it obvious that they should go for this project? They might have followed a sort of Heathite corporatism just as much. Why did they go for Thatcherism? Not because they believed in a free market; they certainly did not, and nor did the Thatcherites really. Perhaps one reason they went for this politics lies in one element of the nineteenth-century entrepreneurial ideal: that the owner-manager should be allowed to do what he wants with his own property. What the private-sector professionals have done is to con everybody into thinking that they are nineteenth-century owner-managers. They are not, of course. They are employees – hired by the shareholders who fix their remuneration and fringe benefits and everything else – and there is no free market at all. It is an absolute scandal what has happened here if you think about it. But if they can trick everybody into thinking that they are actually nineteenth-century entrepreneurs, they can justify their massive claims on society in a way that they could not in terms of a Heathite corporatist ideology.

And when you look at the rhetoric about top salaries, the remuneration of chief executives, all that sort of debate, it becomes starkly clear. It is not very difficult to deconstruct at all. The argument of this group is that there has to be a market for talent. We have to pay these people this money because that is what the market economy is all about. But of course it is a rigged market. The so-called talent is actually dictating the behaviour of this market. Obviously, there is also the political dimension of the Thatcher project to consider, especially the creation of a new social coalition with a new rhetoric. I think the question of changing our identity is very important in this, through the rhetoric of national greatness and so on.

I developed a related idea in my inaugural lecture here at Sheffield University.[36] I was trying to argue that there were three dominant visions of the British state. One was what I called Whig imperialist, the second was democratic collectivist, and the third was authoritarian individualist, a label I took from Jonathan Clark. The imperialist argument gave its proponents a strong identity. It was the view held by the historian G.M. Trevelyan, Winston Churchill and many others. The postwar Labour government entirely accepted this perspective. The administration was democratic collectivist at home but effectively imperialist abroad. However, the imperialist argument collapsed in the 1970s. We no longer had an empire. You could not plausibly maintain the vision of the British state and the identity that went with it. The authoritarian individualist alternative, of which Enoch Powell was one of the earliest exponents, is not British but English. Very powerful rhetoric has been deployed to construct this in England. It is very potent, but has the unfortunate consequence that it does not work elsewhere in the United Kingdom. So the growing gap between Scotland and England, which is one of the most interesting features of British politics now, is partly the result of this. The myth of nationhood which the Thatcherites constructed in the 1980s, and which is the emotional cement binding their new coalition together, is really only about England. I remember a wonderful example of this when Mrs Thatcher addressed the Conservative Party Women's Conference at the time of the Falklands War. She was talking of the recreation of pride and greatness. She quotes Shakespeare's John of Gaunt speech.[37] Suddenly, at the emotional climax of her speech, 'Britain' turns into 'England' without her even realising that the two words are not synonymous. If she had made that speech in Scotland, people would have thought, 'What the hell is this?' It would have gone down like a lead balloon.

There is perhaps a chance for the left to produce a constructive alternative to this version of Englishness. I am not a football fan but I did watch with absolute fascination the game against Germany during Euro '96. I found it utterly gripping. Those St George's flags were absolutely astounding. Now, where did they come from? That does appear to have been a spontaneous development. I also read somewhere that they were cheering Germany in the pubs in Glasgow. There is something significant happening here I think. I now realise I must start watching football very seriously if I want to study national cultures in Britain!

I suppose my reflections on these matters are to some extent autobiographical. I do not regard myself as English. I have lived most of my life in England but was born in Wales whilst my father's family came from the Channel Islands, and his mother was Scottish. My mother's father was Welsh and a Welsh speaker, and his grandmother was Scottish. As a child I grew up virtually entirely in South Wales. I always felt uncomfortable saying I was English. I would say I was British. And I would be hard put so say what else I am, in national terms. There is no logical reason why you cannot have multiple identities. My memory of childhood growing up in South Wales is that people did. They thought of themselves as Welsh, but also as British, completely unselfconsciously. It never occurred to them that there was any difficulty about being both. And if you have that, you can then also think of yourself as European. But I do believe that there is a difficulty about Englishness because in some structural sense this identity involves being unhappy with the notion of multiple identities. In continental Europe one of the very interesting things that has happened, and I think it is partly a function of Europeanisation, has been the reinvention of provincial or regional identities, which antedated the modern nation-state. I do not know how deep these things go or what it means exactly, but people talk about it at least. This just does not seem possible in England. As a matter of historical fact, I think that most people in this country do not see themselves as European in the way in which continental Europeans do, or at least continental Europeans from the original member states of the European Union. It is very difficult for the British to say, 'Forget about the national level. What counts is how far Europe is in decline or not, how far Europe is powerful in the world, and so on. And we, a part of Europe, therefore join in Europe's success or failure.' You can just about imagine that being said in France or Germany. But it certainly cannot be said here, at least not yet.

Arguments about Britain as an economic power in relative decline are bound to continue. Possibly though, debate about decline in the old sense, in the old form, is now totally parochial, and rather irrelevant. The question is with whom are you comparing yourself, really? Certainly if you are talking about clout in the world market, Britain is going to have very much less. I think that some economists' critique of the whole notion of national competitiveness is hard to deny. It is firms that are competitive, not countries. It is a mistake to use the notion of competitors to apply to a national economy as a whole. In a way there are no such entities as national economies. We are probably moving into a phase in economic history where one has to make far fewer assumptions about the nation state. We should be thinking in terms of public power, and this still has an important part to play in economic development, but it does not have to be at the national level. It may make little sense to talk about national decline in an economic sense any longer. In the 1960s people argued that 'We are doing worse than Germany, worse than France, and we soon will be doing worse than the Italians'. There is a good book by Sidney Pollard called *The Wasting of the British Economy*, which lists all the countries which overtook Britain in GDP per head in the course of the postwar period.[38] It was virtually all the European countries, and then Japan too.

But now continental Europe is not performing very well, either, so that if the comparison is between Britain and continental Europe, then Britain is actually doing moderately well, judged by these sorts of indicators. We have to think about such questions in terms of what the architecture of the global political economy is going to be in the next century. It is very difficult to see Britain being a major part of the world economy in any scenario, except as a member of the European Union. The European dimension of the debate is going to remain. And so in all these questions we return to the problem of identity.

When the decline debate really starts, there are two implicit models in play. One is America and the other is Germany. And this is not accidental: these are the first two countries which challenged Britain's pre-eminence. Joseph Chamberlain's imperialist movement is a response to both of these. Its whole argument was that we are now in the age of great empires, not small states, and the British Empire is potentially the greatest of them all, if we could only get our act together. This is rather interesting in view of contemporary debates about 'arranged capitalism'. How resonant the Chamberlainite argument is. We borrowed our national insurance system, for instance, from Germany. And in the 1930s America becomes the model for the left, at least the moderate left. And this was true, I think, in the postwar period. There is a sort of left pro-Americanism there as well. But it is interesting that the features which made these models different have changed in our minds. At one time Germany was represented as Prussian – disciplined and orderly. We were far too sloppy by comparison. Now the Germans are rather nice, cooperative and consensual. They emphasise partnership and talk to their workers. And in the 1930s, and I think a bit in the 1940s as well, America represented ideals – the Tennessee Valley Authority, Keynesianism and so on. This is the America of aggressive movements for freedom and war on the robber barons. And then later on it is the individualistic frontier ethos of 'jungle capitalism' that captured people's imaginations.

Maybe we should take a lead from the arguments of environmentalists, and actually criticise quite severely the whole notion of development, of which decline is the obverse. If you talk about decline, it is the down-side of development. The ideas of development and decline suggest a sort of natural progression towards something. There is a sense of motion. Maybe that whole way of thinking is actually extremely obsolete, and also very dangerous as well. It implies a conception of the economy and the natural environment which is actually wrong, and also getting to be environmentally perilous in its implications. So maybe we should dump this whole language actually because it is no longer appropriate.

This also seems true of other ways in which we still talk about the economy. In the 1960s we used to think there was something called planning, we knew how to do it, and the reason why Britain was doing badly was because of stupid Tories who could not add up, and were run by the fourteenth Earl of Home, with his matchsticks and grouse moors.[39] We would come into power, being technocratic, competent, meritocratic, and we would get rid of grammar schools and scholarships, and we would know how to do things properly because we were clever and properly educated, unlike the old 'fuddy duddies'. Through planning we would reorganise society; we would produce a high rate growth and have more social justice as well.

Now we do not believe in planning anymore. The left has converted to thinking about the supply side. But change the word 'planning' for 'supply side' and you have exactly the same sort of simplistic view: 'We know how to make the supply side more efficient'. And there is this supposedly marvellous methodology, 'endogenous growth theory', which is now the equivalent of planning ideology in the 1960s. This form of thinking seems to me to be very akin to our assumptions in the 1960s. Yes, I think there is something in the notion that what is being attempted is a rethinking and restructuring of the welfare state, so that it is not seen any longer as being the consumer of resources. Instead it is being presented in a developmental role as the investor in resources. But there are problems here; in particular, training, which figures largely in this sort of thinking, is not in itself enough. Training is only one half of the story. The rest is about what you do with people after they have been trained. The idea that you can, by producing more inputs of highly-trained people into various labour markets, transform the way these markets behave, is totally simplistic. The problem is that it may be hard to absorb trained personnel when you produce them. So we have to think of the demand side for trained people. Supply and demand should actually go together and this means some degree of economic restructuring. It is not enough to say, 'Here you are, personnel managers in big corporations, I am going to supply you with a lot more trained people'. What do you train them for? I think the Labour Party's thinking in this respect is confused. But I am not saying this in criticism of Blair; he is doing the best he can to try to make sense of a very inchoate situation.

Notes

1. See his collection of essays, *The New Reckoning: Capitalism, States and Citizens* (Oxford, 1997), especially his autobiographical essay, 'Journey to an Unknown Destination', pp. 1–33.
2. D. Marquand, *The Progressive Dilemma: From Lloyd George to Kinnock* (London, 1991).
3. D. Marquand, *Ramsay MacDonald* (London, 1977).

4. D. Marquand, *The Unprincipled Society: New Demands and Old Politics* (London, 1988).
5. D. Marquand, 'Journey to an Unknown Destination', p. 12.
6. He was Parliamentary Private Secretary to the Minister for Overseas Development.
7. He served as Junior Opposition Frontbench Spokesman on Economic Affairs.
8. D. Marquand, 'Journey to an Unknown Destination', p. 14.
9. *Ibid.*, p. 13.
10. *Ibid.*, p. 26.
11. D. Marquand, *The Unprincipled Society*, pp. 6–7.
12. *Ibid.*, p. 7.
13. *Ibid.*, p. 2.
14. *Ibid.*, p. 8.
15. *Ibid.*, p. 115.
16. *Ibid.*, pp. 246-7.
17. D. Marquand, 'Journey to an Unknown Destination', p. 29.
18. P.J. Cain and A.G. Hopkins, *British Imperialism: vol i, Innovation and Expansion 1688–1914* (London, 1993); and W.D. Rubinstein, *Capitalism, Culture and Decline in Britain 1750–1990* (London, 1994; 1st edn, 1993). See also the interview with Rubinstein, pp. 61–75 of this book.
19. P. Anderson, 'Origins of the Present Crisis', *New Left Review*, vol. 23 (1963), pp. 26–53.
20. M.J. Wiener, *English Culture and the Decline of the Industrial Spirit 1850–1980* (Harmondsworth, 1992; 1st edn, 1981). See also the interview with Wiener, pp. 25–36 of this book.
21. J.C.D. Clark, *English Society 1688–1832: Ideology, Social Structure and Political Practice during the Ancien Régime* (Cambridge, 1985); and J.C.D. Clark, *Revolution and Rebellion: State and Society in England in the Seventeenth and Eighteenth Centuries* (Cambridge, 1986). See also the interview with Clark, pp. 137–152 of this book.
22. J.C.D. Clark, 'The History of Britain: A Corporate State in a *Europe des Patries*?', in J.C.D. Clark (ed.), *Ideas and Politics in Modern Britain* (Basingstoke, 1990), pp. 32–49.
23. C. Leys, 'The Formation of British Capital', *New Left Review*, vol. 160 (1986), pp. 114–21.
24. See R. Dore, 'Industrial Policy and how the Japanese do it', *Catalyst* (1986), pp. 45–58.
25. A reference to the theories of the Scottish philosopher and political economist, Adam Smith (1723–1790).
26. R.J. Cain and A.G. Hopkins, *British Imperialism*.
27. A. Shonfield, *British Economic Policy since the War* (Harmondsworth, 1958).
28. C. Barnett, *The Audit of War: The Illusion and Reality of Britain as a Great Nation* (Basingstoke, 1987; 1st edn, 1986). See also the interview with Barnett, pp. 37–49 of this book.
29. The Right Honourable Hilary Marquand, MP, served in government throughout the 1940s; in the 1945–51 Attlee administrations, he held the posts of Secretary for Overseas Trade, 1945-47, Paymaster General, 1947–48, and Minister of Pensions, 1948–51.

30. C.A.R. Crosland, *The Future of Socialism* (London, 1956).
31. John Mackintosh was MP for Berwick and East Lothian from 1966 to February 1974. After 1977 he was Professor of Politics at Edinburgh University. See D. Marquand (ed.), *John P. Mackintosh on Parliament and Social Democracy* (London, 1982).
32. H. Perkin, *The Rise of Professional Society: England since 1860* (London, 1989); see also H. Perkin, *Professionals, Property and English Society since 1880* (Reading, 1981).
33. See, for instance, J. M. Buchanan and G. Tullock, *The Calculus of Consent: Logical Foundations of Constitutional Democracy* (Ann Arbor, Mich., 1962).
34. See, for instance, J. K. Galbraith, *A History of Economics: The Past as the Present* (Harmondsworth, 1989); and *Economics and the Public Purpose* (London, 1974).
35. A. Gamble, *The Free Economy and the Strong State: The Politics of Thatcherism* (Basingstoke, 1988). See also Chapter 1 of this book by Gamble.
36. This lecture is published in D. Marquand, *The New Reckoning*, as 'Henry Dubb versus Sceptred Awe', pp. 166–78.
37. A reference to John of Gaunt's speech about the decline of England in Shakespeare's *King Richard II* (act two, scene one).
38. S. Pollard, *The Wasting of the British Economy: British Economic Policy 1945 to the Present* (London, 1982). See also the interview with Pollard, pp. 76–91 of this book.
39. A reference to Sir Alec Douglas-Home, leader of the Conservative Party, 1963–65.

10

Jonathan Clark

Introduction

Born in 1951, and educated at Downing and Corpus Christi Colleges in Cambridge University, Jonathan Clark is one of the most distinguished of British historians. After working in the City of London, he returned to academic life as a Fellow of Peterhouse, Cambridge from 1977 and then of All Souls, Oxford from 1986. He currently holds the Hall Distinguished Professorship of British History at the University of Kansas. Clark's work has related to decline debates in a number of ways. In particular, his arguments challenge implicit historical assumptions underpinning declinist theses. One example is provided by his critique of David Marquand, whose view 'explained why economic recovery built around radical individualism was impossible: it was therefore wholly unable to explain what happened after 1979'.[1] Marquand, Clark argued, relied here on the notion of a bourgeois, individualist revolution in the seventeenth century which, first, replaced the *ancien régime* and laid the foundation for the industrial revolution; second, meant that individualist Britain was ill-suited to the late twentieth-century industrialism which required a corporate state and central planning; and, third, therefore ensured that Britain in the late twentieth-century found itself unable to break from the pattern of decline. In contrast, Clark argues that this view of the death of the *ancien régime* is false. It is mistaken to think of a seventeenth-century bourgeois, individualist revolution drawing an old order to a close. Indeed, there was a marked survival into the eighteenth century of values and assumptions which linked science, technology and trade with constitutional royalism, hierarchy and order. This social nexus survived at least until 1828–32, so that the last two centuries are to be understood as a natural and creative association of old and new rather than as the revolutionary or counter-revolutionary triumph of either.[2]

This subversion of the view of a seventeenth-century bourgeois revolution is typical of Clark's approach. It undermines an assumption which one finds in much declinist writing: that history should be interpreted in directional, teleological terms. In his iconoclastic *English Society* ('This is a revisionist tract'),[3] Clark opposed a linear, Whig reading of English history[4] (a reading which 'focuses attention on those lines of development in the past which seem to culminate in present arrangements').[5] Rather than looking in the eighteenth century for the origins of what we know to have developed in the nineteenth, Clark prefers to reinterpret those origins in the light of survivals from the preceding period (patriarchal and hierarchical characteristics of social structure rather than class conflict; the doctrine of the divine right of kings; traditional piety; the aristocratic ideal; the domination of national politics by the aristocracy and of local by the gentry; the symbiosis, not the antagonism, of land and trade).

Indeed, Clark questions the teleological sense of ineluctable progression which has been widespread in English historiography. In challenging the view of a transition from English feudalism to capitalism, in rejecting the reading of the English Civil War which sees it as a bourgeois revolution, and in arguing that eighteenth-century England was an *ancien régime* society, he attacks both Whig and Marxist readings of Britain's past. Moreover, these historical judgments have major implications for modern British politics. By dismissing the notions of class (socialists/Marxists) and caste (Whigs), and by showing the location on the extremes of the spectrum of both Filmer and Locke, Clark argues that it is hierarchy and royalist constitutionalism which represents the successful, progressive middle ground. Therefore, we see executive government, the monarchy, religion and relations between local and national government differently. According to such scholarship, English national consciousness has had less to do with class or ethnic consciousness, local autonomy, popular sovereignty or the plural society, than with religion, the rule of law, the state's defence of the individual, rights of private property, freedom of trade and long-shared historical experience. Plainly, such arguments carry a powerful political charge, their relevance to political developments in the 1980s being perhaps the most obvious. According to Clark, England has historically been characterised by an authoritarian individualism, echoing Alan Macfarlane's[6] thesis that English individualism formed part of English societal structure for hundreds of years before the seventeenth century.

Clark's work stresses that historians in several fields have recently been drawn to see the English past more in terms of hierarchy, allegiance and authority than of class conflict or economic revolution. And the former triumvirate operates powerfully in the fields of law and religion.[7] He draws out the implication of other historians' demonstrations that class stratification and economic consciousness do not adequately explain people's choices of allegiance in the English Civil War. Moreover, Clark's work also challenges the foundations of much declinist thinking by questioning the appropriateness of the very notion of 'characterising' a period or a nation in terms of its position along a stadial pathway: 'How far can we characterise a nation or a period? It seems better that we should avoid using "character" in this reified sense at all.'[8] There are clear implications here for notions of late nineteenth-century or twentieth-century British decline. Much declinist writing rests upon precisely such stadial characterisations (of a nation once great, now comparatively weak), and is perhaps open to the charge of being insufficiently sensitive to detailed variations (regional, social, sectoral).

Clark has commented sensitively on the relationship between academic argument and political projects, and has noted that the discipline of history is 'resistant to assimilation in present-day political programmes'.[9] But political figures have been involved with his work,[10] and he has argued that the discrediting of left-wing historiography has gone hand in hand with the practical disproving of many predictions based on such historiography: 'academic history can be an important analogue or anticipation of public events'.[11] In the following interview statement Jonathan Clark amplifies such arguments, offering sceptical reflections upon declinism, and importantly setting decline debates within appropriate international and historical perspectives.

Interview[*]

I am somewhat sceptical of the generalised notion of declinism. There is nothing intrinsically wrong with theses of decline provided that they are clearly formulated and provided that they relate to a clearly specified phenomenon. It is the generalised jeremiads about which I am more sceptical. They remind me of the truth that an aircraft does not have a life-span, but that its component parts have life-spans. The more generalised one's notion of decline, the more implausible it necessarily is. It becomes much more plausible as soon as it becomes a precise argument: that some specific national institution might have a trajectory, or that some specific set of

* Interviewed by Richard English: Oxford, 25 March 1997.

national values might have a trajectory. Only if you define precisely what it is that you are talking about, might a theory of decline make more sense. It might or might not: you would have to look to know, and you would also need to quantify the argument.

But the chief reason why I am sceptical of declinism is that I am aware that theories of decline have a very long history. They can probably be found in all periods, though they take different forms at different moments, being formulated differently in different ages. They tend to recur towards the end of centuries. In ages of faith, theories of national decline tend to take the form of laments about the decline of piety; sometimes they take the form of literally apocalyptic expectations. In the 1590s, for example, this found expression in Puritanism. In the doom-laden 1690s, one finds theories of national decline expressed in terms of pessimism about Protestant England's military fortunes vis-à-vis Catholic France and also in terms of claims that the church was in danger, and one finds a response, for example, in Societies for the Reformation of Manners. In the 1790s one finds theories of decline articulated by the people we anachronistically call radicals (they did not have the term then) – people like Richard Price, for example, the man who provoked Burke to write his *Reflections on the Revolution in France*. Price was a statistician and an actuary, but he nevertheless believed that the population of England was in decline at the end of the eighteenth century (disastrously the opposite of what was actually happening). He held that the phenomenon of urbanisation was diminishing the population by leading people into a life of luxury and vice, and that life in towns produced a higher death rate than birth rate. His solution to England's problems was not some more just organisation of industrialisation but a return to the rural life. The same argument can even be found among French Jacobins. Some French Jacobins in the 1790s, reviewing the question of poverty in France, were of the mind that France's population was vastly too great for its means of support and they looked forward to a steady diminishing of that population. I am not an expert on the 1890s and one would need to ask an historian of the nineteenth-century *fin de siècle* how one would characterise that mood.

How do we characterise the declinist literature of the 1990s? Perhaps in some ways it represents the complaint of a section of the bourgeois intelligentsia who feel that life has passed them by, and that their careful solutions to the nation's problems are no longer as relevant as they were? It might, more particularly, be a lament at the amorality of a successful capitalism in a secular age, a happy hedonism which the bourgeois intelligentsia finds difficult to live with because the intelligentsia does not have any metaphysical basis for its rejection of the morality of the man in the street. Their appeal to custom therefore fails. And it is a lament of decline by implicit comparison with a posited antiquity – a recent antiquity – in the 1960s in which morality was consensually and communally based. I remember the 1960s well enough to be sceptical of the comparison.

It might be suggested that declinism offers psychological rewards similar to those offered by some brands of Marxism: things are shown to be dreadful; dramatic change is said to be required; specific prescriptions for change are less specific, and perhaps less important, than the condemnation of present ills. True believers would almost certainly be hopeless if in a position of power, with the opportunity to effect practical change; and yet the analysis is not wrong about everything, has a powerful intellectual attraction, and can be expressed in terms which are quite simple and appealing. The analysis is validated more by identifying the problem and denouncing the enemy than by producing a thought-through account of the benefits of the changes which are recommended. And so it has always been.

Decline debates have to be self-referential because as soon as one adopts a wider perspective or tries to quantify the phenomena that are claimed to be in decline it becomes quite clear that there are usually very few grounds for deploying these grandiose explanatory schemes. As soon as one tries to measure, it becomes clear that, far from everything being just about to fall to pieces, the present looks rather more like the past, and the future turns out to be rather more like the present. Reality is dull and inconvenient for the intelligentsia, but not for the majority of the population who never have to face apocalypse.

If this declinist and apocalyptic mood is one which regularly recurs, what happens when the apocalypse does not materialise? People in the street are quite happy when the apocalypse never actually happens. That is convenient for them, as it should be. Our problem is with the doomsters because they tend not to go away when their predictions do not materialise. They tend to try to create the apocalypse in order to validate their analysis. And the problem with doomsters is always that they resist the reduction of their general vision to a series of quantifiable, particular problems: individual problems which can be quantified can be solved. What we see with doomsters is a mood, a vision which can hardly be dealt with in that way, and a vision which they wish to realise: they need the doom to come true. They therefore sometimes adopt a remarkably overstated pessimism. An example might be Will Hutton. Hutton's book – *The State We're In*[12] – was the sort of book which provoked me to ask: what is your evidence, can you quantify this? It contained a series of propositions all of which would, if true, be important and interesting, but all of which I wish to see quantified. And as soon as one tries to quantify them one realises that the rhetoric is considerably out of line with the statistics. I am quite happy to look back on British economic policy in the last twenty or thirty years and say that some things were done badly, some were done well, and some were done indifferently; that some areas of life are getting better and some getting worse. But I am not sure how I can generalise that into such a vision of gloom as Hutton's.

Indeed, the phenomenon to be explained is not national decline, but the mood of declinism itself. The two are not wholly separable because, certainly, there are some things in society of which we can legitimately be critical. But nevertheless looking back over the long history of declinist thought what matters more is its independent vitality, the way in which it develops a life of its own almost irrespective of objective circumstance.

Let us put this phenomenon into a wider context. It is a characteristic of all those groups which attempt to reverse decline that they largely accept the declinist thesis in order to work against it. In order to provide a solution to it, they have to accept that the problem as it has been described is real. So in a sense the counter-declinists are playing the same game as the declinists; whereas the further one stands back from the phenomenon the more one wants to see long continuities, or at least longer continuities. Because the declinists are never completely wrong, the counter-declinists are never completely wrong either. People do make a difference: if they persuade themselves that they are locked into a situation of irreversible decline, that is a prophecy that becomes self-realising. To the extent to which they persuade themselves otherwise then they are freed to do new things. The 1970s, and the arrival of Mrs Thatcher, provide a telling illustration. In the 1970s I remember well that a large number of commentators seemed unable to come up with answers to questions which they posed in declinist terms. And the Keith Josephs and the Margaret Thatchers were the people who clearly thought of themselves as being able to answer precisely those questions. Now there are two problems for the historian. Firstly, were the declinists of the 1970s right in persuading themselves that there were no solutions? And secondly, were the Thatcherites justified in claiming that they had found the answers? The two questions have to be asked together.

My position is that the continuities in English history tend to be longer than both the declinists and the counter-declinists claim, although both do make a difference. My own work, in so far as it bears on this question, does so in the following way: I have tried to point to the integrity of one particular period of the English past that I work on, to show the sense in which it ought to be understood as a thing in itself rather than as a hangover from some earlier period, and not as a seedbed for some later period. So that, for example, one disengages what I call the long eighteenth century, or England's *ancien régime*, from the nineteenth-century perspective which argued that in a traditional society economic growth is hampered and that only by bursting the shackles of a restrictive old order could a new industrial society suddenly emerge. Or, for example, in a moral sense that *ancien régime* England was a sink of corruption and vice and therefore of administrative inefficiency which was transformed by Benthamite utilitarian reform. It is certainly true that there was economic growth in the nineteenth century, but it did not relate to the society which had gone before in that way. And indeed society, as it had preceded the industrial revolution, was economically viable in many ways which did not depend on the existence of the phenomena of industrialisation. Similarly, its value system was a thing in itself and it is not necessarily to be condemned by its failure to anticipate nineteenth-century values – Victorian values if you like. So I come back to the claim that an aircraft does not have a life-span; its component parts have life-spans. It follows, too, that the system as a whole may experience a trajectory (using the metaphor, the aircraft may crash) while almost all of its parts are in perfect order. If you are looking at the hegemonic value system of a society then I am not suggesting that nothing changed; I would argue that one can see in British history a series of hegemonic value systems being established, flowering, coming to maturity, developing problems, and being negated. And I see the long eighteenth century as a period in which one such value system is devised; its institutions are developed, refined, defended, then vainly defended, and it comes to pieces. So my perspective tends to undermine both Whig and Marxist interpretations, both of which are essentially teleological.

Now, to the degree to which the assumptions of the 1970s involved problems being presented in terms characteristic of the hard left, it was necessary for Mrs Thatcher and her colleagues to engage with them on those terms. And since the question had been posed in that way the only way of solving it was to answer the question as set. There is no point in the exam candidate answering another question. That is not the only question that the historian might ask, however. It may indeed be the case that supply side reforms can be instituted in society and can have an effect similar to that which the triumphalists claimed. It may not be the case that that is the only way to go. It may not necessarily be the case that the supply side reforms have involved as dramatic a transformation as the triumphalists have asserted.

There were many people on the left who appreciated that left and right shared an analysis and so were interested in what Mrs Thatcher was doing even if they put a different valuation on the whole thing. The doomsters of the late 1990s tend to come from the centre of English politics, not from the hard left. The hard left have moved on. The professional doomsters are often the ex-SDP people or their spiritual heirs, whose analysis of politics was always primarily a moral one, whose objections to capitalism were always primarily aesthetic, and whose objections to Mrs Thatcher were class objections.

Some have suggested that the notions of left and right often seem inadequate (partly because people shift ground, but partly also because of shared analyses) and that these categories are increasingly redundant in terms of analysing politics. It might be worth considering here Sir Samuel Brittan's view that the 1980s were beneficial in reducing the power of the trade unions, that something simply had to be done. There, I think, is an example of the right sharing an analysis with the left, but just putting a reverse set of values on it. It does not mean that these analyses are wholly wrong. It may be a good and quantifiable argument that economic growth can be increased by supply side reforms which would demand some redefinition of the function of trade unions. It might be the case, as Wiener[13] has argued, that you can demonstrate the adverse economic impact of Victorian public schools. You would need to look to know. But even if it were demonstrable in some quantified form it would not necessarily prove the apocalyptic consequences which were supposed to stem from trade union power or from public schools. That is the point that I would make: although it might be the case that supply side reforms did act as a prerequisite for the changes of the 1980s, those changes may seem, in a longer perspective, to be less momentous than both their champions and their opponents claimed. Perhaps their significance lay more in returning Britain to longer-term patterns of development.

Both the left and the right share a hard-nosed statistical attitude to national questions which allows them to move forward. It is the centre which is stuck with this problem of inconclusive subjective analyses. In some ways Will Hutton would be a good case in point. I would find it hard to describe the mind-set of a person who would not be open to the argument that some things have been done well, some things have been done badly, that in some senses things are getting better while in others they are getting worse. I would find it hard – and indeed this is why the historian is attracted to this problem – to explain the mind-set of somebody who is so pessimistic. I can take points of Hutton's analysis, look round the Western world and say that they might fit in some areas for some periods. I would find it harder to think that they were a complete fit with English experience now. Clearly the declinist mentality has something to do with the intellectual formation of these figures in the early 1980s, or earlier.

An important feature of declinism is this: to posit as the only solution to the problem a solution which cannot be attained is a way of heightening the importance of declinist rhetoric. The most difficult challenge to a declinist is: if you were dictator, precisely what would you do that would cure the problem as you have diagnosed it? It is not enough to say that we need a new moral code. Precisely what would you do? If there are specific answers to the question then they should be looked at on their merits. Usually, talking to declinists, there are no specific answers; their complaint about the world is more a comment on their own state of mind. The key subject is not national decline, but theories and theorists of national decline: why certain people at certain times have had these doom-laden theories. The least plausible hypothesis is that some people at some times have theories of national decline because the nation is really in the terminal condition that they find fashionable ways of describing.

Biographical details can sometimes provide clues to explaining this predilection for declinism, and such personal experiences are not to be neglected; they tell us something which is real. But it does not follow that the explanations of individual states of mind are also equally powerful explanations of national trajectories. The most revealing question to ask of declinists is, who is your enemy, who is the guilty party? And in theories of decline the guilty party can often be quite clearly identified: there is usually a particular social institution or group. In Martin Wiener's vision the guilty party is the English public school culture of the nineteenth century. In Correlli Barnett's[14] vision it is an amateurish attitude to military power which has some relation to the same phenomenon. In Will Hutton's vision the enemy is the culture of the City of London, before the Big Bang. Hutton's account of what burden our financial institutions place on our economy is one which is related to a particular vision of what financiers are like and therefore by extrapolation what capitalists are like – essentially rentiers. Reading Hutton's book, I had a vision of men in top hats and pin-striped trousers. I am not sure you would have seen many such people in the City of London since the 1950s. Nor are cartoon-strip parodies a sufficient shortcut to historical understanding of why the City has been so successful, and for so long.

As well as explaining the individual declinist's mentality, one also has to ask why it is that these arguments resonate with enough people to gain such popular prominence. Why is it that hostility to these various enemies is so easily mobilised? The answer is that the declinists appeal to social stereotypes in the same way that Dickens' novels appealed to social stereotypes. Just as people say that Dickens is always exaggerated but never wholly wrong, so one can recognise the stereotypes in Martin Wiener, Correlli Barnett and Will Hutton; and one cannot say that they, too, are wholly wrong. The historian might find, on the other hand, that these caricatures are only fully developed once the institution has changed out of recognition. Caricatures only come onto the scene after the enemy has gone away. While the public school culture was in full force in Victorian England it did not typi-

cally generate Wiener's sort of critique, and this was so for a number of reasons: partly because too many people were caught up in it, partly because it
was too powerful and too successful. While the people whom Correlli Barnett
criticises were actually running a worldwide empire and doing it through
armed services which tended to win their battles, people tended not to develop the critiques that we now read. While the City of London was a gentle-
man's club, people did not tend to complain about it in Will Hutton's terms,
for a variety of reasons. It was successful, probably more so than manufacturing industry. It was quite good at self-regulation, better than it is now. It is
only when these institutions are no longer with us, at least in the same
terms, that they become open and vulnerable. Declinist critiques tend not to
be intellectually very powerful. They are often quite well-informed, but they
rest to too large a degree on the construction of ideal types. They are rarely
properly quantified. They have too narrow a frame of reference. They are not
comparative: they do not compare the phenomenon to similar phenomena at
other times and places. So although they might have some brief currency,
they are not powerful or profound historical analyses and for that reason
they would not have been persuasive if they had been formulated at a time
when the phenomena were there to be appraised by anybody who could
pick up a newspaper or could walk into the City of London and see how it
was doing. There is nothing necessarily wrong with painting with a broad
brush, as these critiques tend to do, but arguments if deployed on a wide
canvas are *more* demanding of quantifying proof, they are *more* demanding
of comparative analysis, not less.

Now, that is not to say that there are not in human history periods of setback and disaster. The phenomena which typically do generate periods of
catastrophe for humanity are disease, famine and war. Natural catastrophe
and war do have profound influences on Western culture; but then we
analyse such phenomena as disease or as war. We do not collapse them
into a general apocalypse. Similarly, why should we depress ourselves now
with some sense of national decline? The problems to be explained are the
declinist theories, and the declinist mentality. People encourage each other
in this declinist mentality, just as in the early seventeenth century people
encouraged each other in the thought that the apocalypse was just around
the corner. Shared indignation does not validate the analysis.

The declinist mentality has to argue that *everything is wrong*: things are
wrong across the board; there is some fundamental malaise which perme-
ates every aspect of national affairs. The declinist mentality is not one which
can point to specific remedies to specific institutions. The declinist mentality
is not melioristic, it is apocalyptic. It needs to find the most generalised
scapegoat. It is convenient, therefore, for the declinist mentality to focus on

those most general aspects of our national affairs which we call the Constitution. The more specific one is about constitutional remedies the less plausible the declinist thesis becomes. As soon as we start pinning down the declinist political theorist to say what exactly would be gained by removing hereditary peers from the House of Lords, for example, the less plausible the specific solution seems to a problem which is defined in such grandiose and general terms – however desirable or undesirable the individual proposal might be. Reform of the House of Lords or the electoral system might be very interesting. We might be more sceptical of the idea that it could produce some general transformation of national fortunes. The most ironically appropriate response to declinism would be to conscript its theorists and make them civil servants in charge of the implemention of some piece of reformist legislation.

Political parties tend to engage in triumphalist rhetoric while in power and declinist rhetoric when in opposition: when major parties alternate in office, this polarity tends to be mitigated. The problem is much greater for centre parties, which (in the British system) never enjoy power, or for a party long out of office. In the second case, the Labour Party in opposition was tempted to adopt the declinist rhetoric of the permanently marginalised, and now has the task of translating it into practice. Constitutional change currently takes place in this unreliable and over-emotional setting, as people look to specific, technical electoral arrangements as if they were solutions to apocalyptic ills. It is hard to judge the outcome of prospective Labour reform of the Constitution. The responsibilities of office will probably have a very moderating influence on anyone who tries it. As soon as they lift the lid on the Constitution they will be appalled at the complexity of constitutional change. But there are real possibilities. If the Union were to break up it would not be the end of the world for England by any means. It would encourage us all to become little Englanders. The consequences would be greater for people who might find themselves living in Scotland, Ireland or Wales. Yet debates about decline normally refer to England without considering the other constituent parts of the United Kingdom. This actually echoes an older phase of historical writing, in which we assumed that England was paradigmatic. Again, that was not wholly wrong. Because England is dominant within the British Isles, England's categories of explanation tend to be paradigmatic. But we now see that the history of declinist thought is different in England, Wales, Ireland and Scotland: it will follow a different pattern and will have a different logic. To be proper historians we will need a history of declinist ideas in these four different cultures which relates them to their intellectual origins and to the practical life experience of the four societies.

So declinism is not as simple a thing as the metropolitan bourgeois intelligentsia of the 1990s would lead us to think. They may indeed encourage each other to think the same thoughts. But as an historical phenomenon across the British Isles and over many decades the problem is much more complicated. It is actually quite easy to deal with the modern declinists and to analyse them historically. They tend to be fairly intelligible to us; they are academics; they are the higher journalists. We know them; they are people not wholly unlike ourselves. We know their life experience; we know their background. And because we know them and have thought about them for quite some time they are not really a danger. But there are nevertheless in our polity more serious forces which are not within the pale of academe. Government policies tend not to be as successful at dealing with these (as we see in Ireland). Of relevance here are questions concerning the social cohesion of the population, especially in inner city areas. Ireland clearly is a society with a long-term record of political violence. In the British Isles the prospect of apocalyptic racial conflict is a very small danger, because Britain is historically relatively tolerant on racial questions. Nevertheless Britain has been at different times more subject to religious and sectional conflict and may be again, given suitable declinist encouragement.

Yet some of the premises of declinist writers' work are undoubtedly correct. Let us consider Correlli Barnett. British military strength is not what it was in 1897. The question is, could this realistically have come out differently? And at what price could it have come out differently? Had Britain turned itself into a militarist power in 1900 and acted as such throughout the twentieth century, would things be different and better now? We can ask these questions only because the military was successful in two world wars. But the most aggressive military power in western Europe paid a very high price for its militaristic efficiency. *(Yes but elsewhere?)*

Declinist theories also raise important questions of methodology, for they fly in the face of the most important scholarly innovations. The two big developments in historical method during my professional lifetime have been the recovery first of the contingent and then of the counterfactual. Both of these trends undermine the force of the doomsters' arguments. They also, in the same way, undermine the force of the triumphalists' arguments. Even if the triumphalists are right, things can nevertheless go wrong. Even if the doomsters are right, things can nevertheless shortly afterwards go well. So I do not see us being locked into any pattern of national decline. I do not think that there are such logics in history. There are real choices, and the reasons for choosing between different paths, each of which is valid, are often contingent ones. So there are mistakes in national policy. There are also helpful decisions in national policy. And I am afraid there are few general answers. During the 1960s and the 1970s historical analysis was often deeply teleological, whatever the position of the historian. It has taken a lot to distance ourselves from all that (and I do not think we should exaggerate our success in having permanently eliminated these errors). There are many people who still have a deeply teleological attitude to their subject who did not share in that crusading process of re-emphasising the contingent and the counterfactual. The ability to frame contingencies and counterfactuals undermines the old teleologies, whether of Marxist progress/doom or of Whig progress/ doom. I too wrote of 1832 as an end. But what I meant more restrictively was that it was the end of a particular state form as I had defined it, not the end of everything. So I was not as attached to a declinist thesis as some of my colleagues on the left were. The people I am least impressed by now are the declinist theorists of the centre, who were never enlisted in the hard left but who were never part of those developments in historical method in the last twenty years which have made so much difference to our view of British history. Indeed they would react indignantly against emphases on either the contingent or the counterfactual.

If Britain and the USA are each other's major counterfactuals, however, it may throw some light on the declinist mentality in Britain to look at the American case. I have recently written a counterfactual piece on the American Revolution,[15] and there one is touching on a national myth: Americans could not conceivably internalise the idea that this triumphalist event might not have happened. There will be no reaction to this argument in the USA. The methodological shifts to which I have referred have not occurred in the United States; they have made a big difference in England, but not in America. When I gave my inaugural lecture,[16] I made some comparisons between the general shape and course of British historiography and American historiography over the last twenty or thirty years. It seems to me that the shape of British history has changed more in the last fifteen years probably than at any other time in the last hundred and fifty; whereas during the same period the received account of American history in America has changed hardly at all. And in fact those challenges to it which were framed in the 1960s, and which seemed in the 1960s to be threats to undermine the received version of American history have been absorbed within it. The history of the USA written by its citizens is now more self-absorbed, more self-referential probably than at any other time in the last thirty years. And it is getting more so. The American historical profession, remember, is numerically enormous. Most able US historians write American history. They do it in a very scholarly fashion. There is much secondary literature and they are absorbed in it. Their international horizon is not always wide. Their access to international comparisons is not always as great as it might be.

There is not, therefore, significant American discussion of decline or potential decline in relation to their own empire, or an end-of-century anxiety there which one can compare with British attitudes. Since recovery from Vietnam, America's is not a declinist culture. Its mood at the end of the century is less one of anxiety than of reassertion, of a rallying to the American public myth, which has proved to be a very successful myth in its functional aspect. It might not be true, but it works. The declinist thesis is most obviously, demonstrably true in respect of empire. Empires rise and fall, military strength rises and falls across centuries. But you cannot tell a country which is currently the only superpower left that in a century China might be that superpower. It is not a proposition one can grapple with; it is too long a time horizon, even though the argument is quite plausible. It is not easily quantifiable and it is not easily addressed. What would they do? It is not clear that there are any things which could be done in the USA today which are not being done which would avert that problem. Just as it is not clear that in Britain in 1897 there were any things which could realistically be done which could have averted the outcome; but other counterfactuals were certainly averted, those summed up by the dates 1917, 1933 and 1945.

What should have been done? I can see a limited validity in Correlli Barnett's claims: more professionalism in the armed forces, and more resolute military power might have helped at certain times in achieving limited goals. The problem is that a society which could have converted to extreme efficiency would not have had limited goals. When one has managed to explain why declinists have the mentality they have, and why certain of their ideas resonate widely, one needs to ask a further question concerning the impact of declinism on the wider culture. Declinism can have – and has had – a wider impact in certain cultures at certain times. Societies that persuade themselves that the end is nigh are societies which tend to behave irrationally and to enter into armed conflict. A sense of the decline of Protestantism and parliamentary government led to civil war in Britain in the 1640s. The American colonies from the 1760s came to believe that they were being subjected to a grand international conspiracy and acted on this belief. It was their belief in national decline that led them into armed conflict. Germany in 1914 was preoccupied by the long-term threat of Russia and of German decline relative to Russia.

In a much smaller way declinism is now the stuff of politics in modern Britain. Which party the electorate chooses has a great deal to do with which of the competing versions of declinism is most widely believed. For that reason macro-economic decisions can often be swayed by declinist theories, even if those declinist theories do not rest on quantifiable analysis. The difference in GNP between many major industrial nations in western Europe is only a matter of a few years' growth. It is quite possible that supply side reforms, or successes or failures in macro-economic policy, in these different nations could over ten or twenty years significantly change the current order. Although it is hard to do much better, it is very possible to do much worse. For example, the European continent would have been far more advanced in its industrialisation but for the French Revolution which had a short-term effect of deindustrialising France and a disastrous effect on the long-term structure of French population, with results we see in 1914. But in general the long-term pattern is that Britain and the continent are roughly comparable in economic terms. If one country gains in one century and another gains in another century that should not cause triumphalism or despair. You might argue that Thatcherism was extremely successful in terms of supply side reforms but relatively unsuccessful in terms of macro-economic management; had the recessions of the early and late 1980s not occurred then GNP per head would be comparable to that of Germany.

If somebody were to find their way into 11 Downing Street on the strength of having a declinist theory of the national economy then there might well be consequences. I would rather have a triumphalist in Downing Street than a declinist. I am more sceptical of declinism as a theory than of triumphalism because triumphalism is describing the future, which is variable; declinism is describing the past, which is quantifiable. The future could be better than the past has been bad, at least in respect of England. But I am not sure to what degree practical politicians are really respectful of declinists. It would be interesting to see to what extent the Labour Party disengages from declinism and adopts managerial or triumphalist attitudes when in office. It would be interesting to see whether the Liberal Democrats turn their declinist theories against a Labour government. All triumphalists and all declinists ought to be regularly disillusioned. Of the two, declinists have, historically, done far more damage.

Both in practical terms and in historical terms declinist theories are unhelpful, and the process of disillusion, either practical or historiographical, is important. That is why one should be encouraged to think about declinist theories in a larger setting. How many have there been over the centuries? Where have they come from? What do they do? How successful are they? How justified were they as comments on what was actually happening? To what degree were they simple intellectual mistakes? To what degree were they corrected by experience, or to what degree did they continue to be held despite experience? To what degree did different theories of decline lead different western countries into disaster in the twentieth century? Perhaps Germany is the archetypal case of sophisticated declinist theories regularly being made the ground for practical policies. No greater warning is necessary.

Notes

1. J.C.D. Clark (ed.), *Ideas and Politics in Modern Britain* (Basingstoke, 1990), p. 2.
2. J.C.D. Clark, *English Society 1688–1832: Ideology, Social Structure and Political Practice During the Ancien Régime* (Cambridge, 1985), esp. ch. 6; J. C. D. Clark, *Revolution and Rebellion: State and Society in England in the Seventeenth and Eighteenth Centuries* (Cambridge, 1986), pp. 154–5, 161.
3. J.C.D. Clark, *English Society*, p. 1.
4. He refers elsewhere to 'Whig sins of teleology and anachronism' (J.C.D. Clark, *Revolution and Rebellion*, p. 13).
5. J.C.D. Clark, *English Society*, p. 11.
6. A. Macfarlane, *The Origins of English Individualism: The Family, Property and Social Transition* (Oxford, 1978).
7. 'Law and religion dominated men's understanding of the public realm [in the mid-eighteenth century]'; 'Hierarchical social order, monarchy and religion formed an interlocking matrix of national identity for British subjects into the nineteenth century' (J.C.D. Clark, *The Language of Liberty 1660–1832: Political Discourse and Social Dynamics in the Anglo-American World* (Cambridge, 1994), pp. 1, 49).
8. J.C.D. Clark, *English Society*, pp. 63-4.
9. J.C.D. Clark (ed.), *Ideas and Politics*, p. 1.
10. John Patten and John Redwood were, for example, both involved in *Ideas and Politics*.
11. J.C.D. Clark, *Ideas and Politics*, p. 32.
12. W. Hutton, *The State We're In* (London, 1996; 1st edn, 1995). See also the interview with Hutton in pp. 50–60 of this book.
13. M.J. Wiener, *English Culture and the Decline of the Industrial Spirit 1850–1980* (Harmondsworth, 1992; 1st edn, 1981).
14. C. Barnett, *The Collapse of British Power* (Stroud, 1984; 1st edn, 1972); *The Audit of War: The Illusion and Reality of Britain as a Great Nation* (Basingstoke, 1987; 1st edn, 1986); *The Lost Victory: British Dreams, British Realities 1945–1950* (London, 1996; 1st edn, 1995).
15. J.C.D. Clark, 'British America: What if there had been no American Revolution?' in N. Ferguson (ed.), *Virtual History: Alternatives and Counterfactuals* (London, 1997).
16. A verson of this lecture has been published as J. C. D. Clark, 'The Strange Death of British History? Reflections on Anglo-American Scholarship', *Historical Journal*, vol, 40, no. 3 (1997).

Part II

Thematic Analysis

11

Party Ideology and National Decline

ROBERT ECCLESHALL

The now extensive historiography on Britain's relative decline in the global economy tends to be long in perspective and pessimistic about the prospects of national recovery. Common to most explanations of the country's slippage from the premier league is an argument that obstacles to current attempts at modernisation emerged somewhere along the relatively smooth passage of an *ancien régime*. The premature bourgeois revolution which created an Hanoverian elite of gentlemen disinclined to escape entirely from the feudal past; the Revolutionary settlement of 1688 which arrested constitutional development by replacing monarchical with parliamentary absolutism; the gentrification of the Victorian industrial middle classes which stifled entrepreneurial endeavour and scientific innovation by inculcating the upwardly mobile with an ethos of public service and a cult of amateurism; and ambitious oceanic ventures which eventually led to imperial overstretch: these are among the reasons which those on the left and right of the academic debate have given for Britain's loss this century of economic power and international prestige. The assumption tends to be that Britain suffers from long-term structural problems because it peaked too soon on a largely untroubled ascent to modernity; the prognosis is that the halcyon days when in so many ways the country was a world pioneer will not return; while the prescription tends to be radical renovation, cultural and institutional, to enable Britain to keep pace even as a small and diminished nation.

Commentary on how decline has featured in party ideology tends to assume some sort of correlation between political utterances and the enormity of the British problem as characterised in much of the historiography. Andrew Gamble, though acknowledging that decline is primarily a matter of perception rather than objective measurement, nevertheless suggests that the connection between political realities and ideological discourse has been fairly close. Since the 1880s, according to him, the ideological agenda has been dominated by anxieties about Britain's economic malaise – the preoccupation with national efficiency at the turn of the century, for instance – at those key moments when the country's precarious position in the world order has been particularly evident.[1]

According to David Cannadine, by contrast, the immensity of Britain's long-run problems has prompted the bulk of politicians to keep a safe ideological distance from them. Only a handful in the past century – emboldened by enlarged egos, and probably by messianic impulses and delusions of grandeur – have set themselves the task of halting or reversing apparently inexorable trends. Among the adventurous few were Joseph Chamberlain, Churchill and Thatcher.

Cannadine's claim that in a British context politicians need to be exceptionally reckless and self-regarding to take on the mission of reconnecting the nation with its glorious heritage has a certain resonance with ideological discourse, particularly that of the right with its tendency to romanticise the past as a series of momentous events in which extraordinary leaders have rescued Britain from nemesis by harnessing the qualities of its people for an heroic project of national delivery. At the end of the Second World War, Ernest Benn, who promulgated Herbert Spencer's version of Social Darwinism long after it became unfashionable, pronounced that only a leader of unusual vision and iron resolve – an 'Economic Churchill' – could turn the tide of half a century of collectivist stagnation by giving political direction to the latent British characteristic of robust individuality.[2] Margaret Thatcher, of course, portrayed herself with growing conviction as some kind of Churchillian reincarnation. Cannadine's point is that only rare politicians have dared give ideological priority to the problem of Britain's backwardness, and in doing so their careers have been frustrated by inevitable failure to retrieve a world that is forever lost. Other politicians have been sufficiently modest, or at least cautious enough, to leave 'the issue of national decline very much alone'.[3]

Analysis of this sort makes the ideology of decline – whether avoidance of the issue, as Cannadine contends, or sporadic obsession, as Gamble claims – too dependent upon historical developments. The postwar connection between the two has been looser and more complex because ideology, as Stuart Hall reminds us, 'has its own modality, its own ways of working and its own forms of struggle. These have real effects in society which cannot be reduced to, nor explained as, merely the secondary or reflexive effects of some factor which is primary or more determining'.[4] Politicians have been flexible and creative in articulating the British malady for electoral purposes, sometimes denying its existence but often fabricating it into some pressing crisis for which they purport to have a panacea.

At times when, on Gamble's reading, Britain's slippage from the top league should have induced a fresh bout of national neurosis, politicians have not been unsuccessful in reassuring the public that business continues as usual. The end of Empire, for example, was hailed as yet another demonstration of Britain's global pre-eminence: as beneficiaries of those civilised values and democratic institutions pioneered by the mother country, colonies had naturally matured into independent nations; while Britain, released from the 'burden' of dependent territories, would scale the uplands of even greater prosperity, and also enhance its international prestige at the apex of a new tripartite relationship of the Commonwealth, the United States and an increasingly integrated Europe. On other occasions, when the signs of decline were less visible, politicians have indulged in apocalyptic warnings about the nation's possible termination unless remedial action is taken. Far from refusing to touch the issue with a bargepole, as Cannadine claims, they have rushed to embrace it. And not all have been egomaniacs on the scale of Churchill or Thatcher. At the core of several successful postwar electoral projects – those of Wilson, Heath, Thatcher and Blair – has been a promise that Britain, as Wilson was fond of putting it, would no longer 'lag behind' other nations.

The British malady has been used by politicians as a stick with which to beat their opponents for implementing measures that temporarily disconnect the nation from its steady progression towards modernity; as a means of identifying the enemies within – amateurish industrialists, imperious trade unions, or whatever – who must be dealt with if Britain is to do as well in the future as in the past; as a way of spotlighting some cultural impediment – habits of dependency, a two-nations mentality, and so forth – to the harnessing of national energies; and not least as a pretext for ditching former policies, usually statist, of their own parties.

In dramatising the problem of decline, however, politicians have portrayed themselves neither as Canute-like figures, eager to preside over the nation's submergence beneath the historical tide, nor as custodians who can be trusted to take the country on the least uncomfortable route to its inevitable destination as a little place living in much reduced circumstances. Their message has been that with appropriate political direction happy days will soon be here again. Their electoral pledges have been projects that will enable Britain to remain, in Wilson's words, 'a first-rate nation';[5] and their reassurance has been – as Blair told one of his annual party conferences – that its 'glory days' are not past.[6]

There is clear blue water between the historiography and the ideology of decline.[7] One is pessimistic about the future, arguing that Britain is now a prisoner of past successes; the other is upbeat about the prospects of the country remaining a pathfinder on the ascent to modernity and a significant influence in international counsels. One assumes that some project of structural renewal is necessary to retain Britain even in the second or third league of nations; the other claims to have at its disposal a concoction for ensuring that in every respect the nation will remain a global leader. One suggests that obstacles to modernisation have accumulated from the peculiar evolution of British society over several centuries; the other offers quick-fix solutions to some wrong-turn taken in the recent or more distant past. One identifies inexorable trends towards descent arising from Britain's formerly rapid pace towards modernity; the other emphasises the need to reorientate the nation towards the course which has and will continue to carry it upwards. One concludes that Britain's pioneering spirit is now exhausted; the other announces that another golden age is about to dawn. The postwar ideology of decline has offered a politics of hope rather than despair, promising to key the nation into the future by aligning policies with those achievements and native characteristics which delivered the glory days of the past.

There are two obvious reasons why postwar ideology has been at some distance from the historiography of inevitable descent, both of which have been recognised by commentators such as Cannadine and Gamble. The first is that politicians are unlikely to succeed by appearing before the electorate as jeremiahs, prophesying doom and gloom, and seeking a mandate to be put in charge of a nation that is going rapidly and inescapably down the plughole. They are more likely to win votes by orchestrating popular anxieties and aspirations into a broad measure of consent for a project which appears to provide a short-cut solution to perceived problems, and by reassuring the electorate not only that something can be done but that with the correct dose of political medicine all will be well again. Nobody in pursuit of power is likely to announce to the country that there is no alternative to a slippery slope into oblivion.

The second reason is that, as Barry Supple has written, 'relative decline and absolute growth can and do co-exist'.[8] Britain's century-long accelerated rate of economic growth, though slower than in many other countries, has enabled politicians to indulge in bouts of ideological complacency at those moments when by any objective measurement national failures were evident: the dismantling of empire, for example, was accompanied by reassurances about the unprecedented age of affluence enjoyed by Britons at home. Absolute economic growth also in part explains why, contrary to what Cannadine suggests, so many politicians have on occasion been willing to grasp the nettle of relative decline. Britain's relative successes in the past, coupled with some continuing absolute achievements, enable its relatively poor economic performance in the present to be depicted as a brief halt on the long haul to the summit. Politicians have sought electoral approval by claiming to have at their disposal the means of reinvigorating the nation, thereby overcoming any temporary setback in its forward march.

What tends to be neglected in the literature about decline is the historical context which so readily facilitates the ideological transformation of the realities of poor economic performance into a politics of hope and renewal. Historians, we know, are prone to attribute Britain's current difficulties to its longevity as an *ancien régime*. But Britain's exceptionalism, its early and smooth transition to modernity, has deposited in the national psyche a residue of eternal optimism which politicians are eager to choreograph; and its relative historical autonomy has placed at their disposal an iconographic storehouse for illustrating how failure can be turned into success.

There are gripping yarns to be told about a small nation that has been unconquered for a millennium; of how since the first Elizabethan age a swashbuckling and adventurous people have transported British values and institutions around the globe; of how the robust individuality and inventive genius of this island race spurred the development of mercantile and commercial capital, then made Britain the industrial workshop of the world, and eventually contributed many of the innovations which inaugurated a new age of global technology; of how the nation took a European lead in demolishing royal absolutism, and then in eliminating other forms of arbitrary power by extending civil liberties and democratic rights; of how the country introduced a structure of social welfare and a national health service that are envied by much of the world; and of how in moments of heroic endeavour and of stoicism in the face of adversity, from the Armada to the spirit of Dunkirk, the sturdy inhabitants of this small place have refused to capitulate to military might and oppressive forces.

The legacy to politicians of this enduring state are two types of ideological discourse, both of which are celebratory, patriotic and optimistic. Each is distinct, though in political usage they often overlap. One is evolutionary, the other is episodic. The former weaves Britain's long procession towards modernity into a narrative of linear progression; the latter assembles heroic leadership, memorable events and persistent virtues into a saga of momentous achievements and rugged endurance in which foes have been vanquished and the country has survived against the odds. Each is used to depict the nation's relegation from the top league as a temporary arrest in its pioneering mission as a global leader; and both are pressed into service on behalf of programmes of national recovery that promise to succeed through fidelity to what is essentially British.

A prevalent assumption of commentators is that contemplation of this *ancien régime* is likely either to animate right-wing impulses to recapture the grandeur of the past or to mobilise the forces of the left into an assault upon an archaic political frame. The view of left intellectuals, reinforced by the prolonged ascendancy of Thatcher, tends to be that the peculiarities of British evolution have given rise to an insular and primarily English form of nationalism that can be most readily appropriated by the right. Their argument is that the legacy of Britain's premature rush to modernity is a post-imperialist state which wallows in the glories of a once-conquering nation and induces a domestic culture of subjecthood: a deferential and pro-monarchy culture in which a supine people, fixated by the symbols of social ascription, are too willing to acquiesce in a national soap opera of hereditary pageantry and ceremonial; and in which any potential for social transformation through class allegiances is suffocated by a resonant image of hierarchy that makes the fine gradations of a lingering feudal regime appear as a natural order of leaders and led.

Conservatives have certainly not been slow to colonise the terrain of this 'empire state', and in doing so have skilfully articulated both types of ideological discourse: the evolutionary in the form of a Whiggish judicious statecraft in which the orderly, upward movement of the nation through the centuries is attributed to the sagacity of an establishment that is the product of an unusual symbiosis of aristocratic and bourgeois wealth; the episodic in the form of fables of how often in the past right triumphed over wrong, of picturesque illustrations of how on occasion courageous leadership and the perennial qualities of the people bonded in pursuit of some grand enterprise, and of celebrations of golden historical moments when political arrangements and native characteristics fused in exemplary displays of British greatness. The episodic discourse facilitates particularly dramatic invocations to the nation to rally against a sluggish present by reconnecting with a glorious past: in portraying Victorian Britain as a sort of prelapsarian era before the onset of a corrupting corporatism, for example, Thatcher was able to persuade a sufficiently large section of the electorate to collude in her offensive against the postwar settlement. Since at least the time of Disraeli Tories have used both forms of discourse to portray themselves as the custodians of a land of hope and glory in which the mass of people gladly respond to sound leadership, whether that of patrician prudence or of entrepreneurial dynamism.

Yet Labour has not been uncomfortable occupying the same terrain. Living in an old country provides opportunity for ideological contestation across the political spectrum, and for teasing from a long past diverse prologues to the present. The peculiarities of British development may well explain the lack of popular clamour for a democratic republic with the kind of vibrant civil society favoured by commentators on the left, and also why the route to modernisation chosen by the postwar Labour Party has been through landscape which more fervent socialists barely recognise. From the intellectual heritage of British exceptionalism, however, Labour has not been unsuccessful on occasion in summoning the nation to a project of economic recovery, and there is no compelling reason to suppose that the party is intrinsically disadvantaged in the struggle for cultural hegemony.

Labour has been no less inclined than its principal rival to deploy an episodic discourse in presenting itself as the party most in touch with the cultural residues of a thousand glorious years. Take the following megaphone invocation of the buccaneering British spirit against the complacency which had arrested national ascent:

> What is it we want to change? It is not the enduring values which have made Britain great, it is not the qualities of independence and personal freedom, the democratic right of dissent, the right to argue. What we want to change is the clammy unimaginativeness at the top, which has prevented our people exercising these qualities and energies in full measure.
>
> The fault lies not in our people, but in the form and pattern in which our national system of government has come to be ordered . . .
>
> (W)e want a Britain . . . proud of its past and willing to rediscover the true traditions of our nation as a guide to our role in the future: because the real traditions of Britain are not to be found in the so-called qualities that have been exalted and disproportionately rewarded in these past few years. It was

our people's ingenuity, innovation, sometimes their brashness and saltiness, and political irreverence, our energy, determination, and merchant-adventuring spirit which gave us our influence in the world.

(W)hat we offer is an exciting programme calling forth all the finest qualities of our people: their energy, their skill, their tenacity, and their spirit of adventure.[9]

This was not Margaret Thatcher at full throttle against the stultifying effects of too much government, but Harold Wilson in 1964 advocating more extensive state activity in the form of a national plan to rescue Britain from the relative decline it had endured during the 'wasted years' of misrule by those inculcated with a cult of patrician amateurishness. In his speech to the annual Labour Party conference in 1996, Tony Blair also promised to take 'an old country' forward into 'a new age' by unlocking those durable virtues which had been stifled by an even longer period of Conservative mismanagement:

> Consider a thousand years of British history and what it tells us. The first parliament in the world. The industrial revolution ahead of its time. An empire, the largest the world has ever known. The invention of virtually every scientific device of the modern world. Two world wars in which our country was bled dry, in which two generations perished, but which in defeat of the most evil force ever let loose by man showed the most sustained example of bravery in human history. Our characteristics? Common sense. Standing up for the underdog. Fiercely independent. But the outstanding British quality is courage. Not just physical bravery. The courage to think anew. To break convention when convention is holding us back. To innovate whilst others conform. To do it our way.

The left are prone to castigate the Blairite project as Thatcherism *sotto voce*. In doing so they perhaps neglect the skill with which the postwar Labour Party has sometimes put its own ideological gloss on an old regime by attributing a languishing economy to Tory suppression of indigenous characteristics which made Britain a global leader in the past.

Nostalgia for a fading grandeur which inhibits the task of national renewal; preference for an antiquated class structure which wastes talent; and a knee-jerk inclination to revert to free-market dogma which dissipates energy by splitting Britain into two antagonistic nations: these have been the ideological stock-in-trade by which postwar Labour has sought to persuade the electorate that national advance has been halted by Conservative attachment to institutional ossification and class divisions. The promise is always to apply British grit to some fresh challenge by instigating a fairer, more inclusive and meritocratic society; and in doing so to modernise through policies which are in harmony with those qualities which have carried the country forward for a millennium. The nation is to be reborn by the reinvigoration, not the destruction, of an *ancien régime*.

Labour has also fashioned its own evolutionary narratives from Britain's longevity. The early rush to modernity may account for the persistence of aristocratic remnants in the national culture. But this old regime accommodated free-born Englishmen and a new model army in the seventeenth century, and by European standards has pioneered various attempts to give institutional expression to civic virtue and social solidarity. There is a rich vein to be tapped by those on the left eager to formulate a discourse of a linear progression from Britain's exceptionalism. Such narratives tend to suggest either that a benign teleology can be discerned in the gradual ascent to modernity, or, if less deterministic, that through a combination of popular agitation and moral sensibility the nation forged ahead of its European neighbours in safeguarding individuals against arbitrary power, in introducing a democratic franchise, and eventually in providing a safety net of economic security for all citizens.

As a consequence of the extensive debate at the turn of the century about the shift from individualism to collectivism, Labour has inherited a repertoire of these progressivist narratives. There is the conviction, appearing in Fabian and other guises, that through conscious planning – the application of brain power to problems of economic growth and social justice – capitalism can be incrementally improved, tamed, transformed and even abolished. But there is also a kind of Hegelian optimism, diluted and anglicized in the manner of T.H. Green, that closer attention by the state to the promotion of the common good will eventually induce in every citizen a moral determination to transcend sectional interests. Tony Blair has articulated this latter intellectual heritage in a bid to present himself in the vanguard of broad liberal forces that will renew the nation's movement in a benevolent direction. Hence his tendency to highlight the contrast between the ranting sectarianism of the Thatcher years and his own inclusive, irenic leadership of a centre–left coalition; and also the inclination to package his ethical socialism in the form of T.H. Marshall's reassuring account of British evolution over three centuries as a staircase to citizenship by which, through a combination of popular will and enlightened leadership, the nation gradually stepped towards a fuller recognition of civil, then political, and eventually social rights.[10] Progressive liberalism provides firmer anchorage than the ideology of old Labour for the morality of citizenship that is central to Blair's brand of market communitarianism.

In Britain, then, the ideology of decline across the political spectrum is about rescuing and renovating an old regime by recapturing the values and dynamic spirit which have consistently piloted the nation in the right direction. The objective is to equip the country for the future by rejoining it with the past, the tone is upbeat, and the message is that 'things can only get better'. Old nation, new age; modernisation by channelling those stirring qualities which made Britain the wonder of the world through fresh political formulae for national advance; renewing Britain's forward march by reversing some recent 'wrong-turn': such are the themes of postwar political debate.

British exceptionalism may have elicited a type of ideological contestation that is too parochial and insular for some tastes. Those on the intellectual left, however, who suppose that the evolution of an old state has provided the right with an intrinsic ideological advantage make the same mistake as conservative thinkers such as Michael Oakeshott who compress the components of the national culture into a single entity or 'way of life'. Their 'reimagination' of the nation results in cultural reductionism. The specificity of British historical development has bequeathed to Conservative and Labour politicians alike a heterogeneous ideological legacy which they have moulded into diverse projects for national recovery, but which in their various ways promise continuity with what has gone before.

Since 1945 the ideology of relative decline has gone through four historical phases. In the first, which lasted until the early 1960s, politicians used episodic and evolutionary modes of ideological discourse to insist that the nation was unfolding in a beneficent direction, and their disagreements focused on the measures needed to ensure the continuation of this comfortable progression. In the second, more alarmist phase politicians announced that the engine of historical advance had been derailed, and they mingled stories of the enduring British spirit of adventure with the narrative of linear progression as they attempted to convince the electorate that their party had the only reliable mechanism for putting the engine back on the tracks. Less use was made of evolutionary discourse during the third phase, which began in 1975 with Margaret Thatcher's election as Conservative leader. The British past was now depicted not as a continuum of steady ascent but as discrete golden moments when the polity was in harmony with a natural economic order, and of periods of inertia whenever politicians neglected the science of political economy. Thatcherites melodramatically pre-

sented their project as a grand scheme of national rejuvenation by cele-
brating those epochs when vibrant leadership had given the British
temperament opportunity to respond to the rhythms of the market. In
the final phase, which began when Tony Blair was elected Labour
leader, the two modes of ideological discourse were again blended to
affirm the party's ability to channel persistent British qualities into a
resumption of the long march to modernity. In this sense the language
of New Labour marks a return to the ideological *status quo ante*
Thatcher.

In the first phase Conservatives claimed that Britain could remain at
the forefront of global developments without some mighty project of
national recovery. For about twenty years after the end of the Second
World War Tories argued that the country would continue its civilised
ascent to modernity if government was entrusted to grandees who were
accustomed to the art of prudent statecraft. They repudiated any suggestion that Britain suffered from structural economic weaknesses or
was somehow failing as a great power, and they raised the spectre of
long-term decline only to scoff at those intent on frightening the electorate with the prospect of encircling gloom by ideologically fabricating a sense of imminent crisis. The predominant Conservative theme in
these years was that Britain would continue its orderly procession so
long as power was denied to those wayward ideologues who were
intent on implementing some grand design or intricate blueprint of
national renewal. There was to be no place for dramatic gestures in a
politics by conventional means.

The tone was set by Labour's landslide victory in the general election of 1945, which seemed to vindicate wartime economic planning
and closer attention by government to social welfare. During the next
few years Conservatives adjusted to postwar realities by eventually
accepting the efficacy of a Keynesian-style mixed economy, and by
ideologically repositioning themselves as the legitimate tenants of a
halfway house between unbridled capitalism and regimented socialism.
They did so by suggesting that Britain had been quick off the mark to
modernisation because of a creative partnership between the state and
the private sector which began in the Tudor age. On this account
Victorian free-enterprise did not represent the apogee of national economic and cultural achievement, as Thatcherites were to pronounce,
but was an unfortunate interlude in conventional political practice
which Tories were prominent in ending by remedying the social injustices of the industrial revolution. According to R.A. Butler, who was
instrumental in designing the postwar Conservative middle way,

Britons had rarely been spellbound by the nostrums of political economy. And he dismissed as socialist propaganda any suggestion that the nation's prolonged and successful economic ascent had been interrupted before the war by Conservative inactivity.

> It is often represented, and especially by Socialists for their own purposes, that all this great progress came to a halt during the 1914–1918 war and that the two decades between the wars were a period of stagnation and indeed decay under a regime of increasingly monopolistic exploitation. Nothing could be farther from the truth.[11]

In the interwar period, Butler argued, productivity, employment and wages had all risen because of careful Tory economic management which prefigured the measures implemented after 1939.

In government from 1951 to 1964, Conservatives sought to reassure the electorate that in steering a middle course between individualism and collectivism they were ensuring that Britain rode with the historical tide. Measured Tory statecraft, unencumbered by excessive ideological baggage, would enable the nation to remain in the vanguard of technological innovation and to enjoy unprecedented prosperity. There was a reasonable expectation, according to Butler, that the country would 'surf-ride upon the new Industrial Revolution' and double its living standards within a quarter of a century,[12] and he resorted to a quotation from fiction to underline the enduring mission of this *ancien régime* as a global pioneer:

> We may no longer be the world's workshop: but we lead all countries in the quality of our products and in the range of our inventive genius . . .
> It will be the enthusiasm and ability of our scientists and engineers . . . that will propel this country forward. As H.G. Wells made one of his characters remark: 'This 'ere progress keeps going on. It is wonderful 'ow it keeps going on.'[13]

National ascent would be impeded only if prudent statecraft was displaced by political dogma. The Labour Party could not be entrusted to carry the nation forward because it was irretrievably doctrinaire: liable to veer towards collectivist extremes, motivated by envy to stifle entrepreneurial endeavour with punitive rates of taxation, prone to monetary incontinence, and eager to reduce the careful art of politics to simplistic solutions and scientific blueprints. With 'balanced' and 'responsible' political management, however, Britain would remain a pathfinder to modernity. Lord Hailsham told Conservatives at their annual party conference in 1957 that they represented the essence of a nation forever 'dedicated to endless adventure in pursuit of liberty under the law':

> We are determined to secure social justice without sacrificing individual enterprise. We are determined to defend our currency without creating mass unemployment, to secure tax reductions without destroying our social services . . . (W)e are determined to produce . . . an Opportunity State, in which the ideas of liberty and law will continue to be co-partners. In short we intend to hold fast to the path of greatness, a path we know involves sacrifice and difficulty, but the failure to maintain which would mean the abandonment of some essential purpose of our national well-being.[14]

With the national party in its proper place as the advance guard, the spirited British would proceed with their sometimes arduous, but invariably successful, task of exploring the uplands of modernity.

Conservatives were no less sanguine when extolling the nation's persistent role as a great power in the international order. Even the Suez debâcle was represented as another instance of how the plucky inhabitants of a small island remained constant in their determination to withstand 'predatory nationalism', and as a reassurance to dependent territories and other vulnerable regions that Britain had not abdicated its moral responsibility to protect them against aggressors intent on arresting international progress by trampling upon liberty and the rule of law.[15] The rapid collapse of Empire barely punctured this buoyant mood. Little ideological fuss was made, by Tories themselves or their opponents, about African decolonisation after 1959. Conservatives were successful in representing colonial withdrawal, not as a symbol of a once great power on the wane, but as an enlightened decision to grant independence to nations which had reached political maturity by imbibing the values and acquiring the political skills of the mother country. Here, as John Darwin has written, was 'Whig history large as life and twice as shameless'.[16] Imperial retreat, on this account, was a conscious and orderly endeavour to spread the spirit of progress abroad. Britain, released from former commitments, would continue its global leadership by sagacious coordination of a new constellation of relationships that focused on the Commonwealth, Europe and the United States.

A vivid illustration of the Conservative devotion to measured statecraft is a book, *Rebirth of Britain*, that was published in 1964 under the auspices of the Institute of Economic Affairs, a free-enterprise think-tank which was to be influential in shaping the Thatcherite agenda. The 18 essayists engaged in the usual advocacy of a market economy by attributing Britain's economic problems, which became increasingly apparent in the early 1960s, to the suppression of private enterprise by Keynesian-style planning for full employment in a welfare state. Their argument was that the country's postwar revival had been slower than that of comparable nations because economic activity was confined within a political straitjacket. Restrictive work practices which accounted for Britain's failure to compete in the global economy; capricious and cack-handed efforts at economic regulation in the form of 'stop–go' measures and incomes policies; indiscriminate public expenditure which rewarded the incompetent by robbing the efficient; excessive rates of taxation which discouraged entrepreneurial initiative; monetary indiscipline which resulted in inflationary overheating of the economy; and well-intentioned but ill-conceived egalitarian policies which created a dependency welfare culture by eroding habits of self-reliance: these were the reasons given for a failing economy, all of which were to be assembled by Thatcherites into a dramatic project for rolling back the frontiers of the state.

The difference was that, unlike Thatcherites, the contributors to *Rebirth of Britain* denied the need for some mighty endeavour to replace the nation on the rails that would take it onwards to modernity. There was no sense of overwhelming crisis requiring a radical political response, no call for exceptional political leadership to repair the damage done by a busybody state, and no injunction to the electorate to join a crusade of national recovery. All that was required were modest measures to revive the enterprising spirit which had carried the country forward in the past. The 'scale of Britain's economic problems', wrote Graham Hutton, 'is really not large. Informed leadership would not need courage of heroic proportions'.[17] The conclusion to the book was written by Enoch Powell, an iconic figure for Thatcherites because of his oratorial skill in evoking successive crises of British identity. In *Rebirth of Britain*, however, Powell endorsed the opinion of the other contributors that the postwar siege economy could be unravelled by moderate statecraft rather than a politics of melodrama. The restoration of free enterprise was easily within the scope of 'political practicability'. Powell used his classical knowledge to castigate those who exaggerated Britain's global and economic decline, both absolute and relative, by contrasting the nation's current weaknesses with its rousing performance during some imaginary golden age:

> The myth of the Ages of Gold and Iron (the contrast between a glorious past and a decadent present), and the twin myth of the Isles of the Blest (the con-

trast between other lands where all is well and our own where everything is wrong) – these myths have been and no doubt always will be embraced in every age and clime. They belong to humanity's stage properties for dramatising its lot. There is no need to be surprised or indignant when they turn up again in our time and country . . . [18]

Pessimistic prognoses about the country's plunge into perpetual decline were unwarranted, according to Powell, because the electorate was more likely to be persuaded to support the modest steps needed to retrieve a market economy than to embrace utopian promises of a bright new tomorrow that would take the nation further into a cul-de-sac of economic stagnation and cultural malaise.

The reason for this Tory vindication of cautious statecraft was that others were demanding a drastic programme of social transformation to reorientate Britain towards the path of progress. *Rebirth of Britain* was written in response to *Suicide of the Nation?*, in which 18 contributors to the July 1963 issue of *Encounter* had attributed Britain's long-term structural problems to a rigid class structure deriving from the early and relatively comfortable progression to modernity. The outcome was a fusion of aristocratic and bourgeois values which had created a cultural barrier to economic advance by installing a regime of gentrified mediocrity in both government and industry. It was this kind of analysis, reinforced by the investigations of historians, which the Labour opposition used in its advocacy of a programme to arrest national decline by sweeping away obstacles to the creation of a more meritocratic society. Hence the concern of free-marketeers who contributed to *Birth of Nation* to combat the suggestion that Britain needed some herculean project to eliminate the inequalities of wealth and status which, according to them, were the principal initiatives to entrepreneurial endeavour.

An old country in need of renovation was Labour's principal theme when orchestrating a sense of national crisis in the general election campaign of 1964. The same theme, though without a warning of imminent danger, had informed the party's expectation in the 20 years since the war that the application of professional expertise to social problems would succeed in filtering from Britain its feudal remnants and capitalist injustices. The Labour victory of 1945 appeared to confirm the lesson of wartime economic planning that mechanisms were at hand to maintain the ascent of an *ancien régime*. The goal, declared Hugh Dalton in the aftermath of Labour's postwar electoral success, was the erection of a durable framework capable of sustaining wartime achievements for years to come. 'There is a great tide running in the hearts of men. This tide will wash away much of our evil heritage of inequality, injustice and insecurity in this old land. The tide is still rising.'[19] In the early postwar years the engine of national advance was to be more extensive public ownership, with its prospect of the painless evolution of an old state into a fairer, more prosperous future in which good times would become universally available. Nationalisation was considered at the time to be, in Raphael Samuel's words, 'the political economy of socialism, asserting itself aggressively against capitalism, and setting in train an irreversible process by which the private ownership of the means of production would become extinct'.[20] Even during the 1950s, when Labour was too consumed by internal squabbles about the continuing relevance of Clause Four to be an effective opposition, there was little doubt among the protagonists that Britain could easily undergo a post-capitalist transformation. Disagreements between the old guard and revisionists such as Anthony Crosland were primarily about which levers the planners in an enlarged state should pull to ensure optimum economic growth and equitable distribution. There was little dissent from the prevalent assumption that Britain could flow with the historical tide, however intense were Labour quarrels about the mechanisms of rapid advance.

A few discordant voices did question whether a combination of Keynesian demand-management and high public expenditure was sufficient to carry the nation to a future as glorious as its past. Roy Jenkins, for example, made much of the country's relative decline in the international economy. His target, in a Penguin Special written for the general election of 1959, was Tory nostalgia for imperial grandeur, and he argued that the economic future would be buoyant only if illusions were shed about the nation's unique global role. But his call for 'a touch of realism about Britain's world portion', though intended to highlight Conservative nonchalance, was hardly the stuff of a rousing invocation to the nation to engage in renovation. And his suggestion that the country should adjust to its diminished international position by becoming a co-partner with other nations in an increasingly integrated Europe was not a recipe for unifying an introspective and bickering Labour Party.[21] Hugh Gaitskell, the Labour leader, pressed more familiar ideological buttons when, in his speech to the annual conference of 1962, he reminded those such as Jenkins who would take Britain into the European Community of the continuing global responsibilities of an old and successful island state. The outcome of British integration into Europe would be the closure of:

a thousand years of history . . . And it does mean the end of the Commonwealth. How can one seriously suppose that if the mother country, the centre of the Commonwealth, is a province of Europe (which is what Federation means) it could continue to exist as the mother country of a series of independent nations?

What the party needed to distract it from navel-gazing was not 'a touch of realism', but the promise of a dose of collectivism that would carry the nation onwards into another glorious millennium.

In a 1963 Fabian lecture, 'Scientists in Whitehall', Richard Crossman said that during its period of internal wrangling the Labour Party lacked 'a new, creative socialist idea' capable of reconciling the differences between traditionalists like himself and revisionists such as Crosland. What had been needed was a repackaging of the political and moral case for socialism in 'ultra-modern terms': the political in the form of a national plan to exploit the potential for technological innovation; the moral in the form of a guarantee that the application of expertise to the problems of social injustice would quickly eliminate poverty by doubling living standards 'in a dozen years'[22] – which was about half the time predicted by that skilful exponent of the art of prudent Tory statecraft, R.A. Butler! What had provided the balm for healing intra-party wounds was Harold Wilson's notion that socialism was somehow equivalent to science.

By recasting socialism as the application of science to industrial modernisation, Wilson inaugurated the second, more alarmist phase in the postwar ideology of decline. He summoned the electorate to engage in a quasi-Fabian project of national efficiency by suggesting not only that the 'winding up of Empire has been accompanied during the last ten years by what many overseas observers regard as an alarming decline in Britain's standing in the world, due chiefly to two reasons: a loss of purpose in the central direction at Westminster, and a languishing economy outside',[23] but also that the rot had set in during the industrial revolution. For the first time the historiography and ideology of decline appeared to coincide in recognition that Britain was suffering from long-term problems requiring a major overhaul of the engine of economic advance. Too much dead wood at the top because of the peculiar fusion of aristocratic and bourgeois values which had left the industrial workshop of the world with a feudal cultural residue that became a brake on subsequent economic development; the need to ensure that brain rather than blood prevailed in government and industry; and the claim that Britain would slip further down the international league unless burnished by the heat of technological innovation: these were themes now common to the analysts and ideologues of the nation's structural defects.

But the convergence was not that close. In highlighting Britain's century-long problems Wilson's purpose, unlike that of the historians of decline, was not to persuade the nation to adjust to its diminished status, but to mobilise it for a dash to recover global prominence. His fabrication of a sense of national peril that had to be understood within historical context was ideologically effective on several levels. It enabled him to rally Labour troops, bloodied by internecine warfare, with the suggestion that wrangles about public ownership and the mechanisms of wealth distribution were a distraction from the party's persistent and pragmatic endeavour to ensure a future of economic dynamism of benefit to all:

> It was no ideological dogmatism but . . . the empirical search for a solution of the relative decline, ever since 1919, of Britain's economic fortunes – and thus of her international influence – that led the Labour party step by step to socialist planning, planning based on social justice and a substantial publicly-owned sector.[24]

The identification of socialism with scientific planning also gave Wilson opportunity to denounce the Conservative Party as the preserve of that patrician antipathy to expertise which had been the main cause of Britain's sluggish economic performance; and his promise to create a new, properly trained elite was calculated to appeal to the upwardly-mobile, grammar-school educated section of the electorate.

Where the Labour project was at furthest remove from the historiography of relative decline was in the claim that Britain could easily resume its place at the centre of the world stage. Wilson, who was no more inclined than Gaitskell to exacerbate divisions within his party by advocating European integration, announced that the country was resourceful enough to recover its global position without external assistance:

> The Conservatives are prepared voluntarily and complacently to accept second-class status for our country. Loss of influence in the counsels of the nation is the price of economic weakness. And when ten years of Tory freedom were seen to have failed they sought a different escape route – entry into Europe . . .
>
> We are not in Europe. Our economic strength and influence depend on our own efforts, and on them alone, and we believe this country has the skill, and craftsmanship, the power of innovation, and the determination to put forth the efforts that are needed. We reject this defeatism.[25]

What the country needed was not a 'touch of realism', but a blueprint to engage the enduring spirit of sturdy individuality. Wilson, unlike Thatcher when she castigated the dependency culture, rejected 'any suggestions that we have gone soft, that there is any deterioration in our moral fibre, our determination, our will to work'.[26] If the country's mission as a global pathbreaker had been arrested by outmoded policies and failure to displace a defunct elite, purposeful direction would soon 'enable Britain to regain her rightful place in the world, and her rightful influence'.[27] A glorious restoration was at hand.

Wilson's tenure in office is remembered less for a visionary programme of national recovery than for his preoccupation with political intrigue and the minutiae of decision-making. Yet his ideological agility prior to the general election of 1964 succeeded in enlisting much of the nation for another adventurous project; and even some sceptical commentators of the left, for whom Britain's premature rush to modernity had ground to a halt somewhere around the time of the Williamite revolution, were almost persuaded by his confident assertion that a quick-fix formula was available for renewing the nation's ascent.

Wilson's ideological assault upon the class-ridden attitudes and practices of an old regime, though briefly successful in capturing the public imagination, quickly 'unravelled as economic crises and political pressure sapped the will of the party's elite to carry forward the programme of expansion in social expenditure and state-led reorganisation of the economy'.[28] The collapse of the Labour project reinforced a growing assumption that Britain was idiosyncratic in resisting attempts to modernise. The initial Conservative response was to resort to Whig statecraft rather than rumbustious political gestures as a means of replacing the engine of economic advance on the rails. Edward Heath, Tory prime minister from 1970 to 1974, echoed Wilson's invocation to the nation to rediscover the path of greatness. 'Given the right economic policies,' he announced before the 1970 general election, 'there is nothing that the British people, by their own efforts, cannot achieve'.[29] Heath wanted to repair the damage of Labour corporatism by curbing public expenditure, eliminating restrictive work practices, and releasing entrepreneurial initiative from suffocating rates of taxation. But his 'quiet revolution' had closer affinity with the moderate measures advocated in 1964 by the authors of *Rebirth of Britain* than with the herculean project of rejuvenation that was to be urged on the nation by Thatcherites. The country was in need of modernisation because innovation had been stifled by an hyperactive state, but the task could be accomplished without an excess of sweat and tears.

A suspicion that the British disease was peculiarly resistant to conventional remedies appeared to be confirmed when the Heath government was propelled by economic and political pressures to abandon its cautious free-market strategy after only two years, and it now became fashionable for commentators to suggest that the country was essentially ungovernable. The Conservative Party's response was to replace Heath by Margaret Thatcher in 1975, and as a consequence the structures of state and civil society were battered through the 1980s by a kind of permanent, and certainly unprecedented, revolution from the right.

The ideological architecture of Thatcherism was largely in place before 1975. One of its two main pillars was the familiar argument for a low-tax market economy in which entrepreneurial innovators, emancipated from the shackles of Keynesian demand-management, could renew the task of national wealth-creation. The other was the claim that economic inertia and cultural malaise were interconnected. A culture of welfare dependency which undermined self-reliance and sapped any incentive to self-improvement; an increase in vandalism, hooliganism and other forms of anti-social behaviour; the penchant of rebellious youth for drug-taking and mass protest; the spread of pornography, and the use of foul language on television: these and other threats to 'the organic unity of our society' were the outcome of an indulgent state which had enacted egalitarian legislation while dismantling traditional mechanisms of social control.[30] The Thatcherite message was that the state had to be rolled forward and backward to remove the constraints on private enterprise while simultaneously displacing the permissive society by a more disciplinary regime.

Much of the ideological packaging used for the Thatcherite project was recycled. Exposure of Britons to the discipline of the market was represented as an attempt to engage those perennial virtues of stamina and independence upon which national greatness had always depended. Margaret Thatcher's chief reason for optimism about Britain's future in the global economy, she told an interviewer in 1983, was:

> the character of the British people. We've always shown great industrial ability and enterprise. From Elizabethan times this country has thrived because her people have gone overseas seeking trade; so I believe we have a world perspective.
>
> Above all, we have never lost the will and capacity to defend our freedom and the rule of law. This love of freedom is something for which we have been willing to stand up and fight. In the Second World War, we were involved from day one to the end. This was the record of Britain fighting for freedom. I believe that same spirit burns today . . .

(A) massive welfare state has been built up. Unfortunately, this has tended to become a 'nanny' state, leading some people to expect government to provide a grant, a subsidy, a magical solution to every problem. But Britons do not like an overbearing state. And I believe there came a point – with the general election of May 1979 – when people realised the state had acquired too many powers over housing, incomes, jobs, industry. My government is trying to redress the balance of power between the citizen and the state. . . .

The country might in some ways be a chillier, bumpier, less cosy place – but infinitely more invigorating. For as George Bernard Shaw aptly put it, 'liberty means responsibility. That is why most men dread it.'

For many years, our friends have never tired of telling us that Britain is drifting – that having lost an empire, we have not yet found a role. Well, I want the 1980s to be the decade when we get back on course. We have courage, compassion and inventiveness – all the ingredients of a great nation. What can hold us back? Only ourselves. We must never again allow state monopoly to replace competition; or collectivism to strangle individual endeavour. Let this be an era of enterprise.[31]

This summoning of the adventurous British spirit against cultural and institutional torpor was the ideological stock-in-trade of politicians: the difference lay in the shifting identification of the obstacles to national renewal.

Thatcher's invocation of enduring British grit for yet another project of national recovery was consistent with the postwar ideology of decline. In urging the British people to join a crusade to smash the nanny state, however, she discarded the usual account of how, notwithstanding setbacks, the nation had proceeded on its long haul to modernity. A narrative of Britain's steady evolution was not the natural discourse of someone eager to proclaim after nearly a decade in office that she had engineered an escape from 'the long, dark tunnel of socialism'.[32] There was little reference in the third phase of the postwar ideology of decline to a largely uninterrupted continuum of national ascent. The Thatcherite message was that history had flowed backwards since 1945 because of the 'ratchet effect' of collectivism. Successive Labour and Conservative governments, mesmerised by Keynesian orthodoxy, had burdened themselves with increasingly impossible responsibilities. The outcome had been not the unfolding of a beneficent teleology but inexorable descent into what Keith Joseph described as a 'totalitarian slum'.[33]

Thatcherite sights were focused more on the postwar slippery slope to corporatism than on a wider historical canvas, and they made little use of the familiar narrative of three hundred years of linear progression. There are no 'easy ways to reverse long-term decline', said Geoffrey Howe in 1982. 'And it is *long-term* decline which we have to reverse'.[34] But the long term, on his reckoning, amounted to no more than a couple of decades during which governments had side-stepped the market by planning for full employment in a welfare state. More cerebral Thatcherites did make the occasional excursion into the historiography of decline to account for the lack of entrepreneurial dynamism in pre-Thatcher Britain. A favourite historian was Correlli Barnett because of his contention that Victorian enterprise had been arrested by the gentrification of the bourgeoisie, with the public schools imparting to the upwardly mobile the skills needed to run the empire and to staff the Anglican priesthood and other professions instead of firing them with a hunger for capitalist success. There was also a tendency to cite commentators who suggested that collectivism had been inaugurated in the late Victorian period by those who, obsessed with middle-class guilt, had sought to appease the working class through redistributive taxation.[35] Generally, however, Conservatives displayed little interest in much of the past; and while extolling the Victorian age as the apogee of British endeavour, they were largely silent about the period from the 1870s to 1945.

Instead of subscribing to a developmental narrative, Thatcherites opted for a snakes-and-ladders version of the past which celebrated those occasions when government had harnessed the enduring qualities of an ancestral people for some grand enterprise. These occasions had coincided with moments of national danger, such as the Second World War, when Britons had responded to courageous and imaginative leadership; and also with periods when the polity had given scope for those vigorous virtues of adventure, thrift, self-reliance and national loyalty which were both peculiarly British and the moral bedrock of a market economy. Thatcherite history provided not a chronology of gradual progress but didactic warnings about how easily the nation could be blown off course whenever the state tampered with a natural economic order. The lesson was that Britain had plunged into decadence, and some of its people had become undisciplined, when politicians had neglected the science of political economy. The need was not to attend to a derailed engine of evolutionary ascent but to ensure that government refrained from encroaching upon a natural harmony of economic interests. In depicting the Victorian age of unfettered private enterprise as a vision of what Britain might become again, Thatcherites indulged in the kind of golden ageism which Enoch Powell had gently ridiculed in *Rebirth of Britain*.

Golden ageism enabled Conservatives to discount the argument that there were endemic obstacles to national recovery. Victorian free-enterprise provided an exemplar of how Britain could again be at the fore-front of global developments. All that was required to set this blessed isle on yet another glorious adventure was a form of government which engaged the British instinct for liberty and order, one which did not sti-fle the natural play of economic interests. Economic decline was reversible because nothing was historically inevitable. Britain had slipped from its premier position in the international league not through ineradicable structural problems, but because since 1945 politicians and the chattering classes had been in the grip of a false ideology. The corrective was a counter-revolution of ideas to alter the climate of pub-lic opinion. What was needed was a battle of minds and hearts to per-suade people of the folly of the Keynesian consensus and to instil in them the resolve never again to install a regime which impeded the operations of the capitalist market.

In an address given in 1982, Nigel Lawson commented on the grim diagnosis of the British condition made by so many commentators, among them the contributors in 1963 to *Suicide of the Nation?*, during the previous two decades. The debate had now virtually ceased, he said, and

> the bottom has fallen out of the market for predictions of gloom and doom . . .
>
> A neurotic obsession with decline and a national mood of defeatism have been replaced, not, to be sure, by Panglossian optimism, but by a reawaken-ing of national confidence in our ability to overcome our difficulties and to shape our own destiny. . . .
>
> Defeatism has not disappeared, but it at last seems to be on the retreat. What has happened?[36]

What had happened, according to Lawson, was that a mood of realism and self-confidence had swept the nation once its members were reac-quainted with the precepts of political economy, particularly on the shop-floor where there was growing recognition of the community of interest existing between management and the workforce. For Conservatives the defining moment in this process of ideological regen-eration was the Falklands war which had been successfully waged against the advice of cynics and defeatists. The 'spirit' of the South Atlantic 'born in the economic battles at home and tested and found true 8000 miles away', Thatcher intoned, indicated a resurgence of those ancestral virtues of stamina, intense patriotism, heroism, and political determination which were eternally and essentially British. The task now was to use this renewal of national confidence to vanquish the remaining foes at home – a rail strike was threatened – who clung to the illusions of corporatism.[37]

Thatcherite contemplation of the past provided neither bland reassurance about the inexorability of British progress nor discomforting discoveries about the prospects of a nation exhausted by having set the international pace to modernity in earlier times. What history disclosed was the pageantry of an island race: inspirational examples of how national greatness was assured when daring leadership and innate individuality coincided at moments of challenge or in epochs of entrepreneurial achievement; and cautionary tales of how easily the nation languished whenever government failed to engage the virtues of old Britain. Thatcherites resorted to an episodic discourse to portray British backwardness as a matter of political will rather than endemic deficiency.

If some critics of the Blair government are correct, the fourth phase in the postwar ideology of decline is remarkable indeed. For not only does a party which claims to represent the 'progressive centre-left' genuflect in the manner of Thatcherites to a self-regulating market, it came to office convinced that the nation-state is largely powerless to influence international economic developments. This was the contention of most of the contributors to a one-off issue of the defunct journal *Marxism Today*, which in 1998 was briefly resurrected to castigate New Labour for failing to escape from a Thatcherite terrain. The charge is that the Labour party is enchanted by globalisation – the fashionable idea that scope for economic regulation by national governments is now curtailed by the operation of international finance and by the spread of information technologies – and is therefore willing to be supine when confronted by what it regards, in Stuart Hall's words, as an 'implacable Force of Nature'.[38] Having subscribed to free-market orthodoxy about the error of tampering with a natural harmony of economic interests, the Labour government has restricted itself to the task of equipping citizens for their activity as competitors in the global marketplace. And whereas Thatcherites at least depicted the mission of tutoring British people in the vigorous virtues as preparation for yet another glorious national adventure, the Blair government assumes that adjustment to international imperatives is an issue of prudent management rather than some grand endeavour. According to David Marquand, another critic of the left, though from outside the stable of the contributors to *Marxism Today*, Tony Blair's rhetoric is that of 'a management consultant, advising a company to redesign its products, not of a political leader, mobilising his followers for a rendezvous with destiny'.[39]

The Blair government has certainly justified fiscal rectitude by emphasising Britain's entanglement in the international economy, and the left may have a point in censuring New Labour for being more concerned to preserve incentives for entrepreneurial dynamism than to embark upon a programme of redistributive taxation – even though the criticism seems odd from contributors to *Marxism Today*, who through the 1980s chastised Old Labour for failing to adjust to the realities of globalisation. As an assessment of Blairism as an ideology, however, this sort of analysis is inadequate. The problem stems from the tendency to conflate the political and ideological projects of New Labour. Politically, Blairism may indeed be engaged in the modest enterprise of conscripting people to forces beyond the control of the nation-state. Ideologically, however, New Labour has sold its ambition to modernise the British state as yet another grand rendezvous with destiny, and there is no reason to suppose that Blairites are determined to cut themselves adrift from those ideological discourses which political parties have persistently used in their appeal to the electorate.

In no way do the ideological contours of Blairism mark a radical departure from the familiar postwar mapping of decline. There is the same use of British exceptionalism to summon the nation to resume its place in the international vanguard on the hard road to paradise. Blair's speeches are full of reassurances that the relative historical autonomy of the British state provides a deep well of resources that can be drawn upon in responding to fresh challenges of modernisation. Post-imperial Britain may not be the biggest or mightiest nation but it can still be the 'best', 'the model 21st century nation, a beacon to the world'. Britain has pioneered many of the new technologies, and the characteristics of an ancestral and successful people will ensure that it remains a global pathfinder:

> From the Magna Carta to the first Parliament to the industrial revolution to an empire that covered the world; most of the great inventions of modern times with Britain stamped on them: the telephone; the television; the computer; penicillin; the hovercraft; radar.
> Change is in the blood and bones of the British – we are by our nature and tradition innovators, adventurers, pioneers . . .
> Even today, we lead the world, in design, pharmaceuticals, financial services, telecommunications. We have the world's first language.[40]

The nation will be transported into a glorious future by the same indigenous attributes which ensured its ascent for a millennium.

'Building the greatness of our nation through the greatness of its people',[41] however, requires resolute statecraft to remove obstacles to renewal. The irenic Blair is less ferocious than Thatcher about the enemies within who must be vanquished if Britain is to rise to the challenge of modernisation. They are nevertheless identified. There are the 'fatalists', condemned by Thatcher, who spread the message that Britain has lost the race to be a 'pivotal' influence in the world; and there is also the old guard, berated by Harold Wilson, who would stifle the innovative British spirit by clinging to 'old boy networks', 'cosy cartels', a divisive educational system and all the other manifestations of an antiquated class structure: 'these are Labour's enemies'.[42]

New Labour promises to pilot the nation through the choppy waters of globalisation neither by anchoring it to a natural economic order, as Thatcherites were intent on doing, nor by resorting to quasi-Fabian statism, as was the wont of Old Labour, but by a 'third way' which will repair the social fabric torn by the 'two nations' dogma of the New Right. And this requires a revitalised civil society in which all citizens, conscious of their rights and responsibilities, will engage in a common endeavour of national reinvigoration. The nation is called to respond to the challenge of modernisation by means of a progressivist narrative that celebrates the long struggle, in which liberals and other radicals as well as socialists have participated, to make the country a place where everyone can feel a citizen with a 'stake' in the public good. 'We are part of the broad movement of human progress. The marriage of ambition with justice, the constant striving of the human spirit to do better and better. It is that which separates us from Conservatives'.[43] With a 'people's party' at the helm of a nation united by 'the strength of our character' and by policies that cultivate a strong sense of civic virtue, Britain will safely 'navigate' through the turbulence of globalisation.[44]

Living in an old country provides politicians with abundant opportunity to distance themselves from the historiography of British decline. There is nothing startling in the fact that Labour, no less than the Conservative Party, should articulate a robust nationalism when appealing to the electorate. The only surprise is that so many commentators of the left are naïve enough to suppose that a serious political party would rush to discard the ideological discourses fashioned from an *ancien régime*.[45]

Commentators in search of the origins of 'the present crisis' have assembled a mass of evidence to demonstrate the malady of British culture and 'the decline of the industrial spirit'.[46] When dealing with ideology their assumption tends to be either that British backwardness has induced a sense of anxiety in the national psyche or that the cultural sediments of an old imperialist state have been a brake to modernisation. What they neglect is the distance of ideological utterances from the analysis of economic decrepitude. Perhaps the issue which ought to be addressed is not why Britain has long been in decline, but the extent to which the ideological buoyancy generated by its exceptionalism has made the nation more at ease with itself than is warranted by any objective criteria as well as giving it the confidence to remain, if not a global leader, a not insignificant player on the world stage.

Notes

1. A. Gamble, 'The Decline of Britain', *Contemporary Record*, vol. 2 (Spring 1989), pp. 18–21.
2. E.J.P. Benn, *Benn's Protest: Being an Argument for the Restoration of our Liberties* (London, 1945), p. 110.
3. D. Cannadine, 'Apocalypse When? British Politicians and British 'Decline' in the Twentieth Century', in P. Clarke and C. Trebilcock (eds), *Understanding Decline: Perceptions and Realities of British Economic Performance* (Cambridge, 1997), p. 284.
4. S. Hall, *The Hard Road to Renewal: Thatcherism and the Crisis of the Left* (London, 1988), p. 9.
5. H. Wilson, 'A First-Class nation', in *The New Britain: Labour's plan* (Harmondsworth, 1964), pp. 42–56.
6. T. Blair, '*Speech at the Labour Party Annual Conference* (London, 1996), p. 14.
7. The distinction made between the historiography and the ideology of decline will not be to everyone's taste. Much of the academic literature about decline is itself ideological, while strictly there is no such phenomenon as the ideology of decline or 'declinism' but rather various articulations of the problem of British backwardness within ideological discourses. The distinction is intended to highlight, if a touch simplistically, two divergent approaches to the 'British disease' which I think commentators have tended to conflate.
8. B. Supple, 'Introduction: National Performance in a Personal Perspective', in P. Clarke and C. Trebilcock (eds), *Understanding Decline*, p. 10.
9. H. Wilson, *The New Britain*, pp. 10–13, 40–1.
10. T. Blair, 'My Vision for Britain', in G. Radice (ed.), *What Needs to Change: New Visions for Britain* (London, 1996), p. 7.
11. R.A. Butler, 'About the Industrial Charter', in *Conservatism 1945–1950* (London, 1950), p. 45.
12. R.A. Butler, *Our Way Ahead* (London, 1956), p. 11.
13. R.A. Butler, *Address . . . Delivered in the St Andrew's Hall* (Glasgow, 1958), p. 5.
14. Viscount Hailsham, *Toryism and Tomorrow* (London, 1957), pp. 10, 23.
15. R. Butler, *Our Way Ahead*, pp. 18–19.
16. J. Darwin, 'British Decolonization since 1945: A Pattern or a Puzzle?', *Journal of Imperial and Commonwealth History*, vol. 13 (1983), p. 189.

17. G. Hutton, 'The Ruin in the Nation', in *Rebirth of Britain: A Symposium of Essays by Eighteen Writers* (London, 1964), p. 29.
18. E. Powell, 'Is it Politically Practicable?', in *Rebirth of Britain*, p. 259.
19. H. Dalton, 'Our Financial Plan', in *Forward From Victory! Labour's Plan Based on Six Essays Prepared by the Fabian Society* (London, 1946), p. 50.
20. R. Samuel, *Island Stories: Unravelling Britain. Theatres of Memory*, Vol. II (London, 1998), p. 251.
21. R. Jenkins, *The Labour Case* (Harmondsworth, 1959), pp. 9–12.
22. R.H.S. Crossman, *Planning for Freedom* (London, 1965), pp. 134–47.
23. H. Wilson, *The Relevance of British Socialism* (London, 1964), p. 9.
24. H. Wilson, *The Relevance of British Socialism*, p. 99.
25. H. Wilson, *The New Britain*, p. 132.
26. H. Wilson, *The Relevance of Socialism*, p. 17.
27. H. Wilson, *The New Britain*, p. 47.
28. M. Kenny, 'Harold Wilson', in R. Eccleshall and G. Walker (eds), *Biographical Dictionary of British Prime Ministers* (London, 1998), p. 340.
29. E. Heath, *Conservatives and Industry* (London, 1970), p. 8.
30. R. Boyson, 'Right Turn', in R. Boyson (ed.), *Right Turn: A Symposium on the Need to End the 'Progressive' Consensus in British Thinking and Policy* (London, 1970), p. 10.
31. M. Thatcher, 'Britain's Era of Enterprise', *Reader's Digest*, December 1983, pp. 24–5.
32. M. Thatcher, *Speech . . . at the 58th Conservative Women's National Conference* (London, 1988), p. 12.
33. K. Joseph, *Stranded on the Middle Ground? Reflections on Circumstances and Policies* (London, 1976), p. 79.
34. G. Howe, *Conservatism in the Eighties* (London, 1982), p. 6.
35. See, for example, D. Howell, *Freedom and Capital: Prospects for the Property-Owning Democracy* (Oxford, 1981), pp. 23–5.
36. N. Lawson, *What's Right with Britain* (London, 1982), pp. 4–5, 8.
37. M. Thatcher, *The Revival of Britain: Speeches on Home and European Affairs 1975–1988* (London, 1989), pp. 160–4.
38. S. Hall, 'The great moving nowhere show', *Marxism Today*, November/ December 1998, p. 11.
39. D. Marquand, 'Can Labour Kick the Winning Habit?', *New Statesman*, 23 October 1998, p. 26.
40. T. Blair, *Speech at the Labour Party Annual Conference* (London, 1997), pp. 1, 7.
41. T. Blair, *Speech at the Labour Party Annual Conference* (London, 1996), p. 14.
42. T. Blair, *The Third Way: New Politics for the New Century* (London, 1998), p. 4; *Speech at the Party Annual Conference* (London, 1997), p. 17; 'Power for a Purpose', *Renewal*, 3 (1995), p. 13.
43. T. Blair, *Speech at the Party Annual Conference* (London, 1996), p. 12.
44. T. Blair, *Speech at the Party Annual Party Conference* (London, 1997), p. 19; 'My vision for Britain', in G. Radice, *What Needs to Change*, p. 16.

45. For an exception see A. Finlayson, 'Tony Blair and the Jargon of Modernisation', *Soundings*, vol. 10 (1998), pp. 11–27.
43. M.J. Wiener, *English Culture and the Decline of the Industrial Spirit 1850–1980* (Harmondsworth, 1992; 1st edn, 1981).

12

Institutional Approaches to Britain's Relative Economic Decline

MARTIN J. SMITH

Some of the most prominent and influential explanations of Britain's economic decline focus on the role of institutions. However, various analysts take a very different approach to what constitutes an institution, and to how institutions affect the issue of decline. There is no single agreement on what constitutes institutionalism as either a method or an explanation.[1] There are, subsequently, a large number of institutional accounts of Britain's decline that focus on a range of institutions and different elements of the relationships between institutions. This chapter examines the various institutional accounts of Britain's decline. It points out that whilst institutional approaches are very different and often focus on different phenomena, they also share much in their explanation of Britain's decline. Rather than analysing particular institutional explanations, it examines the common institutional variables these authors use to explain Britain's decline. The chapter demonstrates that whilst there is much to commend the institutional approach, it does have a number of problems. In particular, there is a tendency for institutional prescriptions for reform to ignore institutional analysis of decline. The chapter begins by defining institutionalism.

There is currently much dispute in the social science literature concerning the nature of institutionalism.[2] Hall and Taylor[3] argue that institutionalism 'does not constitute a unified body' and indeed that 'at least three different analytical approaches, each of which calls itself "a new institutionalism" have appeared in the last fifteen years'. Institutional accounts cover a vast array of different methodologies and theoretical accounts of politics. There are at least four broad forms of instituional-ism: first, structural accounts derived from Marxist approaches analyse how the institutions of the state and the structured relations between classes influence and constrain policy options; second, 'old institution-alism' concentrates directly on the impact of formal political institu-tions such as parliament, the civil service and the executive on policy makers and policy outcomes;[4] thirdly, 'new institutionalism' sees insti-tutions in a broad sense of the values, cultures and the 'rules of the game' of organisations which create a particular social reality and so it examines how these norms limit the possible options;[5] finally, rational choice institutionalism acknowledges the role of institutions in deter-mining preferences and examines how institutions affect the choice of rational actors.[6]

Despite differences in the methods and definitions of these various forms of institutionalism, there are a number of shared assumptions within what might be called an institutional position. Institutional accounts are based on the premise that institutions, however defined, do matter.[7] Institutions are not just the sum of human behaviour. For insti-tutionalists they affect the way humans act. Institutionalism sees human interests and behaviours as exogenously affected by the institutional context. Consequently, institutional methodology involves investigating the formation, action and influence of institutions. In explaining out-comes the focus of institutionalism is not on the actions of individuals but on the impact of institutions on individuals. This is not to say that individuals do not matter. Following Giddens,[8] individuals create insti-tutions through recreating organisational rules, but they are also reflex-ive. They have the ability, if not always the resources, to reflect on rules and so change them. As a result they can change institutions.

Institutional accounts vary between those that are institutional in the strict sense (concentrating on the impact of formal institutions) and 'new institutionalism' (which focuses on institutions more broadly, analysing the structure of relationships that exist between actors either through organisations or values). These different forms of institutional-ism have produced a range of accounts of Britain's decline. This chap-ter will highlight how various institutional accounts have focused on different elements in explaining decline. Nevertheless it will show that despite very different methods and definitions there are a number of shared elements in institutional accounts of decline.

Whilst many explanations of Britain's decline focus on the impact both of institutions and the institutionalisation of various forms of behaviour, few explicitly call themselves institutionalist. Anderson and Nairn's explanation is largely neo-Marxist;[9] Finer and Middlemas provide accounts that derive from mainstream history and political science[10] whilst Olson is a rational choice theorist.[11] However, what is clear is that all these accounts do examine how institutions have affected Britain's economic performance, and despite coming from very different traditions they do share certain assumptions concerning Britain's decline. For the sake of simplicity it is possible to identify four different ways in which institutions are used to explain British decline but as the chapter demonstrates there is considerable overlap between these approaches.

Institutional accounts of decline can be roughly characterised as follows. First, one of the most influential institutionalist accounts is that developed by Anderson and Nairn but reflected in the work of many others such as Wiener and Hutton.[12] This view sees Britain's decline deriving from the maintenance of an *ancien régime* combining a premodern state, an anti-industrial commercial class and the remnants of the landed aristocracy. Second, and strongly overlapping with the Nairn/Anderson thesis, are explanations based on the nature of the British state. Following Dyson's[13] argument that Britain is a weak state, it is argued by a number of authors[14] that the British state never developed the capabilities to implement a coherent industrial policy that would enable Britain to adjust to the demands of the postwar era. Third, a different form of a state-centred argument is the adversarial politics explanation.[15] This sees economic decline deriving from the conflict that is inherent in the British political system as a result of the combination of parliamentary sovereignty and the electoral system producing disciplined parties. Fourth, one important institutional rational choice explanation of Britain's decline is Olson's argument concerning the impact of interest groups on Britain's economic performance. This has been developed in a more polemical and normative fashion by those concerned with government overload.[16]

Despite the range and variation of institutional accounts of decline, these perspectives do have much in common and frequently use a common set of variables to explain Britain's supposed economic malaise. Institutionalists tend to focus on Britain's historical context and how it has shaped the nature of the state and its relationships to the outside world and to civil society. For institutional accounts, to explain decline it is necessary to understand the British state and the structure of its relationships with other institutions and actors. The following section of this chapter will focus on the common elements in institutional analysis demonstrating how different accounts focus on path dependency, the nature of the state, the role of the City of London, and Britain's relationship with the world.

Path Dependency

A key feature of various forms of institutional accounts is the notion of path-dependency. By making a particular choice in the past, future actors are prevented from making certain decisions later because institutions (the institutionalisation of past policy choices) bias later options.[17] By industrialising without a strong state and therefore not creating the machinery to intervene in industry, it is more difficult for later policy-makers to decide to become involved in detailed intervention. The ideological and institutional structures set the agenda for later economic decisions. According to Gamble:

> The history of external expansion and internal compromise ... left important legacies and allowed the accumulation of specific internal weaknesses. The legacies were the patterns of external dependence of the British economy and the international orientation of the British state and British business. The weaknesses were the institutional organisation of the principal classes and interests, and their relations to the state. In the social democratic era that opened in 1940 the interaction of these two elements established the constraints within which government operated.[18]

The ways in which these path-dependencies have been conceived has varied greatly in different forms of institutional accounts.

Nairn and Anderson's famous account of decline focuses on the ways in which the maintenance of the *ancien régime* in the nineteenth century, despite the process of industrialisation, set Britain on a path which prevented political and economic modernisation into the late twentieth century. For Anderson and Nairn, Britain's crisis is linked inextricably to features and events that unfolded in the nineteenth century. Unlike Britain's European counterparts, Britain never experienced a revolution that destroyed the aristocracy and its attendant state organisation. The industrial bourgeoisie gained political power without undermining the *ancien régime*. For Anderson, the absence of a thorough bourgeois revolution meant that the bourgeoisie was incorporated into the aristocracy rather than overthrowing it. The capitalist class developed from within the aristocracy and no purely industrial class has developed. Therefore the interests of capitalists have always been overlaid with those of the old regime and the political subordination of industrial capital. The result has been the development of a commercial class concerned with land and the City and not the grubby world of manufacturing industry. Nairn claims that:

> one may read the history of late nineteenth century Britain as first the containment, then the defeat of industrialism by an older more powerful and more political bourgeoisie. This was of course, the southern, London-based elite, first mercantile and then financial in its interests, which during this epoch built up about itself what Rubinstein calls 'its London-based associates of great influence in twentieth-century society, like the Civil Service and the professions – the familiar Establishment of fact and fiction'. This strong hegemonic bloc then colonized and took over the growing state power of the Edwardian decade and afterwards.[19]

As Britain industrialised it was the City, not industry, that was handed the mantle of the aristocracy's cultural, political and economic hegemony. With the ease of transition from agricultural to industrial society, the bourgoisie gained entry to the political system without any structural change in the state. Through this evolutionary process of co-option and adaptation, the landed classes were able to retain considerable influence. Britain was condemned to developing modern industry with a premodern state and later fell behind its competitors who had adapted their states to the needs of the twentieth century. For Hutton this indicates that the Conservative ruling class was never really removed from office. It was protected by a:

> self-reinforcing network – monarch, church, the law, the City, the army and the landed aristocracy – [which] came to represent the gentlemanly ideal and thus England itself. Educated in the main at the great public schools, its denizens were above and not part of society. They shared a similar world view and spoke a common language . . .[20]

Their culture, because it was aristocratic and landed, was anti-industrial. Business was seen as dirty and lowly and those who aspired to mobility looked to the land and the City, or perhaps Whitehall.[21] In Nairn's[22] view this culture is hegemonic and exists in order to prevent a modernisation process that could undermine the privileges of the ruling elite.

A very different path-dependency account is offered by Elbaum and Lazonick, who focus on the institutionalisation of particular production techniques. They attribute:

the decline of the British economy in the twentieth century to rigidities in the economic and social institutions that developed during the nineteenth century, a period when Britain was the world's leading economic power and British industry was highly atomistic and competitive in organisation.

These institutional structures in terms of patterns of ownership, relationships with banks and poor management training 'constrained the transformation of Britain's productive system'. In Britain competitive capitalism was institutionalised, whilst in the USA, Japan and Germany corporate capitalism 'characterised by industrial oligopoly, hierarchical managerial bureaucracy, vertical integration of production and distribution' created the conditions for the development of large-scale, modern industry.[23] A similar argument is also developed by Hobsbawm, who highlights how industrial adjustment was irrational in the context of imperial markets which ensured returns without additional investment.[24]

Whilst Anderson and Nairn, and Elbaum and Lazonick, have offered very different accounts of decline, they are all concerned with how the processes and decisions of the nineteenth century became institutionalised and therefore affected the choices of decision-makers in the twentieth century. Whilst there is much that is convincing in these historical arguments, there are a number of problems. Anderson sees British capitalist development as peculiar, but this pejorative sense of peculiarity only derives from Marxist or historicist perspectives that see state/society complexes developing in particular ways. If we see history as particular there is nothing peculiar about Britain (any more than any other nation). Britain's history is Britain's history; the state and the economy took the form they did because of the conditions of Britain's industrialisation, which affected economic development into the twentieth century. What Anderson provides is a normative account of the British state rather than an analysis of Britain's economic growth that presumes, within a structural account, that the ruling elite had choices and options and could have seen the error of their ways, and so prepared Britain for the late twentieth century.

There is also little evidence that the ruling class in Britain was any more aristocratic than the ruling class in other countries. It was the Prussian aristocracy that was behind much of the industrialisation in Germany. As Barrington Moore[25] highlighted, Japanese and German modernisation were revolutions from above without any real break with the past. Likewise, whilst the British state may in many ways seem premodern, it is indeed more modern than many other societies. Britain is a largely industrial and urban society where there is very little day-today connection with the land – much less so than in France, Spain or even Germany. Britain in many ways has adapted more to industrialism than most other societies. With the Northcote–Trevelyan reforms in the mid-nineteenth century, Britain established a professional, meritocratic and largely non-corrupt civil service. In doing so it created a professional ethic that allowed it to challenge some of the more class-based and ideological policies of politicians.[26] This was part of a wider change in the British state during the nineteenth century that saw the shift from Parliamentary government (which was largely dominated by landed interests) to executive government. This change created an arena within which complex economic decisions could be taken and then implemented by a professional bureaucracy. Perkin illustrates how new classes did become institutionalised in the political and social structure and avers: 'By mid-century the entrepreneurial class could feel well pleased with the new society which they had created and persuaded the other classes to accept'.[27]

Wiener emphasises not so much the nature of the state but the value system underpinning it and suffusing the ruling class, and he sees the rural and anti-industrial idyll as the core aspiration of the ruling class. The problem with this approach is the assumption that the desires for rurality amongst Britain's elite were greater than in any other industrial nation. Rubinstein[28] makes the point that every cultural system in the world is anti-business and anti-capitalist. There is indeed little evidence that this failure of the bourgeois revolution or the pre-eminence of non-industrial values stopped Britain industrialising or developing a large manufacturing base. Moreover, Wiener does not demonstrate the causal relationship between Britain's culture and economic decline.[29] The British aristocracy may value the rural but in a society where industry is so important it is difficult to sustain an argument that it has stopped industrial development.

According to Johnson, E. P. Thompson characterised the nature of nineteenth-century hegemony in a very different way. For Thompson, the landed aristocracy was not hegemonic but was exercising power in the interests of industrial bourgeoisie. What Anderson and Nairn provide is a history of failure when the reality is one of success – of a class that is very adept at protecting its economic and political interests as the aristocracy decline and the working class are on the whole excluded.[30] Much of the Nairn/Anderson thesis is based on the presumption that the aristocracy remained dominant. Whilst this argument may have had more resonance in the early 1960s, when Anderson first wrote on decline, the shifting nature of the Conservative Party and the petit bourgeois character of its recent leaders does not seem to sustain the idea of aristocratic hegemony into the 1990s.

Turning briefly to Elbaum and Lazonick's account, it is true that many industries suffered from institutional rigidities, but it is very difficult to apply this thesis to the British economy as a whole. Kirby[31] indicates how in a number of very traditional industries such as steel and shipbuilding there are examples of industries undergoing significant technical and organisational change. This suggests that Elbaum and Lazonick's account cannot provide a generalisable explanation of Britain's decline. Despite their claims, many British industries have been highly innovative and competitive worldwide. In the 1930s, in particular, a whole range of light industries developed to replace the increasingly inefficient nineteenth-century industries. Indeed Harris[32] suggests that this was largely a result of the attempt to create corporate capitalism of the kind that existed in other nations.

To understand Britain's decline it is important to understand the particular patterns of British history and how past decisions influence present day options. Nevertheless there is a tendency to overgeneralise in historical explanations and to assume that Britain is exceptional in relation to the rest of the industrialised world. Moreover, many historical accounts do not explain the causal links between past behaviour, old state forms and contemporary problems. What is crucial about the notion of path-dependency is that it underpins all other institutional approaches. In particular, when we examine the role of the state, it is apparent that its nature very much reflects past actions and choices.

The Nature of the British State

An important variable that is clearly related to historical developments and which is central to most institutional accounts is the nature of the British state. Whilst some institutional accounts focus on formal institutions such as Parliament and the civil service, and others look more widely at the nature of the British state, all agree that the form of the state has prevented the development of the capabilities to intervene in the economy in order to develop a modernising industrial policy. The predominent concern of the state has not been with industrial policy but with maintaining the market (a *laissez-faire* approach). Because of the institutionalisation of this ideology and the absence of a culture of, or machinery for, intervention, later attempts at increased state intervention failed.

The weakness of the British state has been explained in terms of a

number of factors. Crucially, Britain's early and self-motivated industrialisation made state-led development unnecessary. Economic development appears to have been spontaneous and without external competition and so the state had no incentive to protect the home market or
subsidise production for export. What capitalists desired was state facil-
itation, not involvement in their industries. Moreover, the requirement
for raw materials and access to overseas markets strengthened the
desire for free trade. The *laissez-faire*/free trade ethos was institutionalised both within the British state and in the attitudes of economic
groups to the British state. For Grant and Wilks, 'The *laissez-faire*
compulsion has proved astonishingly powerful',[33] so even when economic circumstances changed and Britain faced more competition there
was neither the desire nor the ability to increase state intervention or
introduce protectionism. All shades of government have been reluctant
to intervene in industry in any systematic way. Nairn and Anderson
suggest that this reluctance about intervention derives from the maintenance of a premodern state that did not develop the professional civil
service or administrative machinery necessary to accommodate and
implement economic intervention. Zysman supports this position by
pointing to civil servants' lack of experience or knowledge of industry.
Consequently, 'Interventionist policies run against the training and traditions of the civil service'.[34]

Whilst the civil service is seen in several accounts as limiting the
industrial capacities of the state,[35] more particular blame is placed on
the Treasury. The latter is seen as pursuing policies inimical to economic growth. The Treasury is probably the strongest department within the
British core executive and it has almost a complete monopoly on economic and public expenditure policy. Consequently, its impact on economic policy has been much greater than departments such as Trade
and Industry or Employment which tend to be more concerned with the
interests of manufacturing. The result has been an economic policy
dominated by what Pollard[36] calls the 'Treasury view': an over-anxious
concern with inflation and the balance of payments. These preoccupations have a detrimental effect on the economy. The Treasury's focus
has been concentrated largely on macro-economic policy rather than
micro-economic industrial policy, and on demand measures such as
taxation and overall public expenditure rather than supply-side policy
to improve the production of goods. At the same time, even macro-economic policy goals such as sustained demand to stimulate growth are
repeatedly sacrificed to the goals of low inflation and reducing imports.
Pollard's argument accounts for the ever-present stop-go cycle.

Because supply-side problems were never tackled, increases in demand produced more imports and higher inflation which led to cuts in public expenditure and increased taxation to cool down the economy. This view has developed as a result of the Treasury's concerns with the interests of the City, which favours low interest rates, rather than with manufacturing production, which favours sustained demand.

An alternative conception of the problems created by the nature of the British state concerns the notion of the 'Westminster model of British Government'.[37] The Westminster model was the dominant conception of the British state amongst academics until the 1970s and remains so amongst politicians up to the present day.[38] It is based on the presumption that authority within the British political system lies with the crown-in-parliament. Parliament is sovereign – it is the final arbitrator in terms of legislative decisions; there is no higher authority. With the development of strong, disciplined parties Parliamentary sovereignty has effectively become executive dominance of the political system in a highly centralised state. The problems of this highly-centralised, party dominated system are two-fold.

The centralised nature of the British state with its monocratic view of decision-making and its inability to share power, creates great difficulty in terms of intervening in the economy. If the executive is unable to share power and is generally unwilling to negotiate on policy, it is extremely difficult to create the arrangement where groups and the state work together in order to develop a modernising industrial policy.[39] The Westminster model presumes that economic policy is made within the executive and implemented by Whitehall and so power sharing with economic interests is neither necessary nor desirable. For Hutton the dominance of the Westminster model means that:

> British public authority is incapable of being anything other than top-down and centralised. Constructive forms of intervention and public/private partnerships, used in other capitalist countries to capture the gains from co-operation, have worked much less well in Britain. The state has developed a rentier culture that complements 'gentlemanly capitalism', in which the state stresses the financial targets over investment and production.[40]

Hutton's position emphasises the link between the historical and state-centred approaches. The failure of a bourgeois revolution and the lack of state directed industrialisation created a state without the means or desire to intervene in the economy and so entrenched the aristocratic and City values of financial capital and overseas trade.

The second consequence of the Westminster model has been to

encourage adversarial politics. The argument concerning adversarial politics is developed at three levels: party; state/civil society; and management/labour. From this perspective the ideological and adversarial nature of British politics, which derives from the first-past-the-post electoral system and the nature of parliamentary sovereignty, means that parties find it unnecessary and to some extent undesirable to compromise. The consequence of the winner-takes-all nature of the electoral and parliamentary systems is parties disagreeing over policy not out of fundamental opposition but because of the electoral need to be seen as different. When there is a change of government, there is a change of policy. The consequence is that industry cannot make long-term investment plans because even medium-term economic policy is unknown. One obvious example is the continual nationalisation and denationalisation of the steel industry. This situation is exacerbated by the electoral cycle. The first-past-the-post system implies that governments are concerned with winning a majority of seats and therefore economic policies are aimed at winning elections by producing a boom at election time rather than doing what it best for the economy. Electoral considerations explain why the economy is continually plagued by a boom and bust cycle as re-elected governments correct the inflationary tendencies of the pre-election period.

The adversarial nature of politics is reflected in relationships between the state and society. The relationship between groups and government is not one of cooperation, as in some Christian Democratic and East Asian traditions, but one where groups pressurise government for their own sectional goals and government imposes policies on groups against their will. These relationships are replicated in that between capital and labour which is continually characterised as one of exploitation rather than cooperation. Consequently, the role of employer is to gain labour for least cost and for unions to achieve the best possible wage increases regardless of the impact on the firm or the economy more widely. There is a strong thread between the adversarial politics thesis and the stakeholding concept. Both see economic policy as being based on conflict rather than working together and creating loyalty within economic organisations.

The weakness of the British state in terms of the economy is illustrated by a brief review of its industrial policies. Britain's postwar industrial policy is a succession of failed attempts at state-led development. At the end of the Second World War Britain did have some of the necessary means for planning industrial growth. However, the response of the Labour government was not to build on this machinery but rather to initiate a 'bonfire of controls'.[41] Until the late 1950s governments followed large *laissez-faire* industrial policies within the context of demand management for macro-economic policy. When Britain's relative decline was first becoming apparent in the late 1950s there was increased interest in the indicative planning of France. In order to catch up, Harold Macmillan, in 1959, set up the National Economic Development Council. However, the NEDC lacked any of the necessary teeth for planning and remained largely an arena for discussion rather than the source of effective action.[42]

The Labour government of 1964 attempted to take planning and industrial policy further with the creation of the Department of Economic Affairs and the publication of a national plan. This attempt at intervention was destroyed by the concern of the government with deflation and the value of sterling, rather than its efforts to modernise industry and the unwillingness of the Treasury to forgo any economic power.[43] In the 1970s further attempts were made at constructing effective industrial policy but rather than being positive modernisation programmes these collapsed into measures for bailing out ailing sectors of British industry.[44] Repeatedly, the British state failed to develop either the administrative machinery or the necessary relationships with civil society to develop a coherent, modernising industrial policy that was more than a response to crisis.

This is a theme revisited in the work of Marquand and Hutton. They see Britain's economic failings as deriving from the inability to build a 'developmental' state. Marquand and Hutton look to the states of continental Europe and East Asia to demonstrate that there is an alternative to Anglo-Saxon capitalism. It is based on states that were prepared to intervene in the economy both directly and through facilitating cooperative relationships between industry, workers, banks and the state. Britain's political authorities have repeatedly failed to promote more adaptive economic behaviour.[45] The dominant view was that economic development is market-led. This nineteenth-century view of the state was no longer appropriate and a move to developmental intervention had to take place.

State-centred accounts have a certain intuitive appeal in understanding Britain's decline and they can, potentially, be substantiated by empirical evidence. Nevertheless, a number of problems are raised. Despite the claims of many analysts, the British state did grow substantially in the nineteenth and twentieth centuries. Both in terms of public expenditure and public employment it is comparable in size to other Western states.[46] Moreover, there has been a long tradition of a theoretical discourse concerned with the nature of the British state.[47] Indeed, Greenleaf[48] believes that the dominant ethos in Britain has been one of collectivism, and therefore state intervention, rather than *laissez-faire*.

Undoubtedly, the postwar British state, even after many years of Thatcherism, intervenes substantially in a large number of areas: particularly welfare, but also to a large degree in the economy.[49] The statists make two errors. First, they confuse the failure of intervention with an unwillingness to intervene. Postwar British economic policy has seen many occasions when the British state has tried to improve the competitiveness of the British state and developed many of the mechanisms of a developmental state from the National Economic Development Council (NEDC), to the Department of Economic Affairs (DEA), the Industrial Reorganisation Commission (IRC) and the National Enterprise Board (NEB). Various governments have established policies for encouraging mergers, investment and improved productivity. In the 1970s, sector working parties were created with representatives of government and industry to examine particular industries in order to find ways to overcome supply-side problems. These policies failed to end Britain's relative economic decline but they have been tried.

The second mistake is to treat the state as a unified object that is, or is not, developmental. The state *per se* is of limited analytic usefulness. It cannot act and cannot be explained. It represents a range of connected institutions, each with their own form and containing actors who carry out specific roles. Each institution – department or agency – has a particular pattern of development and its own *modus operandi*. Therefore it is impossible to say that Britain lacks an interventionist state or is dominated by *laissez-faire* because it depends on the department or agency concerned. The Board of Trade tended to be dominated by a *laissez-faire* ethos whilst the Ministry of Agriculture appears to have all the features of an interventionist state.[50] Likewise, Edgerton demonstrates how aircraft production has been encouraged to a large extent by the state.[51] Throughout the Department of Industry there was a strong preference towards protecting industries. The department contained a series of 'sponsorship divisions' which acted as advocates within the department for the industry and provided very close institutional contact between officials and industry.

It is difficult to make general claims about the growth of the British state. It has grown in various ways at different times for a range of reasons. The British state had, by the 1970s, become very large and interventionist. In 1978 one in 12 employees worked for public corporations and the government directly intervened in the running of many industries. 'Direct state provision of welfare state services has also made British social policy distinctive with only a minimal role for voluntary provision'. The state controls most provision of education and housing and 'the UK pattern of social insurance income maintenance has also focused on constructing a comprehensive set of universalised and fully tax-based benefits including pensions, unemployment insurance and "safety net" social security provision'.[52]

Within the developmental-state tradition, the British state is seen as both highly-centralised and little constrained and at the same time unable to intervene in the economy. Whilst this position seems somewhat contradictory, it is also a simplification. Although political authority in Britain is highly centralised, both the development and implementation of policy have been decentralised and largely fragmented. In a whole range of services much of the control and provision, at least until the 1980s, has been delivered at the local level. Much of the British political system is based on negotiation with service deliverers at the local level.[53] The problem may be that the British state is too fragmented rather than too centralised.

Marquand and Hutton seem to recognise the fragmentation, rather than the centralisation, of the state when they propose the creation of a developmental state. Developmental states tend to be highly-centralised and even authoritarian because they exist to impose industrialisation. Hence the notion of a developmental state is based on the imposition of a highly directive state on a society even when there may be no desire for industrialisation. Moreover there is little evidence that should such a state develop in Britain it would work. The developmental state worked in Japan because it related to its particular needs, economic circumstances and culture. Those conditions do not exist in modern-day Britain. With the blurring of the boundaries of national economies and national sites of production and with many states disengaging and liberalising, it is not evident that the sorts of developmental states that were relevant earlier in the century are appropriate to increasingly globalised and integrated economies. Moreover, many elements of a developmental state would not be legal within the context of European Union regulation.

The adversarial politics argument also provides a questionable account of Britain's decline. For whilst the rhetoric of British politics is one of conflict, the reality for much of the postwar period is consensus – or at least policy convergence. A detailed examination of postwar economic policy demonstrates that the significant changes in economic policy were not between governments of different complexion but rather occurred within governments.[54] The shift from *laissez-faire* to planning occurred under Macmillan and was continued, and later dropped, by the Labour Government of 1964–70. Edward Heath returned to intervention in 1972 and this approach was continued by the 1974 Labour Government until they shifted towards a monetarist policy in 1977–78. Changes in policy were not necessarily the cause of economic problems, but they could have been a response to economic failure.

The role of the state is crucial in understanding the nature of economic policy in Britain. There is fairly widespread agreement that Britain did not develop the capabilities for detailed economic intervention and this largely derived from the nature of Britain's economic development. However, to see the British state as anti-interventionist is a simplification. Different parts of the state, and governments at various times, have been highly interventionist. Perhaps the greater problem is not the lack of intervention but rather its nature, and it is often argued that this has been highly influenced by the relationship between the state and the City.

The Role of the City

The structure of relations between the state and the City is seen as one of the key elements in explaining Britain's economic problems and it is strongly related to Britain's historical development and imperial connections. Many analysts subscribe to what Stones calls the City Hegemony Thesis: Britain's manufacturing industry has been undermined by the hegemony of the City over economic policy, producing an economic policy which has served the interests of the City at the expense of industrial capital.[55] From this perspective the City has maintained its position by building a hegemonic bloc with other fractions of capital to ensure its dominance over productive capital.

The strength of this position is derived from the close links that the City has to the state through the Bank of England and through Britain's long-term commitment to the sterling area.[56] Sterling became a reserve currency due to overseas holdings of the pound. Consequently other countries held in principle more than the Bank of England could pay – liabilities were greater than holdings of sterling. The British government could not afford for the holders of sterling to sell and this explains why devaluation was never an option.[57] Fear of devaluation would have caused a run on the pound, thereby bankrupting Britain. So the City always had a lever over the British government – if the policies followed by the government did not satisfy the City, there would be a loss of confidence and the pound would collapse. This situation explains why Labour governments were forced to adopt policies which were in the interests of the City, and why the economic policies followed in Britain were concerned with low inflation and high interest rates. High interest rates protected the pound and increased the return to finance capital. Such a policy, however, was a constraint on industrial capital. Its economic interests could be better served by low interest rates (so borrowing for investment was cheaper); a low pound (reducing the price of exports) and more concern with growth than inflation.

Hutton takes a slightly different line on the role of the City, focusing not so much on the structure of the relationship between the City and the state – although he does see this as important – as the actual structure of the City. He argues that the way the capital markets have developed 'fails the corporate sector, affecting companies negatively at all stages of their life cycle'. The structure of the City produces the problem of short-termism because the Bank of England does not have a reserve 'float' and so is dependent on short-term money markets: 'The way the Bank of England manipulates and guarantees the vast short-term money markets is the first of many incentives that forces the banks into keeping their lending as short-term as they can'.[58]

This short-termism is exacerbated by the stockmarket, through which many British companies, unlike most other countries, raise finance. The stockmarket expects very high returns preventing companies developing over the long term and reinvesting their profits. Moreover, the nature of the stockmarket forces companies to be constantly on guard against the prospect of takeovers, and so both the stock market and companies do look very much to the short term. Investors are concerned with the best investments and companies are concerned with keeping shareholders happy. There is no long-term relationship between bankers and firms as exists in Japan and Germany.

The City has exerted a high degree of influence on Britain's economic policy but there are problems with equating its success with Britain's decline. Analysis of the role of the City places much blame on it when it is one of the most dynamic, innovative and competitive sectors of the British economy. The CBI and the Wilson committee[59] have argued that there has never been a shortage of finance for investment in Britain, and that the City will invest where there is a prospect of an adequate return on capital. The problem may be the nature of the investment opportunities rather than an unwillingness to invest.

Much of the analysis of the City assumes the existence of a coherent fraction of capital called finance capital and that its views are hegemonic. In reality, the relationships between finance and productive capital are much more complex than the City Hegemony Thesis allows. The City is one of the key owners of British industrial capital, particularly with the development of the large pension funds, and therefore members of 'finance capital' are on the boards of many industrial firms and have an interest in their success.[60] There is little evidence of agreement within the City on economic policy. For example, there is no unified view concerning Britain's participation in European monetary union.

The critics of the City argue that it has frequently opposed devaluation because it is against the interests of finance. However, when devaluation did occur in 1967 it was not an economic elixir but led to deflation to avoid the corresponding inflation and therefore increased unemployment. Consequently, Stones[61] argues that Wilson's failure to devalue was not a result of the hegemony of the City, but of his desire to maintain full employment. The strength of the City has undoubtedly distorted Britain's economic development but it is difficult to blame an economic success for Britain's economic problems.

Britain's External Orientation

The nature of the British state and the structure of the City to some extent derive from Britain's external orientation. Britain's economic and political dominance derived in large part from Britain's Empire. The central role of the Empire in economic development undoubtedly created a number of important path-dependencies. Crucial in terms of expanding the Empire and reaping the economic benefits was the development of free trade. Whilst this was economically advantageous when Britain had competitive advantage, it was an economic liability once other countries developed and could flood British markets. The access to other markets through enforced free trade also meant that British industrial development could occur without state direction and subsequently accounts for the *laissez-faire* tendency in economic policy.

Likewise, the international orientation created as a consequence of the Empire also led to a high degree of overseas investment by the City. Much of the City's concern has been with international companies rather than the domestic market. For instance, between 1860 and 1914 the value of British assets abroad increased from £235 million to £4 billion and this was at a time when Germany and the United States were investing greatly in their domestic industry.[62] Finally, the continuation of the empire in the postwar era led to a significantly higher degree of defence spending than all Britain's competitors except the United States.[63] The result was imperial overstretch[64] and money spent on the military and defence related industries rather than the domestic economy. The role of the Empire in the development of Britain underpins many of the aspects of the institutional organisation and is important in understanding how British institutions have developed in the way they did.

The Relationship between the State and Civil Society

Crucial to the institutional explanations of Britain's decline is the structure of relationships between groups and the state. However, different institutional accounts provide diametrically opposed views on the nature of the relationships between the state and civil society. There are broadly three types of explanation. The first suggests that, due to the power of capital and labour, the British state attempted to incorporate groups into the British state and this created a 'corporate bias'. This relationship was undermined in the 1960s due to economic pressures and consequently the breakdown exacerbated the problems of political and economic management.[65] The second sees the British state as having difficulty establishing regularised and consensual relationships with pressure groups,[66] and this has limited the state's ability to intervene in the economy. A final approach is associated with institutional rational choice theorists who maintain that relationships between groups and the state have become institutionalised in ways that enable special interests to dominate the policy process and so prevent economic change and create governmental overload.[67] All these positions are based on the presumption that interest groups in Britain – particularly those representing capital and labour – are strong. Nevertheless, they provide very different interpretations of how the state has dealt with this power.

Middlemas argues that following the 1926 general strike, the British state dealt with class conflict by incorporating both representatives of capital and labour into the British state, and details how, particularly during the Second World War, outsiders were given prominent roles in government and an important input into wartime policy. This led to the emergence of 'corporate bias': 'the tendency for industry, trade unions and financial institutions to make reciprocal arrangements with each other and with government while avoiding conflict'.[68] Economic interest groups became 'governing institutions' as trade unions and business were incorporated into many levels of government through positions on advisory boards, Quangos, royal commissions and direct contact with both officials and ministers. By 1966, the CBI was represented on 57 advisory bodies including organisations like ACAS, the NEDC and the price commission. More generally, Middlemas maintains that in the postwar period, the main centre of activity returned to an informal network of contacts between the TUC, the British Employers Confederation and the government. Nevertheless, under the strains of the 1960s economic problems this relationship began to break down as unions, government and employers disagreed over the means of solving Britain's economic problems and fought over the distribution of declining resources.

Hall sees a similar problem in slightly different terms. He argues that whilst British trade unions and businesses are strong at the local level, their peak organisations are weak. Hall accepts Middlemas's argument that the strength of the trade unions forced the government to create the conditions for industrial peace. For Hall, rather than this power resulting in the incorporation of the trade unions, unions and business supported voluntarism and *laissez-faire*. They wanted government to provide the framework for industrial relations and industrial policy but not to be involved in the detail. At the same time government was happy to remain aloof from difficult political problems. The combination of strong local organisations and weak peak organisations with a voluntarist and *laissez-faire* ideology 'prevented the state from using these associations to impose industrial reorganisation on their members, as nations with more corporatist industrial arrangements were able to do'.[69] The lack of corporatist institutions was an important loss of capability for the British state. As Mann[70] has indicated, close, stable relationships with groups in civil society are important forms of infrastructural power. By not establishing integrated relationships with interest groups the state lost the ability to intervene in the economy and to restructure when new economic challenges developed.

A very different interpretation of the role of interest groups is developed within a framework of institutional rational choice. Put simply, Olson[71] maintains that interest groups are concerned with protecting their special interests through developing distributional coalitions. These coalitions slow down the adoption of new technologies and so retard the ability of societies to adapt to new economic conditions. This produces slower economic growth. Therefore Britain, with the longest period without dictatorship or growth, will suffer low rates of growth, given the uninterrupted period in which such groups had grown in influence. This argument has been developed in a more normative form by the proponents of overload.[72] Many on the new right in the 1970s believed that Britain's economic problems were due to the actions of special interests who were concerned with increasing public expenditure for their members and protecting their own privileges. The result was sclerosis of the state and society, making politicians unable to adapt to the economic condition resulting from the oil crisis and the collapse of Bretton Woods.

There are empirical problems with the rational-choice argument. Britain never developed the sorts of corporatist arrangements that existed in the rest of continental Europe and which do not appear to have damaged their economic growth in the postwar era. Grant[73] suggests that dictatorship and military defeat in Germany did not necessarily undermine the relationships between business groups and the state. Many of the state–business links in Germany were established at the end of the nineteenth century and remain in existence today.

Two important points emerge from these interpretations of the impact of the relationships between the state and civil society. First, all the accounts at least implicitly accept that the adversarial nature of the relationships between groups and the state is very different from the more consensual attitudes that exist within Germany and Japan. Second, there is agreement that the 1970s saw a degree of interest group anarchy with a whole range of groups pressing government to deal with their problem or interest without there being any agreement over how these problems could be solved. However, the main problem with the focus on interest group intermediation is that these difficult relationships are more a consequence of decline than a cause.[74]

Institutional accounts of Britain's decline provide a convincing theoretical and empirically rich account of Britain's economic decline. Despite the criticisms raised of various aspects of institutional approaches throughout this chapter, they do provide a coherent picture of the relationship between Britain's historical development and the economic problems of the twentieth century. Britain's early economic development, assisted by an expanding Empire, allowed the economy to grow without the need for a strong state. A state developed with the capability to maintain free trade and free markets but without disrupting economic growth through regulation. This suited Britain well when there was a lack of economic competitors, a surfeit of untapped markets and sources of raw materials. It led to a dominant and internationally orientated financial sector with close contact with the economic powerhouse in the Treasury through a supportive Bank of England.

While this position was highly advantageous in the nineteenth century, it institutionalised a set of problems for the economic challenges of the twentieth century. When competitors developed behind the door of protection and with the aid of relatively strong states, Britain lacked the means of adaptation. The British state did not develop the administrative capabilities to intervene in the economy. The main economic ministry, the Treasury, was concerned with finance rather than industry and macro rather than micro-policy. An alternative to state machinery was to develop infrastructural power through developing networks with groups within civil society. This was made difficult by the Westminster orientation of British politics and its adversarial nature. There was no provision within the British system for decisions to be made outside Whitehall and Westminster through civil society. In addition, the adversarial nature of British politics created distrust between the Conservatives and the unions, and between Labour and the private sector. Unions saw state intervention as a prelude to reducing their rights in wage bargaining and business saw intervention as a prelude to nationalisation. These views produced conflict in economic policy and consequently economic interest groups preferred, if possible, to keep their distance from the state.

The precarious situation was made more difficult by Britain's external economic policy. Due to Britain's world role sterling had become a reserve currency. This position had advantages in terms of trade and borrowing but major disadvantages in terms of domestic industry. The overhang on Britain's liabilities prevented Britain from devaluing the currency without major economic consequence. Buoyed by the demands of the City, governments preferred high interest rates and low inflation as mechanisms for preserving the value of the pound, to a policy aimed at the needs of industry. Moreover, the need to contain inflation without a distinct industrial policy led to the stop–go economic policy that undermined the long-term confldence of industry.

Peter Hall demonstrates in his excellent account of Britain's economic policy how the configuration of institutions within the modern state can have an independent impact on policy. He concludes by seeing five sets of variables as the most:

> important for the course of a nation's economic policy: the organisation of labour, the organisation of capital, the organisation of the state, the organisa-

tion of the political system and the structural position of the country within the international economy.[75]

We have seen in the course of this chapter how these variables interacted to constrain Britain's economic growth. However, there are some dangers with institutionalist accounts. There is a tendency for them to become tautological. Britain has a political and economic crisis because of its political and economic institutions. The explanation can become circular with the institutions making the crisis and the crisis making the institutions. A further danger arises from its tendency to explain everything. By explaining everything, and including every variable in an explanation, it is not entirely clear what variables actually account for Britain's decline. With an account that is based on institutions, the explanation would be the same whether Britain succeeds or fails economically – the institutions always explain performance. Such a position can underplay the role of agency. Economic problems may occur because policy-makers have made the wrong decisions. Institutionalists can place too much emphasis on the structural and ignore the contingent. Poor economic decisions may be due to political conflicts at a particular time which, although influenced by institutional context, explain outcomes more effectively. There is also the possibility that it is economic problems that have led to particular institutional developments and not *vice versa*.

Perhaps the greatest danger is the tendency for institutional accounts to contradict their analytical methods with their normative prescriptions for change. Institutional analysis sees policy development as path-dependent, and therefore state policy is the result of the institutional, cultural and economic context. Germany and Japan developed developmental states within the context of late industrialisation within authoritarian and communitarian societies where they were isolated from the world economy. It seems highly unlikely that policies that worked for Germany and Japan could work in Britain. Analytical institutionalism in this sense undermines normative institutionalism. Explanations of why Britain did not produce a developmental state highlight why such a state cannot easily be tacked on to Britain's institutional, cultural and ideological structures. As Hall in his clearly analytical account suggests:

> Given the longstanding continuities that we have observed in national patterns of economic policy and their organisational correlates, we can say that many of the most fundamental organisational features of state and society are not readily susceptible to change.[76]

From this perspective, Thatcherism is a more understandable response to Britain's economic decline because it acknowledges the institutional constraints on economic success, and rather than trying to import an alien state form it attempted to release the economic traditions that had a long history in Britain. Even when Thatcher was working with the institutional grain, institutional constraints slowed the progress of policy change,[77] demonstrating the difficulty of radically changing institutional structures.

Analytical institutionalism can also explain why Tony Blair has shifted away from stakeholding to a more competitive supply-side policy that is focused on Britain's relationship with the world economy, not its internal institutional organisation. To bring about changes that fundamentally alter the nature of the British state and its political culture are extremely difficult – if not impossible – and very costly. Moreover, there is no guarantee that they will succeed given the interests that are likely to oppose such changes. Such institutional opposition was Harold Wilson's problem in the 1960s. An attempt to develop an interventionist policy prevented by Britain's precarious international position, the power of the Treasury and the opposition of economic interest groups. The proponents of a developmental state are not forthcoming on how these factors can be overcome.

Considering the foundations of institutionalism and the nature of the British state, the electoral system and the economy, proposals for reform need to take account of the institutional context and not its complete dismantling. Moreover, many institutionalists' prescriptions are political and concentrate on the need for reform of the system of government, the electoral system and the constitution without really explicating the link between political reform and economic success. It may appear obvious that Britain requires democratic modernisation, but there is no certainty that this will produce economic modernisation. In many cases (Japan, Korea and Taiwan), economic modernisation has been a result of authoritarianism (as is to some extent implicit in the developmental model) and not a process of opening up the state.

Despite a wide array of institutional methods and approaches, therefore, institutional accounts of Britain's decline share a high degree of agreement on the causes of Britain's decline. They focus on the weakness of the state, the relationship with the City and other interest groups, and Britain's overseas orientation.

Notes

1. R.A.W. Rhodes, 'Institutionalism' in D. Marsh and G. Stoker (eds), *Theories and Methods in Political Science* (London, 1996).
2. P. Hall and R. Taylor, 'Political Science and the Three New Institutionalisms', *Political Studies*, vol. 44 (1996); R.A.W. Rhodes, 'Institutionalism', S. Steinmo *et al.*, *Structuring Politics: Historical Institutionalism in Comparative Perspective* (Cambridge, 1992).
3. Hall and Taylor, 'Political Science', p. 936.
4. J. Linz, 'Presidential or Parliamentary Democracy: Does it Make a Difference?' in J. Linz and A. Valenzuela (eds), *The Failure of Presidential Democracy* (Baltimore, 1994).
5. J. March and J. P. Olsen, *Rediscovering Institutions: The Organizational Basis of Politics* (New York, 1989).
6. K. Dowding and D. King (eds), *Preferences, Institutions and Rational Choice* (Oxford, 1995).
7. R.K. Weaver and B.A. Rockman (eds), *Do Institutions Matter?* (Washington, 1993).
8. A. Giddens, *The Constitution of Society* (Cambridge, 1986).
9. P. Anderson, 'Origins of the Present Crisis', *New Left Review*, vol. 23 (1963); P. Anderson, 'The Figures of Descent', *New Left Review*, vol. 161 (1987); T. Nairn, 'The Twilight of the British State', *New Left Review*, vol. 101 (1977); T. Nairn, 'The Future of the British Crisis', *New Left Review*, vol. 113 (1979).
10. S. Finer, *The Changing Party System 1945–1979* (Washington, 1979); K. Middlemas, *Politics in Industrial Society* (London, 1979); K. Middlemas, *Industry, Unions and Government* (London, 1983); K. Middlemas, *Power, Competition and the State,* Vol 1: *Britain in Search of Balance 1940–61* (London, 1986).
11. M. Olson, *The Rise and Decline of Nations* (Yale, 1982).
12. M.J. Wiener, *English Culture and the Decline of the Industrial Spirit 1850–1980* (Harmondsworth, 1992; 1st edn, 1981); W. Hutton, *The State We're In* (London, 1996; 1st edn, 1995).
13. K. Dyson, *The State Tradition in Western Europe* (Oxford, 1982).
14. P. Hall, *Governing the Economy* (Oxford, 1986); A. Gamble, *Britain in Decline: Economic Policy, Political Strategy and the British State* (Basingstoke, 1994; 1st edn, 1981); J. Zysman, *Governments, Markets and Growth* (Ithaca, 1983).
15. S. Finer, *The Changing Party System*; A. Gamble and S. Walkland, *The British Party System and Economic Policy 1945–83* (Oxford, 1984).
16. A. King, 'Overload: Problems of Governing in the 1970s', *Political Studies*, vol. 43 (1975); D. Held, *Models of Democracy* (Oxford, 1986).
17. P. Hall and R. Taylor, 'Political Science'.
18. A. Gamble, *Britain in Decline*, pp. 99–100.
19. T. Nairn, 'The Future of the British Crisis', p. 53.
20. W. Hutton, *The State We're In*, p. 43.
21. M.J. Wiener, *English Culture*.
22. T. Nairn, 'The Future of the British Crisis'.
23. B. Elbaum and W. Lazonick, 'An Institutional Perspective on British

Decline' in B. Elbaum and W. Lazonick (eds), *The Decline of the British Economy* (Oxford, 1986), pp. 2, 4.

24. E. Hobsbawm, *The Age of Empire* (London, 1967)
25. B. Moore, *The Social Origins of Democracy and Dictatorship* (Harmondsworth, 1966).
26. G. Savage, *The Social Construction of Expertise* (Pittsburgh, 1996).
27. H. Perkin, *The Origins of Modern English Society* (London, 1969), p. 408.
28. W. D. Rubinstein, 'Cultural Explanations of Britain's Economic Decline' in B. Collins and K. Robbins (eds), *British Culture and Economic Decline* (London, 1990).
29. *Ibid.*
30. R. Johnson, 'Peculiarities of the English Route: Barrington Moore, Perry Anderson and English Social Development', *Stencilled Occasional Papers* (University of Birmingham Centre for Contemporary Cultural Studies, 1975).
31. M. W. Kirby, 'Institutional Rigidities and Economic Decline: Reflections on the British Experience', *Economic History Review*, vol. 45 (1992).
32. N. Harris, *Competition and the Corporate Society* (London, 1972).
33. W. Grant and S. Wilks, 'British Industrial Policy: Structural Change, Policy Inertia', *Journal of Public Policy*, vol. 3 (1983), pp. 25–6.
34. J. Zysman, *Governments, Markets and Growth* (Ithaca, 1983), p. 202.
35. K. Theakston, 'Whitehall,Westminster and Industrial Policy' in D. Coates (ed.), *Industrial Policy in Britain* (Basingstoke, 1996).
36. S. Pollard, *The Wasting of the British Economy* (London, 1982).
37. J.P. Mackintosh, *The Politics and Government of Britain* (London, 1977).
38. M.J. Smith, 'Reconceptualizing the British State: Theoretical and Empirical Challenges to British Central Government', *Public Administration*, vol. 76, no. 1, 1998.
39. D. Marquand, *The Unprincipled Society* (London, 1988), pp. 175–206.
40. W. Hutton, *The State We're In*, p. 22.
41. J. Leruez, *Economic Planning and Politics in Britain* (Oxford, 1975).
42. K. Middlemas, *Industry, Unions and Government*.
43. P. Hall, *Governing the Economy* (Oxford, 1986); M. Shanks, *Planning and Politics* (London, 1977).
44. W. Grant, *The Political Economy of Industrial Policy* (London, 1982).
45. D. Marquand, *Unprincipled Society*, p. 144.
46. B. Hogwood, *Trends in British Public Policy* (Milton Keynes, 1992).
47. J. Meadowcroft, *Conceptualising the State: Innovation and Dispute in British Political Thought* (Oxford, 1995).
48. W.H. Greenleaf, *The British Political Tradition,* Vol 1: *The Rise of Collectivism* (London, 1983).
49. K. Middlemas, *Politics in Industrial Society, op. cit.*; W. H. Greenleaf, *The British Political Tradition,* Vol 2: *The Ideological Heritage* (London, 1983).
50. M.J. Smith, *The Politics of Agricultural Support in Britain: The Development of the Agricultural Policy Community* (Aldershot, 1990).
51. D. Edgerton, *England and the Aeroplane* (London, 1991); see also S. Lee, 'Manufacturing' in Coates (ed.), *Industrial Policy*.
52. P. Dunleavy, 'The Paradoxes of Ungrounded Statism' in F. Castles (ed.), *The History of Comparative Public Policy* (Oxford, 1989), pp. 244–5.

53. See R.A.W. Rhodes, *Beyond Westminster and Whitehall* (London, 1988); J. J. Richardson and A. G. Jordan, *Governing Under Pressure* (Oxford, 1979).
54. A. Gamble and S. Walkland, *The British Party System and Economic Policy 1945–83* (Oxford, 1984).
55. R. Stones, *The Myth of Betrayal: Structure and Agency in the Government's Policy of Non-devaluation 1964–67* (University of Essex PhD Thesis, 1988); F. Longstreth, 'The City, Industry and the State' in C. Crouch (ed.), *State and Economy in Contemporary Capitalism* (London, 1979), B. Fine and L. Harris, *The Peculiarities of the British Economy* (London, 1985); G. Ingham, *Capitalism Divided? The City and Industry in British Social Development* (Basingstoke, 1984).
56. S. Strange, *Sterling and British Policy: A Political Study of an International Currency in Decline* (Oxford, 1971).
57. R. Stones, 'Government-finance Relations in Britain 1964–67', *Economy and Society*, vol. 19 (1990).
58. W. Hutton, *The State We're In*, pp. 133, 149.
59. Wilson Committee, *Committee to Review the Functioning of Financial Institutions* (London, 1977); C. Leys, *Politics in Britain* (London, 1986).
60. G. Ingham, *Capitalism Divided?*; J. Scott, *Corporations, Classes and Capitalism* (London, 1979).
61. R. Stones, *Myth of Betrayal*.
62. P. Hall, *Governing the Economy*, p. 40.
63. D. Sanders, *Losing an Empire, Finding a Role: British Foreign Policy 1945–90* (London, 1990).
64. P. Kennedy, *The Rise and Fall of the Great Powers: Economic Change and Military Conflict from 1500 to 2000* (London, 1989; 1st edn, 1988).
65. K. Middlemas, *Politics in Industrial Society*.
66. P. Hall, *Governing the Economy*.
67. M. Olson, *The Rise and Decline of Nations* (New Haven, 1982); A. Birch, 'Overload, Ungovernability and Delegitimation: The Theories and the British Case', *British Journal of Political Science*, vol. 14 (1984); A. King, 'Overload: Problems of Governing in the 1970s', *Political Studies*, vol. 43 (1975).
68. K. Middlemas, *Power, Competition and the State*, p. 1.
69. P. Hall, *Governing the Economy*, p. 60.
70. M. Mann, 'The Autonomous Power of the State: Its Origins, Mechanisms and Results', *Archives Europeennes de Sociologie*, vol. 25 (1984).
71. M. Olson, *The Rise and Decline of Nations*, *op. cit.*
72. A. King, 'Overload'; A. Birch, 'Overload'; D. Held, *Models of Democracy*.
73. W. Grant, *Business and Politics in Britain* (Basingstoke, 1987).
74. D. Cameron, 'Distributional Coalitions and other Causes of Economic Stagnation', *International Organisation*, vol. 42 (1988).
75. P. Hall, *Governing the Economy*, pp. 19, 258.
76. *Ibid.*, p. 66.
77. P. Jackson, 'Economic Policy' in D. Marsh and R.A.W. Rhodes (eds), *Implementing Thatcherite Policies* (Milton Keynes, 1992).

13

British Decline and European Integration

MARIE-THERESE FAY AND ELIZABETH MEEHAN

The editors of this volume have asked us to consider whether the European agenda is merely a backdrop against which arguments about British decline have occurred, or whether developments in European integration have substantially affected, positively or negatively, the prospects of a national road to recovery. In our view, to speak of European integration as a 'mere backdrop' would understate what is going on. We suggest that the contested nature of the notion of 'decline' – and of 'sovereignty' – means that the question of positive or negative effects cannot be answered conclusively but can only be explored in the light of competing beliefs about economic interests and sovereignty among those who make policy or try to influence it. We do, however, argue that it may not be valid to speak of a 'national road to recovery' in the British context: 'sub-national' features as well as global trends and transnational sectors could invalidate discourses of national economies (and therefore also much of the debate on British national decline).

More than a backdrop, European integration is central to much discourse about British decline. The first flirtation with 'Europe' arose from a glimmer of recognition of Britain's declining world power. Serious efforts to accede were symptomatic of acceptance that Britain was no longer the powerful state it had been. These later forays into 'Europe' coincided with increasing doubt about whether national economies could prosper as discrete entities, and involvement in European integration began to be seen as the only way to modernise and to improve economic performance. But there are conflicting views about whether EU membership is the right strategy both to compensate for political decline and to halt relative economic decline and, hence, whether or not it has positive or negative consequences for recovery. So intense is that debate, particularly in the Conservative Party, that it has become commonplace to suggest that EU membership could affect the British party system as dramatically as did the repeal of the Corn Laws and Gladstone's Irish Home Rule Bills. Nonetheless, the very public conflict in the Conservative Party, which contributed to its loss of office in 1997, has not broken the dominance of cross-party consensus in favour of EU membership.

Current disputes are more vitriolic than they have been for 20 years – and the most vocal opposition has shifted from the Labour Party to the Conservative Party – but their terms have not changed much over the last 40 years. The general displacement of the discourse of political decline by one of economic underperformance is not fully replicated in disputes about EU membership. There were and are two main features to the debate. One is about the economic merits of integration and the best way to promote national economic interests. The second is about sovereignty, not merely in connection with national control over economic policy but also more generally about institutions and traditions. In the first section of this chapter, we explore competing claims about whether economic integration helps to limit the century of decline outlined by Gamble[1] or reinforces the deterioration of Britain's relative economic position. In the second section, we discuss the debate about whether sovereignty is strengthened through being 'pooled', or undermined with each new stage of integration. Connections between these two dimensions come into sharp focus when, instead of treating the United Kingdom (UK) as a whole, we consider 'sub-national' interests and how the constituent parts view EU membership. This is the subject of our third section. The conclusion drawn from these three sections is that, while the editors' questions cannot be answered definitively, it can be said that competing beliefs about the European agenda have been central to debate about the halting of decline and that this agenda does call into question the idea of 'national recovery' – not, however, in conventional senses but by encouraging the view that the means of recovery must be regionally differentiated.

In 1945, 'Britain had not been conquered or invaded; she felt no need to excoriate history'.[2] In 1950, the British economy was the healthiest in Europe. These differences between the UK and continental countries elevated Britain's prestige in Western Europe immediately after the

Second World War but soon became problematic – because they gave rise to different approaches to the means of reconstruction. When the UK declined to join the European Coal and Steel Community in 1951 or to attend the Messina Conference in 1955, which led to the creation of the European Economic Community (EEC), there was disappointment across Western Europe. The UK's perception of itself as less a European power than a global one – in partnership with the USA and with Imperial or Commonwealth trading and political links – was not, however, sustainable.

The Suez crisis of 1956 marked a turning point in the UK's global role. It was followed by a period of national self-examination in which the centrality of foreign and defence policy began to be rivalled by scrutiny of economic performance.[3] Between 1956 and the withdrawal in 1967 of the British military presence from Suez, the costs of partnership with the USA had become evident, the Empire had largely gone (with adverse effects on exports), and economic performance, relative to the founding EEC members, was poor. By 1961, when Harold Macmillan applied for membership, standards of living in the original six had doubled. At the time of Harold Wilson's application in 1967, the continental economies were outstripping that of the UK in rates of growth and in the expansion of trade. Trade between the UK and the continent was almost non-existent. The third and successful application was made by Edward Heath in the belief that a reorientation of policy towards the EEC was the only way to induce the economic and industrial modernisation necessary to improved performance.[4]

There was, and is, controversy over whether this strategy was mistimed and even whether or not it was inherently correct.[5] The period of rejection coincided with the most successful economic stage of integration. Conversely, accession took place at what could hardly have been a worse time. The world recession caused by the 1973 oil crisis flattened European economies and integration was undermined by the adoption of national responses to the effects of international economic instability. The relative weakness of the UK, increasingly evident after 1950, meant that such effects were felt more keenly in Britain than elsewhere in Europe.

Nevertheless, '[m]embership of the Community was an integral part of [Heath's] programme for economic revival which involved the reform of industrial relations and the reduction of Britain's increasingly high levels of inflation'.[6] This view was shared by 'the intellectual and political elite at the centre of British politics': pragmatic Conservatives, the social democratic wing of the Labour Party, and the Liberal Party.[7]

Little was done, however, about the 'hearts and minds' of voters.[8] Despite elite consensus that joining the EEC was the only means of halting decline, the agreed terms of entry were not auspicious.

The budgetary funding system, then in the process of reform, and the domination of the budget by the Common Agricultural Policy (CAP), determined 20 years previously by the original six in accordance with their interests, were particularly disadvantageous to Britain. The CAP was unlike the British agricultural support system. In the UK, agricultural prices were allowed to find their own levels and deficiency payments compensated farmers for shortfalls in incomes. Under the CAP, farmers' incomes were supported through annual price fixing by Agricultural Ministers. The introduction in the early 1970s of the Community's 'own resources' meant that part of its revenue was raised from levies on imported food, fixed at levels to ensure that imported products were not cheaper than those produced inside the Community, and from common external tariffs on industrial goods. The new budgetary system and the established CAP combined to produce three disadvantages for the UK. First, there was a large increase in food prices upon accession. Second, little was gained from the price-support system compared to countries such as France where agriculture was, and is, a larger sector of the economy. And, third, since levies and tariffs were raised at the point of entry into the EEC, they fell more heavily on the UK as a larger importer than other states of industrial and agricultural goods from outside the Community. Thus, the UK emerged as a net contributor to the budget, despite being among the poorer member states.

Heath knew that there would be these problems and sought to off-set budgetary losses through securing a new European Regional Development Fund. The ERDF became 'almost the centre piece of Heath's campaign to make the EC acceptable to the British people and to resolve the increasingly obvious problem of the British budgetary contributions',[9] though he was less successful than he had hoped. Nevertheless, the ERDF did develop in the 1980s into a systematic programme of structural funding, displacing some of the dominance of Community agricultural expenditure. This had perhaps unexpected effects on the idea of a British national recovery, a matter to which we shall return.

Though Harold Wilson had made the second accession bid, he led a party which had always been opposed to (or, at least, divided about) British membership. Indeed, 'Europe' contributed to the splitting of the Party's social-democratic wing, some of whom formed a break-away party which subsequently merged with the Liberals. Though Labour's

social-democrats were part of the cross-party consensus that membership was in Britain's economic interests, the Party as a whole embodied
the same ambivalence as that of leftist parties throughout Europe in the
first years of integration – 'an uneasy alliance of nationalism and internationalism', believing that the EEC was designed to benefit industrialists and farmers rather than workers.[10]

Wilson's intra-party compromise after winning the General Elections
of 1974 – renegotiated terms of entry, put to the people in a referendum
– was not an instance of a new socialist consensus that was then emerging on the continent. Continental socialists were adopting the view that
the real issue was not whether to be for or against integration, but to
secure the right kind of integration and, eventually in France in particular, that it was only on a European level that 'social justice, internationalism and independence from the USA' could be established.[11]
Wilson's renegotiation conditions were distinctly national: the British
budgetary contributions, reform of the CAP, access to Community markets for Commonwealth products and protection of national methods of
recovery through the operation of industrial and regional policy without
EEC interference. Renegotiations completed, there followed the unusual spectacle of a Prime Minister recommending voters to support continued membership, while it was official Party policy to oppose it, a
contrary position vigorously advocated by some senior colleagues.
Despite calls to reform the EEC from within, withdrawal remained the
official policy of the Labour Party until the election of Neil Kinnock as
leader, on the ground that it ruled out a national road to recovery – the
Alternative Economic Strategy.

Wilson's efforts to renegotiate budgetary and CAP terms did not
eliminate the paradox that Britain as one of the poorest economies was
also one of the larger net contributors to the EEC. By 1980, 'British
output and productivity were little better than half the levels in comparable economies'.[12] Margaret Thatcher, having led the Conservatives to
electoral victory in 1979, soon began to tackle this issue, warning that
'Britain cannot accept the present situation. It is demonstrably unjust. It
is politically indefensible . . . [T]he imbalance is not compatible with
the spirit of the Community.'[13] The budgetary question dominated
UK–EEC relations until 1984 under a style of leadership which
shocked many member-states. Nevertheless, agreements were reached
throughout the 1980s first over the formula, then over flat-rate rebates
and, later, a rebate of 66 per cent of the difference between what the
UK paid in and received back. It can be argued that a better deal might
have been possible. But wider international factors also played a part in

Thatcher's final acceptance: namely, Britain's need to be integral to Europe in order to continue to attract investment from America and Japan in technological production and to protect the position of the City of London at the centre of the European Economic zone.[14]

To counteract the doubts raised by budgetary disputes about the UK's commitment to the EEC, the government presented a paper at the 1984 Fontainebleau summit which outlined British views on the direction of the Community. In *Europe – The Future*, constructive dialogue was promised. The signalling of a positive attitude culminated in the signing of the Single European Act (SEA) in 1986, much of its preparatory work having been carried out by one of the British Commissioners, Lord Cockfield. At the time, Margaret Thatcher thought that the SEA facilitated her liberalising national road to recovery – reform of the CAP and the creation of a free, internal market in which the UK was a key player. But the internal market can also be seen as undermining the replacement of intervention by liberalisation as the means of improving economic performance. Two aspects of the SEA came to be perceived as inimical: the social dimension, and Economic and Monetary Union (EMU).

Since 1969, there had been indications of a new institutional discourse of relative economic decline: namely, that trade unions, relationships between the two sides of industry and relationships between them both and government encouraged inflexibility and inhibited entrepreneurialism. It was with the election of a radical Conservative government in 1979 that this became a sustained element of a national regeneration strategy. Thus it was galling to the Prime Minister to find that the social dimension of the Single European Market appeared to justify more regulation of socio-economic life and, worse, through 'social partnership' between the two sides of industry and through European institutions rather than according to the judgement of governments: 'The separate political culture of Britain is announced and announced with pride . . . We have not successfully rolled back the frontiers of the State in Britain only to see them re-imposed at a European level with a European Superstate.'[15]

Despite her successor's different tone, John Major continued to resist the social dimension and secured a Protocol in the Maastricht Treaty of Union under which other members could pursue social issues but from which the British would be exempt (now in the main body of the 1997 Amsterdam Treaty following the new Labour Government's 'opting-in'). Major, too, defined British interests as being attractive to inward investors, more likely in a less-regulated labour market.

While the precursor to EMU – the coordination of national currencies – revealed differing views within the Conservative leadership about the Community's impact on a British road to recovery, the impending EMU profoundly affected Party unity. The first clashes took place between the Prime Minister and her Chancellor of the Exchequer, Nigel Lawson, who was shadowing the pound as though it were part of the Exchange Rate Mechanism (ERM), in which the UK did not formally participate. Mrs Thatcher's view was that, since this entailed periodic intervention to support sterling, the policy impeded freedom to fight inflation. The Chancellor's approach was backed by the British Commissioner, Sir Leon Brittan, and full participation in the European Monetary System was the preferred policy of the Foreign Secretary, Sir Geoffrey Howe. These disagreements led to the resignation of the Chancellor and the Foreign Secretary and, eventually, contributed to the departure from office of the Prime Minister herself. Ironically, Nigel Lawson's successor at the Treasury, John Major – soon also to become Mrs Thatcher's successor – took Britain into the ERM in 1990 at what many felt was a dangerously high level of DM2.95 to the pound. The position of weaker currencies at the end of the recession of the late 1980s, the fall of the Soviet bloc, and the reunification of Germany all placed the ERM under great strain. On the morning of 'black Wednesday', 16 September 1992, desperate measures to hold the pound in the ERM caused interest rates to be raised twice, to 15 per cent. But by the afternoon it was inevitable that sterling would have to be withdrawn from the ERM. For the next year the ERM was in crisis until an emergency meeting of the EC Finance Ministers agreed to relax its constraints. Though this succeeded as a political agreement, it rather defeated the original purposes of the ERM (in which the narrower the fluctuation bands, the closer, effectively, is a single currency), by widening the bands within which currencies could fluctuate to 15 per cent – 'little short of floating'.[16]

The ERM's collapse, during the period of ratification of the Maastricht Treaty, occasioned the opening up of deep splits in the Conservative Party about the best way to pursue UK economic interests. Following the withdrawal of sterling from the ERM, freedom to make unilateral decisions to adjust interest rates and the money supply increasingly came to be seen as a virtue and scepticism grew about the view that 'EMU was a logical consequence of the 1992 programme'.[17] The sceptics became more and more unconvinced by Major's claim to have protected economic interests by securing agreement in the Maastricht Treaty that the UK need not participate in EMU if the conditions were inappropriate; and he had the increasingly difficult task of appealing to incommensurate audiences.

On the one hand, he tried to persuade, not only pro-Europeans at home but also the partner-states, that he wanted to be 'at the heart of Europe'. In a speech in 1994 he insisted that the EU needed the UK: 'We have the world's sixth largest economy – London is one of the world's largest financial centres. Our trading links and global connections bring substantial benefits to Europe. We are the second largest net contributor to the European Union's budget.'[18] On the other hand, he had to douse fears that his, and his Chancellor's, strategy was wrong. In the same speech, he confessed that Britain had learned the painful lesson from the ERM that, in global currency markets, inflexibility between currencies could not be defended. In March 1995, he told the House of Commons that Europe was not ready for a single currency and, if a single currency 'were used to bind together artificially countries which were not marching in step economically, the strains upon the economies of Europe would be immense and unsustainable'.[19] Later, in the *Daily Telegraph*, he tried to reassure Euro-sceptics that 'our opt-out from a single currency protects us from being forced into an unworkable system'. [20]

As the growing virulence of intra-party opposition made his policy position increasingly untenable, so too did conflict obscure, according to the Liberal Democrat leader, the merits of EMU: namely, that under the right conversion criteria, monetary union would boost trade, stable exchange rates would be helpful to trade, and inflation rates could be brought closer to those of Britain's competitors'.[21]

In summarising the European dimension to the debate about British decline since the 1970s, three issues need to be addressed: economic costs and benefits; the political status of the UK in the EU; and the state of the mainstream political consensus that membership is the best strategy for the UK economy. First, the CAP has been a significant cost and remains a factor in the size of the net contribution – though, as noted earlier, its significance has declined in favour of regional expenditures, a form of redistribution intended, as the then Chancellor, Kenneth Clarke, pointed out to the House of Commons in 1994,[22] to ensure that companies have purchasers throughout the EU. A potential cost, according to the Chairman of the House of Commons Foreign Affairs Committee, David Howell,[23] is the prospect of missed opportunities in markets outside the EU which are increasingly important. He argued that more than half of British visible and invisible trade now takes place outside the EU.

On the other hand, the Single Market accounts for 58 per cent of the UK's visible exports and exports from the UK to other EU countries have grown at an above-average rate – by 6.5 per cent in 1993, 11.1 per cent in 1994 and 18.0 per cent in 1995, contributing very significantly to the recovery of the economy. But the significance of the financial sector to the UK economy should not be overlooked, its share of world exports of financial services being well ahead of its share of world trade in manufactures. Slow progress in bringing about an effective common market in financial services in the EU has not been to the advantage of the UK.

Few people other than ardent Euro-sceptics think that withdrawal would be the answer. According to Pilkington, the USA 'has made it clear that their interest in Britain is solely as a link with Europe and, if they were offered a choice between Europe and Britain alone, they would choose Europe'[24] – a view shared by potential investors from Japan. He also observes that the Commonwealth countries have all found new markets.

Despite perceptions among pro-Europeans, EU partners and potential inward investors that Britain is an 'awkward partner', it is not the case that the UK has been poorer than other members at affecting developments in integration that are regarded as appropriate to common and national interests. Indeed, the UK has adapted quite well to a redefined political leadership role, albeit in a regional not global arena. As George[25] suggests, British opposition in situations requiring unanimity is sometimes convenient to other countries. He also argues that the British are better than is sometimes recognised at the fluid alliance-building that occurs in situations of qualified majority voting. The success of British diplomacy and bargaining can be seen in the existence in the Maastricht Treaty of separate 'pillars' for Justice and Home Affairs and for Foreign and Security Policy, as well as the 'pillar' for common, Community business. It can also be seen in the 'opt-outs' on social policy and EMU,[26] in the inclusion of 'subsidiarity' and in extensions to authority at the centre that are more limited than in original proposals.

Despite the self-destructive conflict in the Conservative Party and the continuation of less-disruptive opposition in the Labour Party, there is still a consensus that Britain's economic needs are best met through EU membership. And there is little difference over the shape of Europe that is seen as appropriate to national needs. As George[27] points out, key points for Margaret Thatcher and John Major were virtually the same: a Europe of nation-states, common action which focuses on practical problems instead of theoretical constructs, competition, free trade, and defence through NATO. Moreover, the Labour Party's vision of the UK and Europe is also similar; even though it shares the continental view that economic progress and social inclusion are interdependent, the government is against a raft of social measures. But, if perceptions of the right kind of Europe for British economic interests are similar, discourses on sovereignty are more complicated. It is to these that we now turn.

The Euro-sceptics' anxieties, and the concern of Conservative and Labour leaders to assure voters that neither party will 'give up the British veto', are related to a particular conception of sovereignty which symbolises national distinctiveness. Yet the notion of sovereignty is multi-faceted and, as Newman[28] points out, invoking lost national sovereignty as a rallying-cry may say more about the general ideologies of the rallier than about what kind of power is in question and in what way its exercise is changing. He suggests that it is more illuminating to use different concepts to describe different things: for example, authority and power. Barry,[29] too, distinguishes between sovereignty as legal authority and as the capacity to act; and Teague[30] refers to 'outer' and 'inner' sovereignty, of which more will be said later. An influential exponent of the history of postwar Europe, Alan Milward,[31] argues that European integration, far from undermining the nation-state, has reinforced its authority and capacity. States remain legally sovereign actors in domestic politics, recognised as such in international affairs; moreover, their capacity to protect citizens' core interests (and, hence, to maintain their moral authority) is reinforced through cooperation instead of reduced as otherwise it might be in the modern world of globalisation.

It is likely that it is the coexistence of several meanings within the apparently single concept of sovereignty that explains what Barry observes about UK accession to the EEC: 'that reaction to this apparent diminution in sovereignty has been both favourable and hostile in about equal measures from all sides of the political spectrum'.[32] From this, he concludes that accession may have destroyed a defining characteristic of British political culture: fundamental agreement on institutions. Just how strong that fundamental agreement was can be questioned, as we do in the next section. For the moment, there is another dimension of the diversity noted by Barry which needs to be explored. This is that, broadly speaking, the use of 'loss of national sovereignty' as a rallying-cry has moved from the Labour Party to the Conservatives. Conversely, 'loss of sovereignty' as a calculated decision to 'pool' certain powers in order to increase capacity to act, characterises Labour discourse more now than that of the Conservatives.

Though Ernest Bevin had hoped to build a European imperial bloc to help maintain equality with the United States, this foundered partly on his disquiet over the supranational elements of early continental integration.[33] Murray[34] reminds us that later Labour fears that the EEC would inhibit socialist economic strategies were regularly couched in terms of loss of national sovereignty – notwithstanding other voices in the Party.

At the same time, Conservatives were increasingly converted to the idea that sovereignty in the sense of capacity to act pointed to EEC membership. If most converts were unenthusiastic, this was not so for Edward Heath, who remains convinced. Interviewed by the *New Statesman and Society*,[35] he pointed out 'with pleasure, that the British gave federalism to Australia'. On being asked if the UK was 'ready to be another New South Wales', he replied that 'New South Wales is a very powerful government'. After Heath, the most articulate exponent of the power to be gained from 'pooling sovereignty' was Foreign Secretary, Sir Geoffrey Howe. He, too, remains convinced.[36] But, even while he was in office, his outlook was beginning to be overtaken by the Euro-sceptics' claim that sovereignty was diminished by being pooled.

Such colleagues, including the then Prime Minister, were horrified by Jacques Delors' assertion to MEPs in 1988 that, in ten years, 80 per cent of economic legislation and, possibly, fiscal and social legislation would be of European rather than national origin. Since then, they have been alarmed by the expansionary consequences of old Directives, and the introduction of a new one, on women's working conditions, and by other rulings in the European Court of Justice (ECJ). Of note are those in 1990 and 1991 (arising from proceedings in the domestic courts in 1989 brought by *Factortame*) against the 1988 British Merchant Shipping Act which had intended to stop 'quota hopping' by 'creating new nationality and residence requirements for the registration of fishing vessels'.[37] A 1996 ruling, in favour of the Council of Ministers over the UK's challenge to the legal basis of the 48-hour working week Directive, was similarly unwelcome.

As Conservative discourse was becoming more nationalistic, that of Labour was becoming more international. Murray[38] draws attention to Tom Nairn's view that, by opposing the EC, the Party had 'sold out class interests for the sake of the nation', and the Scottish MEP Ken Collins' ironic comment on Labour's opposition at a time when 'the idea of sovereignty and socialism in one country hardly appears on any other left-wing party's agenda'. Movement between 1979 and 1982 was rapidly consolidated under the leadership of Neil Kinnock who repudiated a nationalist approach to international relations, cooperated with the European Parliament's Socialist Group and promoted the idea of a European-wide policy to deal with unemployment. The sea-change was nowhere more evident than in the rapturous reception given to Jacques Delors when he addressed the annual conference of the Trades Union Congress at Birmingham in 1988. The new approach may have stemmed from a hope that Jacques Delors' vision of Europe – which in some ways survived his retirement from the Presidency of the Commission – might serve to defend welfare-democracy against the aims of a deregulatory government. Nevertheless, the changing outlook of the Labour Party and its increasing contacts with European socialists or social democrats seems to have led 'New Labour' to agree that 'the good society' can be achieved only at the European level. Thus – albeit that the emphases in social democracy and Christian Democracy are not the same – the prevalent approach to 'Europe' in the Labour Party of the 1990s is not so different from that of Conservative MEPs who have recently aligned themselves with the European People's Party whose version of 'the good society' is quite different from that of neo-liberal Conservatives at Westminster.[39]

However, EMU represents a more substantial ground for fear of loss of sovereignty than were previous innovations. For example, though proceedings were taken later against the 48-hour working week, the UK did not vote against it when the proposal was considered by the Council of Ministers in 1993. Such a measure is similar to those in, for example, higher education and unemployment, which Teague[40] calls matters of 'outer sovereignty' where it is safe, even advantageous, to acknowledge the EU as an important catalyst for cooperation. Also in this category are 'forged exchange rate links through the ERM' since 'participating in the ERM did not atrophy the national peculiarities of economic and political life in Europe'. This differentiates it from full EMU which undermines 'inner sovereignty' because it may be seen to threaten national distinctiveness.

Even so, there are leaders elsewhere who are determined to proceed with EMU because they believe that it will enhance capacities to act. Notably, it is a central aspiration in the Republic of Ireland even though being in EMU while the UK remains out would be problematic for its other prime goal of a settlement within the islands of Ireland and Great Britain. That EMU is likely to entail a 'multi-speed' Europe creates further difficulties for conceptions of sovereignty, power and authority in the UK. Margaret Thatcher, for example, had to wrestle with the contradiction that: '[a] central European Bank in the only true meaning of the term means surrendering your economic policy';[41] while being in the 'slow lane' would be 'difficult to present as anything but humiliating and would undermine her claim to have brought Britain back to the centre of events'.[42] Despite yet more harmful divisions among Conservatives in the 1990s, lack of confidence in the Maastricht opt-out, and the unpopularity of a single currency (not only in the UK), it is not necessarily obvious that the concern in the first quotation above is stronger than that of the second, particularly if we bear in mind the distinction between economic decline and political decline.

There is, of course, a uniquely British concept of sovereignty which, theoretically, is inconsistent with EU membership: Parliamentary Sovereignty. This is the doctrine that laws can be made only by Parliament, that one Parliament cannot bind its successors, and that only succeeding Parliaments can overturn the acts of their predecessors. Thus, constitutionally speaking, the Parliament of 1970–74 could not bind its successors to comply with existing or future Community law. Nor, under British constitutional conventions, could Acts of Parliament be subject to judicial review in the ECJ.

The problem was addressed in section 2(4) of the 1972 Act of Accession which states that: 'any enactment passed or to be passed . . . shall be construed and have effect subject to the foregoing provisions of this section'. Thus, 'the whole meaning of the Act gives priority to European law over domestic law', a hierarchy confirmed in domestic courts – even in *Factortame* where, in the Act in question, Parliament appeared deliberately to have contravened Community law.[43] Though EU accession overturned Parliamentary Sovereignty, the doctrine may be problematic irrespective of EU membership. Usher,[44] for example, points out that, taken to its logical extreme, the doctrine makes unsafe all Acts that granted independence to former colonies. Yet, it is implausible that any Parliament would repeal them, while it is the case that alterations to the legal status of Commonwealth countries take place through political negotiation. Similarly, in this view, it is less important that Parliament cannot deliberately contravene Community law than it is that governments are in a position to negotiate the terms of integration. That EU member states are so is evident in the forty or so special protocols in the Maastricht Treaty.

From a different standpoint, it should be noted that there may be less affection than supposed for the formal doctrine of Parliamentary Sovereignty in those parts of the UK where the majority party in Parliament (the holders of *de facto* sovereignty) does not reflect regional voting preferences. It is to the diversity of the UK and its significance for a national road to recovery that we now turn.

British politicians all accept the validity of the idea of a national economy and, hence, that decline can be understood mainly as something generated within Britain. As shown, however, they have differed over whether the EU can serve as an instrument of internal modernisation. The consensus that it can prevails over two forms of opposition. The 'Old Labour' view is that the EU precludes national measures and that its free market approach cannot bring about national recovery. To neoliberal Conservatives, the free trade basis of the EU has been subverted: overregulated markets cannot bring about national recovery either. All approaches – the consensus, the Alternative Economic Strategy or extensive deregulation – assume the need for and appropriateness of a unified strategy for a single territory applied, albeit, with some variations in different parts of the UK. In exploring the assumption that there is a national economy upon which the EU might have positive or negative effects, we are confronted with complicated issues.

First, the EU, like national governments, has to deal with the co-existence of common and diverse interests – giving rise to some inconsistencies in policy. Second, the issue of whether or not there is **a** national economy for which there can be **a** national road to recovery may be questioned not only in terms of sectoral variation and global interactions, but also on the basis of domestic geo-political differentiation.

Dealing first with EU policy, it can be argued that traditional Labour opponents have a *prima facie* case. The conventional instruments of national and internal regional regeneration increasingly became subject to the principle of non-discrimination by one member state against another. As Allen[45] points out, competition policy – encompassing not only control of mergers but also state monopolies, public procurement, subsidies to industries and aid to regions – became central to the removal of all non-tariff barriers to the single market. Moreover, it did not escape the notice of 'Old Labour' that such moves were promoted by Conservative UK governments in the 1980s, as the European adjunct to their internal deregulatory solution to poor competitiveness, and carried forward by Commissioners Sir Leon Brittan and Peter Sutherland. But this may oversimplify matters.

On the one hand, the early period of Labour's critique coincided with a time when very little action was in fact taken. As Allen points out, competition policy in the 1960s and 1970s, more or less confined to the control of mergers, did little to undermine national measures, including state aids, aimed at the recovery of national industries. Though there was some constraint on regional aids, 'the large industries in decline – shipbuilding, textiles, and steel in particular – all received substantial national subsidies'. Despite the stepping-up of state aids policy in the 1980s, most publicly evident in 1989 when national 'flagships' (Rover in the case of Britain) had to repay subsidies, the Commission continued to approve the granting of aids where these had been notified, while increasing its efforts to find out about those which had been granted without notification.[46]

Another reason for scepticism regarding the 'Old Labour' view is Allen's[47] identification of a contradiction between 'competition objectives of the treaties designed to enhance the working of the market and the idea of using structural funds to overcome regional disparities', the latter of which 'has to be seen as inhibiting the working of the market'. The use of structural funds for this purpose stems from the idea that the market cannot work as intended if there are serious disparities of wealth between and within member states. Insofar as common policies to promote competition limit member states' capacity to reduce internal disparities, then alternative or additional means are needed to promote cohesion. Hence, the transformation of the ERDF, together with other structural funds, into coordinated programmes of development and regeneration. These developments bring to the foreground the relevance of Britain's multinational economic and political character to the question of whether the EU can have a positive impact 'on an unmodern British state'.[48] Despite its importance, this is a neglected topic: 'An even more serious gap in the treatment of Britain and Europe is the absence of any sustained account of the relationship between the multinational character of the British state and the issue of the European Union'.[49] A 'sustained account' would need to explore several aspects which can only be touched upon here. First, there is the history of British regional policy. Secondly, there is the question of whether there are distinctive regional economies upon which the EU might have variable impacts. And, thirdly, there are constitutional issues of sovereignty and the role of the EU which are viewed differently in different parts of the UK.

Most writers trace the beginnings of British regional policy to the 1930s and note that a principal part of the postwar consensus was agreement to use 'regional aid to stem the outflow of jobs and people from the less favoured regions and to achieve some sense of territorial equity or balance between the more prosperous parts of Britain and those which were less well-to-do'[50] – much the same reasoning that informs the socio-political aspect of EU cohesion policy. It also came to be believed that overall national output could be raised by regenerating those regional resources which were unused because of regional imbalances in industrial structures – similar to EU reasoning about the economic case for cohesion. The system of 'differential regional incentives and controls operated by the UK central government in favour of assisted areas'[51] began to change in the 1970s and more rapidly in the 1980s. This meant that 'the spatial coverage of the assisted areas was cut back', grants became more selective and intervention took a different form, shifting from 'investment in capital intensive projects' [largely manufacturing] designed to take 'work to the workers' to a diverse range of instruments intended improve the human capital aspects of 'regional enterprise' and to bring about competitiveness through market forces.

It is very difficult to determine the effects of regional policy on economic performance relative to other factors, such as international cycles, North Sea oil and diversification. But there is some consensus that regional policy contributed to an improvement in 'Scotland's economic position relative to the UK up to at least the middle 1970s' and that 'the jury must still be out on the efficacy of the radical policy changes introduced in the 1980s'.[52] Equally vulnerable to 'peripherality' explanations for poor performance, Scottish trends contrast with those of Northern Ireland which has continued to be granted 'hard' assistance when policy elsewhere has become 'soft' but where 'relatively high levels of state aid' have done little 'to improve performance'.[53] The persistence of this contrast may indicate distinctive regional economies rather than regional components of a coherent British whole.

Indeed, it could be argued that 'the Troubles' do not in themselves account for the huge employment shortfall in the province, and this might suggest the existence of 'routine' distinctiveness in the economies of Northern Ireland and Scotland. That there may be a Northern Irish economy distinguishable from that of Great Britain is hinted at by Gibson[54] who 'suspects' that 50 years of conformity with British policy, albeit through a devolved assembly, may have 'distort[ed] the industrial and social structure with adverse effects on economic performance' and created an undesirable financial dependency. That we may be able to speak of a Scottish economy is evident in 'Scotland's historic tendency to perform relatively worse in UK cyclical upturns and relatively better in downturns',[55] in the view that 'macro-economic policies targeted at economic problems specific to the south-east of England' are not suitable for Scotland[56] and in the existence of 'distinct policy-networks and institutions' which articulate a 'separate Scottish national economic interest'.[57]

In one sense, except in the special case of Northern Ireland, the existence of distinctive regional economies with distinctive regional needs does not seem to matter to central government. The 1980s changes in domestic regional policy are consistent with the approach the government was promoting in the EU; in both cases, increased competitiveness through market forces. It would seem, then, that a relatively uniform solution was seen as universally appropriate regardless of different situations. On the other hand, while the EU acknowledges the significance of regional variations, its policies may be able do little about this, particularly in the UK.

Beyond the truism that the volume of EU regional expenditure is, and can be, only infinitesimal compared to governmental assistance, assessments of the costs and benefits of EU regional policy are controversial. On the one hand, Ashcroft[58] and Brown, McCrone and Paterson[59] identify problems in certain kinds of inward investment, mergers and takeovers inherent in a single market to which insufficiently 'developmental' states are vulnerable. Branch plants, licensing and mergers may reinforce disadvantage in less-favoured regions if they import most of their components, and by leaving regions bereft of headquarters, subject to ownership and control that is outwith the region and, hence, worse-off in terms of the entrepreneurial culture that 1980s domestic policy was supposed to stimulate. The promotion of entrepreneurship by the EU is 'commendable' but it is unlikely to be of sufficient scale to offset the centralizing tendencies of the integration process.[60]

The perceived difficulty of making the most of EU membership is doing more than inducing circumvention of central institutions. It is also augmenting demands for the division of Parliamentary Sovereignty or at least some devolution of political power. Unionists in Northern Ireland sometimes feel compelled to resist the grander claims about the EU's potential impact on the island because they can be perceived as putting at risk the union with Great Britain, a fear that is compounded by nationalist hopes that integration in Europe may, indeed, contribute to local change. But they are not averse to Northern Ireland's having greater and distinctive influence in the EU. The debate in Scotland about its place in Europe is intimately linked with that about its place in the UK. There, opinion is not divided between those seeking radical constitutional change and those preferring none. Majorities do want substantial reform but differ as between independence or federalism. Thus, there is a particular twist in Scotland to discussions of subsidiarity. Conventional wisdom elsewhere is that the definition of subsidiarity in Article 3b of the Maastricht Treaty is preferred by central government because it protects the legal authority of member states *vis-à-vis* common institutions. Conversely, advocates of participatory democracy, whatever the shape of the political regime, like the definition in the Preamble which refers to decisions being made 'as closely as possible to the citizen'. In Scotland, all parties (except Conservatives), other organisations and citizens – 30 000 of whom demonstrated in its favour at the Edinburgh summit in 1992[61] – like the Preamble's definition but they also are 'much more likely than people in the south of England to think that the best level of decision-making might be above the nation-state',[62] thereby 'squeezing out' the authority of the nation-state as currently constituted. According to Brown, McCrone and Paterson,[63] 'European membership and European policies provide a potential alternative to the free market ideology . . . of Conservative administrations post-1979'. Given the same 'minority government' of Wales, it is likely that similar views would be found there though less so in Northern Ireland where, as noted above, 'hard' regional policies have not been applied as extensively. But shifts in the focus of electoral politics to 'Europe as an alternative site for Scottish aspirations' are not narrowly instrumental. In Scotland and Wales, many people 'increasingly feel frustrated by comparison with their counterparts in regions in other European states which allow regions a much greater opportunity to participate'.[64]

According to Young's historiography of the UK and the EU, a plethora of questions, not yet answerable, would need to be answered in a full response to our editors' questions. These include: Why did Macmillan change tack from the European Free Trade Area to the EEC? Why did Wilson, unenthusiastic at first himself and leading a divided party, also apply? Why did both Prime Ministers do so when they must have known that President de Gaulle would veto their applications? How, precisely, was Wilson's decision linked to continuing economic problems, division in the Commonwealth over Rhodesia's Unilateral Declaration of Independence, and withdrawal in the same year from Suez? Young's speculative reply to his own questions is that 'given the disappearance of Empire, the declining value of US alliance and the relative underperformance of economy', there may simply have been 'no alternative'. That the new orientation was adopted in a mood of resignation may explain the lack of eagerness for accession when it came.[65]

The same reluctance to welcome the inevitability of the EEC route to national recovery may also underlie the vulnerability of the dominant consensus to opponents who pitch their appeals on notions of sovereignty (notions which, to left and right respectively, seem capable of realising dreams of autarky or *laissez-faire*). Perhaps what no-one realised in the 1960s – though maybe they should have done so by the 1970s – was that the EEC was not merely the means of national recovery but that it might also clarify fundamental questions about the economic and political interests of the different parts of the UK. It remains to be seen precisely how radical the explicit differentiation between regional interests will prove. But the variation between sub-national regions of the UK undoubtedly helps to qualify overly general assumptions concerning Britain's experience of national decline.

Notes

1. A. Gamble, *Britain in Decline: Economic Policy, Political Strategy and the British State* (Basingstoke, 1994; 1st edn, 1981).
2. Jean Monnet, quoted by G. FitzGerald and P. Gillespie, 'Ireland's British Question', *Prospect*, vol. 12 (October 1996), p. 25.
3. S. George, *An Awkward Partner: Britain in the European Community* (Oxford, 1990), p. 10.
4. A. Gamble, *A Conservative Nation* (London, 1974).
5. See, for example, L. J. Sharpe, 'British Scepticism and the European Union: An Explanation' (Paper presented at ECPR Joint Sessions, Oslo, April 1996).
6. S. George (ed.), *Britain and the European Community: The Politics of Semi-Detachment* (Oxford, 1992), p. 31.
7. R. Dunphy, 'Conservative and Christian Democrat Debates on European Union', in P. Murray and P. Rich (eds), *Visions of European Unity* (Boulder, 1996), p. 133.
8. *Ibid.*; see also J.W. Young, 'Britain and "Europe": The Shape of the Historiographical Debate', in B. Brivati, J. Buxton and A. Seldon (eds), *The Contemporary History Handbook* (Manchester, 1996).
9. George, *Awkward Partner*, p. 65.

10. P. Murray, 'Nationalist or Internationalist? Socialists and European Unity', in P. Murray and P. Rich (eds), *Visions*, pp. 160, 162–5.
11. *Ibid.*, p. 168.
12. A. Gamble, *Britain in Decline*, p. 13.
13. Quoted by S. Letvin, *The Autonomy of Thatcherism* (London, 1988), p. 281.
14. S. George, *Awkward Partner*, p. 165.
15. Mrs Thatcher, Bruges Speech, 20 September 1988.
16. L. Tsoukalis, 'Economic and Monetary Union', in H. Wallace and W. Wallace (eds), *Policy-Making in the European Union* (Oxford, 1996), p. 289.
17. *Ibid.*, p. 291.
18. John Major, Second Annual William and Mary Lecture, 7 September 1994.
19. HC Debates, 1 March 1995, vol. 255, col. 1065.
20. *Daily Telegraph* 8 December 1995.
21. P. Ashdown, 'Ashdown on Europe: The Case for a Single Currency', *The Economist* 10 June 1996.
22. Debate on European Communities Finance Bill, 28 November 1994, HC Debates, vol. 250, cols. 932–1049.
23. D. Howell, 'Britannia's Business', *Prospect*, vol. 15 (January 1997).
24. C. Pilkington, *Britain in the European Union Today* (Manchester, 1995), p. 248.
25. S. George, 'The Approach of the British Government to the 1996 Intergovernmental Conference of the European Union', *Journal of European Public Policy*, vol. 3, no. 1 (1996).
26. R. Dunphy, 'Conservative and Christian Democrat Debates', p. 153.
27. S. George, 'Approach of the British Government'.
28. M. Newman, *Democracy, Sovereignty and the European Union* (London, 1996).
29. N. Barry, 'Sovereignty, the Rule of Recognition and Constitutional Stability in Britain', *Journal des Economistes et des Etudes Humaines*, vol. 4, no. 1 (March 1993).
30. P. Teague, 'The European Union and the Irish Peace Process', in P. Gillespie (ed.), *Britain's European Question: The Issues for Ireland* (Dublin, 1996).
31. A. Milward, *The European Rescue of the Nation-State* (Berkeley, 1992).
32. N. Barry, 'Sovereignty', p. 160.
33. J.W. Young, 'Britain and "Europe"', *op. cit.*, pp. 210–11; K. Larres, 'Integrating Europe or Ending the Cold War? Churchill's Post-War Foreign Policy', *Journal of European Integration History*, vol. 2, no. 1 (1996), p. 31.
34. P. Murray, 'Nationalist or Internationalist?', pp.169–70.
35. *New Statesman and Society*, 26 May 1995.
36. BBC, *Any Questions*, 16 June 1996.
37. R. Harmsen, 'Integration as Adaptation: National Courts and the Politics of Community Law' (Paper presented at the Annual Conference of the Political Studies Association of Ireland, October 1994).
38. P. Murray, 'Nationalist or Internationalist?', p. 170.

39. R. Dunphy, 'Conservative and Christian Democrat Debates'.
40. P. Teague, 'The European Union', p. 62.
41. *Independent* 4 October 1988.
42. S. Letvin, *Autonomy of Thatcherism*, p. 284.
43. N. Barry, 'Sovereignty, the Rule of Recognition', *op. cit.*, pp. 167, 169; see also R. Harmsen, 'Integration as Adaptation'.
44. J. Usher, *European Community Law and National Law: The Irreversible Transfer?* (London, 1981).
45. D. Allen, 'Competition Policy', in H. Wallace and W. Wallace (eds), *Policy-Making*.
46. *Ibid.*, pp. 159, 177, 179.
47. D. Allen, 'Cohesion and Structural Adjustment', in H. Wallace and W. Wallace (eds), *Policy-Making*, p. 211.
48. W. Paterson, 'Britain and the European Union Revisited: Some Unanswered Questions', *Scottish Affairs*, vol. 9 (1994), p. 10.
49. *Ibid.*, p. 3.
50. M. Goldsmith, 'UK Regional Policy, Northern Ireland, the Republic and Developments in the European Union', in P. Gillespie (ed.), *Britain's European Question*, p. 93.
51. B. Ashcroft, 'Regional Policy and the Scottish Economy', *ibid.*, p. 103.
52. *Ibid.*, p. 115.
53. M. Goldsmith, 'UK Regional Policy', pp. 93–4, 95–6.
54. N. Gibson, 'Northern Ireland and Westminster: Fiscal Decentralisation. A Public Economics Perspective', in Northern Ireland Economic Council, *Decentralised Government and Economic Performance in Northern Ireland* (Belfast, 1996), pp. 60–1.
55. B. Ashcroft, 'Regional Policy', p. 114.
56. Cited in A. Brown, D. McCrone and L. Paterson, *Politics and Society in Scotland* (Basingstoke, 1996), p. 76.
57. *Ibid.*, pp. 69–70.
58. B. Ashcroft, 'Regional Policy'.
59. A. Brown, D. McCrone and L. Paterson, *Politics and Society*.
60. B. Ashcroft, 'Regional Policy', p. 117.
61. A. Brown, D. McCrone and L. Paterson, *Politics and Society*, pp. 22–4.
62. W. Paterson, 'Britain and the European Union Revisited', p. 4.
63. A. Brown, D. McCrone and L. Paterson, *Politics and Society*, p. 86.
64. W. Paterson, 'Britain and the European Union Revisited', pp. 4, 8.
65. J.W. Young, 'Britain and "Europe"', p. 212.

14

Globalisation and Britain's Decline

HENK OVERBEEK

This chapter discusses the decline of Great Britain from the perspective of the global political economy. It explores how the rise and decline of Britain as a hegemonic power have been inextricably intertwined with the changing world economy, and argues that the weaknesses in Britain's relative position in the postwar period had their roots in long-term structural factors. Finally, I ask how the restructuring of the global economy since the mid-1970s has affected Britain.

Since the recession of the years 1973–75, the world economy has undergone an intensive transformation, a rapid 'intensification of economic, political, social, and cultural relations across borders'.[1] When viewed in this essentially quantitative way, there is nothing very new about globalisation. The ratio of international economic linkages to domestic linkages (trade, but also investment) is not extraordinarily high in the current epoch: the late nineteenth century was, in these terms, probably more global than the late twentieth century. In fact, in the quantitative sense of the 'expansion of economic transactions across borders', globalisation had its roots in the epoch of the creation of the capitalist world market after the so-called discovery of the Americas at the end of the fifteenth century.[2] The expansion of the world market was an uneven process characterised by periods of rapid intensification alternating with periods of stagnation and even reversal, wrought with contradictions and deflected by obstacles often of its own making.

The premise of this chapter is that the fundamental dynamic underlying this process is the dialectic between *privatisation* – the commodification of all spheres of human life, the competition of market forces,

the individualisation and atomisation of people – and *socialisation* –
the progressive replacement of personal bonds by widening circles of
impersonal dependence and coherence through the division of labour.
This dialectic (or 'double movement' in Karl Polanyi's words) is mani-
fested in the alternation of waves of revolutionary transformation and
periods of retrenchment during which the forces of the market are constrained by a strengthening of social protection.[3] Put thus, we can see
that the true essence of 'globalisation' is not quantitative, but qualitative: it does not just denote 'more' (trade, investment, cultural
exchanges), and flows across 'more' borders, but also signifies a 'different' kind of economic order. Each new phase of globalisation and
each new phase in the development and expansion of the capitalist
world economy brings (and is brought about by) at once a quantitative
and a qualitative change. There have been three waves of globalisation
over the past five centuries, characterised not only by geographical
expansion and increased flows of goods and finance across borders, but
in a deeper sense by changes in the nature of the dominant production
and circulation relations and in the structures of governance. My objective in this chapter is to situate the examination of Britain's decline in
this global context. Great Britain cannot be regarded as a self-contained
social formation, the dynamics of which are determined internally. The
process of capitalist development is fundamentally global in nature,
and the specificity of a national formation can be adequately grasped
only if it is seen as the outcome of the dialectical interplay between
external (systemic) and internal factors.

Most contributions to the debate on the causes of Britain's decline
have indeed recognised the international context. Britain's relations
with the world economy as well as the domestic configuration of interests resulting from those relations have been crucial ingredients of a
wide variety of approaches.[4] However, few if any of these contributions
have taken as their point of departure the *totality* of the global political
economy and the crucial role of British capital and the British state
therein. The decline of Britain is not the decline of a hegemonic power
within the context of an international system with which it is closely
linked but which is fundamentally external to it. The decline of Britain
must be conceived as a transformation *of* the global system, rather than
as a transformation of Britain *within* that system. Adopting such a global perspective does not necessarily imply the suggestion that the world
system should be ontologically privileged over its constituent units, as
Wallerstein and many of his fellow world systems theorists claim.[5] The
question is not one of simply deciding whether to consider the system

as prior to the units or, as is the position of most of mainstream international relations theory, rather declare the unit to be ontologically prior to the system. Dialectical or structurationist theories provide us with the tools to transcend this dichotomy and to comprehend how system and unit are mutually constituted.[6] It is therefore imperative that we look beyond the state-centric discourse which is so common in most approaches to world politics, wherein the sovereign territorial state is seen as the prime actor, separate from society at large which is treated as the 'environment'. Social forces are at best recognised as 'non-governmental actors' influencing the behaviour of states. Yet the state can also be seen as the institutional expression of political power, as the 'repository of certain social and political practices'.[7] To underline this view that the state is embedded in the wider social system, Robert Cox has introduced the concept of the 'state/society complex' as the basic unit in world politics.[8] Cox bases his views on an innovative reading of the work of Antonio Gramsci, applying Gramsci's core concepts such as hegemony, historic bloc and civil society to an analysis of world politics. Cox distinguishes between two basic types of state/society complexes – hegemonic and non-hegemonic.[9]

In hegemonic state/society complexes, political power is based on consent rather than on domination. The economic basis of the state is a self-regulating market, social relations are subject to the rule of law and the state plays a facilitating rather than a leading role in social and economic life. This type of state/society complex may be called *Lockean*.[10] The first Lockean state/society complex came into being in England, with the Glorious Revolution of 1688. From the very beginning, its essence was transnational. Its sphere of operation was not restricted to the territory of England proper, but was expanded by the transnational extension of the English historic bloc. Emigration and colonisation projected 'English' civil society across the seas, and the coherence of this emerging transnational civil society was cemented by the rise of cosmopolitan banking families such as the Rothschilds and transnational elite networks such as the Round Table Society. Through this gradual expansion there emerged a hegemonic 'core' of the state system, or a Lockean 'heartland'. The infrastructure of the heartland has two crucial features: the transnational spread of civil society, and the establishment of a single state, or a group of states with quasi-state structures, serving as the world's banker and providing the power to safeguard capitalist relations of production around the globe.

The expansion of this heartland has historically taken place in confrontation with a variety of 'Hobbesian' contender states where the state/society complex is based on mobilisation by one single dominant class. The 'Hobbesian' state/society complex is characterised by a fusion of ruling class and governing class into a single 'state class' which is constrained in its capacity to articulate [its] interests in the transnational space dominated by the Anglo-Saxon ruling class.[11] Hobbesian states are thus propelled by a continuous catch-up drive which mostly ends in failure, collapse, or violent defeat by the Lockean heartland. This defeat is followed either by gradual incorporation into the heartland (as with Germany after 1945) or by disintegration (as has so far been the case with the Soviet Union).

In this chapter I utilise the notion of a hegemonic state/society complex and review the rise of the British ruling classes to global hegemony and the decline of their hegemonic position. This was inevitably accompanied by a relative decline of the British domestic economy and society. These processes are explained in relation to the transformation of the global system as a whole. My argument utilises the two ideal-typical state formations described above.

Mercantilism

The first wave of expansion of the global capitalist economy – the era of the great discoveries – ushered in the age of mercantile capital. It created a genuinely global market through the expansion of international trade and the establishment of an international division of labour. The rise of capitalist production in Europe and the growth of the world market were mutually constitutive, each presupposing the other for its consolidation. In terms of the structures of governance, the first spurt of globalisation conditioned, but was in turn also conditioned by, the formation of the system of 'sovereign' territorial states in Europe, collectively called the Westphalian system. The Peace of Westphalia of 1648 was followed by a century of consolidation, during which the further expansion of European capitalism was subjugated to the exigencies of stabilisation and mercantilist rivalry.[12]

As Wallerstein puts it:

> the core countries reacted [to the stagnation of the seventeenth century] by attempting to concentrate all the major sources of capitalist profit within their frontiers: world-market oriented cereals production, the new metallurgical and textile sectors, the new transport infrastructure, and the entrepôts of Atlantic trade.[13]

Similarly, Cox argues that 'states sought to establish and protect monopolies in trade, access to resources, and colonial settlement as adjuncts to their domestic sources of power'.[14] And Arrighi speaks of a 'new synthesis of capitalism and territorialism', with three major components: 'settler colonialism, capitalist slavery, and economic nationalism'.[15] The name which was given to this new synthesis was mercantilism. It was the means of self-defence adopted by the commercial late-comers of the era – the United Kingdom and France – to the liberalism and universalism of the declining hegemonic power, the United Provinces.

The Ascendancy of the British Ruling Classes

During this phase capital internationalised through the circuit of commodity capital, by means of a steady expansion of the scope of international trade. The period between 1450 and 1750 hence saw the rise of a commercial bourgeoisie, first in the Italian city-states, then in Holland, and finally in England. These merchants played the leading role in the expansion of the capitalist world market. Only later, from 1750 onward, did the English and Scottish industrial bourgeoisie gradually rise to economic prominence. However, politically the industrial bourgeoisie remained subordinate to the older commercial, shipping and financial interests controlling the foreign trade routes on which industry depended. The internal power base of the British bourgeoisie, however, was initially not very different from that of its Dutch counterpart: its social power was derived from its control of trade and commerce (particularly the Atlantic trade) and the associated activities. This economic foundation of power determined the composition of the historic bloc in Britain, and therefore the nature of Britain's hegemony in the world system, which, following Cox, should be understood as the 'outward expansion of the internal (national) hegemony established by a dominant social class'.[16]

These ascendant capitalist classes required from the state a very specific form of support, namely support against external commercial rivals. This is what Gerstenberger called *merkantile Aussenvertretung* – external mercantile representation.[17] In England, this function was fulfilled by the state created by Oliver Cromwell which implemented the transition from royal privilege to generalised class ('national') interest especially through the Navigation Act of 1651. The defeat of the Dutch in the Anglo-Dutch wars decisively weakened the strongest commercial rival and thereby eclipsed much of the English bourgeoisie's demand for *merkantile Aussenvertretung*. The Glorious Revolution of 1688 eventually laid the foundations for a 'Lockean' state–society complex in Britain, in which a 'civil' society emerged, characterised by the self-regulation of private affairs and the withdrawal of the state from direct interference with the spheres of production and exchange.[18]

The Transnational Expansion of the Lockean Pattern

The Lockean pattern of state–society relations was from its very inception transnational. In fact, the principles of self-government were already firmly established in the colonies in New England by the middle of the seventeenth century and were further developed in interaction with developments in England after 1688. Emigration from the British Isles during the eighteenth century transmitted these patterns to the new areas of settlement in Canada, Australia and New Zealand, thus creating an integrated *Lockean heartland* in the global political economy.[19] Writing about the resulting structures a century later, H. Duncan Hall captured their essential transnational quality:

> The Commonwealth, like the United States, was being formed by one of the great population movements of history . . .The peoples of the Commonwealth were circling back and forth between the new homelands over the seas and the old homelands in Europe . . . the 'great society' of the Commonwealth . . . had long since begun to overflow the political boundaries of its nations. It operated as a system of interlinked groups, organisations and societies within the greater community of the family of the Commonwealth.[20]

The age of mercantile capital was really the pre-history of capitalism. It was an era during which the main means of accumulation was the trade in goods produced under non-capitalist relations of production. It is true, of course, that this trade took place for profit, but the dynamics of a trade-based system are fundamentally different from those of a production-based system like that which became dominant after 1750. It is only then that capitalist production relations, in which human labour is directly subjected to the exploitation by capital in the production process, came to dominate society at large. Only then did capital become what Marx called self-expanding value. And with the rise of industrial capitalism, the process of the socialisation of labour was accelerated enormously, and the state gradually became a nation-state. In that process, the British were faced with a sustained and serious challenge to their supremacy, a challenge which it would take more than half a century to defeat. What exactly was the nature of that challenge?

The Challenge of France

The emergence and hegemonic expansion of Lockean state/society relations through the emigration of the English and their reproduction of self-governing polities in the areas of settlement (though not in the other colonies) called forth in the countries resisting their subordination a counterpoint to the Lockean pattern, in which the state, through a revolution from above, led the attempt to catch up. This can be termed the Hobbesian state, following van der Pijl.[21] In contrast with the Lockean pattern of the separation of powers, ruling class and governing class tended in these cases to merge into a state class. As Elsenhans pictures this class, it '. . . does not appropriate surplus product on the strength of its competitiveness on the market, but through the instruments of state economic policy'.[22] In the eighteenth century, the main Hobbesian contender confronting Britain's preponderance in the expanding world economy was France. By the middle of that century it was by no means clear that the struggle between Britain and France would be decided in favour of the former. True, Britain did have a slight competitive advantage which was gradually enhanced by the increasing importance of the Atlantic trade.[23] In terms of the power struggle between the two countries, the British victory in the Seven Years War (1756–63) signalled the end of the struggle for supremacy. In terms of the economic struggle between the two core states, the break-up of the commercial-industrial power of the French Atlantic coast around Nantes eliminated the French as a serious contender for control over the Atlantic trade. The American War of Independence reinforced this result. Ostensibly, the British lost the war, but in fact the dynamism unleashed by the rise of America could benefit only the British because no other European competitor was in a position to take advantage of the new opportunities. A further consequence was that the French state debt continued to rise, whereas the British (partly thanks to Dutch investments) were able to repay their public debt swiftly. Consequently the 1780s were a decade of rapidly growing disparity between France and Britain.

The outcome of the struggle between Britain and France decisively shaped the resulting structure of the global political economy, in both political and economic terms, both internationally and in Britain. Politically, power in Britain remained firmly in the hands of the old power bloc, consisting of the landed aristocracy and the 'monied interest'. The upper classes closed ranks around patriotic slogans against the radicalism threatening their privileges. Domestic hegemony and hegemony in the world economy mutually reinforced each other. Economically, however, the changes which occurred during the years 1789-1815 were far-reaching. As a result of the French occupation of Holland, the Dutch role as major creditor was also taken over by England. London replaced Amsterdam as the most important financial centre of the world economy. The French Revolution further provided an effective shield behind which English manufacturers were able to prosper. French domination of the Continent drove British industrial and commercial capital to seek expansion across the Atlantic Ocean instead of across the Channel and this turned England into the workshop of the world in the following century. During the same decades, the British effectively destroyed all industry (particularly textiles) in India by levying heavy import duties on Indian textiles. It was only when Indian competition had been disposed of that the British manufacturers became free traders, propagating *laissez-faire* and free trade liberalism throughout the world.[24]

Liberal Internationalism

The second wave of globalisation occurred with the expansion of industrial capitalism from the middle of the nineteenth century until the 1890s. The defeat of the Napoleonic challenge to Britain's hegemony, and later the Repeal of the Corn Laws, ushered in the era of the Liberal World Order, with its dramatic expansion of industrial production and global trade and finance. The expansion of the world market until the early twentieth century was basically *extensive*. It was only in the twentieth century that geographical expansion lost some of its central importance to forms of intensive growth. Just as Dutch hegemony in the seventeenth century was accompanied by the articulation of a liberal ideology, so was the British. Britain's liberal internationalism was not only embraced by the hegemonic forces but it was also shared (this is the essence of hegemony) by key subordinate forces in the nineteenth-century global political economy.

The era of industrial capital was further characterised by the rise of a new form of state. Urbanisation and the creation of an industrial working class dissolved traditional social and familial relationships and transformed the local or regional frame of reference for social relations into a national one. State and nation merged; sovereignty, territoriality and nationality were 'bundled' together; and the 'popular nation-state' was created.[25] Towards the end of the nineteenth century the expansion of European capitalism reached its zenith with the partitioning of the globe into colonial and semi-colonial spheres of influence. With the rise of new Hobbesian challengers in the form of Japan and the unified Germany the international system again entered a phase of international rivalries and internal consolidation. The period of the two World Wars represents the climax of that period, with two successive German bids to break Britain's hegemony, and with an unprecedented 'closure' of national economies and societies.

Balance of Power

The Napoleonic wars ended in British victory, and the restoration of the Westphalian state system in the Settlement of Vienna of 1815. Of all major powers only Britain was involved in every region where European power expanded, giving it overwhelming preponderance. Britain put in place a mechanism (the balance-of-power system) for the maintenance of its strategic preponderance which was to a large extent self-regulating and therefore quite cheap. This system left the British free to pursue their colonial expansion in other parts of the world. This mix of commercial and territorialist expansion is what distinguished global hegemony in the nineteenth century from global hegemony in the seventeenth.[26] Britain's role as the 'balancer' of the European system made possible the bourgeois-liberal transformations in Western Europe as well as the independence of the Spanish and Portuguese colonies in South America in the post-1815 decades, thus reinforcing those social forces within these continents supportive of the liberal organisation of the world economy to suit the interests of the dominant power bloc in Britain which was ultimately able to reinforce its economic interests with its naval omnipotence.

Empire and Free Trade

The rapid expansion of British naval and industrial power notwithstanding, it was several decades before Britain truly ruled the waves and free trade could be adopted wholeheartedly. British tariffs did not fall below 20 per cent until 1855.[27] However, after the Companies Act of 1844 and the Repeal of the Corn Laws of 1846, industrial capital expanded swiftly. Between 1850 and 1870 industrial production in Britain doubled. Whereas in 1750 the level of industrialisation in Britain was approximately the same as in France and Germany, and about double the level in Russia and the United States, in 1800 Britain was twice as industrialised as its main competitors, and at the height of its 'great leap forward' (in 1860) the lead had increased to between three times (France and the United States) and eight times (Russia).[28] As the logical corollary of this rapid industrialisation, British exports in the mid-nineteenth century accounted for approximately 40 per cent of world trade.[29] Throughout most of the nineteenth century imports existed for roughly 90 per cent of raw materials and foodstuffs, while industrial products made up about 85 per cent of exports.[30] The international division of labour both deepened and widened decisively: almost all regions of the world were linked, through a complex hierarchy of commercial and financial ties, to the core. Britain's commercial predominance reinforced its financial superiority as well, which depended on its ability to maintain a balance of payments surplus with the rest of the world. The control over the Empire, and especially India, was crucial in this respect.[31] The continuous outflow of investment capital from Britain to the rest of the world led to a compensating flow of investment income from abroad which overtook the outflow of new capital from 1875 onward.[32]

The Liberal State

Britain's hegemony in the global system rested on the hegemony of the power bloc consisting of the financial bourgeoisie and the commercial aristocracy (and it reproduced and reinforced this at the same time). Throughout the first three quarters of the century, this power bloc held all the reins of control in what Nairn has aptly described as the 'patrician' British state.[33] The patrician classes always pursued their interests in a transnational context. British emigration and the projection of British influence throughout the world contributed crucially to the spread of Lockean patterns of state–society relations, of which 'constitutionality' is a major component.[34]

The hegemony of the internationally oriented historic bloc, when challenged, was restored through the 'de-nationalisation' of the British ruling class.[35] The recurrent discussion about protectionism vs free trade emerging during the Depression of the late nineteenth century was repeatedly decided in favour of the free traders. With the movement for Tariff Reform in 1905, 'the political hour of heavy industry seemed finally to strike', but the movement was defeated once more because it was unable to gain the support of the old liberal capitalists in such industries as textiles, coal and shipbuilding, who at this time 'remained loyal to Free Trade'.[36] The exercise was repeated, with further increased costs to the domestic social economy, with the return to the Gold Standard after 1919.

The Rise of America

The British 'pacification' of Europe through the balance of power system, coupled to its domination of the East, cleared the way for the rapid further incorporation of the Americas into the world economy. British merchant bankers, such as Brown Shipley and Barings, played an essential role in the economic unification of the United States and toward the end of the nineteenth century, after the Civil War had resolved the struggle between Southern agro-commercial interests and Northern industrial interests, this enabled the United States to become a serious imperialist rival. In the process, the economies on both sides of the Atlantic were integrated through multiple links of trade, investment and migration to such an extent that their cycles became demonstrably interlinked. However, the global role of the British financial oligarchy changed fundamentally during the Depression of 1873–96: 'British capital moved fast towards specialisation in financial speculation and intermediation',[37] and out of productive investment. At the outbreak of the First World War the role of the London merchant bankers as the financiers *par excellence* of trans-Atlantic investment was taken over by American financiers such as J.P. Morgan, making New York the new world centre of world investment (even though the City remained strong in the funding of international trade).[38]

The rise of America, prophesied in the nineteenth century by de Toqueville and Marx, became an undeniable fact fundamentally changing the world order, and thereby transformed the conception of the world entertained by the statesmen of the time. Throughout the Commonwealth it was now recognised that Britain depended upon the United States for the ultimate protection of its imperial interests,[39] for which it would have to pay a heavy price in the form of the admission of the USA into most of its sphere of influence.

The Final Days of Hegemony

The debates over how to respond to the Great Crash of 1929 and the surge of protectionism that followed signalled the arrival of a new dominant class coalition in the capitalist world. The coalition of the first two generations of the bourgeoisie, the financial/commercial aristocracy and the old liberal bourgeoisie dominating the first wave of industrialisation in textiles and coal, had still prevailed in the struggle over the return to the Gold Standard. When the crisis of 1929 hit, these industries were so severely affected that the old liberal bourgeoisie could no longer effectively defend its position. Instead, on the wave of protectionism engulfing the globe, a third generation of the bourgeoisie came to the fore – the state-monopolistic bourgeoisie: the iron-and-steel capitalists (and other entrepreneurs in heavy industry) with their almost 'natural' preferences for protection and state intervention. This newly-prominent fraction of the bourgeoisie was able to claim its share of power as a result of the development of global capitalism in the 1930s. In Britain the decisive step on the road to 'closure' was taken in 1932 at the Ottawa Conference of the British Empire and Commonwealth, which ended with the adoption of Imperial Preferences.[40]

The position of the emerging corporate liberal bourgeoisie based in the industries producing mass consumer goods, which had crystallised during the 1920s in the USA, was ambivalent. Economic development behind protective tariffs favoured the new mass production branches, which boomed during the 1930s. As these new branches developed, their share of overall employment also grew; the rise of these new sections of the working class strengthened 'reformist' tendencies. In the United States this trend culminated in the New Deal, reflecting the growing influence of corporate liberalism, the synthesis between liberal internationalism and state-monopolism. In Great Britain, however, the corporate-liberal bourgeoisie proved unable to articulate its fractional interests into a hegemonic concept of control that could also express the interests of other social forces. This failure reinforced and reproduced the structural tendencies towards the decline of Britain against the backdrop of the rise of American hegemony.

Corporate Liberalism

The third wave of globalisation must be subdivided into two phases: the gradual return to an open world market through the internationalisation of capital in the years after 1945 and what is commonly called globalisation since the mid-1970s. The years after the Second World War witnessed the reestablishment of an open world market through the reconstitution of an international monetary system and gradual liberalisation of trade, both under decisive American guidance. Foreign direct investment in manufacturing became, for the first time, the leading mode for the internationalisation of capital, and the mechanism for exporting the Fordist mode of accumulation (or the corporate liberal concept of control) developed in the USA in the 1920s.[41]

American hegemony was founded on productive superiority, projected into the world economy by America's corporations through foreign direct investment (FDI). New York became the undisputed economic capital of the world, with the Stock Exchange (rather than the banking community) now symbolising its pre-eminence. By 1960 American superiority in this field peaked: nearly 60 per cent of all FDI originated in the United States, primarily moving into Western Europe to exploit competitive advantages in Europe's expanding markets. The era of American hegemony combined the liberalisation of world trade and finance with the development of Keynesian welfare states within an essentially national framework, premised on restricted access to citizenship rights if not outright on closed borders. The resulting governance structure has been dubbed 'embedded liberalism'.[42]

It is important to understand that hegemony in the state system is intricately interwoven with the class structures within the hegemonic state and in the transnational sphere. Epoch-making changes such as those taking place during 1914–45 do not occur in either one or the other sphere, not even in both spheres (conceptualised as separate) at the same time, but by their very nature transcend the boundaries between them and constitute them as fundamentally one. They involve changes in the relative power of social groups and the formation of new historic blocs resulting from the transformation of the underlying social structure of accumulation.

Adapting to American Hegemony

Declining hegemons do not relinquish their privileges easily or voluntarily. The adaptation of the British ruling classes to the realities of American hegemony in world politics has been a slow and painful process. It started with the wartime concessions to the United States, and was followed by the postwar acceptance of American commercial and military supremacy, the dissolution of the British Empire, the experiences of the Suez expedition, and the difficulties involved in restoring the 'Special Relationship' after Suez. Britain was initially able to maintain the integrity of the Commonwealth and the Sterling Area with the aid of the 1945 American loan, but had to pay the price of the untimely return to convertibility in 1947 which led to a severe crisis. The United States took advantage of Britain's problems to press for concessions in the sphere of access to the markets of the Empire. The Americans did agree to the resurgence of Sterling as an international reserve currency, which formed the basis for the City's postwar revival as an international financial centre and its renewed predominance internally. However, this revival of the City was not truly autonomous: rather it was shaped and conditioned by American hege-mony in the world system.

Another central element in the compromise shaping the postwar international economic order was the need to raise the standard of liv-ing in Europe, both as a preservative against communist contagion and as a precondition for the transatlantic expansion of Fordism. The Marshall Plan secured the replacement of the Pax Britannica by the Pax Americana, begun prior to the First World War but temporarily sus-pended by the imperial retrenchment of the 1930s. The Marshall Plan not only cleared the way for the progressive liberalisation of trade and the return to convertibility foreseen in the Bretton Woods agreements, but it was also instrumental in restructuring the industrial economies and the configurations of social forces in Western Europe.

In the military-strategic sphere, the division of Europe into West and East and the establishment of NATO enabled Bevin to commit the Americans permanently to Europe. Of course, there were conflicts between the USA and some of the European states including Britain – particularly with respect to the issue of decolonisation and the freeing up of trade and finance. However, two factors explain why these con-flicts never seriously endangered the underlying consensus over the new order. The first is the existence, in the form of the Soviet bloc, of a powerful common enemy. Whatever the differences between the Western powers, the West's rulers were united in their anti-Communist stance. This has meant, throughout the Cold War era, that conflicts of interest among Western powers have eventually always been resolved through a combination of economic pressure and ideological arm-twist-ing. Differences of opinion over the nature of the Soviet threat and over the desired policy *vis-à-vis* the East were usually the function of domestic political struggles rather than a reflection of 'real' Soviet threats.[43] The second reason is that in Western Europe the Marshall Plan was part of a more encompassing restructuring of the economy along the lines suitable for the expansion of the mass production sys-tem known as Fordism. The next step was the launching in 1950 of the Schuman Plan for a supranational authority to oversee the restructuring of the European coal and steel industries. The formation of the European Economic Community in 1958 was also actively supported by the Americans as conducive to the further expansion of Fordism in Europe.

The Failure of Fordism in Britain

Fordism, defined here as the combination of new mass production techniques with state-guaranteed mass consumption, had been the foundation of the restoration of growth in the United States with the New Deal, and with the adoption of the Marshall Plan and the formation of the Organisation for European Economic Cooperation (OEEC) also in Western Europe. In Japan too, economic recovery was organised under American tutelage on the basis of a restructuring of social and economic conditions along the same lines.[44] In this way, Fordism had become the basis for the rapid growth of the world economy. However, the expansion of global Fordism to an important extent by-passed Britain. When compared to the performance of the member states of the European Community and Japan, the British economy consistently lagged behind. Notwithstanding the economic growth that did take place (which was in fact more rapid than at almost any time before in the twentieth century), Britain was clearly again in relative decline as it had been between the 1860s and 1930s. How should we explain this return to decline in a period of rapid growth of the world economy?[45]

The first explanation involves the effects of the international character of British capital. This international orientation was reinforced by the resurrection of the City of London as a central 'locus' in the international circuits of money capital after 1945. The City was so successful that it became an 'off-shore' centre, particularly after the floating of the dollar in 1971. Nevertheless, the question remained as to why British capital chose to expand externally rather than internally. A number of factors have contributed to this continued decline of Britain after 1945: the feebleness of the British state, and, connected to this, the weakness of the British industrial bourgeoisie as a consciously organised class 'für sich', whose demands might otherwise have forced the state to engage more actively in the reconstruction of the British productive apparatus. The specifically British relationship between civil society and the state (a 'lean' state and a loosely organised hegemonic coalition of aristocracy and bourgeoisie), which had been temporarily modified by the transformations of the 1930s and 1940s, were reproduced in contemporary form, adapted to and determined by the conditions of the new organisation of world capitalism in the form of the Pax Americana. And the City's hegemony over monetary and economic policy forced the economy (through the 'stop–go' cycle' into constant relative stagnation.

A second explanation sees working class strength as a major factor.[46]

Kilpatrick and Lawson emphasise the historical development of the trade union movement in Britain. That development was characterised by its early-capitalist organisational forms (craft based, focus on the workplace, with weak national organisation), and by its relative continuity. The result was strong and successful resistance to the restructuring of work practices and the introduction of technological innovation. The British trade union movement in the post-war period did indeed have a strong defensive position within firms. Even if this strength was not used, or was insufficient, to oppose technological innovation with success (as is argued by Fine and Harris[47]), it did succeed at the national level in enforcing the adherence to full employment until the latter half of the 1960s, and this has contributed to British capital's tendency to expand abroad rather than domestically. The full employment priority also probably contributed to the slow rate of restructuring of British industry and again reinforced the propensity of British capitalists to invest abroad. The working class organisations were too weak however to induce the state to adopt a conscious industrial policy to make up for the negligence of capital. The organisations of both the industrial working class and the industrial bourgeoisie were weak, decentralised, unaccustomed to dealing with each other constructively, and faced with a state that was just as weak and unaccustomed to intervening in industrial relations and the industrial structure.

The Demise of the Corporate-Liberal Consensus

When by the late 1960s the world economy was hit by recession, the impact on the British economy was disproportionate. The last chance for the corporate-liberal bourgeoisie to impose its concept of control on the historic power bloc was frustrated when Macmillan's bid for entry into the Common Market failed in 1963. From then on, the corporate liberals fought a losing battle. Domestically, the needs of industrial capital were insufficiently met by the externally oriented City, and the export markets growing most rapidly, those on the Continent, were increasingly difficult to penetrate. Major British manufacturing companies responded by investing heavily in Europe to circumvent these problems. By the time Britain finally did enter the European Community in 1973 these companies had already become global companies. They would play a major role in the next phase of the internationalisation of capital in the global economy.

Globalisation

By the mid-1970s, the postwar world order, based upon American hegemony, the Keynesian welfare state and the Fordist mode of accumulation, entered a structural crisis. The first response to the crisis on the part of capital was to intensify its internationalisation, which resulted in what became known as the New International Division of Labour, and which represented a qualitative transition from an international to a global or transnational world.[48] The abolition of the gold–dollar standard in 1971 led to a rapid expansion of international money capital, which found its political expression in the rise of monetarism and neo-liberalism. Productive capital decisively outgrew its national confines too. Its paradigmatic scale of operation became global, and productive capital accelerated its rapid internationalisation, to reach a qualitatively new intensity in the 1980s and 1990s. With this quantum leap in globalisation, the capability of national states to regulate key economic processes has been seriously eroded. In response, states sought to re-establish their control over the economy through the creation or reactivation of regional structures (such as the European Community) which is one of the factors explaining the phenomenon of regionalisation. In Britain, the crisis of the postwar order and the transition to neo-liberalism were deeper and earlier than in other OECD states: the severity of the crisis in the 1970s, culminating in the 'Winter of Discontent' in 1978–79 and an unprecedented degree of 'deindustrialisation', attests to this, as does the first free election of a neo-liberal government in 1979.

Thatcherism in Perspective

Towards the end of the 1980s I argued that:

> Thatcherism is a reasonably coherent and comprehensive concept of control for the restoration of bourgeois rule and bourgeois hegemony in the new circumstances of that decade – that is in the context of the transformation of world capitalism now taking place.[49]

I interpreted Thatcherism as 'the expression of the outlook of *circulating capital* and *transnational capital* inside Britain, which expressed a 'general interest' through its reactionary-populist elements'.[50] I went on to identify four key areas in which Thatcherism had made significant political interventions: the redefinition of Britain's European and global role, the defeat of the organisations of the left, the elaboration of a neo-liberal accumulation strategy, and the shaping of a neo-liberal power bloc. My conclusion was that Thatcherism had been very successful in its deconstructive mission defined thus: 'Neoliberalism is . . . directed towards disarticulating the old formation which is in crisis, that is, towards *deconstructing corporatism and the Keynesian welfare state*'.[51] But I also thought that it was too early to judge the durability of its constructive enterprise – 'towards the formation of a new configuration, the *construction of a post-Fordist accumulation regime*'.[52]

A key debate at the time of the publication of the book in late 1989 focused on the question of the sustainability of the neo-liberal regime. How could an essentially de(con)structive project be anything but transitional, and how could such an unpopular (if not anti-popular) project be hegemonic in the longer run? Both of these questions were informed by the assumption that corporate liberalism (to be found in social democratic, Christian democratic and progressive liberal parties) still represented a possible alternative to neo-liberalism: a return to the old ways – even if they would have to be amended slightly – was regarded as the most likely alternative. We are now in a better position to see that this assumption was false. The best way to understand this is to take a closer look at the phasing of the process of global restructuring and the neo-liberal ascendancy. When we look beyond the more superficial components of 'globalisation', such as the growth of global finance and the rise of foreign direct investment, the era of global restructuring can be disaggregated into four distinct 'moments':

- The first moment (*deconstruction*) was that of the organic crisis of the postwar order: the recession, oil 'crises', stagflation and worker militancy of the 1970s, culminating in the global debt crisis erupting in 1982. This was the phase in which the limitations of Keynesianism became clear and neo-liberalism emerged as the concept with the most convincing analysis of what went wrong. This first moment lasted until the mid-1980s during which neo-liberalism struggled with and defeated corporate liberalism and social democracy in one country after another. Neo-liberalism became dominant but was not yet hegemonic.
- The second moment (neo-liberalism as a *constructive* project) was the imposition of structural adjustment, liberalisation, deregulation and privatisation. These processes can be roughly dated from 1982 until 1990 but they continue in some places until today. By 1990 neo-liberalism had become hegemonic: corporate liberalism was discredited, no new alternative can be articulated, and the tenets of

neo-liberalism were increasingly accepted as valid and legitimate. Political opposition was neutralised by a combination of demoralisation and criminalisation (the 'enemy within') of the left, and the creation of a social basis for neo-liberalism through privatisation and deregulation.

- The third moment (of *consolidation*) has been that of the post-Cold War era, starting with the appointment of Gorbachev in 1985, through the opening of the Berlin Wall in 1989 to the collapse of the Soviet Union in 1991, and the proclamation by President Bush of a New World Order. With the collapse of the Soviet Union and of 'real socialism', and with the rapid turn to capitalism of China, any notion of an alternative (however unattractive in many ways they had become) to the global rule of capital became utterly 'unrealistic' and discredited.
- Finally, the fourth moment has been that of the gradual shift of the centre of gravity in the world economy from the Atlantic to the Pacific since the mid-1970s and still continuing, though this has been temporarily interrupted and reversed by recessions such as the Japanese one of the late 1980s and the problems in East and South East Asia which have surfaced since 1997.

The combined effects of these 'moments' of global restructuring are twofold:

- the parameters of political debate have shifted radically, and
- the spatial co-ordinates of the discourse of decline have been transposed.

First, globalisation has fundamentally shifted the parameters of the political, social and economic struggles and debates throughout the global system, especially in the OECD area, and also in Britain. The pressures for liberalisation and deregulation since the late 1970s have come from similar neo-liberal quarters in all the major Western countries. In the United States organisations such as the Heritage Foundation and business lobbies such as the Business Roundtable led the struggle of the neo-liberals to gain control of the political agenda.[53] In Canada, the counterparts of these organisations were the Business Council on National Issues (BCNI) and the Fraser Institute.[54] In Britain, the torch of neo-liberalism was carried by the Institute of Economic Affairs, the Adam Smith Institute, the Centre for Policy Studies, and the Institute of Directors.[55] Internationally, the cohesion of the neo-liberal drive was greatly enhanced by the work of the Mont Pelerin Society led by Hayek and Friedman. In all cases, the neo-liberal ascendancy has entailed a strengthening of (quasi-)authoritarian structures and practices, and an assault on established forms of progressive or left popular participation.

In a more structural sense, too, globalisation reinforces the increasing difficulty for political leaders in parliamentary democracies to legitimise the policies they are committing themselves and their countries to in the transnational arena.[56] This erosion of democratic control has been termed by Stephen Gill the 'New Constitutionalism', '. . . the move towards the construction of legal or constitutional devices to remove or insulate substantially the new economic institutions from popular scrutiny or democratic accountability'.[57] In the process, the state tends to lose its redistributive function (a slow and painful process in Western Europe, but a process swiftly and mercilessly executed in much of Eastern Europe and the Third World), and its repressive nature becomes more apparent, as does its role as transmission belt for the exigencies of transnational capital (*casu quo* the IMF, the World Bank and the EBRD). Crucial areas of state action have been 'internationalised', including even the function of policing. On the ground, in the different national political systems, both corporate-liberalism and social democracy have been eclipsed as potentially hegemonic projects. The parties representing these paradigms of course still exist but they now articulate variants of neo-liberalism, which has become hegemonic across the spectre of mainstream parties.[58]

Second, globalisation is not a harmonious and even process. It proceeds through regionalisation, meaning that global economic interactions are increasingly concentrated in the major regions of the world. Regionalisation is further complemented and reinforced by *political* integration projects. The three most prominent regions in this context are North America (NAFTA), Western Europe (European Union), and East and Southeast Asia (EAEG, ASEAN). In the years since the mid-1970s the growing economic and political importance of East and Southeast Asia and the reorientation of the United States – particularly in the Reagan years – from an Atlantic to a Pacific power, expressed by the formation of APEC, have contributed to a relative decline of Western Europe when compared with the two other main regions. This is clear in terms of economic dynamism as expressed in the growth of employment, productivity and world trade share.

Since the early 1980s Britain's economic performance in comparison with that of the rest of Europe has not deteriorated any further.[59] In

terms of such indicators as GDP growth, unemployment rates, investment rates and productivity growth, Britain performs at least as well as
its major European competitors. However, 'the increased growth rate of
the late 1980s was generated largely by the financial and property sectors of the economy, while the contribution of manufacturing industry
to GDP continued to decline'.[60] Now, although this last observation is
applicable to practically all OECD economies, the degree to which it is
true for Britain underscores at once that old problems in Britain's political economy persist, but at the same time that the accumulation strategy developed under Thatcher (spearheaded by the liberalisation of foreign exchange dealings and the deregulation of the City) has been relatively successful. And furthermore, the success of the financial and services sectors in Britain has once more given Britain a special place in
the global political economy.

For, although international production and trade concentrate more
and more in the major regions of the world economy, global finance
keeps the system together by locking the spatially dispersed sites of
production and accumulation into one integrated global system. Britain
has been successful in attracting a disproportionate share of global
finance to London as is amply illustrated by the details provided in a
recent survey.[61] This success may be an example of 'short-termism',
and it may slow or even hinder the revival of British manufacturing, but
it is profitable for those interests involved in it, it does create employment, and it is strategically inserted in the new globalised world economy.

We have ceased to be a nation in retreat. We have instead a newfound confidence – born in the economic battles at home and tested and found true 8000
miles away . . . (Margaret Thatcher, 3 July 1983)

Thatcher's comment reflects a sentiment expressed repeatedly by neo-
liberals at the time. In their eyes the decline of Britain had been
reversed with the election victory of 1979, and Britain has restored its
status as a great power. For most observers of varying other persua-
sions, the verdict was much more cautious, if not outright critical: at
best Thatcherism produced a statistical, not a real, improvement in economic performance, while there was also much reason to be sceptical
over the early foreign 'successes' of the Thatcher government, such as
the victory in the Falklands War or the row over the EC budget.

The conclusion of this essay is that the structural transformation of the global political economy, of which the ascendancy of transnational neo-liberalism was one aspect, also transformed Britain. The 'decline of Britain' is a concept that is inherently linked to the era of the 'closure' and gradual internationalisation of the global system. The notion of the decline of a national polity and economy loses much of its cogency when global restructuring erodes the exclusivity of the principle of national sovereignty. Ironically, therefore, although Britain's neo-liberals are right to claim that they have stopped or even in some respects reversed the decline of Britain relative to its major European rivals, the significance of this achievement is considerably reduced by the transformation of the global order. In this sense, the 'decline of Britain' no longer exists, which also explains why the fascination of writing about it has waned. The globalisation of the world economy, the end of the Cold War, and the rise of macro-regional groupings in the world have all strengthened the impression that in important respects Britain's decline has been overtaken by (or become part of) the 'decline' of Europe *vis-à-vis* North America and East Asia.

The precise future trajectory of this process is by no means clear. What seems irreversibly true, however, is that the direction will not be determined in strictly national arenas, but that the social struggles which will be decisive are increasingly taking shape at the transnational level, in terms of simultaneous developments within national contexts, in inter-national contexts, and beyond national contexts. The fate of British society (if not of global finance in Britain) has become irrevocably intertwined with that of Europe.

Notes

1. H.-H. Holm, and G. Sörensen (eds), *Whose World Order? Uneven Globalization and the End of the Cold War* (Boulder, Colorado, 1995), p. 4.
2. As Malcolm Waters states, 'globalization could not begin until that time because it was only the Copernican revolution that could convince humanity that it inhabited a globe. More importantly, until then the inhabitants of Eurasia–Africa, the Americas, and Australia lived in virtually complete ignorance of each other's existence. So the globalization process that is of most interest here is that associated with modernity', in *Globalization* (London/New York, 1995), p. 4.
3. See K. Polanyi, *The Great Transformation: The Political and Economic Origins of our Time* (Boston, Mass., 1957).
4. For examples, see P. Anderson, 'Origins of the Present Crisis', *New Left Review*, vol. 23 (1964), pp. 26–53; R. Bacon and W. Eltis, *Britain's Economic Problem: Too Few Producers* (London, 1978); C. Barnett, *The Audit of War: The Illusion and Reality of Britain as a Great Nation*

(London, 1986); P.J. Cain and A.G. Hopkins, 'Gentlemanly Capitalism and British Expansion Overseas I. The Old Colonial System, 1688–1850', *Economic History Review*, vol. 39, no. 4 (1986), pp. 501–25; D. Coates and J. Hillard (eds), *UK Economic Decline: The Key Texts* (London, 1985); B. Elbaum and W. Lazonick (eds), *The Decline of the British Economy* (Oxford, 1986); A. Gamble, *Britain in Decline: Economic Policy, Political Strategy and the British State* (London, 1994); G. Ingham, *Capitalism Divided? The City and Industry in British Social Development* (London, 1984); T. Nairn, 'The Twilight of the British State', *New Left Review*, vol. 101-2 (1977), pp. 3–61; S. Pollard, *The Wasting of the British Economy; British Economic Policy 1945 to the Present* (London, 1982); S. Pollard, *Britain's Prime and Britain's Decline: The British Economy 1870–1914* (London, 1989); W.D. Rubinstein, *Capitalism, Culture and Decline in Britain, 1750–1990* (London, 1993); E.P. Thompson, 'The Peculiarities of the English', *Socialist Register* (1965), pp. 311–65; and M.J. Wiener, *English Culture and the Decline of the Industrial Spirit 1850–1980* (Harmondsworth, 1992; 1st edn, 1981).

5. See I. Wallerstein, *The Modern World System I: Capitalist Agriculture and the Origins of the European World-Economy in the Sixteenth Century* (New York, 1974); I. Wallerstein, *The Modern World System II: Mercantilism and the Consolidation of the European World Economy 1600–1750* (San Diego, Cal., 1980); and I. Wallerstein, *The Modern World System III: The Second Era of Great Expansion of the Capitalist World-Economy 1730–1840s* (San Diego, Cal., 1989).

6. See the discussion of these paradigms in A.E. Wendt, 'The Agent-Structure Problem in International Relations Theory', *International Organization*, vol. 41, no. 3 (1987), pp. 335–70.

7. R. Palan, 'The Second Structuralist Theory of International Relations: A Research Note', *International Studies Notes*, vol. 17, no. 3 (1992), pp. 22–29.

8. R. Cox, 'Social Forces, States and World Orders: Beyond International Relations Theory', *Millennium*, vol. 10, no. 2, (1981), pp. 126–55; and R. Cox, *Production, Power and World Order: Social Forces in the Making of History* (New York, 1987).

9. These types must be understood as *Idealtypen,* abstractions towards which real historical systems gravitate without ever being complete replicas of these ideal types.

10. K. van der Pijl, *Transnational Classes and International Relations* (London, 1998), pp. 64–87.

11. *Ibid.* pp. 78–83.

12. For a discussion of these processes, see I. Wallerstein, *The Modern World System II.*

13. I. Wallerstein, *The Modern World System III*, p. 59.

14. R. Cox, *Production, Power and World Order*, p. 115.

15. G. Arrighi, 'The Three Hegemonies of Historical Capitalism', in S. Gill (ed.), *Gramsci, Historical Materialism and International Relations* (Cambridge, 1993), pp. 148–85, 167.

16. R. Cox, 'Gramsci, Hegemony and International Relations: An Essay in Method', *Millennium*, vol. 12, no. 2, (1983), pp. 162–75, 171.

17. H. Gerstenberger, 'Zur Theorie der historischen Konstitution des bürgerlichen Staates', *Prokla*, vol. 8-9 (1973), pp. 207–26.
18. K. van der Pijl, *Transnational Classes and International Relations*, pp. 64–7.
19. *Ibid.* pp. 67–74.
20. H.D. Hall, *Commonwealth: A History of the British Commonwealth of Nations* (London, 1971), p. 106.
21. K. van der Pijl, 'The Second Glorious Revolution: Globalizing Elites and Historical Change', in B. Hettne (ed.), *International Political Economy: Understanding Global Disorder* (London, 1995), pp. 100–28.
22. H. Elsenhans, *Development and Underdevelopment: The History, Economics and Politics of North–South Relations* (Delhi, 1991), p. 78.
23. For a discussion of this, see I. Wallerstein, *The Modern World System III*, p. 68.
24. K. Polanyi, *The Great Transformation: The Political and Economic Origins of our Time* (Boston, Mass., 1957; 1st edn, 1944), pp. 135–41.
25. See J.G. Ruggie, 'Territoriality and Beyond: Problematizing Modernity in International Relations', *International Organization*, vol. 47, no. 1 (1993), pp. 139–74.
26. For a fuller consideration of these developments, see G. Arrighi, *The Long Twentieth Century: Money, Power, and the Origins of Our Times* (London/New York, 1994), p. 199; and R. Cox, *Production, Power and World Order*, p. 25.
27. R. Reuveny and W.R. Thompson, 'The Timing of Protectionism', *Review of International Political Economy*, vol. 4, no. 1 (1997), pp. 179–213.
28. P. Kennedy, *The Rise and Fall of the Great Powers: Economic Change and Military Conflict from 1500 to 2000* (London/Sydney/Wellington, 1988), p. 149.
29. M. Barratt Brown, *After Imperialism* (London, 1970), p. 62.
30. E. Krippendorff, *Internationales System als Geschichte: Einführung in die internationalen Beziehungen 1* (Frankfurt/New York, 1975), p. 107.
31. G. Arrighi, *The Long Twentieth Century*, pp. 263–4.
32. S. Pollard, 'Capital Exports 1870–1914: Harmful or Beneficial?', *The Economic History Review*, second series, vol. 38, no. 4 (1985), pp. 489–514.
33. T. Nairn, 'The Twilight of the British State'.
34. P.J. Taylor, *The Way the Modern World Works: World Hegemony to World Impasse* (Chichester, 1996), p. 112.
35. B. Rowthorn, 'Imperialism in the 1970s – Unity or Rivalry', in H. Radice (ed.), *International Firms and Modern Imperialism* (Harmondsworth, 1975), pp. 158–80.
36. P. Anderson, 'The Figures of Descent', *New Left Review*, vol. 161 (1987), pp. 20–77, 43.
37. G. Arrighi, *The Long Twentieth Century*, p. 221.
38. See W.M. Clarke, *The City in the World Economy* (Harmondsworth, 1967), pp. 24–5, 128–9; and G. Ingham, *Capitalism Divided?*, pp. 187–8.
39. See G. Barraclough, *An Introduction to Contemporary History* (Harmondsworth, 1967), p. 73.
40. See K. van der Pijl, *The Making of an Atlantic Ruling Class* (London, 1984), pp. 76–90; and H. Overbeek, *Global Capitalism and National Decline: The Thatcher Decade in Perspective* (London, 1990), pp. 59–70.

41. See van der Pijl, *The Making of an Atlantic Ruling Class*; and M. Rupert, *Producing Hegemony: The Politics of Mass Production and American Global Power* (Cambridge, 1995).

42. See especially J.G. Ruggie, 'International Regimes, Transactions, and Change: Embedded Liberalism in the Postwar Economic Order', *International Organization*, vol. 36, no. 2, (1982), pp. 379–415.

43. See A. Wolfe, *The Rise and Fall of the 'Soviet Threat': Domestic Sources of the Cold War* (Washington DC, 1979).

44. See M. van den Berg, 'Culture as Ideology in the Conquest of Modernity: the Historical Roots of Japan's Regional Regulation Strategies', *Review of International Political Economy*, vol. 2, no. 3 (1995), pp. 371–93.

45. What follows summarises my earlier survey of explorations of Britain's postwar decline in H. Overbeek, *Global Capitalism and National Decline*.

46. See particularly A. Glyn and J. Harrison, *The British Economic Disaster* (London, 1980); and A. Kilpatrick and T. Lawson, 'On the Nature of Industrial Decline in the UK', *Cambridge Journal of Economics*, vol. 4 (1980), pp. 85–102. And see the similar account of the neo-liberals F. Hayek, '1980s Unemployment and the Unions', in D. Coates and J. Hillard (eds), *The Economic Decline of Modern Britain: The Debate between Left and Right* (Brighton, 1986), pp. 106–14; and K. Joseph, 'Solving the Union Problem is the Way to Britain's recovery', in D. Coates and J. Hillard, *The Economic Decline of Modern Britain*, pp. 106–14.

47. B. Fine and L. Harris, *The Peculiarities of the British Economy* (London, 1985).

48. See C.A. Michalet, *Le Capitalisme Mondial* (Paris, 1976); and F. Fröbel, J. Heinrichs and O. Kreye, *Die Neue Internationale Arbeitsteilung. Strukturelle Arbeitslosigkeit in den Industrieländern und die Industrialisierung der Entwicklungsländer* (Hamburg, 1977).

49. H. Overbeek, *Global Capitalism and National Decline*, p. 178.

50. *Ibid.*, p. 180.

51. *Ibid.*, p. 180.

52. *Ibid.*, p. 180.

53. T. Ferguson and J. Rogers, *Right Turn: The Decline of the Democrats and the Future of American Politics* (New York, 1986).

54. See W.K. Carroll, 'Canada in the Crisis: Transformations in Capital Structure and Political Strategy', in H. Overbeek (ed.), *Restructuring Hegemony in the Global Political Economy: The Rise of Transnational Neo-Liberalism in the 1980s* (London, 1993), pp. 216–45.

55. See H. Overbeek, *Global Capitalism and National Decline*; and R. Cockett, *Thinking the Unthinkable: Think Tanks and the Economic Counter Revolution, 1931–1983* (London, 1995).

56. M. Zürn, 'The Challenge of Globalization and Individualization: A View from Europe', in H. Holm and G. Sörensen (eds), *Whose World Order?*, pp. 137–64, 154.

57. S. Gill, 'The Emerging World Order and European Change: The Political Economy of European Union', *Socialist Register*, vol. 1992, pp. 157–195, 165.

58. The main variants of neo-liberal thinking might be dubbed 'hyperliberal-

ism' (R. Cox, *Production, Power and World Order*) and 'embedded neo-liberalism' (B.van Apeldoorn, 'Transnationalisation and European Transformation: Contending Social Forces in the Construction of "Embedded Neoliberalism"', paper presented at the 38th Annual Convention of the International Studies Association, March 1997, Toronto).

59. See A. Cox, S. Lee and J. Sanderson, *The Political Economy of Modern Britain* (Cheltenham/Lyme, 1997).
60. *Ibid.*, p. 60.
61. *Ibid.*, pp. 248–9.

15

The End of Empire

RITCHIE OVENDALE

In the preface to his recent text, *Great Power Complex*, John Callaghan contends that at a time when opposition to imperialism was growing within the Empire, 'British politics effectively ignored the signs of national decline and persisted with the country's over-blown world role'. Overtones of a Marxist approach are discernible in his assertion that Britain's decline as a world power was 'inevitable'. It was the apparent refusal to acknowledge that its Great Power days were over that leads to Professor Callaghan's endorsement of Paul Kennedy's verdict that Britain became 'one of the weakest and least successful of the second-rate powers'. This is committed history, and takes the political stand that it was Britain's imperial world role and an overestimation of its economic and political influence that deluded the British establishment into thinking that it could stand aside from European involvement.[1] This assertion is in line with a school of thought which offers the 'imperial thesis' as an explanation of Britain's so-called 'decline',[2] though another, taking a longer-term view extending the analysis back to the late nineteenth century, challenges the assertion that it was Britain's conversion to 'imperialist values' that was the real reason for Britain's decline.[3] Some economists have also argued that, until 1950, the Empire inhibited modernisation, and, by implication, that the end of Empire enabled necessary reform.[4] Much of this literature focuses on aspects of imperial trade and emphasises economics. It is perhaps important to examine the political aspects of the end of Empire as well.

In 1939 Britain went to war as the head of a united Commonwealth and Empire, a great achievement of the Prime Minister, Neville Chamberlain.[5] A.J.P. Taylor has observed that the Second World War ended in a victory for every imperial cause. The logical expectation might have been that the Commonwealth would have been strengthened. Instead, sentiment about it faded, and the postwar Labour government decided to cultivate the special relationship with the United States. Taylor suggests that the Commonwealth was confused with the 'coloured colonies' which the British once ruled in despotic fashion.[6] The British Commonwealth became 'the Commonwealth' in 1949: with the admission of India as a republican member the common bond which had kept the members together, the British monarch as head of state, faded. With the outbreak of the Korean War, London began to discriminate between the old 'white' dominions which had gone to war alongside Britain in 1939, and the new Commonwealth members: the old dominions continued, on the whole, to receive the same confidential information as was laid before the British Cabinet, whereas the new Commonwealth members were considered a security risk. The Suez crisis of 1956 marked this change with respect to the old 'white' dominions.

By the early 1960s, Britain's international preoccupation has changed. Harold Macmillan's 'wind of change' speech to the South African parliament on 3 February 1960 signalled the British abdication in Africa. The Middle East, which in the years immediately following the Second World War had been regarded as one of the three crucial 'pillars' of British strategy, had lost its strategic significance, and Britain was successfully transferring power in that area to the United States, a country not always eager to take over Britain's responsibilities. With South Africa's exclusion from the Commonwealth in 1961, Macmillan started to move Britain towards Europe. The Commonwealth-Empire was increasingly viewed by British politicians and the wider public as having little significance. This is often seen as marking the 'end of Empire'.

This is one of the greatest and least noticed changes of our age. Historians and commentators have offered various explanations for the end of the British Empire. Indeed, as John Darwin has observed, the phrase 'end of Empire' is 'deceptively enigmatic'. The notion of the British Empire can be taken to cover 'a constitutional hotch-potch of independent, semi-independent and dependent countries, held together not by formal allegiance to a mother country but by economic, strategic, political or cultural links that varied greatly in strength and character'.[7] At the end of the Second World War that assemblage of countries was surprisingly intact. By the early 1960s there was little of the world map that was coloured in imperial pink, and the metropolitan power seemed anxious to dispose of those areas if it could.

Predominant amongst the explanations for the end of empire is the economic argument: Britain could no longer sustain the cost of empire and the assumption of world responsibilities that went with it; the British people were tired of rationing and looked to the improving standards of living enjoyed by their former enemies, Germany and Japan. Brian Lapping argues that the bankruptcy brought about by fighting the Second World War 'was the principal reason why the British Empire ended so much more quickly than anyone expected'. Faced with the reality of a weak economy Britain could not sustain an Empire.[8] Another interpretation, offered by R. F. Holland, is that of 'disengagement': the British and imperial economies were no longer complementary. It is notable, however, that British officialdom clung to the belief that Britain depended on the economies of the great primary-producing countries of the world and remained convinced until a very late stage that membership of the European Economic Community would not conflict with Britain's preferential trading relationship with Commonwealth countries.[9] This analysis is partially at odds with that of authorities like Wallerstein and Wasserman whose case rests on the assumption that successive British governments were insensitive to the fate of the white settlers or the morality of colonialism, and ended the British Empire as a matter of convenience necessitated by the recognition of the multinational nature of Western capitalism.[10]

Linked to this economic argument is the issue of domestic pressure: in the end Macmillan was forced to try to convince the British public that it had never had it so good before. Correlli Barnett has argued that there was a change in the British psyche, and that a sentimentality combined with hesitations over the morality of an imperial role led to a collapse of the will to rule, assisted by the 'humbling' of British world power by Washington, 'a long-cherished American ambition'.[11] While John Gallagher suggests that the British public was just not interested in the Empire,[12] A.P.Thornton attributes a sense of alienation from Empire to the rise of the welfare state with the new power given to the working classes who had little interest in what they regarded as a relic of an aristocratic past.[13]

Related to these questions is a change in British defence policy from the global strategy of the postwar Labour governments, 1945–51, to the Conservative policy of deterrence and limitation evident between 1952 and 1964. With the advent of this new defence policy, the Commonwealth-Empire was of decreasing significance.[14] Other explanations also include the rise of nationalism in the colonies, and some attribute the end of the British Empire to movements within the colonies and territories themselves.[15] Some authorities have viewed the end of Empire in a long term perspective, and have suggested that it was well under way even before the outbreak of the Second World War. Indeed one, John Gallagher, dismisses the idea of looking at the fall of the British Empire in 'a briskly functionalist way' and concludes that it was the damage wrought by the Second World War that brought it down. Gallagher suggests that the British world system had been showing signs of decay long before 1939, and that the Second World War reversed the trend, observable at the end of the First World War, of Britain moving from a system of formal rule towards a system of influence, back towards Empire. Gallagher argues that, in military terms, India exploited Britain during the Second World War. But Britain's decision to quit India was not intended to mark the end of Empire: 'Quitting India has to be seen in the light of the simultaneous decision to push British penetration deeper into tropical Africa and the Middle East'.[16]

The assertion that decline began before the Second World War has also been challenged on economic grounds in a recent 'deconstructionist' work which proposes the thesis that Britain's determination to retain its Empire and its informal influence was undiminished after both world wars:

> the idea that there was a "long retreat" from Empire fits ill with evidence not only of the revitalisation of the colonial mission after the two world wars, but also of the firm grip which Britain retained in the areas of policy which mattered most. . . [17]

This was the dominions (except Canada), India, and the tropical colonies. This substantiates the case made by R.F. Holland that 'the organisation of the Commonwealth was one way that the British state attempted to stem political and economic decline after 1918'.[18]

With the opening of the British official papers in the Public Record Office it is now possible to test many of these assertions against the documentary record. An examination of the primary sources perhaps illustrates the danger of attempting any single explanation or indulging in any over-arching theory. Assessment of them reveals the importance of the role of individuals, their perception of the cost to Britain of sustaining an Empire, the issue of moral authority and the need to sustain a policy abroad that had to be seen as not differing from that at home, and the significance for British policy of the methods pursued by the other colonial powers in Africa. Underlying the overall process is the overriding importance attached to the special relationship with the United States as the cornerstone of British foreign policy. This is the consideration which dominated British policy at the time of the end of Empire.[19]

The official papers show that the key shift in emphasis of British policy occurred during the Foreign Secretaryships of Ernest Bevin. At the end of the Second World War, the British Chiefs of Staff were convinced that British armies should not fight again on the European continent. They developed a military policy which re-established the 'three pillars' strategy under which the security of the British Commonwealth depended on: protecting the United Kingdom; maintaining vital sea communications; and securing the Middle East as a defensive and striking base against the Soviet Union.[20] Bevin opted for the Anglo-American special relationship as the way to counter the Soviet threat. The Foreign Secretary was the architect of the Western alliance. He evolved a global strategy under which the democratic nations, Britain, the European democracies, the United States and the Dominions should cooperate to meet the Soviet threat.[21] At the conference of Commonwealth Prime Ministers in October 1948, Bevin tried to involve the Dominions in Western defence. The British Chiefs of Staff suggested to the Dominion Prime Ministers that, in the event of war, five aims should be pursued in cooperation with the allies: to secure the integrity of the Commonwealth countries; to mount a strategic air offensive; to hold the enemy as far east as possible in Western Europe; to maintain a firm hold on the Middle East; and to control sea communications. The early support and action of the United States had to be ensured; the Commonwealth had to coordinate defence plans with the Western Union; and the allied scientific and technical lead had to be maintained and increased.[22] Following the Commonwealth Prime Ministers' Conference, bilateral defence discussions were started between Britain, Australia and New Zealand. Talks began with South Africa in 1949.[23]

It was against the background of the Cold War in Europe and Asia that a Foreign Office Committee, the Permanent Under-Secretary's Committee, under William Strang, considered long-term questions of British foreign policy and how Britain could in the future maintain its status as a great power. This Committee recommended in 1949 that neither the Commonwealth alone, nor Western Europe alone, nor even the Commonwealth plus Western Europe, would be strong enough, either economically or militarily, to stand on their own against the forces opposing them, and that the full participation of the United States was essential to sustain the free world which the Soviet Union was trying to undermine.[24] Effectively the British Government, at the end of 1949, endorsed the conclusions of this Committee that the prevailing policy of close Anglo-American cooperation in world affairs should continue, and that such cooperation would involve Britain's sustained political, military and economic effort. When, early in 1951, the principle of the Anglo-American special relationship as the cornerstone of British foreign policy was seriously challenged in Cabinet against the background of Western reverses in the Korean War, a dying Bevin, assisted by Strang, and Hugh Gaitskell, fought to sustain the recommendation of the Permanent Under-Secretary's Committee. What Britain had to do was to 'exert sufficient control over the policy of the well-intentioned but inexperienced colossus on whose cooperation our safety depends'.[25] London, in 1951, also felt that it was helped by the responsibilities undertaken by Australia and New Zealand working with the United States in the Pacific. The tripartite security pact, ANZUS, was regarded by the Prime Minister, Clement Attlee, and most of his colleagues as being in line with their idea of the evolution of the modern Commonwealth in which member states would take the lead in areas of their particular interest.[26]

During Bevin's tenure at the Foreign Office, the emphasis in British foreign policy was on the Anglo-American special relationship. The onset of the Cold War made this necessary: Western Europe and the Commonwealth together would not be strong enough to face the Soviet threat. This decision coincided with Britain's alteration of the nature of the British Commonwealth as it admitted republican members. The organisation ceased to be the British Commonwealth and became just the Commonwealth. This was in order to maintain the membership of India at a time when it was thought that it should help to stem the spread of communism in Asia.[27] This alteration also changed Britain's attitude to the Commonwealth. It was no longer the intimate body which had gone to war at Britain's side in 1939. With the outbreak of the Korean War in June 1950, Britain distinguished between the information it sent to the old 'white' dominions – Canada, Australia, New Zealand, and South Africa – and the new members which it often regarded as a security risk.[28] Although the Second World War was a victory for the imperial cause, the postwar Labour governments opted for the Anglo-American special relationship. Against the background of the Cold War, with the Labour administrations' determination to maintain the illusion of Britain as a great power, links with the

Commonwealth-Empire declined in importance in relation to the over-riding significance of the Anglo-American special relationship.

The argument has been advanced that for a short time Bevin favoured the development of the Empire-Commonwealth as an alternative to the Anglo-American special relationship, and that as British influence in Asia declined with the withdrawal from India, the Labour administration placed renewed emphasis on Africa.[29] Yet these were, at most, brief flirtations rather than a serious consideration of policy alternatives.

In British defence planning it was the Middle East that retained crucial importance, and with the withdrawal from Palestine in 1948, Egypt and the Suez base became all the more significant. The British agreed with the Americans that the Middle East should be an area of Commonwealth responsibility.[30] But with the deteriorating situation in Malaya and Indochina, British defence planners placed increased emphasis on Southeast Asia. More forces were needed to stop the Communist threat,[31] and more money had to be spent on defence. On 25 January 1951 the Cabinet accepted a huge increase in Britain's defence budget: £4700 million was to be spent over the years 1951–54.[32] In May 1951, however, the Iranian Prime Minister, Muhammed Mossadeq, nationalised the Anglo-Iranian Oil Company, forcing Britain to buy oil for American dollars. The balance of payments crisis helped to precipitate a general election in October 1951, and a Conservative administration was returned with Winston Churchill as Prime Minister.[33] The new Chancellor of the Exchequer, R. A. Butler, after examining the treasury accounts, decided that the British economy was not only incapable of sustaining the rearmament programme, but that the sterling crisis was also likely to challenge the nature of Britain's foreign and defence commitments, and, in effect, the position of Britain as a great power. Churchill gave his Minister of Defence, Earl Alexander of Tunis, the task of economising on Britain's military commitments.

It was Churchill's Conservative administration, with its reassessment of British defence policy and Britain's global role in relation to Britain's living standards, that marked a shift away from imperial thinking, and the crucial importance of the defence of the Middle East as being as important as defence of the United Kingdom itself. Three successive Conservative administrations instigated policies to take into account Britain's economic circumstances: these meant changes in domestic and overseas policy and adjustments in Britain's defence programme. What was common to the policies of all these administrations was the declining importance of the Empire-Commonwealth for the metropolitan power, at a time when priority was given in British planning to the Anglo-American special relationship and what came to be viewed as a relationship of 'mutual interdependence' between the two leading English-speaking nations. Decisions were taken that in effect marked the end of the British Empire, primarily by the Eden and Macmillan governments. These decisions were prompted partly by a realisation of Britain's reduced economic circumstances, and partly by domestic pressures for an increase in the standard of living, but mainly by the decision that the Anglo-American relationship was of overriding importance at the height of the Cold War. Central to this planning was the cost-effectiveness assessment of the value of Empire initiated by the Eden administration and carried through by Harold Macmillan, the British decision to abdicate in Africa, the rethinking of Britain's position in the Middle East and the transfer of power there to Washington.

In a paper dated 17 June 1952, the Chiefs of Staff revised Britain's global strategy. In considering what preparations to make for a war, they argued that it was necessary to take into account three major developments: the increased accuracy and power of atom bombing; the advent of the small bomb for tactical use; and the economic situation. The Chiefs of Staff decided that it was economically impossible to prepare and build up the necessary reserves for a prolonged war. Efforts had to be concentrated on producing forces and equipment for an intense, all-out conflict of short duration. In their view, in the Cold War period effort had to be directed to the prevention of world war. This 1952 Defence Policy and Global Strategy paper outlined what the Chiefs of Staff regarded as 'reasonable' preparations for a 'hot war'. Their recommendations were undermined by the Treasury under R.A. Butler, who was concerned that the rearmament programme would reduce living standards in Britain. The successful test of the American hydrogen bomb in November 1952 also contributed significantly to a further defence review which further undermined the 1952 Defence Policy and Global Strategy Paper. Churchill insisted that Britain needed a hydrogen bomb to remain a great power. Butler hoped that such a thermo-nuclear weapon would lessen expenditure on conventional forces. The Chiefs of Staff concluded that the main British deterrent should be nuclear weaponry.[34]

This move towards a global strategy based upon the nuclear deterrent alongside conventional forces stationed in Europe, with a reduction of British forces in the Middle East, was outlined in the February 1955

Statement on Defence.[35] The Middle East was no longer cardinal for Britain's security. Following the negotiation of the withdrawal from the Suez base in 1954, it was hoped that manpower from there could be diverted to colonial wars in Kenya, Malaya and Cyprus. But the Cold War meant that NATO, in British eyes, had to be strengthened, and there was also the question of the rearmament of West Germany. It was the collapse of the idea of a European army and the proposed European Defence Community, on which the American administration had based its European policy, that forced Anthony Eden, as Foreign Secretary, to announce in September 1954 that British troops would be committed to Europe: Britain would maintain for an indefinite period four divisions in Europe and the tactical air force. Eden did this to allay American threats of a withdrawal from Europe, and to calm French fears about German rearmament.[36]

Churchill, as he told the Cabinet in November 1951, saw the first objective of British policy as the unity and consolidation of the British Commonwealth and what was left of the former British Empire. The second objective was the 'fraternal association' of the English-speaking world. The third was a united Europe in which Britain was 'a separate, closely- and specially-related ally and friend'.[37] In effect it was during Churchill's premiership that decisions were taken that began the abandonment of the British Empire.

Anthony Eden, however, initiated the study that precipitated the process. In June 1956, before the Suez crisis, Eden as Prime Minister asked for a major review of British foreign and defence policy to take account of 'changes in the methods, if not the objectives, of the Soviet Union', its apparent policy of détente. Just after Eden had become Prime Minister in 1955, he had outlined a policy based on the proposition that the main threat to Britain's position was political and economic rather than military. The June 1956 review was instigated by Eden to examine Britain's economic circumstances, to cover changes in domestic and overseas policy and adjustments in Britain's defence programme. The intention of this review was to take account of the recognition of Britain's reduced position in the world, and the need for increases in domestic expenditure. Eden commented that the period of foreign aid was ending, and 'we must now cut our coat according to our cloth'. There was not much cloth. Britain had to find the means of increasing by £400 million a year the credit side of its balance of payments. The Prime Minister thought that Britain, particularly in defence programmes, was doing too much to guard against the least likely risk, that of major war.[38] In a minute dated 5 July 1956, Sir H. Poynton wrote to the Secretary of State for the Colonies, Alan Lennox-Boyd, speculating on the reasons for Britain's financial and economic difficulties concerning colonial development as being mainly a 'result of adversities to which there can be no quick cure'. Poynton further raised the fundamental question of whether Britain could continue 'to afford Colonial development on the present scale at all'. He referred to the school of thought which held that if the resources were too small to go around, Britain 'may have to begin to have a deliberate policy of shedding some of our Colonial burdens'.[39]

When Eden resigned as British Prime Minister on 10 January 1957, Harold Macmillan took over. The new government reassessed Britain's interests and commitments in the aftermath of the Suez crisis. Rather than pursuing a closer military and political association with Western Europe, the Macmillan government chose to emphasise the American link. It was this relationship which enabled Britain to implement the revised defence policy outlined in April 1957, but first mooted by the Eden Cabinet in June 1956, based on nuclear deterrence, limited commitments and personnel necessitated by the desire to reduce expenditure.[40] Colonial and African affairs were part of Macmillan's cost-cutting exercise, one which had been investigated during Eden's premiership. On 28 January 1957, Macmillan wrote to the chairman of the reconstituted Colonial Policy Committee, the Marquess of Salisbury, asking for an estimate of the probable course of constitutional development in the colonies, and also 'something like a profit and loss account for each of our Colonial possessions, so that we may be better able to gauge whether, from the financial and economic point of view, we are likely to gain or lose by its departure'. The Prime Minister emphasised that this was to be weighed against political and strategic considerations. What he wanted was 'the balance of advantage, taking all these considerations into account, of losing or keeping each particular territory'. He suspected that there were places, not of vital interest to Britain, where there would be no interest in resisting constitutional change and secession from the Commonwealth was a possibility.[41] In July 1957 the Cabinet Official Committee on colonial policy observed that a premature grant of independence could lead to a serious deterioration in economic and political conditions and result in a serious loss to the sterling area's dollar reserves. Its conclusion was that 'the economic considerations tend to be evenly matched and the economic interests of Great Britain are unlikely in themselves to be decisive in determining whether or not a territory should become independent'. Canada could be persuaded to share the British financial burden.[42]

The considered reply to Macmillan's request was given in a report by Norman Brook, the chairman of the Official Committee on colonial policy, to the Colonial Policy Committee on 6 September 1957. It identified those territories likely to obtain independence and become members of the Commonwealth within the next ten years. These included Nigeria in 1960, 1961 or soon thereafter, and the Central African Federation after 1960. Brook speculated that there could be demands for self-government in Uganda in 1961 leading to independence by 1967. During the next ten years the African countries likely to achieve self-government were Kenya, Uganda, Tanganyika, Zanzibar, Sierra Leone, the Gambia, Somaliland Protectorate and Mauritius. Brook's general conclusion was that Britain had been 'too long connected with its Colonial possessions to sever ties abruptly without creating a bewilderment which would be discreditable and dangerous'.[43]

At this time also, London and Washington decided that Africa was the next likely area of Soviet expansion. In Britain, the Africa Official Committee decided on a study of how to formulate Britain's policy towards those territories for which it was responsible against the background of a comprehensive policy for Africa generally. This study, 'Africa the next ten years', stimulated internal policy debates in Britain which culminated in Macmillan's 'wind of change' speech to the South African parliament which signalled the British decision to abdicate in Africa.[44] The documents in the Public Record Office suggest that this decision was partly due to international considerations, as well as Cold War politics and the need to prevent Soviet penetration in Africa. The rapidly emerging new British policy towards Africa was based on the acknowledgment of several important facts: that it would be difficult to distinguish between approaches in West, East and Central Africa; that there would probably have to be acceptance of the 'one man one vote' principle by the settler population which would have to hope to survive as an essential element of the new states' economy; that it would be difficult to follow a different policy in East Africa from that which the Belgian government was pursuing in the Congo, which was based on universal suffrage; and that the nature of the future independent British Africa would depend very much on whether the French succeeded in their experiment of linking their African territories to metropolitan France. These calculations were given a jolt by events on the continent itself, and the Labour opposition's attitude towards policy on Africa before the October 1959 general election.

Following a state of emergency in Nyasaland, a commission of enquiry headed by Sir Patrick Devlin, a judge who Macmillan regarded

as 'Irish' and thus anti-government on principle, and who had been bit-
terly disappointed that Macmillan had not made him Lord Chief
Justice, found that Nyasaland was, 'no doubt only temporarily, a police
state'. The Cabinet simultaneously discussed the significance of the
report on the deaths in the Hola camp in Kenya in February 1959 of 11
Mau Mau detainees who had been beaten to death by their black guards
for refusing to work. On 27 July, from the floor of the House of
Commons, Enoch Powell attacked his own government: 'Nor can we
ourselves pick and choose where and in what parts of the world we
shall use this or that kind of standard'. Macmillan was also forced to
consider African policy in relation to the forthcoming general election.
The Labour opposition was capitalising on difficulties in Africa and
was refusing to cooperate with the setting up of a Royal Commission to
look into the difficulties of the Federation of Rhodesia and Nyasaland.
As Iain Macleod wrote to Macmillan on 25 May, black Africa perhaps
remained the Conservative Party's most difficult problem in relation to
the vital 'middle' voters. Macleod urged Macmillan to see David
Sterling, the founder of the Special Air Services and the Capricorn
Africa society – a body whose constitution argued that a policy for
Africa had to come from within Africa, and that it needed to be acceptable to and supported by all races on the continent. The society's
premise was that there had to be a common citizenship which could be
subject to qualifications but had to be open on the same basis to members of all races. Sterling was supported in his ideas by Lord Home, the
Secretary of State for Commonwealth Relations. Home drafted a statement on colonial policy in Africa in which the Commonwealth
Secretary referred to British policy as aiming to achieve a situation
whereby any individual of any race might exercise his political right on
a basis of complete equality. Britain had taken six hundred years to
achieve 'one man one vote': 'Today no one suggest [sic] such a lengthy
apprenticeship but if democracy is to be secure education in its broad-
est sense must underpin the franchise'.[45]

The Conservatives won the general election of 1959. Lennox-Boyd
left the Cabinet for personal reasons and was succeeded as Colonial
Secretary by Iain Macleod. On 26 November Macleod reported to the
Cabinet that the Colonial Policy Committee had approved his proposed
plan for an announcement on constitutional advance in Tanganyika.
This would mean an unofficial (that is, black) majority in the Council
of Ministers in 1960, and a substantial extension of the franchise.
Because of the likely repercussions in Nyasaland and Northern
Rhodesia the franchise would be more limited than had been recom-

mended, and it was hoped that the constitutional conference that could work out the details could be postponed until April or May 1960.

By 1 November, Macmillan had decided to visit Africa. Apparently influenced by Powell's attack in the House of Commons, he wrote to Norman Brook:

> . . . young people of all Parties are uneasy about our moral basis. Something must be done to lift Africa on to a more national plane, as a problem to the solution of which we must all contribute, not out of spite . . . but by some really imaginative effort.

On 5 January 1960, Macmillan left London and over the following six weeks visited Ghana, Nigeria, the Federation of Rhodesia and Nyasaland, and South Africa. Norman Brook recorded that the Prime Minister was conscious of the rising tide of nationalism and wanted to inform himself at first hand. Macmillan also recognised the specific challenge to Britain arising from the problem of constitutional advance in multiracial societies in Africa.

In Ghana he found that opinion was scarcely disturbed by the suppression of the opposition, the declining effectiveness of parliament, and the domination of all aspects of public life by a single party. On 9 January 1960 at Accra, Macmillan declared that 'the wind of change is blowing right through Africa'. While in the Central African Federation he reached the same conclusion as Macleod, that the only way to save it was a rapid advance to self-government in all matters of territorial interest in Nyasaland. In this statement Macmillan 'jolted' European opinion in a major way. In a conversation in Cape Town with Dr H. Verwoerd, the South African Prime Minister, Macmillan explained how the two world wars had forced the pace of the transfer of colonial territories to their inhabitants. For Britain the problem was acute in East and Central Africa where there were many European settlers who had no other home. Rather than following South Africa's policy of separate development, Britain thought it right to work for a non-racial state in which all communities would have a share in government. Macmillan made a comparison with Algeria, 'a white country in North Africa with about a million French settlers'. It looked as if the French had lost the struggle, and not for lack of courage or material strength and expenditure. If the French experiment did fail, it was likely to do so because they had tried to hold down the indigenous population by force.

In his address to both houses of the South African Parliament on 3 February 1960, Macmillan argued that:

In the twentieth century, and especially since the end of the war, the processes which gave birth to the nation states of Europe have been repeated all over the world. We have seen the awakening of national consciousness in peoples who have for centuries lived in dependence upon some other power. Fifteen years ago this movement spread through Asia. Many countries there of different races and civilisations pressed their claim to an independent national life. Today the same thing is happening in Africa, and the most striking of all the impressions I have formed since I left London a month ago is of the strength of this African national consciousness. In different places it takes different forms, but it is happening everywhere. The wind of change is blowing through the continent, and, whether we like it or not, this growth of national consciousness is a political fact. We must accept it as a fact, and our national policies must take account of it.[46]

The policy that Macmillan outlined in Cape Town was regarded by some as the British abdication in Africa and the cynical abandonment of the white settlers. In Britain, right-wing Conservatives formed the Monday club to mark 'Black Monday', the day Macmillan spoke in Cape Town. The Prime Minister, initially absorbed with reviving the Anglo-American special relationship, showed an interest in Africa only in so far as it showed a profit or loss to Britain. By May 1959 the Labour Party's stand over the forthcoming general election, the emergency in Nyasaland, and the Hola camp killings in Kenya, forced him to pay greater attention to Africa. Macmillan, personally, seems to have been largely influenced by the French experience in Algeria. Indeed the policies of the European powers in Africa did a great deal to determine the pace of British policy. Britain thought that Belgium's adoption of the 'one man one vote' solution in the Congo had obvious ramifications for British East Africa. Britain was also influenced by French policy in Algeria, and by the French granting independence to states in sub-Saharan Africa. The 'wind of change', to some extent initiated by the 'profit and loss' accounting exercise commissioned in 1957, and by the Eden Cabinet's reassessment in June 1956 of Britain's position in the world, was possibly moved by French policy in Algeria in 1958, but really began to gain momentum with the internal policy debates in Britain, particularly the initial considerations of 'Africa: the next ten years'.

Alongside the decision to abdicate in Africa, Macmillan's government also oversaw the evolution and implementation of a British policy in the Middle East which put into effect the dramatic change in British defence policy that emerged during Churchill's peacetime administration; the move away from considering the Middle East as one of the three cardinal pillars of British strategy towards the conclusion that it was an area of more limited significance in the age of thermo-nuclear weapons, at a time when Britain's financial strictures meant a limitation of its world role. That policy was also, in effect, helped by Washington's assumption of an increased responsibility in the area. During his first term as President, Dwight Eisenhower had not wanted this. He preferred to leave Britain in the lead in the area, and had wanted her to pay as much as possible for the defence of the area. It was, however, Eisenhower's policy during the Suez crisis of 1956 that led, as Henry Kissinger later observed, to the United States having to take over Britain's burdens in the Middle East. By the time of the crises in Lebanon, Jordan and Iraq in July 1958, the United States had, in effect, acknowledged that it had assumed the leadership of the 'Free World' in the Middle East, and filled the vacuum left by the decline of British influence in the area, particularly with the end of Britain's mandate over Palestine.

In 1958 the British Cabinet and Defence-planning Committees confirmed the view, apparent after 1956, that Britain's 'great' interest in the Middle East lay in Kuwait with its oil and sterling reserves. Initially, this was listed above the only other 'great' interest – Turkey – and later Iran and Aden were added. As Britain moved towards an Anglo-American policy for the Middle East, Kuwait and the Gulf were initially seen as areas of predominant British interest. It was, however, acknowledged that Britain could not act forcibly without American support, and this support did not have to be military. London could not persuade Washington to embark on joint planning for the protection of Kuwait. When Iraq seemed to threaten the invasion of Kuwait in 1961, Washington not only gave diplomatic aid, but allowed for the contingency of possible military support as well, and throughout refrained from imposing a policy on London. The Kuwait crisis of 1961 forced the acceptance on Macmillan and other British officials that the appearance of an Arab solution to an Arab question had to be generated. This constituted a move away from the methods of the previous century, and an acknowledgement of the value of the policy outlined by Eden for the Cabinet in 1953 of the need to harness the social and economic aspirations of the common people of the Middle East at a time when the tide of nationalism was rising fast.

In October 1961, the Defence Committee of the British Cabinet was instructed to reassess defence policy and strategy in the Middle East in accordance with the newly defined political assumptions governing why Britain had a presence there. The political assumptions outlined were: first, the safeguarding of Britain's stake in the oil of the Gulf and support for the independence of Kuwait that this entailed; and, second, that Britain had to discharge its obligation to protect the states in the Aden Protectorate and the Gulf; and, third, to preserve the countries of the area from communist influence.[47]

Following the defeat of Germany and Turkey, and the collapse of the Tsar at the end of the First World War, Britain, with its one million occupying troops, had become the dominant power in an area stretching from India to Constantinople, from the Caspian Sea to the Indian Ocean. The acquisition of this vast new Empire had not been planned. It was in fact unexpected. The results of the military campaigns in the Middle East during the First World War could not have been foreseen. Britain had organised its vast new Empire with the confidence of a nineteenth-century power. Now, Britain was clearly no longer the paramount power in the Middle East and had conceded this position to the United States. By 1961 the British Empire in the Middle East, sometimes referred to as an 'informal Empire', was over.

The documentary record shows how difficult it is to offer any single explanation for the end of Empire. Moves towards a limitation of Britain's imperial role were initiated by the Churchill government as a consequence of the need to reduce expenditure, particularly on defence, to improve standards of living at home. A defence policy based on nuclear deterrence meant that the Middle East lost its strategic importance in terms of a 'hot war'. The British decision to abdicate in Africa was partly due to international considerations and Cold War politics, especially the need to prevent Soviet penetration in Africa. Macmillan, himself, was influenced by the 'moral' dimension of colonial politics, particularly the policies pursued by the Belgians in the Congo, but above all by the failure of French policy in Algeria. But probably the most significant explanation of the moves to end Empire on the part of successive British governments was the overriding emphasis given to the special relationship with the United States. The Anglo-American alliance became the cornerstone of British foreign policy during the Cold War.

Few, if any, today would accept the possibility of 'finite' or closed historical explanations. In 1961, E.H. Carr, in his celebrated volume *What is History?*, reports Sir George Clark's observation that historians expect their work to be superseded again and again: 'They consider that knowledge of the past has come down through one or more human minds, has been "processed" by them, and therefore cannot consist of elemental and impersonal atoms which nothing can alter'. He explains further that faced with this scholars have become sceptical and some have accepted the doctrine that 'since all historical judgements involve persons and points of view, one is as good as another and there is no 'objective' historical truth'.[48] In 1993, R.J.B. Bosworth, in a work as challenging and important as E.H. Carr's, concluded his magisterial study of historical writing and the Second World War with the observation that:

> If the messages of the People's war are to survive "the end of history", historians, proudly accepting the burden of their own "authority", must go on explaining to our societies that our task in exploring the history of the Second World War, and any other issue, is to assess the evidence, find an answer, write it down on a piece of paper, and humbly acknowledge that it is wrong.[49]

Interpretations of the end of Empire and its relationship to Britain's decline might be usefully read against the backdrop of these remarks. The prevailing interpretations have shifted significantly in the last few decades. Sometimes academic arguments have reflected the political preoccupations of the country's leaders. This was particularly evident in the 1960s and 1970s when a generation of journalists, academic commentators and British leaders seemed determined, against the background of successive British applications to join the European Economic Community, to bury once again the Anglo-American special relationship, and saw the Suez crisis as the end of Britain's imperial longings. Yet a number of myths have proliferated about the Suez crisis. Often these were fuelled by Labour politicians for domestic political ends. Anthony Nutting, the Parliamentary Under-Secretary of State for Foreign Affairs, resigned late in 1956 over his disagreements with Eden. Unlike Sir Graham Bower who, after the Jameson Raid in 1895–96, recorded his knowledge of the complicity of Joseph Chamberlain and had his papers closed for fifty years, Nutting published his account of Suez in 1967. This backfired on the sitting Labour government: it led to a spate of memoirs which, arguably, undermined the sanctity of Cabinet confidentiality on which the British political system had been based for over two hundred years.

Despite what Nutting and others have written, Suez was not 'the lion's last roar'. Britain was already retreating from Empire. Suez did not force Britain to turn to Europe. Macmillan only decided on that after South Africa's exclusion from the Commonwealth in 1961. Suez was not an unfortunate break in the Anglo-American 'special relationship'. Britain had been demoted to the status of just one among a number of allies as soon as Eisenhower came into office. Rather, Suez led to the revival of the special relationship on old terms. Eisenhower was particularly anxious to make amends. At the Bermuda Conference in March 1957 there was a return to an Anglo-American management of world affairs. In May 1982, Henry Kissinger, American Secretary of State between 1973 and 1977, publicly regretted the American action over Suez as it generated the perception that Eisenhower had humiliated Britain and France; Kissinger suggested that this event had forced the United States to take over Britain and France's burdens in the Middle East.[50] Eisenhower later went on the record with his view that the revenge he took on Britain over Suez was the greatest mistake of his presidency.[51]

Suez was not the last imperial war. It did not relegate Britain to minor power status, and was not the last wag of the lion's tail after which the British people were prepared to turn inwards and leave the upholding of the international system to others. Admittedly that view gained wider acceptance in Britain than abroad. But it was confounded in 1982 when troops returned from the Falkland Islands, 8000 miles away in the South Atlantic, having fought an imperial war which was designed to maintain an international system as tenuous as that of the 1930s. This war was possible partly because on this occasion the United States backed Britain as, in the words of President Ronald Reagan, 'its closest ally'. Indeed, during her Prime Ministership Margaret Thatcher transformed the image of Britain from that of the 'sick man' of Europe to an industrious, thriving, patriotic nation, with a seat at the Great Table of world politics, a seat which she personally had earned, at the very least, through her role in ending the Cold War. From Pretoria to Peking, regimes across the world have followed her belief in the free enterprise economy, if not in the primacy of the individual. Thatcher's impact on global affairs was enabled by the appearance of an American President for whom she felt a real warmth and empathy, and her cultivation of the Anglo-American special relationship. This was based on the perception that whatever the surface disagreements might be, the current between Britain and the United States flowed deep, and, in the end, the two countries were always prepared to support each other.[52]

In 1949, William Strang's Permanent Under-Secretary's Committee had outlined the basis of British foreign policy, and pointed out that Britain had no real option other than reliance on the United States. The Commonwealth and the nations of Western Europe between them were not strong enough to deter the Soviet Union. Ultimately this rested on a pragmatic calculation as to how Britain could best utilise the special relationship in its own interests. It is this calculation which formed the basis of Britain's Cold War foreign policy. Margaret Thatcher, for instance, developed a foreign policy centred on the special relationship, but based ultimately on what she saw as Britain's best interests. There is little evidence of sentimentality in the attitude of British policy-makers in their understanding and operation of the relationship with the United States. Apart from the era of Harold Wilson and Edward Heath, British leaders in the post-1945 era have consistently tried to capitalise on what they have commonly described as the 'special relationship'.[53] Through this relationship Britain maintained its seat at the world table and its status as a Great Power. This was the decision taken by Strang's Under-Secretary's Committee in 1949, endorsed by the Cabinet then and again in 1951, that subsequently formed the basis of British post-war foreign policy. From that time onwards the realisation dawned that the Commonwealth and Europe together were not strong enough to withstand the advances of the Soviet Union. This was in many respects a pragmatic policy pursued by successive British governments, both Labour and Conservative. In effect it meant the Commonwealth-Empire nexus was of decreasing significance for Britain.[54] Thus, for many in Britain the end of Empire barely registered. Priority had to be given to the relationship with Washington. The Commonwealth-Empire slowly faded as one of the three interlocking circles which Churchill saw as the basis of British foreign policy. The choice between Europe and the United States remains. But as Churchill observed, these spheres of influence are not necessarily mutually exclusive.

Notes

1. J. Callaghan, *Great Power Complex: British Imperialism, International Crises and National Decline, 1914–51* (London, 1997), pp. vii, xi.
2. See A. Gamble, *Britain in Decline: Economic Policy, Political Strategy and the British State* (Basingstoke, 1994; 1st edn, 1981), pp. 34–5.
3. A. Sked, *Britain's Decline: Problems and Perspectives* (Oxford, 1987), pp. 5–6.
4. D. Coates, *The Question of UK Decline: State, Society and Economy* (London, 1994), pp. 270–1.
5. See R. Ovendale, *'Appeasement' and the English Speaking World: Britain, the United States, the Dominions, and the Policy of 'Appeasement', 1937–1939* (Cardiff, 1975).
6. A.J.P. Taylor, 'Lament for a Commonwealth', *History of the English Speaking Peoples*, Vol 1(1) (London, 1969), pp. 12–13.

7. J. Darwin, *The End of the British Empire: The Historical Debate* (Oxford, 1991), pp. 3–4.

8. B. Lapping, *End of Empire* (London, 1985), p. 8.

9. R.F. Holland, *European Decolonization 1918–81: An Introductory Survey* (London, 1985), pp. 205–10.

10. See I. Wallerstein, *The Capitalist World-economy* (Cambridge, 1979), pp. 31–3; and *Historic Capitalism with Capitalist Civilisation* (London, 1995), pp. 61–6, 82–5; G. Wasserman, *The Politics of Decolonization: Kenya, Europeans and the Land Issue 1960–1965* (Cambridge, 1976), pp. 174–5.

11. C. Barnett, *The Collapse of British Power* (London, 1972), pp. 232–3; 589–93.

12. J. Gallagher, 'The Decline, Revival and Fall of the British Empire', in A Seal (ed.), *The Decline, Revival and Fall of the British Empire: The Ford Lectures and other Essays by John Gallagher* (Cambridge, 1982).

13. A.P. Thornton, *The Imperial Idea and its Enemies* (London, 1959), pp. 328–33, 355–6.

14. See R. Ovendale (ed.), *British Defence Policy since 1945* (Manchester, 1994), pp. 18–130.

15. See J. Darwin, *The End of the British Empire*, pp. 85–113, for a summary and discussion of the historiographical debate on the significance of colonial nationalism.

16. J. Gallagher, 'The Decline, Revival and Fall of the British Empire', pp. 73, 139, 144.

17. P.J. Cain and A.G. Hopkins, *British Imperialism: Crisis and Deconstruction 1914–1950* (London, 1993), pp. 308–9.

18. R.F. Holland, *Britain and the Commonwealth Alliance 1918–1939* (London, 1981), p. 24.

19. See R. Ovendale, *Anglo-American Relations in the Twentieth Century* (London, 1998), pp. 120–43.

20. R. Ovendale (ed.), *British Defence Policy since 1945*, pp. 18–41; Public Record Office, London, CAB 128/11, fos 7–8, CM6(47)3, Confidential Annex, 15 January 1947.

21. R. Ovendale, *The English-Speaking Alliance: Britain, the United States, the Dominions and the Cold War 1945–1951* (London, 1985), pp. 29–87.

22. Australian Archives (ACT), Shedden Papers, A5954, 1797/1, Strategical planning in relation to cooperation in British Commonwealth defence – Appendix G(1), Defence appreciation as a basis for military planning between Commonwealth staffs – The threat to world security – United Kingdom Chiefs of Staff Committee paper COS(4)49, 9 February 1949.

23. R. Ovendale, *The English-Speaking Alliance*, pp. 118–84.

24. R. Ovendale, 'William Strang and the Permanent Under-Secretary's Committee', in J. Zametica (ed.), *British Officials and British Foreign Policy 1945–50* (Leicester, 1990), pp. 212–27.

25. R. Ovendale, *The English-Speaking Alliance*, pp. 220–38.

26. CAB 129/45, fos 317–27, CP(51)64, Note by Attlee on Pacific defence and appendices, Secret, 27 February 1951; R.J. O'Neill, 'The Korean War and the Origins of ANZUS', in C. Bridge (ed.), *Munich to Vietnam: Australia's Relations with Britain and the United States since the 1930s* (Melbourne, 1991), pp. 99–113.

27. CAB 128/15, fos 61–2, CM17(49)2, secret, 3 March 1949.
28. Australian Archives (ACT), A5954, Box 1813, Shedden to P.A. McBride, top secret and personal, 23 January 1951; for Britain's relationship with the Commonwealth countries, see N. Mansergh, *Survey of Commonwealth Affairs Problems of Wartime Co-operation and Post-War Change 1939–1952* (London, 1968); J.D.B. Miller, *Survey of Commonwealth Affairs Problems of Expansion and Attrition 1953–1969* (London, 1974).
29. J. Kent, *British Imperial Strategy and the Origins of the Cold War 1944–49* (Leicester, 1993); S. Croft, *The End of Superpower: British Foreign Office Conceptions of a Changing World* (Aldershot, 1994).
30. R. Ovendale, *Britain, the United States and the Transfer of Power in the Middle East, 1945–1962* (London, 1996), pp. 1–23.
31. R. Ovendale, *The English-Speaking Alliance*, pp. 144–84; Australian Archives (ACT), A426/24, P.A. McBride to Menzies, top secret, 24 October 1950; CAB 131/9, DO(50)45, Report by the Chiefs of Staff on Defence Policy and Global Strategy, top secret, 7 June 1950.
32. *United Kingdom Parliamentary Debates, House of Commons, 1950–51*, Fifth Series, vol. 483 (London, 1951), cols 579–84, 29 January 1951.
33. For an account of Britain's position in the world economy at this time see D. Reynolds, *British Policy and World Power in the Twentieth Century* (London, 1991), pp. 206–10.
34. R. Ovendale, (ed.), *British Defence Policy*, pp. 97–109; CAB 131/12, Annex 1, D(52)26, Report by the Chiefs of Staff for the Defence Committee of the Cabinet on Defence Policy and Global Strategy, top secret, 17 June 1952; W. Jackson and Lord Bramall, *The Chiefs: The Story of the United Kingdom Chiefs of Staff* (London, 1992), pp. 281–93.
35. Cmd 9391, *Statement on Defence 1955* (London, February 1955), pp. 1, 6, 9–10.
36. CAB 128/27 Pt 2, CC62(54)1, secret, 1 October 1954.
37. D. Reynolds, *British Policy*, p. 195.
38. CAB 134/1315, PR(56)11, Note by Eden on assumptions for future planning, top secret, 15 June 1956.
39. Public Record Office, London, CO 1025/76, Minute from H. Poynton to Lennox-Boyd, 5 July 1956.
40. Cmnd 124, *Defence Outline of Future Policy* (London, April 1957).
41. CAB 134/1555, PC(57)6, Colonial Policy Committee and future constitutional development in the colonies, secret, 25 February 1957; enclosing Macmillan to Salisbury, 28 January 1957; D.J. Morgan, *The Official History of Colonial Development, v, Guidance towards Self-government in British Colonies, 1941–1971* (London, 1980), pp. 58–60, 96–7.
42. CAB 134/1556, CP(O)(57)6, Cabinet Official Committee on colonial policy, note by secretaries on future constitutional development in the colonies, secret, 4 July 1957.
43. CAB 134/1556, CPC(57)30(revise), Report by chairman of the Official Committee on colonial policy to the Colonial Policy Committee on future developments in the colonies, secret, 6 September 1957.
44. See R. Ovendale, 'Macmillan and the Wind of Change in Africa, 1957–1960', *Historical Journal*, vol. 38 (1995), pp. 455–77, esp. pp. 462–70.

45. CAB 130/164, GEN 688/5, Memorandum by Home on constitutional development in Africa, 25 June 1959; R. Ovendale, 'Macmillan and the Wind of Change in Africa, 1957–1960', pp. 470–3.

46. CAB 129/100, C(60)66, Note by Norman Brook on Macmillan's African tour, secret, 5 April 1960; H. Macmillan, *Pointing the Way 1959–1961* (London, 1972), pp. 116–77; A. Horne, *Macmillan 1957–1986* (London, 1989), pp. 186–200.

47. See R. Ovendale, *Britain, the United States and the Transfer of Power in the Middle East*, pp. 198–215; CAB 131/126, D(61)65, Note by Norman Brook enclosing Macmillan to Watkinson, top secret, 23 October 1961.

48. E.H. Carr, *What is History?* (London, 1961), pp. 7–8.

49. See R.J.B. Bosworth, *Explaining Auschwitz and Hiroshima: History Writing and the Second World War 1945–1990* (London, 1993), p. 198.

50. See R. Ovendale, *The Origins of the Arab–Israeli Wars* (London, 1992), pp. 182–4; *Britain, the United States, and the Transfer of Power in the Middle East*, pp. 140–77.

51. J. Aitken, *Nixon: A Life* (London, 1993), p. 244.

52. See R. Ovendale, *Anglo-American Relations in the Twentieth Century*, pp. 144–56.

53. *Ibid.*, pp. 157–62; and 'W.Strang and the Permanent Under-Secretary's Committee', pp. 212–7.

54. See W.R. Louis and R. Robinson, 'The Imperialism of Decolonization', *Journal of Imperial and Commonwealth History*, vol. 20 (1994), pp. 462–511.

16

Conclusion: Decline or Declinism?

RICHARD ENGLISH AND MICHAEL KENNY

The simplest definition of 'decline' is that the term refers to a traceable process whereby Britain diminished as a world power: an historically observable phenomenon which can be neatly defined, measured and demonstrated. One would need to be specific here about the chronology and scale of the process and, as this book has demonstrated, there is a wide range of answers on these two points. But there can be no dispute about the fact that, relative to key competitors, Britain declined as a world power between the late-nineteenth and late-twentieth centuries. In *absolute* terms, both military power and economic achievement have increased enormously during this period: British weapons were incomparably more powerful and British standards of living considerably higher, for example, in the 1990s than they had been in the 1890s. But the key question concerns *relative* performance and potential, and here there has been a striking diminution in power. This is true both militarily and economically, the two realms being interwoven and each significantly affecting national prestige and confidence.

Between the late-seventeenth and the early-nineteenth centuries Britain had made impressive advances, its naval strength decisively underpinning its progress as a world power. By 1815 Britain possessed most of Europe's colonies, and during the succeeding half century its dominant position was reinforced. In terms of world influence and of economic productivity, Britain benefited from changes between 1815 and the 1860s, probably reaching its peak in the latter decade. In both the economic and the military spheres, however, British dominance subsequently began to be eroded. In the mid-nineteenth century Britain had no international competitors in many industrial spheres. In 1914 this was no longer true. By that year Germany, to take one crucial example, was rivalling Britain in terms of national power, late-nineteenth and early-twentieth century German industrial performance being particularly impressive. By 1914, indeed, both Germany and the United States challenged Britain. Still a great power, Britain was no longer pre-eminent in the way that it had been 50 years earlier. Viewed from our later perspective, it is apparent that the growth of US strength during this half century was in fact the most crucial development: the rise of the United States as the world's leading power signalled the end of such a position for Britain.

Decline, therefore, might be understood as referring to trends upon which observers can largely agree. There *was* a marked fall in Britain's share in world production and trade. Its share of world trade was 23.2 per cent in 1880 and 14.1 per cent just over thirty years later. In 1880 it could boast 22.9 per cent of total world manufacturing output; in 1913 only 13.6 per cent.[1] Britain *has* experienced relative economic decline in terms of international standing, competitiveness and efficiency. Despite those who caution against exaggerating Britain's pre-First World War slippage, it is clear that during 1870–1914 British economic success was less spectacular, in relative terms, than it had been in the preceding decades. Or again, after the Second World War the British economy did decline in the sense that rates of growth (of total and per capita GDP) were lower than those of its rivals. The 1973–88 period represented a marked deterioration; but even the impressively increasing output of the 1951–73 era is sometimes read as an episode of decline since Britain's rivals were making even greater progress and, in some cases, overtaking her. Growth which was high by historical standards could be comparatively weak in relation to contemporary competitors. In military terms, it is also clear that the Britain of the 1890s was relatively much more powerful than 1990s Britain could plausibly claim to be.

It should be noted, however, that while relative decline of this kind is a traceable process, it is also one rich in ambiguities as far as competing commentators are concerned. The debate regarding manufacturing illustrates the point. Undoubtedly, Britain's share of world exports in manufactures fell sharply between, for example, the 1880s and the 1980s; and the troubles of British manufacturing during the post-1960 era have been painful and have appeared prominently in decline debates. But while it is clear that British manufacturing has experienced relative decline, opinions vary greatly as to the relevance of this to the overall economy. Just how significant *is* a reduction in the relative significance of manufacturing? To some, manufacturing industry is the main source of productivity gains, wealth and growth for the economy as a whole and, according to such a view, deindustrialisation represents the key to the decline debate. To others, however, the economy might flourish and might be judged anything other than declining despite the weakness of the manufacturing sector.[2] But the key point for our current purposes, is to recognise that economically and militarily Britain is relatively much weaker in terms of international standing at the end of the twentieth century than it was at the end of the nineteenth.

If 'decline' refers, therefore, to a traceable historical experience, then it might be suggested that the term 'declinism' be used to refer to perceptions of decline, to diagnoses of its condition or causes and, perhaps, to projects explicitly aimed at reversing it. Here it is interpretations which are key, and arguably also a series of mentalities which position their respective possessors in relation to modern British experience. Most of the leading thinkers featured in Part I of this book have, for example, written about decline in terms of specific diagnoses and prescriptions. They are expert examples of the phenomenon of 'declinism', because of their focus on 'decline'. This Conclusion will assess theories which have sought to explain 'decline', and will also evaluate the phenomenon of 'declinism'. In particular, an attempt will be made to answer the questions established at the start of the book. To what extent, and in what precise ways, have arguments about decline improved our understanding of Britain's political and economic development since the late nineteenth century? Why have arguments concerning decline been so frequently and influentially expressed? Are decline debates still pertinent as Britain faces the twenty-first century?

Perhaps the best-known theories of decline are those sometimes referred to under the umbrella term 'cultural critique'.[3] The central notion here, as has been outlined in numerous of the preceding chapters, is that key features of British culture have proved damaging to competitive British performance. In particular, the argument is that British middle- and upper-class culture has had an especially deleterious effect on British economic life: the urge towards enterprise was smothered by a preference for propertied passivity; the British elite preferred continuity, preservation and antiquity to change, innovation and novelty; romantic and pastoral idealism clouded the vision, and obscured from view the realities of hard-headed economic decision-making; public schools and leading universities shared a bias against business, science, industry and technology with the result that the elite products of these institutions were unable to offer first-class economic leadership, universities being a way out of, not into, industry; training and education were inadequate, and short-termism hampered many areas of economic and political life; the twin cults of the educated amateur and the practical man thwarted systematic economic development and science-based progress, while the workforce was ill-trained, ill-educated and obstructive. In the words of Martin Wiener, 'industrialism did not seem quite at home'[4] in Britain, with the period from the late-nineteenth to the late-twentieth centuries being one of psychological and intellectual deindustrialisation.

The arguments of Correlli Barnett as well as those of Wiener himself have been profoundly stimulating and influential here: indeed, the decline debates are unimaginable without their important theses. Another of our contributors, however, has led the criticism of this type of approach. Bill Rubinstein's argument that British strength has rested on finance and commerce, rather than on industry, digs at the roots of much 'cultural critique' thinking: if the economy could flourish primarily on the foundation of finance and commerce, then de-industrialisation need not entail national economic decline at all. Indeed, Rubinstein argues that Thatcherite political economy was a reversion (whether witting or not) to the economic strengths at the heart of the British pattern of development.

Rubinstein is not alone in challenging Wiener's attack on the public schools and the old universities, and other features of the latter's argument have also been assailed.[5] So, too, many aspects of Correlli Barnett's thesis have been questioned (as indeed has his research methodology itself).[6] Rather than seeing Britain as anti-technological, anti-scientific and anti-industrial, it could perhaps be contended that in fact Britain has been a powerful twentieth-century scientific force, that British engineers and scientists have played a leading part in industry and government, and that the British state has been an important supporter of technology and science. Again, Martin Wiener's emphasis on the anti-industrial impact of rural preoccupation has also been questioned. Peter Mandler has recently argued that cultures absorbed in their rural past are not necessarily anti-modern; that England between 1880 and 1914 was actually less characterised by a nostalgic interest in the countryside than were other European countries; and that interwar England was again less absorbed in rural nostalgia than other European cultures and was certainly not backward-looking.[7] Indeed, it is worth asking just how many pre-First World War English people were in fact preoccupied by a rural-nostalgic approach. Intriguing enthusiasts for such an approach can be found, but were they really representative?

The answers to such questions are bound to be complicated, and the most sophisticated adversaries in this field acknowledge the force of at least some of their opponents' arguments. Two general qualifications might, however, be offered when considering the provocative claims of thinkers such as Barnett and Wiener. First, even if the claims about British culture (education, arcadianism, amateurism and so on) are conceded, can one demonstrate beyond reasonable doubt the connection between such features of British culture and the retardation of economic growth? Second, if relative British failure is to be explained, in any substantial measure, by recourse to cultural explanations of this type then it is necessary to demonstrate that Britain's rivals were less flawed by such supposed cultural hindrances. Attacks on the 'cultural critique' have frequently focused on the fact that Britain's competitors were at least as likely to exhibit the same cultural tendencies as those which supposedly inhibited British competitiveness in such a striking way.

If the cultural arguments have been significantly questioned, then what of more directly economic theories? One line of argument involves the identification of problems allegedly associated with particular economic actors. There can be an overlap here with the 'cultural critique', for example in the criticism of trade unions. Much attention has been focused by commentators and politicians on the negative economic impact of poor industrial relations and an obstructionist trade union movement, and on the danger of monopolistic practices with which unions have been associated. According to the commentator, Sir Samuel Brittan, 'the unions played an important role in holding back British performance'. It could also be suggested that organised labour is linked to British decline because it has blocked the full utilisation of existing technologies and the speedy spread of new ones. According to this view, the strength of labour within Britain's manufacturing industry contributed to economic underperformance, with a defensively conservative ethos having been encouraged to prevail. The late 1970s marked the highest pitch of this argument, with Margaret Thatcher and Keith Joseph among those who prepared to give effect to anti-union politics.[8] Other economic players singled out as culprits include British entrepreneurs during the 1870–1914 era. This period has been extensively analysed in an impressively detailed literature, but it remains clear that in many areas Britain was losing ground to its competitors in these years. Can this be attributed to entrepreneurial failure? It has been suggested that British entrepreneurs were reluctant to pick up on new technologies, that they exhibited a conservative attitude to change and improvement, that their businesses were poorly organised and that they operated in an unhelpfully short-termist fashion.[9]

Distinctive economic explanations of British decline have been forthcoming from Marxist sources. These have tended to emphasise the role of class conflict, class interest and the contradictions of capitalism. Particular attention has been focused on the failure to adapt to new technologies in the 1890s (the preference instead being for a retreat into the satellite world of colonies); and it has also been suggested that the failure of British manufacturing resulted from the weakness of that fraction of the owning class dependent for survival on the manufacturing sector of the economy. Perhaps the most significant overarching contribution to decline debates from a Marxist pedigree was Perry Anderson's and Tom Nairn's account of the 'peculiar' pattern of British socio-economic development, which they laid out in a series of seminal articles in the 1960s.[10] In essence, their argument was that British historical development was unique for the absence of a bourgeois revolutionary movement. This had left a major legacy upon indigenous development: the aristocracy absorbed the emergent industrial bourgeoisie from the early nineteenth century onwards, and ruled within a state form that remained *ancien régime* in kind.

This leads to another economic argument proffered as an explanation of British decline, namely that the dominance of finance over industry in the British economy has seriously damaged the nation's competitive performance. If manufacturing is the foundation of the economy, then the predominance of British finance helps explain British under-performance. In part, this relates also to the charge of under-investment: that the comparatively low level of investment in Britain has been one of the most important factors retarding economic growth. The finance–industry relationship has been carefully considered in Geoffrey Ingham's influential study, *Capitalism Divided?* Ingham challenges the idea that the origins of the finance-industry opposition lie in Britain's external relations. Instead, he argues that it is the essentially commercial character of the City which explains British economic development. British capitalism has, according to his view, been characterised by a dual character: it is both industrial and commercial. But the situation is further defined by the fact that while finance dominates industry, so too commerce is dominant within finance itself. This has important consequences for the relations between industry and finance. For new, unproven issues are less surely remunerative of short-term gains than are commercial profits on the secondary market. Ingham argues that it is this short-termist quality of City activities which explains the finance–industry split in Britain. Short-term gains can be made from trading in existing shares more easily than from creating new investment. So the institutional bias, within the City, towards a strong secondary market in already existing shares diminishes the likelihood of finance investing in new, long-termist, industrial projects: short-term returns work against new capital investments.[11]

In other ways, too, economic arguments concerning decline might be modified. Regarding trade unions, this particular argument figures far less frequently in political commentary and academic analysis than it did in the 1970s and early 1980s. With hindsight it looks like a product of the ideological predilections that prevailed then. Given the relative weakness of unions since, it has become clear that many of the structural flaws in the British economy cannot be laid at their door, and that anti-union arguments were exaggerated. Suggestions that entrepreneurial failure lies at the root of British non-competitiveness have also been countered, with some questioning the extent of 'failure' in the first place, and with other causes being suggested for what failure there was (resource endowment might represent one difficulty, and so might the inaction or unhelpful action of government).[12] Marxist theses have come to look threadbare in many cases upon closer inspection, Ingham's book on the city and industry itself challenging the traditional Marxist concentration on the absolute dominance of the economic over the political. Anderson's and Nairn's arguments have encountered some of their most trenchant criticism from within socialist circles: E. P. Thompson's retort, 'The Peculiarities of the English',[13] is an emotive, powerful argument against reading indigenous developments in the wake of the French model of modernity. And the supposed centrality of manufacturing has been brought into question: is manufacturing necessarily a more reliable guide to economic health than other areas of the economy (or society)?[14]

A third group of explanations of British decline might be headed under an 'institutional' label. British decline as a world power has occasioned a search for culpable parties, and the institutions of the political, financial and administrative system have frequently been depicted as the culprits. An example might be found in Will Hutton's influential arguments concerning the sclerotic nature of much British institutional life. As this book has shown, Hutton's work gives prominence to criticisms of key structures in Britain. Clearly it is possible for institutional arrangements to hinder (or foster) productivity. In particular, much attention has been paid to the role here of the British state. As Martin Smith's chapter points out, much declinist writing focuses on the state, some critics having argued that it has done too much. To Samuel Brittan, for example, democracy brought overgovernment, with economic intervention by the state holding back rather than encouraging growth.[15] The perversion of the market order during the twentieth century has indeed been held by some to have caused British decline, with an erosion of British industrial competitiveness being so marked that calls grew for the rolling back of the state. According to this view, government should intervene less in the economy, public expenditure should be cut back and taxation consequently lowered. It has been suggested that the cumulative effect of these policies would be to increase the effectiveness of market forces and therefore produce a more dynamic economy.

To others, however, the state has not done enough. Another contributor to this book, David Marquand, has argued that Britain suffered from not possessing a developmental/entrepreneurial state. Greater priority should have been placed by the state, in postwar Britain, on the modernisation of the economy. Too weak and too distanced from business, the state did not provide the assistance (with funding, research, development and so forth) necessary to promote programmatic modernisation. Marquand pinpoints the exceptional character of British political culture, forged in the hey-dey of Empire and *laissez-faire*, and argues that this shaped the mentality of the political and bureaucratic elites into the twentieth century. This kind of argument has been bolstered recently by Michel Albert's[16] characterisation of a 'Rhenish' model of capitalism, based upon the features of the Japanese and German economies, which is deemed to be the antithesis of the Anglo-American model, with its limited patterns of state intervention, lack of planning instruments and shareholder-driven economic culture.

Others again have argued that the problem with state activity has been less that it did too much or too little, but that it did the wrong things. Sidney Pollard has argued that the comparatively low level of investment in Britain has been one of the most important factors retarding economic growth. Some have held that the state spent too highly on the military. It has been argued that too great a concentration on military expenditure, particularly once a power's relative decline has begun, will further deepen that power's problems by diverting resources away from necessary investment and wealth creation.[17] High military expenditure has been linked to lower growth and lower investment, and it has been argued that it helped ensure Britain fell behind its economic competitors. The thesis here is that high military spending narrows investment in civilian production; absorbs large numbers of research scientists (because of guaranteed governmental purchase), therefore leading to soft management and an uncompetitive spirit in central industrial sectors; and damages the balance of payments by diverting resources away from export industries. This could perhaps be connected to the imperial thesis on decline: in short, that Britain's world role undermined her domestic economy.

While some read possession of a far-ranging and distant Empire as a reflection or source of power, others have argued that it represented a distraction and a drain on resources. Maintenance of Empire necessitated high spending on defence industries; did this distract attention from domestic investment and reconstruction? And was military-financial overstretch crucial to the decline of British power?

As with other theses on decline, the above arguments all carry weight. But they are all now open to political and intellectual challenge, and carry far less conviction than they once did. The argument that rolling back the state from economic life would necessarily bolster the competitiveness of British industrial performance has received a critical pounding since the Conservatives held office in the 1980s/1990s and, broadly, sought to implement such a strategic goal through privatisation programmes, the introduction of quasi-markets and competitive practices within public institutions, and the relaxation of exchange controls. Even former advocates of neo-liberal political economy now express regret about the 'revolutionary' and destabilising impact of such policies.[18] Few now confidently maintain that the neo-liberal argument about decline still holds. In terms of the developmental-state thesis, there are also strong grounds for scepticism. In part this comes from the faltering performance of Germany and Japan since the late 1980s, but also from the argument that the British economy would be adversely affected by the adoption of the institutional structures and cultures of other states.[19] As to the argument that military spending damaged other areas of the economy, it is certainly true that until the late-1960s the state spent more on military research and development than on their civil equivalents. But was the economy as a whole damaged as a consequence? The British state has in fact significantly funded civil research and development. Indeed, by international standards, there has been considerable state and private investment in this area; it is simply not true to argue that military expenditure has occurred at the expense of civil research and development. Moreover, it is far from accepted that higher levels of spending on the latter would in fact have solved the problems of British industry.[20] Of the specifically imperial version of the military expenditure argument, it might be suggested that the causal relationship between economic problems and imperial commitments need not lead from the latter to the former. Cipolla's observation that, 'All empires seem eventually to develop an intractable resistance to the change needed for the required growth of production'[21] possibly hints at this conclusion. Moreover, there might be judged a certain circularity to the argument that declining empires further their own decline by spending too large a proportion of their resources on the military: the reason the empire collapsed was that too high a proportion was spent on the military, and we know that too high a proportion was thus spent because the Empire collapsed.

The question of military expenditure leads us to another wave of declinist arguments, those associated with war. Numerous authors have noted the significance of the First World War in signalling or generating the beginning of British decline. Eric Hobsbawm, for example, has claimed that, 'Britain was never the same again after 1918 because the country had ruined its economy by waging a war substantially beyond its resources.'[22] Certainly, it was Lloyd George after 1918 who was the first British Prime Minister to have to deal with industrial decline and to adjust policy as a result. And during 1914–18, US economic strength had been vitally important in helping to sustain the Allied war effort. By the end of the war, the United States had clearly emerged as the most powerful nation in the world.

While some have therefore identified the First World War as key to the process of British decline, others have focused instead on the 1939–45 conflict. Correlli Barnett has forcefully argued that the years 1939–45 both reflected and reinforced British weakness as a competitive power. He points out the extent to which American support was necessary to sustain Britain during (and after) the war, and he chronicles in great detail the failings which the British compounded during the 1940s. Certainly, if the First World War demonstrated the Empire's lack of cohesion, the Second cruelly exposed its vulnerability and demonstrated British dependence on the USA. It might be suggested that, ironically, being on the victorious side did not help Britain. Complacency worked against the uprooting or dramatic remodelling of outdated structures; where defeated powers remoulded themselves from the foundation upwards, Britain felt no need to do so.

Explanations focusing on the two world wars have the merit of concentrating on external forces as well as internal dynamics, and this is a useful corrective to the sometimes insular character of other lines of enquiry. And each war was, plainly, crucial in determining the development of British experience. But again some doubts might be raised. Correlli Barnett has suggested in this book that Britain came out of the First World War:

> relatively lightly. The Germans were not only financially ruined but politically ruined; their entire society was turned upside down, with revolution and civil strife. The French had a savage war fought over their northern departments, had a great swathe of enormous devastation; they lost twice the numbers of men that we did in proportion to population.

And, while Barnett's thesis concerning the next war highlights British dependence on the United States, there are complications here, too. For after 1945 it was the relationship with the USA which allowed Britain to *continue* to act as a world power. The US connection reflected Britain's diminished place in the world order, but it simultaneously helped to retain for Britain a comparatively lofty position in world affairs.

Powerful theories of decline have therefore been variously called into question. The cultural critique has been assailed by suggestions that its damaging features of British culture were neither as distinctively characteristic of the country, nor as damaging to the economy, as is claimed. Attacks on economic actors such as trade unions or entrepreneurs have been qualified, as have a variety of Marxist declinists' critiques. Institutional arguments have claimed that the state has done too much, too little, or the wrong things; but counterfactual speculation has generated doubts about whether different state behaviour could reasonably be expected to have dramatically altered Britain's relative standing in the world. Military theories about the impact of the two world wars have been questioned; and the notion that military spending drove out civil development has been dismissed as untrue (and, in any case, largely irrelevant).

Indeed, what might be termed chronological explanations of British decline suggest that there is less to account for (and perhaps that there were fewer counterfactual possibilities available) than some of the above mentioned declinist accounts imply. Early industrial success helped make Britain the dominant world power, but it is arguable that a small island with limited resources could not expect forever to lead the world in terms of output of iron and steel, or to maintain its share of cotton textile output indefinitely. Other countries would grow relatively rapidly in part because they were catching up with the pioneer. Britain's early lead could not be maintained indefinitely: techniques pioneered in Britain could be replicated elsewhere, and on a larger scale. Indeed, the very technological and industrial innovations on which Britain had built its strength would undermine its relative lead, as larger countries could deploy them in the context of much greater resources.[23] Thus the post-1870 spread of industrialisation (and the consequent alteration in naval power, among other things) affected Britain's relative position adversely, if for no other reason than that Britain stood to lose most from a change in the status quo.

According to such a view, British decline was a chronological probability, the country lacking the resources needed to compete forever as the leading player in the world economy. This had military implications. Indeed, it might even be suggested that, in terms of military profile, the phenomenon which requires explanation is not British decline, but the persistence of Britain's comparatively prominent role. Broadly, such reflections as these suggest that relative decline should not necessarily be seen as embodying dramatic failure in British performance. As such, they subvert the logic, and the spirit, of much declinist argument.

That Britain should not compete lastingly with larger powers such as the USA is unsurprising. Moreover, if Bill Rubinstein is right that Britain's failure to compete with comparable powers such as Germany has been exaggerated, then there is perhaps less of a mystery to explain than is sometimes suggested in the decline literature. It might be argued, in fact, that what requires explanation is the phenomenon of 'declinism' itself: the obsession, as it has sometimes appeared, with explaining a British failure which is perhaps neither as great nor as surprising as is often assumed.

Decline debates have indisputably enriched our understanding of many features of modern British politics. The contributions to this book variously reflect the fact that decline has provided a unique and emotive terrain upon which important political and ideological argument has emerged, concerning the economy, education, Empire, state institutions and many other important aspects of British life. But while declinist arguments have clarified our understanding of modern Britain, this has often been by their stimulation of corrective responses and revisions as much as by their being persuasive in themselves. Indeed, it might be suggested that decline has been one of the most strategically important yet frequently misapplied concepts in modern political discourse. It seems a prime candidate for membership of the club established by W. B. Gallie of 'essentially contested' concepts.[24]

For is decline really the most appropriate framework within which to consider modern British politics? There is, for example, the paradox that increasing prosperity has accompanied decline as a world power, and that acute anxiety about decline has coincided with a period of unprecedented growth. The 1945–73 period in Britain saw rates of economic growth unsurpassed in the nation's history. Decline in world power status has coincided with rising material wealth, and relative economic decline has been accompanied by absolute economic improvement in people's lives. Postwar Britain has experienced higher living standards than ever, per capita living standards having risen dramatically and uninterruptedly. Are living standards necessarily a less effective measure of economic performance than growth rates? Indeed, if living standards are a valuable measure to deploy, then decline clearly becomes a far less relevant concept in modern British history. Pursuing this line of thought further, one might ask how far people have noticed or been deeply affected by Britain's decline in world power status. Ritchie Ovendale suggests here that 'for many in Britain the end of Empire barely registered'. And if one disaggregates British experience into its separate parts then the picture becomes one of great variety rather than of uniform or evenly consistent decline. As Jonathan Clark argues in relation to the last twenty or thirty years of British economic policy, it might be best to remember that 'some things were done badly, some were done well, and some were done indifferently; that some areas of life are getting better and some getting worse'. Such an approach subverts the broad stroke declinist style of analysis.

For it is important to consider that there exists in Britain, and has existed for centuries, more than a single economic culture. There is a variety of kinds of entrepreneur and of business. There are plural experiences between (and within) England, Scotland, Wales and Ireland/Ulster.[25] Can the notion of unbroken decline, of a downward and continuous experience, be sustained against such considerations? It might be suggested that the extent and the supposed continuity of decline have at times been overstated and are more questionable than much of the literature implies. And if the disaggregation of experience subverts declinist arguments from one angle, then another blow comes in from those who stress the importance of globalisation. With an increasingly global economy, how relevant are the supposed trajectories of national decline? How sustainable indeed are notions of a discrete 'British' economy itself? At the very least, changes identified in relation to globalisation might lead one to question the validity of direct comparisons between the British economy of the 1990s and that of the 1890s. And in assessing whether the rise and decline of nations remains meaningfully traceable, it is instructive to remember that perhaps the most eminent scholar of national powers and their respective historical fates (Paul Kennedy) should subsequently have directed his attention to problems defined in transnational terms.[26]

Commentators vary in their enthusiasm for the globalisation thesis: in their contributions to this book, for example, Stuart Hall perhaps embraces the thesis more enthusiastically than Will Hutton.[27] But there *is* an increasing interdependence of economies, and national economies are less easily distinguishable or comparable as a consequence. Britain's setting within the European Union provides an obvious example. Marie-Therese Fay and Elizabeth Meehan's arguments reflect developments here:

> it may not be valid to speak of a 'national road to recovery' in the British context: 'sub-national' features as well as global trends and transnational sectors could invalidate discourses of national economies (and therefore also much of the debate on British national decline).

And the problems of the British economy are often (and increasingly?) those shared by other leading capitalist states. Indeed, Henk Overbeek argues here that British decline can *only* be meaningfully understood through successive transformations of the global economic system.

Another problem with much declinist writing concerns the question of counterfactuals. Declinists sometimes imply that if only *x* or *y* had been (or were to be) done then Britain would have regained (or would regain) a greater place in the world. But is this true? How reasonable is it to assume that, even if such policies were available, governments should have had the foresight to see them accurately? Could governmental initiatives, even if blessed with the foresight demanded by commentators such as Correlli Barnett, have achieved the desired results? Are historical outcomes so far within the grasp of programmatic planning? Moreover, other methodological questions deserve attention, particularly perhaps the problems inherent in monocausal, generalist theories. Ritchie Ovendale rightly argues that it is difficult to be satisfied with any single explanation for the end of the British Empire, and the same might be said of relative decline as a whole. Despite the many arguments about it, decline has ultimately proved irreducible to any single interpretation or evaluation; in part, this is surely because monocausal explanations of major historical phenomena, and of change over time, tend to be profoundly unpersuasive. The key point is the sheer complexity of the causes of British relative economic decline: theories which lose sight of this are likely to be inadequate.

Moreover, rather than focusing on Britain's allegedly poor performance one might instead consider the question of why her rivals have at times done better. During the years 1951–73 the British economy improved impressively, but not as well as that of some rivals. One answer, deflating in its implications for sharply critical declinist accounts of Britain, is simply that the rivals' relative backwardness in 1951 gave them advantages in relative growth: starting from the experience of war devastation, a country recognises its need for reform, for sustained hard work, for new ideas, institutions and actions. Where Britain saw the Second World War as a triumph to be rewarded, less fortunate countries began the post-war era hungrier for change and improvement.[28] Britain was not in this position; Germany and Japan were. So, too, was France in a different way: the defeat of 1940 led to a sense that those weaknesses which lay behind that defeat must be addressed, and that the economy must be modernised.

In addition to asking whether British decline has been simplified and exaggerated, one might therefore further ask whether – in explaining what relative decline there has actually been – it might be wrong to blame, for example, British culture for what could not really have been avoided. Each of these questions casts doubt over whether decline should be the primary context within which one considers modern British politics and history.

If this is so, then perhaps attention should be directed less at decline than at declinism: a state of mind relatively autonomous of the actual, historical decline of Britain as a world power. For in very different political and historical circumstances people have deployed strikingly similar discourses of decline;[29] and similarities are evident in other countries' declinist literatures as well as within the British tradition.[30] The question is why declinist arguments appeal to intellectuals, to politicians, to writers and their readership. Why have declinist questions been posed so frequently and with such powerful popular resonance?

Just as declinist fears elsewhere have sometimes come to seem exaggerated,[31] so too British politicians' frequent obsession with decline owes far less to any actual decline of Britain than their rhetoric might suggest. Postwar Britain, the setting for the most striking political attention to decline, has been successful in terms of achieving nearly continuous growth, and the picture is certainly not one of unmitigated disaster. Why then has declinist politics been so favoured in this period? Ian Budge has suggested that the appeal of declinism lies in its providing apparent justification for various political parties' programmes for socio-economic change.[32] Certainly, opposition parties can easily be attracted to declinism and both left and right have used it. In analysing this, Jim Tomlinson has traced the ways in which the emergence of the standard of living as a major issue in British politics provided the late-1950s context within which declinism began to flourish; he also points to the significance of the postwar development of calculating shares of world trade.[33] In terms of party politics, Tomlinson examines the ways in which Conservative and Labour politicians began to clothe themselves in declinist rhetoric. The former, initially reluctant to pursue declinist politics, acted partly under pressure from the Federation of British Industries to adopt a modernising strategy, and partly because of a sense that to emphasise the importance of mechanisms for growth would help to justify key political decisions as essential to people's prosperity. By the mid-1960s, the Conservatives were unquestionably working within a declinist framework, a development hastened by pressure from Labour. The latter party had moved in the late-1950s to adopt a declinist perspective, most decisively following their 1959 election defeat. Tomlinson suggests that declinist terrain allowed for a kind of compromise between left-wing and revisionist approaches:

> For revisionists declinism was attractive because it meant an acceptance by the party that the electorate's changing character had to be responded to, in particular its increasing affluence. . . . For the Left declinism seemed to offer an economic programme where one had been so strikingly absent in the 1950s, without any explicit retreat on public ownership. In addition, it provided a rich vein of egalitarian rhetoric for attacking parasitism in the name of efficiency.[34]

This economically-focused declinism which took root in the late-1950s was to survive during the ensuing decades in a variety of guises. The 1970s was, perhaps, the period of high declinism, with the issue of Britain's comparatively poor performance having become prominent during the peceding decade. But as late as 1994 one leading commentator could suggest that, 'Political parties now rise and fall on their ability or failure to arrest economic decline'.[35] The nature of politicians' definitions of decline clearly relates to the nature of the political project proposed to reverse it, and the case of Margaret Thatcher is surely the most significant. The 1970s combination of high inflation, high unemployment and comparatively low growth rendered plausible a pessimistic reading of Britain's postwar economy, and the 1979 election brought to power a Prime Minister who had made a particular interpretation of decline central to her politics, and who claimed to possess the answers to Britain's historical problems. Thatcherites claimed that they would reverse British decline (an approach which had become powerful in the Conservative Party during the 1970s as a response to the perceived British crisis of that period) and, later, that they had in fact done so.

The governments headed by Thatcher urged the need for a new ideological approach in order to reverse decades of decline, and certain declinist arguments appealed in this context. Correlli Barnett provides perhaps the most telling example: Thatcher attacked the consensus built after and upon the Second World War, and Barnett's iconoclasm here was particularly well suited to the needs of her governments, as was his stress upon the necessity of radical reconstruction of key institutions and structures. Even some of those who register dissatisfaction with Barnett's argument concede that there were problems in postwar policy in terms of its lack of attention to modernisation, to planned investment, to training, and to reskilling,[36] or that British industry after 1945 required a radical reconstruction incorporating new technology and drastic reorganisation.[37] For Thatcher, decline was the terrain on which political debate was to be conducted. Declinist historiography provided an important source of rhetorical references and ideological ballast. Those who opposed the Thatcherite project could be represented as purveyors of the mind-set and values that had brought Britain to its knees, be they the miners, Foreign Office mandarins or Tory 'wets'. In fact, insufficient attention has been focused on the degree of energy and legitimacy unleashed by the deployment of declinist rhetoric in such periods.

If the specific conjunction of political, social and economic forces at moments such as the late-1970s helps to explain the emergence of particular versions of declinist politics, then a more general explanation of the wider success of such arguments might lie in the realm of rising expectations. For the irony is that the achievement of ever greater prosperity brings with it an increasing prospect of perceived economic failure. As Barry Supple has observed:

> economic and social progress almost inevitably increases dissatisfaction by making the definition of need more demanding, constantly raising the 'poverty line' as average incomes grow, and transforming the public judgement of what are acceptable standards of social existence.[38]

Thus it is more difficult in the late-twentieth century to satisfy wants than it was a hundred years earlier.

This might suggest that it would be unwise to see declinism as a phenomenon purely of the past. Declinism might frequently be more popular than persuasive, and certain developments have made it less plausible now than in previous eras. But arguments concerning Britain's decline might nonetheless be seen as of continuing relevance by many, albeit in different forms. The appeal of some Huttonite argument to a wide-reading public provides one example, with the declinist rhetoric here focusing on the specific damage allegedly done to Britain during the 1979–97 period of Conservative government. Decline has been a concept central to late-twentieth century discussions of British economic performance and national identity alike. Close inspection of declinist arguments might lead one to be sceptical about their ultimate value – and about the comprehensiveness of the debate to date[39] – but that should not rule out the possibility that influential figures and a wide public audience might continue to think within declinist parameters into the next century.

Notes

1. P. Kennedy, *The Rise and Fall of the Great Powers: Economic Change and Military Conflict from 1500 to 2000* (London, 1989; 1st edn, 1988), p. 294.
2. See, for example, the differing views of Sidney Pollard and Bill Rubinstein, pp. 61–91 in this book.
3. Given that most aspects of British life might be designated 'cultural', this is a phrase which one might prefer not to deploy but for its having already gained widespread use in the literature.
4. M.J. Wiener, *English Culture and the Decline of the Industrial Spirit 1850–1980* (Harmondsworth, 1992; 1st edn, 1981), p. ix.
5. B. Collins and K. Robbins (eds), *British Culture and Economic Decline* (London, 1990), pp. 9–11, 31–4, 81–3. See also Đ. Edgerton, *Science, Technology and the British Industrial 'Decline' 1870–1970* (Cambridge, 1996).
6. D. Edgerton, 'Liberal Militarism and the British State', *New Left Review*, vol. 185 (1991), argues, contrary to Barnett, that in the military sector the British state has been far from neglectful of the relationship between technology, science and industry; see also C. Barnett, 'A Reply to David Edgerton', *New Left Review*, vol. 187 (1991), and D. Edgerton, 'The Prophet Militant and Industrial: The Peculiarities of Correlli Barnett', *Twentieth Century British History*, vol. 2, no. 3 (1991); J. Tomlinson, 'Correlli Barnett's History: The Case of Marshall Aid', *Twentieth Century British History*, vol. 8, no. 2 (1997), attacks Barnett's 'methodological shortcomings' (p. 222), and in particular his ignoring of historiographical context and his questionable use of primary source material; P. Clarke,

'Keynes, New Jerusalem and British Decline' in P. Clarke and C. Trebilcock (eds), *Understanding Decline: Perceptions and Realities of British Economic Performance* (Cambridge, 1997), challenges Barnett's interpretation of Keynes; J. Harris, 'Social Policy, Saving and Sound Money: Budgeting for the New Jerusalem in the Second World War' in *ibid.*, points out that both Keynes and Beveridge were characterised by austerity and economy in their approach to social welfare, and that by European standards postwar British welfare legislation was in fact relatively modest; various lines of criticism are followed in a 'Symposium: Britain's Post-war Industrial Decline', *Contemporary Record*, vol. 1, no. 2 (1987) based around Barnett's work, with Barnett responding in *Contemporary Record*, vol. 1, no. 3 (1987).

7. P. Mandler, 'Against "Englishness": English Culture and the Limits to Rural Nostalgia 1850–1940', *Transactions of the Royal Historical Society*, sixth series, vol. 7 (1997).

8. A. Gamble, *The Free Economy and the Strong State: The Politics of Thatcherism* (Basingstoke, 1988), pp. 33, 94.

9. For treatment of this literature, see S. Pollard, 'Entrepreneurship 1870–1914', in R. Floud and D. McCloskey (eds), *The Economic History of Britain since 1700*, vol. 2 (Cambridge, 1994; 1st edn, 1981).

10. P. Anderson, 'Origins of the Present Crisis', *New Left Review*, vol. 23 (1964); P. Anderson, 'The Figures of Descent', *New Left Review*, vol. 161 (1987); T. Nairn, 'The British Political Elite', *New Left Review*, vol. 23 (1963). On the New Left context, see M. Kenny, *The First New Left: British Intellectuals after Stalin* (London, 1995).

11. G. Ingham, *Capitalism Divided? The City and Industry in British Social Development* (Basingstoke, 1984).

12. H.J. Habakkuk, *American and British Technology in the Nineteenth Century* (Cambridge, 1962); D. N. McCloskey, *Economic Maturity and Entrepreneurial Decline: British Iron and Steel 1870–1913* (Cambridge, 1973).

13. E.P. Thompson, 'The Peculiarities of the English', *Socialist Register* (1965).

14. See, for example, the comments of Rubinstein on pp. 61–75 of this book.

15. S. Brittan, *The Economic Consequences of Democracy* (London, 1977).

16. M. Albert, *Capitalism against Capitalism* (London, 1993).

17. P. Kennedy, *Rise and Fall*, pp. xvi and xxvi.

18. J. Gray, *Beyond the New Right: Markets, Government and the Common Environment* (London, 1993); D. Willetts, *Civic Conservatism* (London, 1994).

19. See Martin Smith's chapter in this book.

20. D. Edgerton, *Science, Technology and the British Industrial Decline*.

21. C.M. Cipolla (ed.), *The Economic Decline of Empires* (London, 1970), p. 9.

22. E. Hobsbawm, *Age of Extremes: The Short Twentieth Century 1914–1991* (London, 1994), p. 30. See also A. Gamble, *Britain in Decline: Economic Policy, Political Strategy and the British State* (Basingstoke, 1994; 1st edn, 1981), p. 134.

23. 'Given the size and natural endowments of other countries, it was inconceivable that Britain could permanently play a very significant or autonomous part in international affairs. It simply lacked the resources necessary to maintain anything like its "historical" role, first as a major policeman in imperial and quasi-imperial affairs, and then as a premier "player" on the world scene' (B. Supple, 'Fear of Failing: Economic History and the Decline of Britain', in P. Clarke and C. Trebilcock (eds), *Understanding Decline*, p. 15).

24. W.B. Gallie, 'Essentially Contested Concepts', *Proceedings of the Aristotelian Society*, vol. 56 (1955–56).

25. For the historically local quality of much English state activity, for example, see D. Eastwood, *Government and Community in the English Provinces 1700–1870* (Basingstoke, 1997).

26. Compare Kennedy's *Rise and Fall* with his subsequent concentration upon cross-border questions of 'overpopulation, pressure upon the land, migration, and social instability on the one hand, and technology's power both to increase productivity and to displace traditional occupations on the other', and with his observation that 'nation-state rivalries are being overtaken by bigger issues' (P. Kennedy, *Preparing for the Twenty-First Century* (New York, 1993), pp. 11, 15).

27. D. Morley and K. Chen (eds), *Stuart Hall: Critical Dialogues in Cultural Studies* (London, 1996), p. 407; cf Will Hutton, pp. 50–60 of the current book.

28. C. Feinstein, 'Success and Failure: British Economic Growth since 1948', in R. Floud and D. McCloskey (eds), *The Economic History of Britain Since 1700*, vol. 3 (Cambridge, 1994; 1st edn, 1981).

29. For stimulating treatment of this theme, see D. Cannadine, 'Apocalypse When? British Politicians and British "Decline" in the Twentieth Century' in P. Clarke and C. Trebilcock (eds), *Understanding Decline*.

30. See, for example, the attention drawn to Spain's supposed weaknesses in modern science and technology: J. H. Elliott, 'The Decline of Spain', in Cipolla (ed.), *The Economic Decline of Empires*, pp. 187–8.

31. See, for example, Krieger's suggestion in 1986 that there had been 'a significant decline in the United States' global pre-eminence' (J. Krieger, *Reagan, Thatcher and the Politics of Decline* (Oxford, 1986), p. 12).

32. I. Budge, 'Relative Decline as a Political Issue: Ideological Motivations of the Politico-Economic Debate in Post-War Britain', *Contemporary Record*, vol. 7, no. 1 (1993).

33. J. Tomlinson, 'Inventing "Decline": The Falling Behind of the British Economy in the Postwar Years', *Economic History Review*, vol. 49, no. 4 (1996).

34. *Ibid.*, p. 752.

35. D. Coates, *The Question of UK Decline: The Economy, State and Society* (Hemel Hempstead, 1994), p. 8.

36. K.O. Morgan, 'England, Britain and the Audit of War', *Transactions of the Royal Historical Society*, sixth series, vol. 7 (1997), p. 146.

37. A. Gamble, *Britain in Decline*, p. 115.

38. B. Supple, 'British Economic Decline since 1945', in R. Floud and D.

McCloskey (eds), *The Economic History of Britain Since 1700*, vol. 3, p. 342.

39. There is, for example, very little sustained consideration of sexual or racial politics within the decline literature.

Select Bibliography

Aldcroft, D.H. (1964) 'The Entrepreneur and the British Economy 1870–1914', *Economic History Review*, vol. 17.

— (1992) *Education, Training and Economic Performance 1944–1990* (Manchester).

Allen, G.C. (1976) *The British Disease* (London).

Alter, P. (1987) *The Reluctant Patron: Science and the State in Britain* (Oxford).

Anderson, P. (1964) 'Origins of the Present Crisis', *New Left Review*, vol. 23.

— (1974) *Lineages of the Absolutist State* (London).

— (1987) 'The Figures of Descent', *New Left Review*, vol. 161.

Barnett, C. (1972) *The Collapse of British Power* (Stroud).

— (1986) *The Audit of War: The Illusion and Reality of Britain as a Great Nation* (London).

— (1991) 'A Reply to David Edgerton', *New Left Review*, vol. 187.

— (1995) *The Lost Victory: British Dreams, British Realities 1945–1950* (London).

Beer, S.H. (1965) *Modern British Politics: A Study of Parties and Pressure Groups* (London).

— (1982) *Britain Against Itself: The Political Contradictions of Collectivism* (London).

Brittan, S. (1968) *The Economic Consequences of Democracy* (London).

— (1971) *Steering the Economy* (Harmondsworth).

— (1973) *A Restatement of Economic Liberalism* (Basingstoke).

— (1978) 'How British is the British Sickness?', *Journal of Law and Economics*, vol. 21.

— (1995) *Capitalism with a Human Face* (London).

Budge, I. (1993) 'Relative Decline as a Political Issue: Ideological Motivations of the Politico-Economic Debate in Post-War Britain', *Contemporary Record*, vol. 7, no. 1.

Buxton, T., Chapman, P. and Temple, P. (eds) (1994) *Britain's Economic Performance* (London).

Cain, P. J. and Hopkins, A.G. (1993) *British Imperialism*, vol. 1, *Innovation and Expansion 1688–1914* (London).

— and Hopkins, A.G. (1993) *British Imperialism*, vol, 2, *Crisis and Deconstruction 1914–1990* (London).

Cipolla, C.M. (ed.) (1970) *The Economic Decline of Empires* (London).

Clark, J.C.D. (1985) *English Society 1688–1832: Ideology, Social Structure and Political Practice During the Ancien Régime* (Cambridge).

— (1986) *Revolution and Rebellion: State and Society in England in the Seventeenth and Eighteenth Centuries* (Cambridge).

— (1994) *The Language of Liberty 1660–1832: Political Discourse and Social Dynamics in the Anglo-American World* (Cambridge).

— (1997) 'British America: What if there had been no American Revolution?' in N. Ferguson (ed.), *Virtual History: Alternatives and Counterfactuals* (London).

— (1997) 'The Strange Death of British History? Reflections on Anglo-American Scholarship', *Historical Journal*, vol. 40, no. 3.

— (ed.) (1990) *Ideas and Politics in Modern Britain* (Basingstoke).

Clarke, P. and Trebilcock, C. (eds) (1997) *Understanding Decline: Perceptions and Realities of British Economic Performance* (Cambridge).

Coates, D. (1994) *The Question of UK Decline: The Economy, State and Society* (Hemel Hempstead).

— and Hillard, J. (eds) (1986) *The Economic Decline of Modern Britain: The Debate between Left and Right* (Brighton).

Colley, L. (1992) *Britons: Forging the Nation 1707–1837* (London).

Collins, B. and Robbins, K. (eds) (1993) *British Culture and Economic Decline* (London).

Contemporary Record (1987) 'Symposium: Britain's Post-War Industrial Decline', *Contemporary Record*, vol. 1, nos 2, 3.

Crafts, N. '(1988) The Assessment: British Economic Growth over the Long Run', *Oxford Review of Economic Policy*, vol. 4, no. 1.

— *Britain's Relative Economic Decline: 1870–1995* (London, 1995).

Darwin, J. G. (1986) 'The Fear of Falling: British Politics and Imperial Decline since 1900', *Transactions of the Royal Historical Society*, 5th series, vol. 36.

Daunton, M. J. (1989) '"Gentlemanly Capitalism" and British Industry 1820–1914', *Past and Present*, vol. 122.

Desai, M. (1996) 'Debating the British Disease: The Centrality of Profit', *New Political Economy*, vol. 1, no. 1.

Dintenfass, M. (1992) *The Decline of Industrial Britain 1870–1980* (London).

Eastwood, D. (1997) *Government and Community in the English Provinces 1700–1870* (Basingstoke).

Edgerton, D. (1991) *England and the Aeroplane: An Essay on a Militant and Technological Nation* (London).

— (1991) 'Liberal Militarism and the British State', *New Left Review*, vol. 185.

— (1991) 'The Prophet Militant and Industrial: The Peculiarities of Correlli Barnett', *Twentieth Century British History*, vol. 2, no. 3.

— (1996) *Science, Technology and the British Industrial "Decline" 1870–1970* (Cambridge).

Elbaum, B. and Lazonick, W. (eds) (1986) *The Decline of the British Economy* (Oxford).

English, R. and Townshend, C. (eds) (1999) *The State: Historical and Political Dimensions* (London).

Feinstein, C. (1990) 'The Benefits of Backwardness and the Costs of Continuity' in A. Graham (ed.), *Government and Economies in the Post-War World: Economic Policies and Competitive Performance 1945–85* (London).

Floud, R. and McCloskey, D. (eds) (1981) *The Economic History of Britain since 1700* (three volumes) (Cambridge).

Gamble, A. (1981) *Britain in Decline: Economic Policy, Political Strategy and the British State* (Basingstoke).

Glyn, A. and Harrison, J. (1980) *The British Economic Disaster* (London).

302   *Select Bibliography*

Gray, J. (1993) *Beyond the New Right: Markets, Government and the Common Environment* (London).

Habakkuk, H.J. (1962) *American and British Technology in the Nineteenth Century* (Cambridge).

Hall, S (1988) *The Hard Road to Renewal: Thatcherism and the Crisis of the Left* (London).

Harris, J. (1990) 'Enterprise and Welfare States: A Comparative Perspective', *Transactions of the Royal Historical Society*, 5th series, vol. 40.

Harrison, B. (1994) 'Mrs Thatcher and the Intellectuals', *Twentieth Century British History*, vol. 5, no. 2.

— (1996) *The Transformation of British Politics 1860–1995* (Oxford).

Harvie, C. (1985) 'Liturgies of National Decadence: Wiener, Dahrendorf and the British Crisis', *Cencrastus*, vol. 21.

Hay, C. (1997) 'A Sorry State? Diagnosing the British Affliction', *Socialism and Democracy*, vol. 1, no. 1.

Hobsbawm, E.J. (1994) *Age of Extremes: The Short Twentieth Century 1914–1991* (Harmondsworth).

Hutton, W. (1995) *The State We're In* (London).

— (1997) *The State to Come* (London).

Ingham, G. (1994) *Capitalism Divided? The City and Industry in British Social Development* (Basingstoke).

Jenkins, P. (1995) *Anatomy of Decline: The Political Journalism of Peter Jenkins* (London).

Kennedy, P.M. (1988) *The Rise and Fall of the Great Powers: Economic Change and Military Conflict from 1500 to 2000* (London).

— (1993) *Preparing for the Twenty-First Century* (New York).

Kennedy, W.P. (1987) *Industrial Structure, Capital Markets and the Origins of British Economic Decline* (Cambridge).

Kenny, M. (1995) *The First New Left: British Intellectuals after Stalin* (London).

Kirby, M.W. (1981) *The Decline of British Economic Power since 1870* (London).

Krieger, J. (1986) *Reagan, Thatcher and the Politics of Decline* (Oxford).

Macfarlane, A. (1978) *The Origins of English Individualism: The Family, Property and Social Transition* (Oxford).

Mandler, P. (1997) 'Against "Englishness": English Culture and the Limits to Rural Nostalgia 1850–1940', *Transactions of the Royal Historical Society*, 6th series, vol. 7.

Marquand, D. (1977) *Ramsay MacDonald* (London).

— (1988) *The Unprincipled Society: New Demands and Old Politics* (London).

— (1991) *The Progressive Dilemma: From Lloyd George to Kinnock* (London).

— (1997) *The New Reckoning: Capitalism, States and Citizens* (Oxford).

McCloskey, (1973) D. N. *Economic Maturity and Entrepreneurial Decline: British Iron and Steel 1870–1913* (Cambridge).

Morgan, K.O. (1997) 'England, Britain and the Audit of War', *Transactions of the Royal Historical Society*, 6th series, vol. 7.

Morley, D. and Chen, K. (eds) (1996) *Stuart Hall: Critical Dialogues in Cultural Studies* (London).

Nairn, T. (1963) 'The British Political Elite', *New Left Review*, vol. 23.

— (1977) 'The Twilight of the British State', *New Left Review*, vol. 101/102.

— (1977) *The Break-Up of Britain* (London).

— (1988) *The Enchanted Glass: Britain and its Monarchy* (London).

Newton, S. and Porter, D (1988) *Modernisation Frustrated: The Politics of Industrial Decline in Britain since 1900* (London).

O'Brien, P. (1988) 'The Costs and Benefits of British Imperialism 1846–1914', *Past and Present*, vol. 120.

Olson, M. (1982) *The Rise and Decline of Nations: Economic Growth, Stagflation and Social Rigidities* (New Haven).

Ovendale, R. (1988) *Anglo-American Relations in the Twentieth Century* (London).

Overbeek, H. (1990) *Global Capitalism and National Decline: The Thatcher Decade in Perspective* (London).

Pavitt, K. (ed.) (1980) *Technical Change and British Economic Performance* (London).

Pollard, S. (1982) *The Wasting of the British Economy: British Economic Policy 1945 to the Present* (London).

— (1989) *Britain's Prime and Britain's Decline: The British Economy 1870–1914* (London).

— (1991) *The Development of the British Economy 1914–1980* (London).

Raven, J. (1989) 'British History and the Enterprise Culture', *Past and Present*, vol. 123.

Robbins, K. (1983) *The Eclipse of a Great Power: Modern Britain 1870–1992* (London).

Rubinstein, W.D. (1981) *Men of Property: The Very Wealthy in Britain since the Industrial Revolution* (London).

— (1987) *Elites and the Wealthy in Modern British History: Essays in Social and Economic History* (Brighton).

— (1993) *Capitalism, Culture and Decline in Britain 1750–1990* (London).

Sampson, A. (1983) *The Changing Anatomy of Britain* (London).

Sanderson, M. (1972) *The Universities and British Industry 1850–1970* (London).

— (1988) 'The English Civic Universities and the "Industrial Spirit" 1870–1914', *Historical Research*, vol. 61, no. 144.

Shonfield, A. (1958) *British Economic Policy since the War* (Harmondsworth).

Sked, A (1987) *Britain's Decline: Problems and Perspectives* (Oxford).

Snow, C.P. (1959) *The Two Cultures and the Scientific Revolution* (Cambridge).

Starn, R. (1975) 'Meaning-Levels in the Theory of Historical Decline', *History and Theory*, vol. 14.

Supple, B. (1994) 'Fear of Failing: Economic History and the Decline of Britain', *Economic History Review*, vol. 47, no. 3.

Thompson, E.P. (1965) 'The Peculiarities of the English', *Socialist Register*.

Tomlinson, J. (1996) 'Inventing "Decline": The Falling behind of the British Economy in the Postwar Years', *Economic History Review*, vol. 49, no. 4.

— (1997) 'Correlli Barnett's History: The Case of Marshall Aid', *Twentieth Century British History*, vol. 8, no. 2.

Walbank, F.M. (1969) *The Awful Revolution: The Decline of the Roman Empire in the West* (Liverpool).

Ward, D. (1967) 'The Public Schools and Industry in Britain after 1870', *Journal of Contemporary History*, vol. 11.

Warwick, P. (1985) 'Did Britain Change? An Inquiry into the Causes of National Decline', *Journal of Contemporary History*, vol. 20.

Wiener, M.J. (1981) *English Culture and the Decline of the Industrial Spirit 1850–1980* (Harmondsworth).

Willetts, D. (1994) *Civic Conservatism* (London).

Index